Democratic Governance in American States and Cities

ABOUT THE AUTHORS

Kim Quaile Hill received his Ph.D. in political science from Rice University in 1974. He is a professor of political science and director of the Graduate Program in Public Administration at Texas A & M University. Previously, he was on the faculty of the University of Houston. His current research is concerned primarily with the democratic process in state government; his earlier research, which considered a variety of public policy questions, has been widely published in scholarly journals. He is the author of *Democracies in Crisis: Public Policy Responses to the Great Depression* and co-author of *The Criminal's Image of the City* and *Texas Government: Its Politics and Economics.*

Kenneth R. Mladenka received his Ph.D. in political science from Rice University in 1975. Currently a professor of political science at Texas A & M University, he has also taught at the University of Virginia and at Northwestern University. His main interest is in the governing of cities, and his present research focuses on how ethnic minorities benefit from the public employment practices of cities. He has written—and published extensively in scholarly journals— about the delivery of public services in urban areas and about the role of government bureaucracies in the service delivery process. He is the co-author of *Texas Government: Its Politics and Economics.* He is the founder and first president of the Urban Politics Section of the American Political Science Association and past editor of the *Urban Politics Newsletter.*

Democratic Governance in American States and Cities

Kim Quaile Hill
Texas A & M University

Kenneth R. Mladenka
Texas A & M University

Brooks/Cole Publishing Company
Pacific Grove, California

Consulting Editor: Roger H. Davidson

Brooks/Cole Publishing Company
A Division of Wadsworth, Inc.

Printed in the United States of America

10   9   8   7   6   5   4   3   2   1

Library of Congress Cataloging-in-Publication Data

Hill, Kim Quaile, [date]
    Democratic governance in American states and cities / Kim Quaile
  Hill, Kenneth R. Mladenka.
      p.   cm.
    Includes bibliographical references and index.
    ISBN 0-534-13602-8 :
    1. State governments—United States. 2. Local government—United
  States. I. Mladenka, Kenneth R., [date]   . II. Title.
  JK2408.H55   1992
  353.9–dc20   91-38687
                                                                       CIP

Sponsoring Editor: Cynthia C. Stormer
Editorial Associate: Cathleen S. Collins
Production Coordinator: Fiorella Ljunggren
Production: Jane E. Hoover/Lifland et al., Bookmakers
Manuscript Editor: Jane E. Hoover
Permissions Editor: Marie DuBois
Interior Design: Quica Ostrander
Cover Design: Roy R. Neuhaus
Cover Photograph: Lee Hocker
Interior Illustration and Photo Research: Gail Magin
Typesetting: Weimer Typesetting Company, Inc.
Cover Printing: Lehigh Press Lithographers/Autoscreen
Printing and Binding: R. R. Donnelley & Sons Company, Crawfordsville

Credits continue on p. 473

PREFACE

As recently as the 1970s, thoughtful observers were predicting the demise of state and local governments as meaningful, independent entities. The federal government appeared to be usurping all the notable powers of those smaller jurisdictions. But the times and the commentary of political observers have both changed dramatically. As the end of the twentieth century draws near, state and local governments are experiencing a remarkable revival in importance and attention.

One reason for this reversal of fortune is the erosion of the power of the federal government. The election of Ronald Reagan and then George Bush to the presidency meant, first, that political conservatives seeking to reduce the power of the federal government were in charge of policy-making efforts in the White House. Although the U.S. Congress has been far less conservative during this period, both of these presidents have been successful in slowing the overall growth of federal power and even in reducing that power in some areas.

Uncle Sam is also less powerful today because he is broke. The 1980s and 1990s have witnessed the largest federal budget deficits in American history. Even political liberals have accepted numerous cuts in federal programs—and, therefore, in federal power—because of financial exigency. And in the face of these budgetary difficulties, many responsibilities have been returned to state and local governments. Those governments have always had more power than many people assumed—even when the federal government was at its strongest. Now, however, they have become even more important.

The states are also getting considerable attention because of the problems they face today. Every newscast and newspaper is full of stories about—to name just a few of the more prominent domestic problems—crime in the streets, the war on drugs, the effort to preserve environmental quality, the problems of educating today's youth, and the difficulties of raising sufficient revenues to pay for governmental efforts. State and local governments have always had the major responsibility for these and many other commonplace but quite vexing difficulties. Because of the federal government's shrinking domestic efforts, the states have taken on even more responsibility in these areas.

If we accept the conventional view of these problems, there is a remarkable irony in the facts cited above. Most people believe that the present-day social and economic difficulties of the United States are far worse than those of the recent past. Thus, the federal government has reduced its commitment to domestic policy at a time when domestic problems are especially acute. Clearly, the states must take up the initiative that Uncle Sam has relinquished.

Grappling with the kinds of discrete problems mentioned above has proven very demanding. Beyond such specific policy concerns, however, the nation faces an even bigger, potentially more disruptive challenge, one that also complicates the response to many individual problems. As we explain in Chapter 1, the United States is on the threshold of a transformation from an industrial to a postindustrial society. The nature of the economy is changing fundamentally. It is possible to envision the tantalizing prospect of a high-tech future, in which economic and social life might be remarkably better than it is under mature industrialism. But getting to that rosy future will entail a difficult passage. And even if the vision is realized, not all Americans may enjoy the benefits.

The reasons for concern about the impending economic transition are already quite evident. Once vigorous industrial sectors of the economy are in decline. High-tech industries are growing, but they have suffered their own growth pains and economic vicissitudes. Whole regions of the nation have experienced dramatic periods of boom and bust, with bust being the more common condition in the late 1980s and early 1990s. Furthermore, the character of life in metropolitan America is evolving with these economic changes, creating a host of difficulties for the governance of cities. And even the nation's economic power is in doubt. The United States not only faces tough economic competition from abroad but is also the world's largest debtor nation.

The economic transition and the immediate problems it poses will dramatically affect Americans' lives in a host of ways. Individuals, families, and governments will be equally touched. And these changes will complicate efforts to deal with other priorities, such as education, the environment, urban decline, and regional economic recessions. How governments respond to those problems will also affect the success of their efforts to accommodate to economic changes.

These observations justify considerable concern with the character and quality of state and local governments. Thus, we begin this book by discussing the difficulties these governments face and why one should read the rest of the book to learn more about them. We argue that the states face an unusual period of stress that will test their policy-making capabilities *and* their commitment to democratic governance. And because their policy decisions over the next several years will dramatically affect the quality of Americans' everyday lives, every citizen can benefit from a better understanding of how they work.

After explaining these policy challenges, we examine the separate parts of state and local governments, the "nuts and bolts," as political scientists say. We subject each nut and bolt—each major institution—to relatively microscopic examination, considering its role in the overall governmental process; the unique technical, political, and decision-making problems it confronts; and how democratic its functioning might be.

This book is heavily shaped, then, by themes implicit in the preceding remarks. We believe that state and local governments, because of their special responsibilities today, merit the close attention of average citizens as well as scholars. We see economic change as causing some of the most serious problems, and we frequently discuss the relevance of economics to politics and policy. We also believe that the greatest threat inherent in today's major problems is to democratic governance. Will the general public interest or narrow special interests be served as state and local governments try to resolve these problems?

The preceding themes are relatively distinctive to this book. Like many other authors in this field, however, we pay close attention to the nuts and bolts of state and local governments in order to demonstrate *how* they function and *why* they function as they do. These are complicated governments, affected by a host of competing external forces. Furthermore, each of these levels of government consists of a fragmented collection of institutions responding in various ways to the social and political pressures in their environments. Thus, understanding state and local governments necessitates a close, careful examination of how their constituent parts function. For this reason, we offer a detailed explanation of what scholars have concluded about these matters—about what is known with some certainty about them. At the same time we recognize that even scholars who specialize in the study of state and local governments disagree on a number of basic issues. We have attempted to present the major points of controversy, too, for they are equally important to a sophisticated understanding of these governments. One must recognize what is unknown along with what is known.

We are indebted to a number of people who aided the completion of this book. Leo Weigman and David Follmer of The Dorsey Press commissioned this enterprise more years ago than we care to admit. Cindy Stormer at Brooks/Cole inherited it as a result of the acquisition of The Dorsey Press by Wadsworth, Inc., and shepherded the project to its completion. Several people offered thorough reviews of earlier versions of the manuscript. They are Robert Albritton, Northern Illinois University; Thad L. Beyle, University of North Carolina at Chapel Hill; John Bibby, University of Wisconsin–Milwaukee; Ed Brazil, Eastern Illinois University; Raymond Cox, Office of the Lieutenant Governor of New Mexico; Charles Dunn, Henderson State University; Larry Elowitz, Georgia College; Richard Foster, Idaho State University; William K. Hall, Bradley University; Tom Holbrook, University of Wisconsin–Milwaukee; Mark Hyde, Providence College; James Jarvis, Wayne State University; Andrew D. McNitt, Eastern Illinois University; Edward J. Miller, University of Wisconsin–Stevens Point; Jim Seroka, University of North Florida. Although we agreed with their suggested revisions on many points, we remained doggedly resistant to their advice on a number of others—whether to our good or ill fortune we must let our readers decide. Finally, a host of people associated with Brooks/Cole contributed characteristically prompt and professional efforts as a tardy, inevitably incomplete, and often inconsistent manuscript was tranformed into the tome you hold today.

Kim Quaile Hill
Kenneth R. Mladenka

Contents

1 The Politics and Economics of State and Local Governments in the Late Twentieth Century   1

THE CURRENT ECONOMIC CHALLENGE   2

THE HAZARDS OF THE IMPENDING ECONOMIC TRANSITION   3

A HISTORICAL ANALOGY: THE TRANSFORMATION FROM AN AGRICULTURAL TO AN INDUSTRIAL ECONOMY   10

     The Transition to Industrialism   10
     The Political Consequences   11

QUESTIONS ABOUT THE ECONOMIC FUTURE   13

     Is There a Pot of Gold at the End of the Economic Rainbow?   14
     What If the Economy Is Not Transformed?   14
     Can States Shape Their Economic Future?   15
     Won't Uncle Sam Be Responsible for the Problems of the Economic Transition?   15

OTHER ECONOMIC INFLUENCES ON THE STATES   16

     Rich versus Poor States   16
     Dependence on an Agricultural Economy   19
     Leaders and Laggards in the High-Tech Race   20

THE IMPLICATIONS OF THE CURRENT ECONOMIC CHALLENGE   22

     The Challenge for Governments   22
     Concerns for Citizens   23

CONCLUSION   25

REFERENCES   25

2 The Legacy of History: Political Cultures and Constitutional Patterns   27

THE STATES' POLITICAL CULTURES   27

     Original Political Cultures of the States   28

Political Cultures of the States Today   31
Cultural Regions   32
THE POSITIVE-STATE ETHOS: A SPECIAL CASE OF A
POLITICAL-CULTURAL VALUE   35
THE STATES' CONSTITUTIONS   37
Constitutional Limits on State Power   37
Style and Language Problems in State Constitutions   39
Special Interests' Influence on State Constitutions   42
Datedness of State Constitutions   44
CONCLUSION   45
REFERENCES   46

3   STATE AND LOCAL GOVERNMENTS WITHIN THE FEDERAL SYSTEM   47

WHAT FEDERALISM IS   47
The Original Federal Design for American Government   48
The Evolution of American Federalism   49
THE ERA OF COOPTIVE FEDERALISM   54
Examples of the Expansion of Federal Power   54
The Methods of Federal Cooptation   69
The Impact of Cooptive Federalism on State and Local
Governments   72
WHAT ROLE IS LEFT FOR STATE AND LOCAL
GOVERNMENTS?   74
Control over Much Public Policy   74
Policy Innovation and Leadership   76
Implementation of Federal Policies   76
CONCLUSION   77
NOTES   78
REFERENCES   78

4   ELECTIONS, POLITICAL PARTIES, AND PARTICIPATION IN STATE
POLITICS   81

HOW STATE ELECTIONS WORK: THE RULES   82
Nominations for Office   82
General Elections   83
HOW STATE ELECTIONS WORK: THE PARTICIPANTS   84
The Candidates   84

Political Parties   85
Campaign Experts   87
HOW STATE ELECTIONS WORK: THE INCREASING
IMPORTANCE OF MONEY   88
Typical Campaign Costs   88
Does Spending More Ensure Victory?   90
Regulation of Campaign Spending   91
STATE PARTY SYSTEMS   93
Mass Partisanship and Ideology in the States   94
Electoral Competition between Parties   96
PUBLIC PARTICIPATION IN ELECTIONS   99
Mass Voting Behavior   99
Individual Voting Behavior   101
OTHER AVENUES FOR PUBLIC PARTICIPATION   102
DIRECT DEMOCRACY   105
The Referendum   105
The Initiative   106
The Recall   106
Utilization of the Mechanisms for Direct Democracy   106
CONCLUSION   108
NOTES   109
REFERENCES   110

5 *INTEREST GROUPS IN STATE POLITICS*   113

WHAT INTEREST GROUPS ARE   113
TYPES OF INTEREST GROUPS   114
Business Groups   115
Occupational Groups   116
Agricultural Groups   117
Public-Interest Groups   118
Single-Interest Groups   119
THE STRATEGIES OF INTEREST GROUPS   120
Financial and Other Electoral Support for Candidates
    and Elected Officials   120
Lobbying the Government   121
Lobbying the Public   126
Bribery   126

THE POWER OF INDIVIDUAL INTEREST GROUPS   127
   Votes   128
   Money   129
   Expertise and Information   129
   Status   129
   Access   130
THE COLLECTIVE POWER OF INTEREST GROUPS   130
   An Extreme Example: Company States   131
   How Many Groups?   132
   How Powerful Are Interest Groups?   133
THE BIAS OF THE INTEREST GROUP SYSTEM   136
CONCLUSION   136
REFERENCES   138

6   *STATE LEGISLATURES*   141

WHAT LEGISLATURES DO   141
THE MECHANICS OF REPRESENTATION   144
   Policy Representation   144
   Constituency Service   146
   Pork Barrel Politics   147
THE MECHANICS OF LAWMAKING   148
   Drafting the Bill   150
   Committee Review   150
   Debate and Vote by the Legislature   152
   The Governor's Approval or Veto   157
THE ERA OF STATE LEGISLATIVE REFORM   157
STATE LEGISLATURES TODAY   159
STATE LEGISLATORS TODAY   163
   Why Do They Run for Office?   164
   Why Do They Leave Office?   167
POLITICAL INFLUENCES ON THE LEGISLATURE   170
   Political Parties   171
   Interest Groups   171
   Governors   172
CONCLUSION   173
NOTES   173
REFERENCES   174

7 GOVERNORS AND STATE EXECUTIVE BRANCHES 177

A HISTORY OF THE OFFICE OF GOVERNOR 178
THE ROLES OF THE MODERN GOVERNOR 180
Policy Leader 181
Legislative Leader 182
Chief Executive Officer 182
Ceremonial Leader 183
Party Leader 184
THE DEMANDS OF THE GOVERNOR'S OFFICE 185
FORMAL SOURCES OF GUBERNATORIAL POWER 188
Tenure Potential 189
The Unified Executive 190
Organizational Control of the Executive Branch 191
Budgetary Power 193
Legislative Powers 194
Powers Associated with Intergovernmental Relations 195
Size of the Governor's Staff 195
Interstate Comparison of Governors' Formal Powers 199
INFORMAL SOURCES OF GUBERNATORIAL POWER 202
Public Expectations for the Office 202
Personal Political Skills 202
The Symbolism of the Role of Chief of State 203
Opportunities for Party Leadership 203
CHARACTERISTICS OF TODAY'S GOVERNORS 204
A Profile of the Contemporary Governor 204
Gubernatorial Ambitions 207
THE STATES' EXECUTIVE BRANCHES 209
The Character of the Modern Executive Branch 209
The Governor and the Executive Branch 211
CONCLUSION 214
REFERENCES 215

8 THE JUDICIAL BRANCH 217

WHAT COURTS DO 218
PUBLIC UNDERSTANDING OF COURTS AND LAW 219
COURTS AS POLITICAL INSTITUTIONS 221

THE ORGANIZATION OF STATE AND LOCAL COURTS   223
Trial Courts   224
Appellate Courts   225
Exceptions to the Typical Oranizational Structure of
State Court Systems   226
THE WORK OF STATE AND LOCAL COURTS   228
Courts of Limited Jurisdiction   228
Courts of General Jurisdiction   229
Intermediate Appellate Courts   231
Courts of Last Resort   232
MAJOR PARTICIPANTS IN THE COURT SYSTEM   232
Judges   232
Trial Juries   234
Prosecuting Attorneys   235
Private Attorneys   238
Litigants   240
METHODS FOR JUDICIAL SELECTION   242
CHARACTERISTICS OF JUDGES   245
CONCLUSION   248
NOTES   249
REFERENCES   250

9   *The Politics and Economics of Urban Life in the United
States*   253

THE FRAGMENTATION OF GOVERNMENT AUTHORITY
IN METROPOLITAN AREAS   254
FRAGMENTATION AND SELF-INTEREST   257
THE PROS AND CONS OF FRAGMENTATION   258
Freedom of Choice   258
The Healthy Effects of Competition   259
The Disparity between Needs and Resources   260
Racial and Class Segregation   261
The Limited Mobility of the Poor   264
Fragmentation and Lack of Intergovernmental
Cooperation   268
Fragmentation—Good or Bad?   269
CAUSES OF SUBURBANIZATION   270
Federal Housing Policy   271
Practices of the Housing Industry   274

Federal Highway Policy 275
ATTEMPTS TO COMBAT FRAGMENTATION 277
Annexation 278
Special Districts 279
Voluntary Agreements 279
Councils of Governments 279
POLITICAL PARTICIPATION IN METROPOLITAN AREAS 280
Voting 283
Contacting 287
Group Activity 290
Nonviolent Protest 296
Violence as Political Participation 298
Exit 300
The Effectiveness of Political Participation 301
CONCLUSION 303
REFERENCES 304

10 THE POLITICAL INSTITUTIONS OF CITY GOVERNMENT 307

THE REFORM OF CITY GOVERNMENT 308
The Effects of Industrialization and Immigration 308
The Reform Movement 311
The Consequences of Reform 317
LEADERSHIP IN THE CITY: MAYORS AND CITY MANAGERS 321
The Special Case of Minority Mayors 326
Differences between City Managers and Mayors 328
CITY COUNCILS 330
CONCLUSION 332
REFERENCES 332

11 COMMUNITY POWER 335

THE ELITIST PERSPECTIVE 336
THE PLURALIST PERSPECTIVE 337
CRITICISMS OF THE ELITIST AND PLURALIST POSITIONS 340
Definitions of Power 340
Methodology 342
Nondecisions and Anticipated Reactions 342

RECONCILING THE ELITIST AND PLURALIST
POSITIONS   344
    The Special Position of Business   345
    The Importance of the Economic Climate   347
    The Power of Public Officials   349
    Policy Arenas and Power   350
CONCLUSION   353
REFERENCES   353

12   *The Delivery and Distribution of Urban Public Services*   355

THE ENVIRONMENT OF URBAN GOVERNMENTS   356
THE DIFFICULTIES OF SERVICE DELIVERY IN URBAN
AREAS   357
EQUITY IN SERVICE DELIVERY   364
    Conceptions of Equity   364
    Implications of Equity Standards   366
THE PATTERNS OF SERVICE DISTRIBUTION   370
    The Determinants of the Distributional Pattern   372
    Historical Change in Distributional Determinants 376
    Racial Bias in the Distribution of Municipal Jobs 378
CONCLUSION   380
REFERENCES   381

13   *Bureaucratic Power in State and Local Government*   383

CHARACTERISTICS OF BUREAUCRACIES   384
BUREAUCRATIC DECISION MAKING   385
    Limitations on Rationality in Bureaucracies   385
    Characteristics of Bureaucratic Decisions   387
THE CONTRADICTIONS INHERENT IN THE
FUNCTIONING OF BUREAUCRACIES   388
THE POWER OF BUREAUCRACIES   391
    Sources of Bureaucratic Power   391
    Limits on Bureaucratic Power   396
ARE BUREAUCRATS RESPONSIVE AND ACCOUNTABLE?   398
    Evidence from Researchers   400
    Bureaucratic Responsiveness in Chicago—A Case Study   403
CONCLUSION   408
REFERENCES   409

14 THE PUBLIC POLICIES OF STATE AND LOCAL GOVERNMENTS 411

    WHAT PUBLIC POLICIES ARE 411

    CHARACTERISTICS OF STATE AND LOCAL
    GOVERNMENTS' POLICIES 413

        Reasons for the Divergence and Convergence of
           States' Policies 413
        The Scope of State and Local Policy Efforts 416
        Extractive Efforts of the States 420
        The Distribution of Benefits and Burdens 423
        Innovativeness of Policy Making 426
        Explaining the States' Rankings 428

    THE MECHANICS OF STATE AND LOCAL FINANCES 430

        State and Local Taxation 430
        State and Local Spending 436

    CONCLUSION 438

    NOTES 439

    REFERENCES 439

15 DEMOCRACY IN THE STATES 441

    IS THERE DEMOCRACY IN THE UNITED STATES? 442

        Democratic Government 444
        Polyarchy 445
        Economic Dominance 445

    EVALUATING THE DEMOCRATIZATION OF THE STATES 447

        The Status of Political Rights 448
        A Scorecard for Democracy in the States 450
        The Meaning of Democratization in the Everyday
           Political Life of the States 455

    PUZZLES IN STATE POLITICS 456

        The Relative Disinterest of Citizens in State Politics 456
        The Limited Development of Two-Party Competition 457
        The Mistrust of Government by Business 458

    CONCLUSION 460

    NOTES 461

    REFERENCES 461

  INDEX 463

1

The Politics and Economics of State and Local Governments in the Late Twentieth Century

The economic news today is troubling. States in the American Midwest—which once were famous for their manufacturing output and, indeed, were the symbol of America's industrial might—have been dubbed the Rust Belt because of the decline of their industries. Farm states—once the symbol of America's natural bounty—suffer because of a long-term recession in the agricultural economy. In the South and Southwest the states of the Sun Belt continue to try to attract new industry to overcome their second-class economic status. Across the nation it is acknowledged that the economic times are uncertain. Many once powerful industries are in decline. Others have uncertain futures, and almost all face stiff competition from foreign competitors. And the buzz words of the day are "high tech." Whether it is wise or even practical, political and economic leaders in every state clamor for high-tech development as the resolution of current uncertainties.

Is all this relevant to state and local governments? We think so; in fact, we think economic concerns will be of critical importance to these governments and their citizens for at least the next generation. This chapter explains how and why economic matters have become central to the politics of state and local governments and, therefore, to the remainder of this book. We will also consider how noneconomic forces shape the policy agendas of state and local

1

governments. Culture, history, and a variety of recent events do have an impact, but economic matters are especially important for state and local governments because current economic conditions are exceptional.

THE CURRENT ECONOMIC CHALLENGE

Although this chapter began with a litany of specific economic difficulties, there is more of concern here than just specific, short-term economic problems. Every age has such problems, and they always affect state and local governments. Today, however, the United States faces a far more serious economic challenge. Its economy is on the brink of a sweeping transformation in character—from an industrial economy to what has been labeled a high-tech or post-industrial one. The economy could pass through that transformation in the next generation or so or remain mired in difficulties of the kind that are currently prevalent. Either way state and local governments will face formidable challenges. To consider what this transformation might mean, we must first look at where the economy stands now.

By 1960 the U.S. economy had reached a highly advanced stage of industrial economic development. Some states had advanced further than others in the process of industrialization, yet in general the nation was highly industrialized. Soon, however, careful observers began to detect significant evolutionary changes in the society and the economy. The most notable of these observers was Daniel Bell (1973), who coined the term "post-industrial society" for what he envisioned was taking shape. Bell argued that the "goods-producing" component of the economy, which was preeminent under industrialism, would be supplanted by the professional, technical, and managerial components. In effect, knowledge-based industries would become the driving force of the economy, and individuals with the greatest technical and professional knowledge would be its leaders.

Clearly there is a great similarity between Bell's early vision and the so-called high-tech image of the future that is popular today. This high-tech future has been described as one in which the economy will be driven by technologically advanced electronics, computer, and automated process industries. This vision is simply a more detailed conception of the postindustrial era, which takes into account recent advances in computer, electronic, robotic, and laser technologies.

Whatever specific form it takes, the transition to a post-industrial economy will fundamentally affect the lives and careers of all Americans. It will offer exciting new opportunities but will also pose significant and, at times, painful difficulties for both individuals and governments. The probable magnitude of these difficulties can be gauged in two ways: by considering some economic problems unique to these times and by looking at those of an earlier economic transformation, that from an agricultural to an industrial economy.

THE HAZARDS OF THE IMPENDING ECONOMIC TRANSITION

One complication of the present economic troubles arises because of the considerable foreign economic competition the United States faces. A number of nations in Asia and Europe, in particular, compete fiercely and effectively in markets for automobiles, manufactured steel and industrial goods, clothing, and electronics. Lower wages and more modern manufacturing processes often give the products from these nations distinct price and quality advantages.

When the United States entered the industrial age, there was little comparable competition. Even as late as 1950—largely because of the devastation many countries suffered in World War II—U.S. industries had few serious foreign competitors for the goods they wished to sell abroad or, for that matter, here at home. Now much of the world has caught up economically. Some say other nations have even eclipsed the United States in worker productivity, product quality, and economic might. And there is just as much international competition in the emerging high-tech industries as there is in the "old-fashioned" industrial ones. Even those states with the most advanced high-tech economies, such as California and Massachusetts, have suffered tough economic times recently, in part because of foreign competition.

A second difficulty arises because some parts of the United States are still highly dependent on agricultural and natural resources production. The farm crisis of the 1980s was only the latest in a series of economic misfortunes faced by agriculture in this century. Similarly, the sharp declines in natural gas and crude oil prices in the 1980s and the recessions that followed in energy-dependent states from Alaska to Texas serve as reminders of how vulnerable these states are to international market forces beyond their control. These states are dependent, too, on exhaustible natural resources whose economic role must one day be played by different kinds of industries.

The problems of agriculture and the energy industry indicate that, while the nation is trying to plan for a twenty-first–century economy, some states (and regions) are still struggling with economic problems of nineteenth-century industries. Those states could face especially notable difficulties in the coming economic transition. These problems indicate that the path to postindustrialism is likely to be an uneven one. It could easily require one or two generations to make the transition. Some states, regions, and even whole nations might still be struggling at the end of the twenty-first century. The hardships of the process, however, can best be typified if we consider some of its effects on individuals and governments.

Consider, as just one example of the effects on individuals, how the economic transition will affect people's careers and personal economic well-being. Most of you reading this book are college students trying to choose and prepare for career paths. In a sense today's students may be lucky—education has been called the key to success in the postindustrial world. In the industrial economy a person with a strong back but little education could often get a good-paying job in construction, manufacturing, or a skilled trade. Today those jobs are rapidly disappearing and mainly being replaced by relatively low-paying service jobs. Now a strong back and little education qualify you to flip hamburgers at the minimum wage. However, even the college-educated face uncertainties. Some of the careers students are training for today may disappear in twenty years. Accountants could go the way of blacksmiths—and of auto workers for that matter. Thus, college students should try to choose careers with a post-industrial future and to acquire skills that will help them adapt to changing economic times.

Another serious concern is that the very best jobs could be quite few in number in postindustrial society. It has already become apparent, for example, that the early years of the high-tech boom produced a great *percent* increase in computer and electronics-related jobs, but the overwhelmingly greater *number* of new jobs arose in relatively low-paying service industries. Figure 1-1 presents, as evidence of this trend, U.S. Department of Labor projections of the occupations that

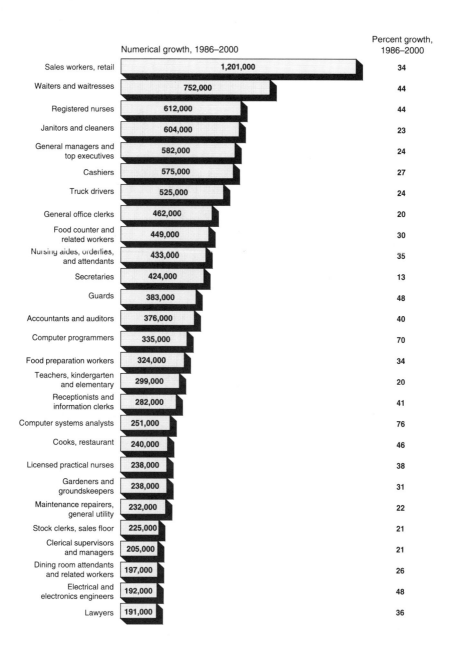

Occupation	Numerical growth, 1986–2000	Percent growth, 1986–2000
Sales workers, retail	1,201,000	34
Waiters and waitresses	752,000	44
Registered nurses	612,000	44
Janitors and cleaners	604,000	23
General managers and top executives	582,000	24
Cashiers	575,000	27
Truck drivers	525,000	24
General office clerks	462,000	20
Food counter and related workers	449,000	30
Nursing aides, orderlies, and attendants	433,000	35
Secretaries	424,000	13
Guards	383,000	48
Accountants and auditors	376,000	40
Computer programmers	335,000	70
Food preparation workers	324,000	34
Teachers, kindergarten and elementary	299,000	20
Receptionists and information clerks	282,000	41
Computer systems analysts	251,000	76
Cooks, restaurant	240,000	46
Licensed practical nurses	238,000	38
Gardeners and groundskeepers	238,000	31
Maintenance repairers, general utility	232,000	22
Stock clerks, sales floor	225,000	21
Clerical supervisors and managers	205,000	21
Dining room attendants and related workers	197,000	26
Electrical and electronics engineers	192,000	48
Lawyers	191,000	36

Source: U.S. Bureau of Labor Statistics, "Changing Employment in Occupations," *Occupational Outlook Quarterly* (Fall 1987), pp. 28–33.

will grow the fastest over the period 1986–2000. Several high-tech and managerial occupations are included in this list, but the greatest numbers of new jobs will be in service and "low-tech" positions. Based on these trends, there will be many more waiters, hospital orderlies, janitors, and hamburger-flippers than high-tech professionals in the postindustrial economy.

Automation continues to take its toll as well, across a surprisingly wide range of occupations. Assembly-line jobs are declining in number because of the use of robotics in manufacturing, but so are jobs for musicians because of the increasing use of computer-synthesized music. Advanced technology for computer-assisted design could devastate the profession of architect. And the creation of increasingly sophisticated computers may mean that one day society will need only a fraction of today's programmers, systems analysts, and electronics engineers.

These observations suggest that all Americans must be concerned about preparing for the economic transition ahead. None of today's college students want to find at mid-career that their profession is disappearing because of economic or technological change. Getting to postindustrialism, in other words, may be a risky and painful process. And postindustrial society may not be a happy place for everyone.

There will be difficulties for governments, too, in this process. Economic recessions have already lowered state and local government revenues dramatically in the Rust Belt, the Farm Belt, and the oil-dependent states. Government expenditures and, therefore, services have often been cut significantly as well, because of these recessions. In addition, those who work in the declining sectors of the economy have quickly pressed for government assistance of various kinds. So state and local governments have already encountered significant policy challenges as a result of economic changes. And these challenges have been especially difficult because demands for public services and benefits have risen at the same time as government revenues have been falling.

State and local government leaders have also been faced with the question of how to spur new economic growth and attract new industries to replace the declining ones. Indeed, as we explain in more detail below, economic development has become a top priority for these leaders in recent years. However, what might be the most efficacious way to ensure such development is controversial and widely debated. At least three strategies for seeking economic development have been especially popular lately.

SUGGESTIVE OF INDUSTRIAL GHOST TOWNS, ABANDONED FACTORIES ARE MODERN CASUALTIES OF ECONOMIC CHANGE.

First, state and local governments have engaged in extensive marketing efforts, touting attributes of their localities that might appeal to businesses. States brag about their large and eager work force, their geographic location and its business opportunities, their favorable "business climate," and, whenever possible, their climate and natural beauty.

Additionally, most states have adopted some kind of tax reduction or public subsidy program to aid new or relocated businesses. Tax exemptions, publicly provided capital, and state-supported training for prospective employees are typical benefits of these programs. Such incentives are also utilized as part of states' marketing efforts. As an example of this combining of two development strategies, the box on the next page presents a page taken from a brochure published by the Oklahoma Department of Commerce to promote that state as a place to locate a business.

The third common strategy for promoting development is to invest in public infrastructure, such as education and transportation facilities, and to maintain high levels of public services. Advocates of this strategy see both short- and long-term benefits from it. In the

Oklahoma Business: A Blueprint of Opportunity.

Oklahoma's healthy business climate is reflected by its active state legislature which has been approving greater pro-business packages each session. Oklahoma's state sales tax is one of the lowest in the nation. Along with a low tax structure, other incentives help point business to Oklahoma. Incentives including:

- A five-year property tax exemption on new or expanding manufacturing or processing facilities.
- No unitary tax.
- No sales tax on industrial machinery and equipment.
- Exempted tax on materials or goods consumed in the manufacturing process, as well as products manufactured in Oklahoma but sold and transported outside the state.
- Oklahoma does not have a state property tax. And its local and county property taxes are significantly lower, averaging 94 cents per $100 of cash value.

short-term they hope business firms will be attracted by the high level of amenities and public services. Business professionals in high-tech firms, for example, are presumed to place great value on quality education for their children; therefore, they might seek to locate their businesses where there are unusually good public schools. In addition, such firms need highly educated employees in some jobs, enhancing their executives' and owners' concern about the education level of the work force in general. Over the long run, spending on infrastructure, and especially on education, is thought to stimulate entrepreneurship and research and development, which in turn promote economic development. Thus, first-class university systems, in particular, have been recommended.

Financial incentives such as these have helped to attract major business in locating manufacturing, warehousing and office facilities in the state. More than $3.4 billion has been invested in the last decade through 460 new plants and 709 expansions, providing nearly 70,000 new jobs.

Companies like AT&T Technologies, American Airlines, Armstrong, Colt Industries, Eaton, Firestone, Ford Glass, Fort Howard Paper Company, General Motors, Goodyear, Hilti, Hitachi, Maremont, Mercury Marine, TRW, Telex, Uniroyal, Weyerhaeuser, Xerox and many others agree Oklahoma was a sound business move.

Their main reasons? A highly productive Oklahoma labor force. The nation's most thorough and effective industry training programs. Central location. Every mode of transportation available. Abundant and affordable energy. Excellent business attitude. A favorable tax structure. And a quality environment to raise a family.

Public agencies offer financing capabilities including the purchase and improvement of industrial sites, financing for equipment and building construction through the issuance of revenue bonds carrying a low rate of interest. Industrial development is further enhanced by a number of Oklahoma communities and districts which offer general obligation tax supported bonds.

Source: "Oklahoma Outlined," brochure published by the Oklahoma Department of Commerce.

All three of these strategies appear to be plausible ways for advancing economic development, and all of them are being pursued to some degree by all the states. But their true potential is uncertain. Recent research has cast doubt on the likely success of tax incentives, subsidies, and state marketing efforts (Ledebur and Hamilton, 1986). Investment in infrastructure has received less critical attention. Yet even if it is a feasible route to development, much of the economic return may not be realized for a long time. That is, a dollar invested in public education today may not return sizable economic benefits for a generation. These doubts about appropriate policy strategies leave the states, as well as most individuals, uncertain about their postindustrial futures.

A HISTORICAL ANALOGY: THE TRANSFORMATION FROM AN AGRICULTURAL TO AN INDUSTRIAL ECONOMY

The preceding remarks indicated some of the ways the transition to postindustrialism will affect Americans and their governments. Much of what lies ahead, of course, cannot be anticipated with certainty. However, we can give some impression of the magnitude of the coming social, economic, and political changes by considering a historical analogy, the only comparable economic transition in U.S. history and its effects on Americans and their governments.

THE TRANSITION TO INDUSTRIALISM

As late as the end of the Civil War, the United States was still an agricultural nation. The majority of the work force was employed in agriculture, and the majority of the population lived in rural areas. During the last third of the nineteenth century and the first half of the twentieth, however, the United States was transformed into an industrial nation. Agriculture declined dramatically, both as a source of employment and as a contributor to the nation's wealth and economic production. Meanwhile the manufacturing, wholesale and retail trading, construction, and services sectors grew enormously. By about the middle of the twentieth century, the nation had attained mature industrialism.

As a by-product of this industrial transformation, a social one came about as well. The growing manufacturing sector required large labor pools concentrated in relatively small areas. And the fact that the trade and services sectors are inevitably linked to concentrated population areas reinforced this development. The results were the urbanization of the population and the growth of large cities. This process has continued throughout the twentieth century, and today almost 80 percent of the U.S. population lives in urban areas. But there is more to this change than a simple switch from a rural to an urban population. Americans do not just live in cities—most of them live in very big cities or metropolitan areas. In fact, more than half of the U.S. population lives in metropolitan areas of 1 million or more. And this majority is experiencing the unique social and political problems attendant on large numbers of people living in such densely settled circumstances.

THE POLITICAL CONSEQUENCES

The decline of agriculture, the rise of the industrial sector, and the growth of cities created a range of new political controversies. The first of those controversies arose in the struggle of the farmers with the railroads. The railroads depended, of course, on a new industrial technology, but the railroad companies typified something else about the age of industrialism. These companies were huge, wealthy, and politically very powerful, capable of affecting the lives and economic fortunes of many Americans to a degree never before experienced.

The farmers, through such groups as the Granger movement and the Populist party, fought a long-running battle against the railroads beginning in the 1870s. The rates charged by the railroads, the character of their services, and even the locations of their lines directly affected the business of farming. The most controversial of such issues was the policy of many rail companies of charging "whatever the market would bear" to transport agricultural goods. The farmers saw a threat to their livelihood in this new industrial entity, and they demanded and got government regulation of the railroads, first at the state and then the national level. Contrary to the traditional laissez-faire ethic that government's powers should be limited, the farmers wanted *positive* functions and powers for government. They wanted government to use those powers to protect their economic interests. This first political skirmish at the dawn of the industrial age foreshadowed much that came after it. The birth of the modern regulatory state in all its broad reach might well be traced back to the farmers' successful fight against the railroads. Over time, more and more groups recognized the value of government protection and demanded it for their interests.

The economic and social transformations associated with industrialism led to other political controversies that resulted in the expansion of governmental powers. Some of those controversies arose because life in the industrial and urban age was full of many new hazards. Factory work in this period was often quite dangerous, since there were few, if any, safety provisions. And it was not just adult factory workers who faced these dangers. Quite young children also worked under unsafe conditions because there were no laws concerning age, working hours, or conditions of employment. It was not long, of course, until reformers demanded that such laws be enacted, that government protect individuals from these new dangers of the industrial era. And it was state government, by the way, that first took up this policy priority.

There were other industrial hazards, too. Urban dwellers began eating more and more processed food instead of food grown by themselves or on a neighbor's farm. They were also taking more and more manufactured drugs and medicines. The muckrakers' exposés of the meat-packing plants brought the safety and sanitation of all these new products into question, and government was eventually called on to help ensure those characteristics.

Big cities and rapid urban growth placed new demands on government, as well. Local and state governments were soon called on to respond to public demands for services. Large accumulations of people in densely settled areas require extensive and costly transportation, public health and safety, sanitation, and related services unimagined by the rustic farmer. These services are admittedly prosaic and easily taken for granted today, but they are central to any conception of the quality of urban life.

The industrial era raised another issue, to which the example of the railroads alluded. Industrial development led to the growth of a variety of huge private corporations with enormous economic power that they could wield over government as well as over private citizens. The historian Richard Hofstadter (1955: 229) has aptly summarized one example of this circumstance with the following observation:

> As early as 1888 Charles William Eliot, in a well-known essay . . . , had pointed out that the great corporations, as units of organization, had far outstripped the governments of the states. He remarked that a certain railroad with offices in Boston employed 18,000 persons, had gross receipts of about $40,000,000 a year, and paid its highest-salaried officer $35,000. At the same time the Commonwealth of Massachusetts employed only 6,000 persons, had gross receipts of about $7,000,000, and paid no salary higher than $6,500. And a really great railroad like the Pennsylvania would overshadow the Commonwealth far more imposingly than the Boston organization.

And the size of the new corporations was not the only matter for concern. Allegations of the abuse of corporate power were common in the 1890s and the early years of this century. Indeed, muckrakers and government investigators documented widespread bribery of public officials and manipulation of governments' agendas by corporate officials. Progressive-era reformers called for new governmental powers to regulate these business entities and limit their political power. A variety of political reforms—of election systems, political party systems, and government administration—were implemented by state and local governments to further this goal.

In sum, the transition to industrialism set in motion a host of social, economic, and political changes. Where Americans lived, how they worked, and the literal quality of their lives changed dramatically and not always for the better. Some skills, occupations, and ways of life became obsolete, and disappeared within a generation or were consigned to a lingering decline. The social and economic changes also brought a host of new demands on government. If the label of laissez-faire was ever an accurate one for governments in the United States, it was no longer so after the Progressive era at the beginning of this century. The problems of the transition to industrialism led Americans to demand that government take responsibility for a number of social and economic goals and for the character of much of their lives. And all levels of government shared this responsibility.

This historic analogy indicates how dramatic socioeconomic change like that impending today leads, first, to sweeping alterations in everyday life and, second, to unprecedented challenges for government. We should note, however, that historians are sharply divided over all the motivations of those groups of Americans who first pressed a broader role on government, as well as about the success of the resulting policy efforts and which interests in society were best served by them. But there is unanimity about the changes in life itself in the industrial age and in the role of government in that society.

QUESTIONS ABOUT THE ECONOMIC FUTURE

We have tried to sound a note of tentativeness about the economic transition facing the United States. We cannot, of course, know with certainty what the future holds. But there are at least four questions about this country's economic future that we should try to answer here, since the economic challenge facing the United States underlies much of this book.

IS THERE A POT OF GOLD AT THE END OF THE ECONOMIC RAINBOW?

Won't it be a good thing, some might ask, when the United States has attained postindustrialism? After all, most Americans would agree that the industrial era brought considerable improvements in their lives—at least after many of its worst dangers were moderated. The "good old days" of the agricultural era were, of course, not precisely that.

We expect that postindustrialism *will* improve the character of American life in many ways. Technological advances will make people's lives easier and safer in many ways. There is also the possibility that many more people will enjoy stimulating work rather than the drudgery of the industrial plants in which their parents toiled. Getting to the postindustrial stage, however, may be a painful and uncertain process, just as the transition to industrialism was. And not all Americans will share in the good postindustrial life. Evidence for this observation consists of the large numbers of poor and economically marginal people who do not share in the good life of the industrial era today. Thus, even if there is a pot of gold ahead, finding it will be a difficult task for both individuals and governments. And those who do not share in the booty will demand that government improve their plight. More fortunate individuals may agree, as well, that society has some responsibility for the welfare of the poor.

WHAT IF THE ECONOMY IS NOT TRANSFORMED?

Some might ask whether there is likely to be any economic transformation at all—at least of the character and magnitude we have described. Maybe the United States will simply remain a mature industrial nation with only some high-tech elements and an expansion of service industries.

This is a possibility, for the transformation that appears to be taking shape may not be inevitable. But the alternative—if the economy does not move into postindustrialism—is frightening. Today the United States finds it tougher and tougher to maintain its economic competitiveness at home and abroad. Many of its traditionally strongest industries are in decline. The banking industry teeters on the brink of insolvency. The population is aging, and future productivity is therefore in question. In fact, worker productivity is presently increasing only at a modest rate. The foreign trade imbalance is embarrassing, and the United States has a huge public debt because the federal government is far bigger than is affordable. If this country does not progress into postindustrialism, then we and our children will live out our lives in this unfortunate situation. And our governments will be fighting to stem the tide of economic decline and increasing public discontent. That is, they will still find the economic challenge a substantial one.

CAN STATES SHAPE THEIR ECONOMIC FUTURE?

Some people might be skeptical about the likely efficacy of the popular strategies for advancing state economic development. They might fear that there is little the states can do to control their own economic destinies. This concern is reasonable, and it is buttressed by recognition of the powerful international forces affecting American economic life. Oklahoma might compete successfully with Iowa or Tennessee for high-tech business. But can it compete with Japan?

There is considerable uncertainty about whether state and local governments can shape their economic futures. Yet we suspect that most Americans believe that their governments should try very hard to do so. And, after all, shouldn't government leaders respond to public preferences in a democratic nation? Thus, it is appropriate for governments to take on this challenge, but as citizens, we should temper our expectations about how successful they might be.

WON'T UNCLE SAM BE RESPONSIBLE FOR THE PROBLEMS OF THE ECONOMIC TRANSITION?

Finally, many people might wish to pose one more question. Won't the federal government, they would ask, be more responsible for the problems of the economic transition than state and local ones?

Undoubtedly, the federal government will play an important role, sharing some policy initiatives with the states and keeping many others as its exclusive prerogative. But the states have always had important independent powers with respect to their social and economic concerns, and there are good reasons to believe that those powers will grow, instead of decline, in the future. We will address this question more fully in Chapter 3. For the present we can simply observe that since 1980 it has been the policy of the federal government to return more and more power to the states. And the ever-growing federal budget deficit means that this trend is likely to continue for some time. For this reason—and for several more to be discussed in Chapter 3—state and local governments will indeed bear significant responsibility for addressing the social and economic problems of the near future.

OTHER ECONOMIC INFLUENCES ON THE STATES

The states face the present economic challenge with differing resources and capabilities. Some are far better advantaged than others to make the transition to postindustrialism. There are many resources that could smooth that transition as well as numerous circumstances that could impede it. We consider three of the most prominent of these resources and impediments here.

RICH VERSUS POOR STATES

Some states are, quite simply, far wealthier than the average, and some are far poorer. Present-day material wealth should be a great advantage for the future. It means that the private sector has more capital to invest in economic enterprises, including high-tech ones. It also means that there is more wealth that can be taxed or otherwise employed by the public sector in its efforts to assist economic development. Furthermore, wealthy states are likely to have a "cushion" against short-term economic difficulties. Poor states are disadvantaged in all these respects.

To illustrate differences in wealth among the states, Table 1-1 presents two kinds of indicators. The first is a comparative index of the average per capita personal income earned in each state in 1988. The index is scaled so that the state with the mean per capita personal income—comparing all fifty states—has a score of 100. Higher scores indicate a proportionately above-average per capita personal

	STATE	INDEX OF PER CAPITA PERSONAL INCOME	INDEX OF STATE AND LOCAL GOVERNMENTS' TAXING CAPACITY
TABLE 1-1 TWO MEASURES OF THE WEALTH OF THE STATES: PER CAPITA PERSONAL INCOME AND STATE AND LOCAL GOVERNMENTS' TAXING CAPACITY, 1988	Alabama	78	76
	Alaska	116	159
	Arizona	91	99
	Arkansas	74	74
	California	114	116
	Colorado	100	107
	Connecticut	140	143
	Delaware	107	124
	Florida	101	104
	Georgia	93	94
	Hawaii	102	114
	Idaho	77	76
	Illinois	107	99
	Indiana	91	87
	Iowa	89	83
	Kansas	96	91
	Kentucky	78	81
	Louisiana	75	83
	Maine	92	98
	Maryland	118	109
	Massachusetts	126	129
	Michigan	100	95
	Minnesota	101	104
	Mississippi	67	65
	Missouri	94	90
	Montana	78	85
	Nebraska	90	90
	Nevada	106	135
	New Hampshire	118	126
	New Jersey	133	124
	New Mexico	76	83
	New York	117	109
	North Carolina	87	91
	North Dakota	78	86
	Ohio	94	91
	Oklahoma	81	84
	Oregon	90	91
	Pennsylvania	98	94
	Rhode Island	102	99

CONTINUED

TABLE 1-1
CONTINUED

STATE	INDEX OF PER CAPITA PERSONAL INCOME	INDEX OF STATE AND LOCAL GOVERNMENTS' TAXING CAPACITY
South Carolina	78	79
South Dakota	77	78
Tennessee	84	84
Texas	88	96
Utah	74	78
Vermont	93	105
Virginia	107	104
Washington	100	98
West Virginia	71	78
Wisconsin	94	90
Wyoming	83	123
Average for All Fifty States	100	100

Source: Carol E. Cohen, "State Fiscal Capacity and Effort: The 1988 Representative Tax System Estimates," *Intergovernmental Perspectives* 16 (Fall 1990), pp. 17–22.

income, and scores below 100 indicate a proportionately below-average one. The second measure presented in the table is an index of potential revenue-raising capacity in each state, based on the forms of wealth and income typically taxed by state and local governments (such as property taxes, sales taxes, income taxes, users' fees, and so on). A state's score on this index is determined by taking its *actual* wealth in taxable terms and calculating the tax income it could derive by applying the average tax rate on each of these revenue sources imposed by those states that now tax each source. A score of 100 means that a state's revenue-raising capacity is at the average among all states. Higher scores mean greater than average capacity, and lower ones the opposite.

A state's ranking on the two measures gives an indication of the amount of resources it can marshal for public or private efforts at economic development and, for that matter, a variety of other purposes. Alaska, California, Connecticut, Massachusetts, New Hampshire, and New Jersey are notably wealthy on both measures. On the other hand, Alabama, Arkansas, Idaho, Kentucky, Louisiana, Mississippi, Montana, New Mexico, South Carolina, South Dakota, Utah, and West Virginia rank especially low on both measures. In fact, per capita income in the states ranking highest on that measure—Connecticut and New Jersey—is about double that in the poorest state, Mississippi.

Undoubtedly, these wealth differences will be important in the future, but it is important to keep in mind a critical fact about them. They are based largely on industrial-era sources and conceptions of wealth. Consider, as an analogy, how someone might have measured the wealth of the states just before the process of industrialization began to accelerate in the late nineteenth century. Wealth then might well have been based on agricultural measures, in keeping with what was the dominant economic mode. That is, wealth would have been gauged by the value of agricultural land and the production from it. Yet those resources did not equip states to enter the industrial era successfully.

What resources will be essential for a successful transition to postindustrialism? Some argue that a highly educated work force will be the most important asset. Some say it will be individual entrepreneurship and innovation. Others say it will be wise government leadership and investment of public resources to stimulate growth. No one can be certain what forms of wealth will be most important in the future. Some assets may quite unexpectedly prove to be critical. Yet it is also true that states that are currently wealthy by the measures in Table 1-1 have the ability to buy some of the needed resources. They can create excellent university systems to educate the work force. They can devote substantial sums to government efforts at economic development. Therefore, industrial-era wealth certainly constitutes one major resource for the transition ahead.

DEPENDENCE ON AN AGRICULTURAL ECONOMY

We mentioned earlier that some states remain heavily dependent on an agricultural economy while the nation as a whole is moving toward postindustrialism. Table 1-2 offers one estimate of the importance of agriculture in each of the states—the per capita amount of gross farm income produced in each one. By this measure, Arkansas, Colorado, Idaho, Iowa, Kansas, Minnesota, Montana, Nebraska, North Dakota, Oklahoma, South Dakota, Wisconsin, and Wyoming have especially large agricultural sectors in their economies. Thus, the fortunes of these states will be particularly dependent on the uncertain future of agriculture and highly affected by the extent to

TABLE 1-2 PER CAPITA FARM INCOME FOR ALL FIFTY STATES, 1988	STATE	PER CAPITA FARM INCOME	STATE	PER CAPITA FARM INCOME
	Alabama	$ 613	Montana	$2,220
	Alaska	64	Nebraska	5,677
	Arizona	589	Nevada	226
	Arkansas	1,787	New Hampshire	128
	California	602	New Jersey	85
	Colorado	1,211	New Mexico	895
	Connecticut	119	New York	151
	Delaware	917	North Carolina	666
	Florida	473	North Dakota	4,751
	Georgia	582	Ohio	372
	Hawaii	522	Oklahoma	1,142
	Idaho	2,476	Oregon	809
	Illinois	682	Pennsylvania	281
	Indiana	853	Rhode Island	80
	Iowa	3,800	South Carolina	333
	Kansas	3,000	South Dakota	4,787
	Kentucky	731	Tennessee	450
	Louisiana	472	Texas	684
	Maine	344	Utah	433
	Maryland	275	Vermont	749
	Massachusetts	69	Virginia	328
	Michigan	322	Washington	672
	Minnesota	1,667	West Virginia	144
	Mississippi	988	Wisconsin	1,132
	Missouri	841	Wyoming	1,640

Sources: U.S. Department of Agriculture, *Agricultural Statistics, 1989* (Washington, D.C.: U.S. Department of Agriculture, 1989), p. 415; U.S. Bureau of the Census, *Statistical Abstract of the United States, 1989* (Washington, D.C.: U.S. Bureau of the Census, 1989), p. XV).

which state leaders can stimulate diversification into other economic endeavors.

LEADERS AND LAGGARDS IN THE HIGH-TECH RACE

A large high-tech establishment may spur economic growth because of the scientific exchange it encourages and the economies of scale it allows. Some states are thus considerably more advanced than others in their progress toward a postindustrial, high-tech economy. Most

HIGH-TECHNOLOGY INDUSTRIES SUCH AS THOSE OF SILICON VALLEY CAN ENHANCE A STATE'S TRANSITION TO POSTINDUSTRIALISM.

Americans recognize the leadership of California and Massachusetts in this regard, because of Silicon Valley and the Boston-area scientific establishment, respectively. In fact, a few other states are also distinguished by the total amount of high-tech resources they possess. For example, California, Illinois, New York, Ohio, Pennsylvania, and Texas have unusually large numbers of employed scientists and engineers (National Science Foundation, 1988b: 115–116). Furthermore, California, Massachusetts, New Jersey, and New York have remarkably large numbers of business corporations engaged in high-technology enterprise (*Directory of Public High Technology Corporations, 1985–1986*, 1985). As a final example, colleges and universities in California, Maryland, Massachusetts, New York, Pennsylvania, and Texas win unusually large amounts of funding from the federal government to support research and development (National Science Foundation, 1988a: 32).

Much of the efforts of these scientists, companies, and schools will be of economic benefit to residents and governments in other states. But those states with large scientific communities on the "cutting edge" of high technology stand to garner the greatest short- and long-run benefits. If there is a race to a high-tech future, some states may have already far outdistanced their competitors.

THE IMPLICATIONS OF THE CURRENT ECONOMIC CHALLENGE

Both general and specific tasks for state and local governments are suggested by the preceding discussion of the current economic challenge. There are also certain concerns that citizens should have about the capabilities of those governments as they go about these tasks.

THE CHALLENGE FOR GOVERNMENTS

When the economy of a state goes into recession, as many have in recent years, state and local governments experience declining tax revenues but greater demands for service. Spending on unemployment rises, and displaced workers and their families seek various kinds of public assistance. Businesses fail, and business owners seek tax breaks or other concessions from government. Meeting these short-run problems is itself difficult. There is, however, also the long-run question of what new economic activities or industries could replace those that have gone into decline. Addressing this question does not have to be the responsibility of state and local governments, but public officials all across the nation have taken it as a top priority. In every state candidates for election to public offices argue over who has the best economic development plan, and a wide variety of such proposals are currently being tested. Even in those states that have not suffered recessions, government leaders have jumped on this bandwagon, possibly out of a fear that other states' aggressive efforts might deprive their state or locality of economic development opportunities. The competition among the states to attract new industries, plants, and, especially, high-tech firms is fierce.

What has occurred, of course, just as in the Progressive era, is that state government has taken on another positive function—responsibility for the future development of the state economy. The states may not all be successful, and that should not come as a surprise, since the task is an imposing one. For good or ill, however, state (and some local) governments have chosen to pursue it. Presumably they have done so because of an explicit public mandate or an implicit public acceptance of the appropriateness of the effort.

CONCERNS FOR CITIZENS

Obviously a major concern of citizens will be the specific policy actions state and local governments take in response to the economic challenge. Voters and taxpayers will want to know what strategies these governments adopt, how quickly they do so, how innovative they are in the process, and what success they achieve. Certain characteristics of these governments may help citizens anticipate how successful the governments are likely to be with such policy efforts.

First, the various economic problems will almost certainly provoke a host of demands for government action. Many economic interest groups, in particular, will have their own agendas for government, because, as we have said, economic interests will be at particular risk. Of course, the broad public interest will be at risk, as well. Therefore, one of citizens' concerns should be with the quality of the democratic process in their state. They can assess the quality of that process in part by considering how well the key institutions of democracy are working. They can also examine past behavior to learn how responsive their governments have characteristically been to special interests, as opposed to the general public. By considering that matter—and the question of which groups are currently politically powerful—the public can learn which interests are likely to prevail in present-day political controversies.

Responding successfully to these economic challenges will also require well-planned government actions based on sound professional and technical rationales. On the other hand, innovation and quick action may at times be necessary, too. People should be concerned, then, with the extent to which their state and local governments are professionally competent and innovative and with how successfully those bodies are developing new professional expertise to meet the challenges of the times. To learn about these matters, citizens must study the institutions of state and local government. How are they structured? What kinds of people serve in them? How and how well do they function?

Attempting to answer all of these questions will take us deep into the "nuts and bolts" of state and local governments and, at times, seemingly very far from the discussion of this chapter. However, these institutions are complex, and they are not fully understood even by the scholarly community that studies them. Simple or superficial examination will not do them justice. We must consider a good many of their fine details to foster a sophisticated understanding of how they function and, therefore, how they are likely to respond to contemporary policy challenges.

Citizens should also recognize that other notable constraints lie in the path of many state and local governments. These governments will be limited in their efforts by such things as the natural resources of their areas, the political values and preferences of their citizens, and the strictures on their powers inherent in the federal system of government. As we noted earlier, some will be held back by the industrial or agricultural orientation of their economies, and some will be advantaged by their relative wealth. Fate, of course, may also shape states' opportunities. Citizens should understand these influences on the states as well, so this book will consider a number of them.

Finally, citizens should be attentive to the effects of the current economic challenge on state and local *politics*. Recall the historical example of the farmers' battle with the railroads for an illustration of the kind of political controversy that might arise in the near future. Just as in that earlier period, certain social and economic interests are in decline today, while others are rising in power. Such shifts in economic power will translate into political power changes. As one example, high-tech companies and their representatives get special attention from, and have special influence over, state and local government officials today.

Another prominent feature of the current political scene has been called the "emerging partnership" between business and government (Mladenka and Hill, 1986: 300–318). In the face of the current economic challenge, government and business leaders have begun to work together in unprecedented ways, collaborating on both general policy strategies and a number of specific economic development programs. This partnership could prove to be a healthy and constructive effort that will lead to unprecedented benefits for the states and their residents. Yet it also gives exceptional influence over government policy making to a group with considerable economic interest in the policy outcomes. Thus, there is the possibility that narrow private interests will be better served than the general public interest. Citizens should be aware of this collaboration, and they should consider its ramifications for both the power of different groups attempting to influence government policy and the benefits deriving from actual policy choices.

CONCLUSION

These are exciting times. This nation—indeed, much of the world—appears on the brink of an extraordinary social and economic transition. But these are also uncertain and demanding times for both individuals and governments. If the United States succeeds in attaining postindustrialism, the process of doing so will be a painful one. If it fails, greater agonies may lie ahead. Whatever the eventual outcome, much of the responsibility for guiding the process and for coping with its problematic consequences will fall on state and local governments. And their successes and failures in these efforts will shape the lives of present and future generations. You should know these governments better, then, to appreciate how they are important to your future and to understand how you might participate in shaping that future.

REFERENCES   Bell, Daniel. 1973. *The Coming of Post-Industrial Society.* New York: Basic Books.

Cohen, Carol E. 1990. "State Fiscal Capacity and Effort: The 1988 Representative Tax System Estimates," *Intergovernmental Perspectives* 16 (Fall): 17–22.

Directory of Public High Technology Corporations, 1985–1986. 1985. Philadelphia: American Investor Information Services, Inc.

Hofstadter, Richard. 1955. *The Age of Reform.* New York: Alfred A. Knopf.

Ledebur, Larry C., and William W. Hamilton. 1986. "The Failure of Tax Concessions as Economic Development Incentives," pp. 101–118 in Steven D. Gold (ed.), *Reforming State Tax Systems.* Washington, D.C.: National Conference of State Legislatures.

Mladenka, Kenneth R., and Kim Quaile Hill. 1986. *Texas Government: Politics and Economics.* Pacific Grove, Calif.: Brooks/Cole.

National Science Foundation. 1988a. *Federal Support to Universities, Colleges, and Selected Nonprofit Institutions, Fiscal Year: 1986.* Washington, D.C.: National Science Foundation.

National Science Foundation. 1988b. *U.S. Scientists and Engineers: 1986.* Washington, D.C.: National Science Foundation.

U.S. Bureau of the Census. 1986. *Statistical Abstract of the United States, 1987.* Washington, D.C.: U.S. Bureau of the Census.

U.S. Bureau of the Census. 1989. *Statistical Abstract of the United States, 1989.* Washington, D.C.: U.S. Bureau of the Census.

U.S. Bureau of Labor Statistics. 1987. "Changing Employment in Occupations," *Occupational Outlook Quarterly* (Fall): 28–33.

U.S. Department of Agriculture. 1986. *Agricultural Statistics, 1986.* Washington, D.C.: U.S. Department of Agriculture.

2 The Legacy of History: Political Cultures and Constitutional Patterns

The states approach today's policy challenges with both the benefit and the burden of their political histories. Many events of their past, that is, influence their decisions in the present, some in constructive and positive ways and some in unfortunate ones. In particular, certain aspects of states' cultures and constitutions affect their contemporary policy efforts. And those two entities have themselves been shaped by historical events. Knowing some of that history will help you appreciate the importance of those two influences.

THE STATES' POLITICAL CULTURES

Political culture refers to the political ideas and beliefs about government held in common by the citizenry. Those ideas and beliefs differ in important ways from state to state, making the politics and governments of the states vary as a consequence. Because you are probably accustomed to thinking that all of the United States share a single set of democratic political values, the preceding idea may sound strange on first reading. Yet you should recall that a principal feature of American history has been the diversity of the people who have migrated to this so-called melting pot.

Immigrants to the United States not only have been diverse but have come in highly specific and identifiable waves—including, to name some of the most prominent, the English colonists who settled at Jamestown in 1607, the Irish and German immigrants of the mid-nineteenth century, the Italians of the early twentieth century, and the Mexicans and Southeast Asian boat people of more recent years (Archdeacon, 1983). And none of the immigrants have settled uniformly across all the states; their settlement patterns have been highly specific. Thus, these groups brought distinctive cultural values about politics to this country, values that have come to affect the states in distinctive ways. As we will explain both here and in several later chapters, political life in the states still exhibits the effects of these different, original cultures.

ORIGINAL POLITICAL CULTURES OF THE STATES

One of the most prominent scholarly explanations of how original cultural values have affected the states is offered by Daniel J. Elazar in his book *American Federalism* (1984). Elazar argues that three distinctive patterns of cultural attitudes toward politics are identifiable in the migrant cultures that originally settled the United States. He labeled these three patterns "political cultures."

The first political culture identified by Elazar is the *moralistic* one, which was brought to the United States by the Puritan settlers of New England and by some Scandinavian groups that settled in the upper Midwest in the nineteenth century. In this culture, government (as well as other aspects of society) is seen as an instrument for achieving a morally pure society. The goals of government are to serve the people and to promote the public good in the noblest sense. Those who work in government, whether filling elected or appointed offices, are to work selflessly to promote the public good. Furthermore, this culture encourages all citizens to concern themselves with government and with public issues. And, like the political leaders, the public should urge government to serve the good of the larger community, rather than particular economic, personal, or ideological interests.

Elazar's second political culture is the *individualistic* one. This culture was brought to the United States principally by non-Puritan

English, Germanic, and Middle European migrants who settled the Mid-Atlantic states. This culture sees government as simply one component of a society intended to allow the fullest pursuit of economic self-interest. Thus, so as not to hinder private economic activity, government should be quite limited in its functions and responsibilities. Furthermore, those functions that government does exercise should be ones that support and maintain the private market economy. Elazar also argues that government itself is a legitimate route to private advancement in the individualistic culture. It offers another career path, just like private business, which some might choose in order to seek fortune and fame. Thus, the pursuit of private gain by those in public life is tolerated or even venerated in this culture. This fact has led to the "professionalization" of politics; that is, those who pursue careers in government attempt to monopolize that arena. To do so, professional politicians in this culture have often sought to develop political party groups or political machines to help them maintain their positions. Members of the party or machine are awarded patronage jobs or other political favors and, as a result, become a part of a larger political organization built on private interests. Mass participation in government becomes, as another result, valued and encouraged primarily when it can be marshaled in the sake of self-interest—the self-interest of those desiring to retain their control over and their positions in government. Public involvement in politics is not, therefore, encouraged for its own sake or for the general public good as it is in the moralistic culture.

Finally, Elazar identifies what he calls the *traditionalistic* culture. This culture arose in the preindustrial, socially rigid, plantation society of the Old South. In that society a rigid class hierarchy dominated by the land-owning elite had already developed by the time of the American Revolution. At the bottom of this society, of course, were the black slaves who worked the plantations and served the semiaristocratic elite. The purpose of government in the traditionalistic culture, according to Elazar, is to preserve the existing social order and the prominence in that order of the social and economic elite. This elite will benefit directly as long as government fills that role, but the benefit is *class*-based and not individualistic as in the second cultural type. In this third culture, as in the other two, public participation in government takes on a distinctive character. Such participation is actually discouraged, according to Elazar, because of the risks it might pose to the elite's control. Political institutions, such as political parties, that might encourage public participation

FIGURE 2-1 CHARACTERIZATION OF THE STATES AS TO DOMINANT POLITICAL CULTURE

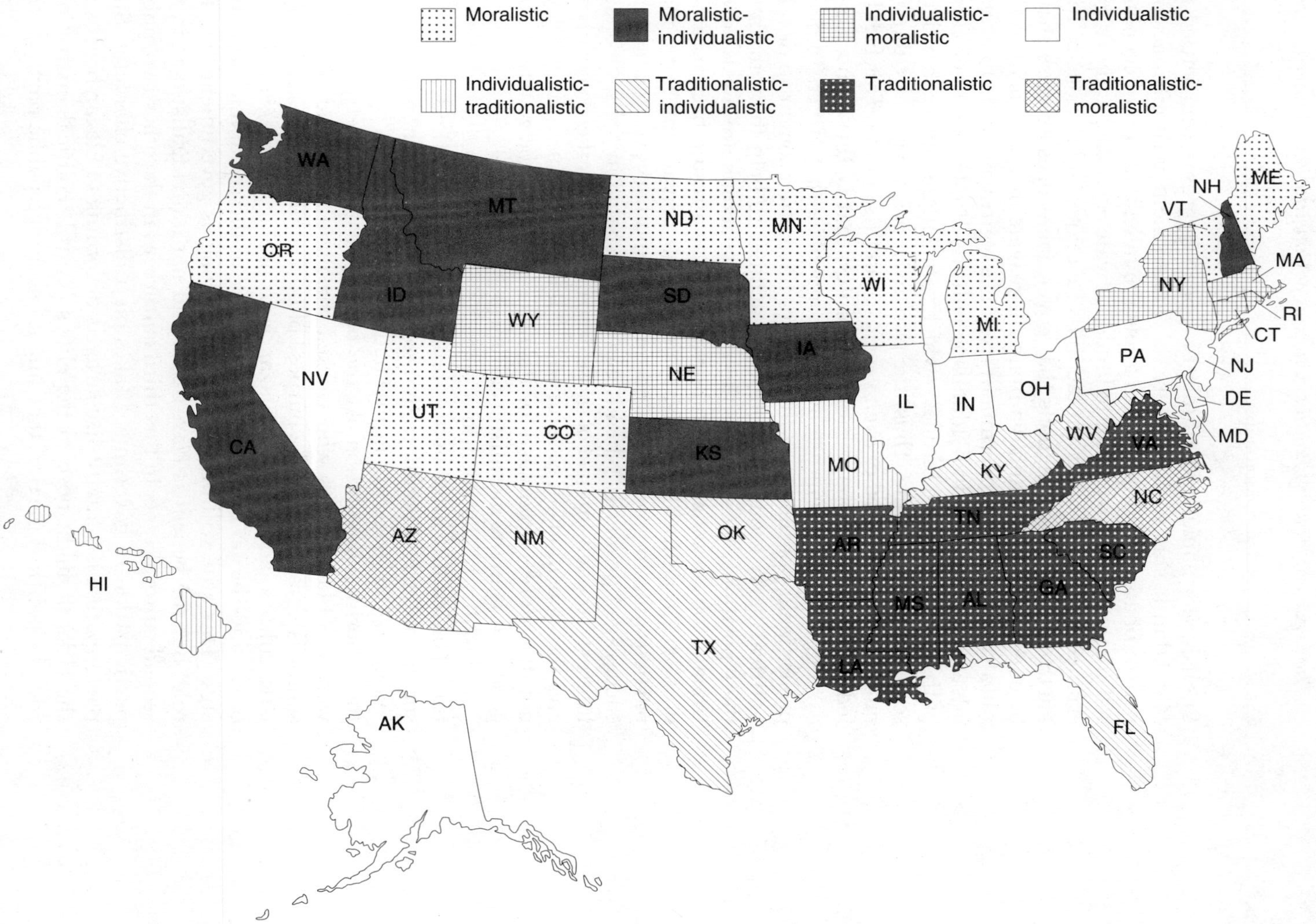
Moralistic
Moralistic-individualistic
Individualistic-moralistic
Individualistic
Individualistic-traditionalistic
Traditionalistic-individualistic
Traditionalistic
Traditionalistic-moralistic
WA
OR
CA
NV
ID
MT
WY
UT
CO
AZ
NM
ND
SD
NE
KS
OK
TX
MN
IA
MO
AR
LA
WI
IL
MI
IN
OH
KY
TN
MS
AL
GA
FL
SC
NC
VA
WV
PA
NY
VT
NH
ME
MA
RI
CT
NJ
DE
MD
AK
HI

Source: Daniel Elazar, *American Federalism* (New York: Harper & Row, 1984), p. 135.

are also discouraged. Instead, the elite organizes personalistic factions to select political candidates and even to control the existing parties "from the top down."

All three of the original cultural groups eventually spawned westward migration across the United States. It is possible to trace their routes of migration and eventual settlement, thus identifying the spread of each political culture across the fifty states. And each state can be characterized in terms of a dominant political culture or combination of two cultures. Figure 2-1 presents those characterizations. The figure reveals three rough bands running east to west— formed from the original home areas of the three cultural groups and the tracings of their subsequent migrations westward. The preponderance of moralism across the northern United States and of traditionalism in the South and Southwest is evident. The mixing of two of the cultures in many states is also apparent. In fact, thirty-two of the states are judged by Elazar to have such mixed cultures. The more prominent of the two cultures in each mixture is named first in the designations in the figure.

POLITICAL CULTURES OF THE STATES TODAY

The original political cultures still have considerable influence on political life in the states. This fact might at first seem surprising, given the time that has transpired since the settling of most of the states. However, cultural dispositions are often passed from generation to generation. In addition, they were frequently embodied in the content and wording of state constitutions and other laws written in the last century, when the original cultural patterns were still young and vital. Many of those laws have been quite enduring, and they ensure the continuing importance of the original cultural values. In later chapters we will indicate a number of other ways in which political cultures influence state government.

But political cultures also evolve over time. They change in part because of the importance of continuing migration—both of indigenous Americans *among* the states and of new immigrants *to* the United States. Thus, for example, migration to the Sun Belt from the Northeast and Midwest in the 1970s surely brought more moralists and individualists to the South and Southwest. To some degree migrants may assimilate the cultural values of their new home states, but they may also be a force for cultural change. In addition, political cultures can change because of evolving economic and social realities. For example, the decline of the plantation elite of the Old South and the commercial and industrial development of that region in the twentieth century have meant, according to Elazar, the weakening of traditionalistic values in favor of individualistic ones. As another example, across the entire United States, higher moral standards have been introduced into government in this century than were typical in earlier times. Evolving public expectations for the behavior of government officials have led to the creation of merit employment systems to replace patronage ones and the enactment of various laws to combat graft, corruption, and conflict of interest. Such *moralistic* legal proscriptions have promoted elements of that type of political culture to some degree in all parts of the nation.

For the preceding reasons every state today probably has some elements of all three of Elazar's political cultures. Yet the original cultural patterns remain influential, and these dispositions indicate some of the goals Americans want their governments to pursue as well as *how* they wish those governments to go about their tasks.

CULTURAL REGIONS

Close scrutiny of Figure 2-1 suggests some regional patterns of political culture. The dominance of traditionalism in the South is one such pattern. The extensive moralism of the upper Great Lakes, upper Midwest, and Northwest is another one. The concept of cultural regions is similar to the more common idea of the cultural identity of separate geographical regions. Indeed, many Americans think of themselves as living in "the South," and many others would say that they live in New England, the Midwest, the Southwest, the West, and so on. Such perceptions are evidence of how shared historical, cultural, and even environmental experiences can bind states into distinctive and commonly recognized groups. Of course, the precise boundaries of those perceived groups are sometimes ambiguous, and there are many ways in which states in a given region differ one from another. For example, although they might all think of themselves as Southerners, many Texans, Virginians, Tennesseans, and Floridians would steadfastly argue that their own state's culture is distinctive in important ways. There are even instances of distinctive cultural areas *within* states. The differences between Northern and Southern California, between upstate New York and the Big Apple, and between northern and southern Florida are some of the better-known

MIGRATION FROM WITHIN THE COUNTRY AND ABROAD HAS MADE SOME AMERICAN STATES AND CITIES TRUE MELTING POTS OF ETHNIC DIVERSITY.

examples of this diversity. These differences suggest how complex cultural regions can be.

These observations suggest that political cultures vary to some degree on a regional as well as a state-by-state basis. That is, some regional groups of states share many political values—and, as a result, governmental priorities. However, there are many ways of defining cultural regions. Some of these are based on geographic distinctions that are presumed to influence cultural patterns, and some are based on specific cultural or political patterns, much like Elazar's characterizations of the states. A notable definition of cultural regions based largely on settlement patterns of immigrants was formulated by Raymond D. Gastil (1975: 29). As shown in Figure 2-2, Gastil identified thirteen distinctive regions, all of which appear to fit some widely held perceptions of regional differences. Gastil's regional groupings are especially notable because they are based on a logic similar to Elazar's state-by-state characterizations. There are,

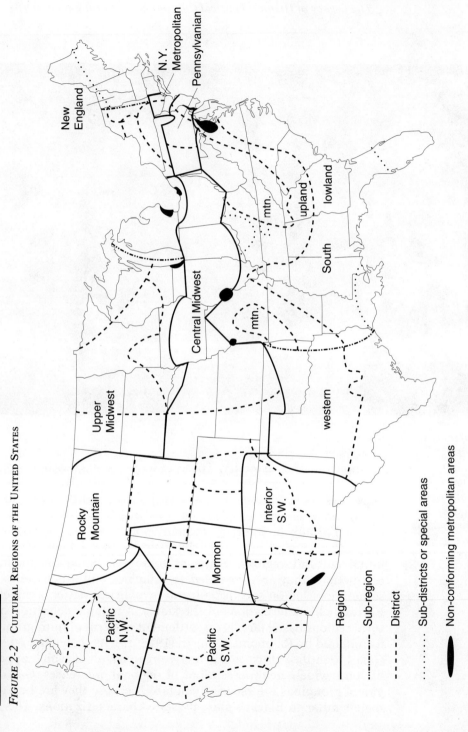

FIGURE 2-2 CULTURAL REGIONS OF THE UNITED STATES

New England

N.Y. Metropolitan

Pennsylvanian

Metropolitan

mtn.

upland

lowland

South

Central Midwest

mtn.

western

Upper Midwest

Rocky Mountain

Interior S.W.

Mormon

Pacific N.W.

Pacific S.W.

—— Region

—·— Sub-region

– – – District

········ Sub-districts or special areas

⬤ Non-conforming metropolitan areas

Source: Raymond D. Gastil, *Cultural Regions of the United States* (Seattle: University of Washington Press, 1975), p. 29.

however, many ways in which to define regional groupings of the states, and several of these different conceptions of cultural regions may have political significance.

THE POSITIVE-STATE ETHOS: A SPECIAL CASE OF A POLITICAL-CULTURAL VALUE

The crux of Elazar's theory is that political attitudes and behavior will differ to some degree across the three types of political cultures. Yet there is one prominent public attitude about government that appears to be widely shared in all states and is an important legacy of twentieth-century politics. We call this attitude the *positive-state ethos.*

A *positive state* describes a government with extensive responsibilities for the quality of social and economic life. It is the opposite of a laissez-faire government, which has highly limited powers. In the United States today all levels of government can be fairly described as being positive states. Over the course of the twentieth century governments in this country have assumed an increasing array of policy and public service responsibilities. The Populist and Progressive eras witnessed the addition of many of these new responsibilities (recall, for example, government's regulation of the railroads, discussed in Chapter 1). The Great Depression of the 1930s saw the instigation of many more. In the 1930s the welfare of the poor, the regulation of many aspects of business, labor, and agriculture, and even the health of the entire economy were added to government's agenda. And this agenda was expanded further in the 1960s and 1970s. The federal government took on the largest number of these responsibilities, but state and local governments assumed many new ones, too.

Many Americans are uncomfortable with the positive state *in the abstract.* They criticize "big government" and question whether it is proper or even feasible for government to assume the burdens of the positive state. But what they think is often quite different from how they act when their personal economic or social status is threatened by strong outside forces. When suffering a personal wrong, many Americans are quick to turn to government for assistance.

Americans learned an enduring lesson from the controversial times of the Progressive era and the Great Depression: if you have a big problem, government can and should fix it (Hill, 1988). Americans demand, that is, that government solve many of their problems. In the process they promote the expansion of government's powers and responsibilities but typically fail to see the contradiction between condemnation of big government on one hand and eagerness to extend it further on the other.

It might seem likely that other political-cultural values would moderate the positive-state ethos, at least in some states. The values of the individualistic political culture, for example, appear to favor a laissez-faire government over a positive state. That may be true in some respects but is contradicted by the recent behavior of some groups that have traditionally been thought of as standard-bearers in the cause of individualism, free enterprise, and laissez-faire government. As a first example, when U.S. auto manufacturers began to reel under a wave of cheap and highly competitive import cars in the late 1970s, they lobbied vigorously for federal government protection: for import barriers against foreign cars; for lowered safety, emission, and fuel-efficiency standards to lower their production costs; and for a financial bailout to save the failing Chrysler Corporation. In addition, the auto companies extracted tax reductions and even direct loans from a number of state and local governments in areas where they had existing plants or contemplated opening new ones.

As another example, consider the recent behavior of the big oil companies and of independent Texas oilmen, classic examples of rock-ribbed individualists. When the oil recession began in the mid-1980s and the price of crude oil dropped to a third of its former level in less than a year, these corporations and individuals pressured the federal government for aid in the form of an import fee on foreign oil and a variety of tax breaks (they did not get all that they had hoped for, however). At the same time they urged the governments in oil-producing states to enact regulations to lower crude oil production and raise prices.

In sum, individualistic values may still be quite important for many Americans. We suspect, however, that individualism has begun to take on a new form. Individualists resist governmental regulation or restraint of their private behavior, but they welcome governmental assistance that enhances their private economic goals. And many groups of Americans, not just executives in the auto and oil industries, turn to government to ameliorate their problems in times of need. We do not judge these actions as either wise or foolish; we simply see them as highly relevant to the broad concerns of this book. They suggest prominent public expectations for governmental performance, ones that will be especially important as the United States faces the economic transition described in Chapter 1.

THE STATES' CONSTITUTIONS

A government's ability to respond to policy challenges or to the public preferences incorporated in the political culture depends on its institutional capabilities—what it is empowered by law, mainly constitutional law, to do. We suspect, however, that most Americans give this matter little thought. They uncritically accept the existing powers and structures of their state and local governments. These governments all appear to be similar in structure, and they all mimic the national government in many respects. Doesn't it seem safe to assume, therefore, that they have the power to do what is necessary or what their citizens desire?

Unfortunately, the history of the states' constitution making has been such that the average state government is not well designed to go about meeting the challenges of the late twentieth century. Instead, its powers are restricted in numerous ways, and it is committed to a number of administrative structures better suited to the nineteenth century than to the present. To explain why this is the case, we must briefly summarize the major movements in state constitutional history.

CONSTITUTIONAL LIMITS ON STATE POWER

One scholar has aptly suggested that state constitutions are compilations of past generations' fears about the gravest political problems of their times (Grad, 1970: 30). Those generations sought to resolve such fears by the adoption of constitutional guarantees or, more commonly, restrictions on government. This tendency began with the earliest state constitutions, which were written very soon after the American Revolution. The greatest fear of that time was of unrestrained power held by executive officers of government—because of the abuse of such power by the king of England and his colonial governors. Thus, the first state constitutions established weak governors, placing a variety of restrictions on their tenure and powers. Indeed, there was little in the way of a balance of power among the branches of state government. The state legislature was made preeminent by the constitution as a further check on executive power.

Succeeding years brought other controversies that left their mark on state constitutions and the capabilities of state government (Sturm, 1982). During the flowering of Jacksonian democracy in the 1820s and 1830s—when the right to vote and participate in government was being broadly expanded—more and more state executive offices came to be filled by popular elections. What, after all, could be more democratic? And the advocates of this kind of reform wanted it written into the state constitution so that future generations might not easily tamper with it. One result, however, was the further weakening of the powers of the governor. In many states the office became not that of a true chief executive, but that of only one of several competing state executives, all of whom had some independent control over this branch of the government.

Similarly, widespread allegations of corruption in state legislatures in the late 1880s led many states to introduce new constitutional restrictions on those bodies, especially with respect to the breadth of their lawmaking and taxing powers. And during the Populist and Progressive eras (briefly discussed in Chapter 1), as reformers lobbied for new state regulatory powers and agencies to assume those powers, they often sought constitutional status for their reforms.

In sum, historical controversies about governmental power were resolved in many states by modifying the constitution to ensure that the resolution would be enduring. What seemed called for with respect to immediate or short-term problems was set in place for all future times. And this lawmaking practice was remarkable for two additional reasons. First, it usually took the form of new limits on action by state or local governments—a setting out of specific requirements for or boundaries on such action. Second, it was contrary to the practice of making fundamental law in the U.S. Constitution. That instrument has always been a general and flexible document. It includes only the broad principles and most essential features of government. All the remaining details, especially with respect to the problems of particular times, are left to be dealt with through laws that can be made and revised by Congress and the President to fit changing times. In contrast, most state constitutions include a good deal of highly particular law. And because it is far more difficult to change constitutional law than to change law made by a legislature, these provisions represent "the dead hand of the past" restraining state and local governments as they grapple with modern problems (Miller, 1968: 183).

State governments are far more powerful today, of course, than they were fifty or a hundred years ago. In particular, they have many new responsibilities and functions that have arisen with the growth of the positive state. Yet the states are still limited in their ability to respond to changing circumstances because many of their new powers have been granted in the fixed, time-bound manner described above.

STYLE AND LANGUAGE PROBLEMS IN STATE CONSTITUTIONS

Another circumstance that has had an unfortunate effect on the typical state constitution is the fact that the writers and amenders of most of these documents ignored more than the philosophy of the national one. They seem oblivious to its spare, elegant style as well. Most state constitutions are excessively wordy and detailed, and they are so because of the zeal of the people who wrote them. The writers and amenders of state constitutions were at times driven by consuming passion for the kinds of government—or restrictions on government—that they sought. And they authored elaborate, painfully detailed constitutional language to ensure that their intentions were explicit and the coverage comprehensive.

Because of this tendency, the typical state constitution is a long instrument. As Table 2-1 indicates, some of them are the length of a novel, and the average length is over 28,000 words. In contrast, the U.S. Constitution is a mere 8,700 words long, shorter than all but one of the state documents! (The exception is Vermont's constitution, adopted in 1793.) Furthermore, the average state constitution has been amended over a hundred times. In contrast, the federal document has been amended a mere twenty-six times, and the first ten of these came in one package as the Bill of Rights. And the ponderous, wordy style of many of the state documents is made even worse by poor organization and arrangement of content. The U.S. Constitution is a relatively terse, lucid, and often inspiring document. The typical state constitution, on the other hand, could quickly deflate the enthusiasm of the most eager student and cure the worst insomniac.

TABLE 2-1
THE AGE AND
LENGTH OF
CURRENT STATE
CONSTITUTIONS (AS
OF JANUARY 1,
1990)

STATE	YEAR OF ADOPTION	APPROXIMATE LENGTH IN WORDS	NUMBER OF AMENDMENTS	
			PROPOSED	ADOPTED
Alabama	1901	174,000	726	513
Alaska	1956	13,000	31	22
Arizona	1911	28,900	198	109
Arkansas	1874	40,700	164	76
California	1879	33,400	781	471
Colorado	1876	45,700	239	115
Connecticut	1965	9,600	26	25
Delaware	1897	19,000	a	119
Florida	1968	25,100	79	53
Georgia	1982	25,000	35	24
Hawaii	1950	17,500	93	82
Idaho	1889	21,500	187	107
Illinois	1970	13,200	11	6
Indiana	1851	9,400	70	38
Iowa	1857	12,500	51	48
Kansas	1859	11,900	115	87
Kentucky	1891	23,500	58	29
Louisiana	1974	51,400	51	27
Maine	1819	13,500	186	157
Maryland	1867	41,100	233	200
Massachusetts	1780	36,700	143	116
Michigan	1963	20,000	47	16
Minnesota	1857	9,500	206	112
Mississippi	1890	24,000	133	102
Missouri	1945	42,000	115	74
Montana	1972	11,900	225	15
Nebraska	1875	20,000	283	189
Nevada	1864	20,800	175	108
New Hampshire	1784	9,200	274	142
New Jersey	1947	17,000	52	39
New Mexico	1911	27,200	231	120
New York	1894	80,000	274	207
North Carolina	1970	11,000	34	27
North Dakota	1889	20,500	222	125
Ohio	1851	36,900	245	145
Oklahoma	1907	68,800	274	133
Oregon	1857	26,000	367	188
Pennsylvania	1968	21,700	25	19
Rhode Island	1842	19,000	99	53

			NUMBER OF AMENDMENTS	
STATE	**YEAR OF ADOPTION**	**APPROXIMATE LENGTH IN WORDS**	**PROPOSED**	**ADOPTED**
South Carolina	1895	22,500	647	463
South Dakota	1889	23,300	185	97
Tennessee	1870	15,300	55	32
Texas	1876	62,000	483	326
Utah	1895	11,000	126	77
Vermont	1793	6,600	208	50
Virginia	1970	18,500	23	20
Washington	1889	29,400	153	86
West Virginia	1872	25,600	107	62
Wisconsin	1848	13,500	168	124
Wyoming	1889	31,800	97	57
Average		28,200	179	113

TABLE 2-1
CONTINUED

[a]Proposed amendments are not submitted to the voters in Delaware.

Source: Council of State Governments, *The Book of the States, 1989–90* (Lexington, Ky.: Council of State Governments, 1990), p. 40.

These stylistic problems might appear trivial at first glance, but they have important consequences. They indicate another way by which constitution writers have curbed the powers of state governments. Highly detailed passages allow no flexibility to suit changing circumstances. The U.S. Constitution, on the other hand, has had an entirely different influence because of the generality of its language. The federal courts, the Congress, and even the President have come to interpret much of this language in light of evolving problems and public expectations for government. Some conservatives criticize such deviation from a narrow construction of the "original intent" of the document, but it is a major avenue by which the national government has been able to respond to new problems and demands.

Additionally, state constitutions lose potential symbolic and educational power when they are badly written and forbidding to read. As suggested above, the U.S. Constitution has a number of inspiring passages. That language has motivated many Americans to pursue political goals they perceived in the document but not in the existing practices of government. Reading the Constitution is a useful educational exercise, too. The student of government can learn much, and

Some Special-Interest Constitutional Provisions

Consider the following examples of special-interest provisions in state constitutions (which were chosen, by the way, from a host of many such items). Many people might agree that compensating the efforts of Vietnam veterans, providing housing for the elderly and the disabled, restricting branch banking, and restricting the taxation of farm supplies and products are worthy public policies. Of course, other people might disagree. The issue we want to raise here is not whether states should adopt such policies, but whether they should include them in their constitutions. These are clearly provisions that benefit particular interests *and* address time-bound issues or controversies. Thus, if they are to be adopted at all, they would better be made ordinary law.

The state may pay an adjusted compensation to persons who served in the armed forces of the United States during the period of the Vietnam conflict. Whenever authorized and in the amounts and on the terms fixed by law, the state may expend monies and pledge the public credit to provide money for the purposes of this section.

Minnesota Constitution,
Article XIII, Section 8

learn it quickly, by doing so. Thus, the U.S. Constitution has important symbolic, educational, and practical political value—something that few state constitutions can claim.

SPECIAL INTERESTS' INFLUENCE ON STATE CONSTITUTIONS

Yet another circumstance that has aggravated the problems of the typical state constitution arises because special interest groups have also recognized what the constitution writers did: if you get a desired policy incorporated into the constitution—rather than simply in a

In the manner provided by law and notwithstanding the limitations contained in section 7, article XI of the Constitution, the credit of the State of Oregon may be loaned and indebtedness incurred in an amount not to exceed, at any one time, one-half of one percent of the true cash value of all taxable property in the state to provide funds to be advanced by contract, grant, loan, or otherwise, for the purpose of providing additional financing for multifamily housing for the elderly and disabled persons.

> Oregon Constitution,
> Article XI-I(2), Section 1

Branch banking shall be authorized only by law approved by three-fifths of the members voting on the question or a majority of the members elected, whichever is greater, in each house of the General Assembly.

> Illinois Constitution,
> Article XIII, Section 8

Farm products, livestock, and poultry in the hands of the producer, and family supplies for home and farm use, are exempt from all taxation unless otherwise directed by a two-thirds vote of all the members elect to both houses of the Legislature.

> Texas Constitution,
> Article VIII, Section 19

law passed by the legislature—it will be much more enduring and more difficult for others to change at a later time. Thus, many special interests have waged successful campaigns for constitutional provisions—employing a variety of rationales, of course. Concerning this phenomenon, Duane Lockard (1963: 91) has observed:

> As a result of such efforts many constitutions contain a wide range of guarantees and prohibitions for the protection of interests powerful enough to push their way into the fundamental law. . . . Veterans, labor unions, farmers, church groups, the gasoline industry, and hundreds of other economic, social, and professional groups have managed to get special exemptions from taxation. For instance, vet-

erans use their political power to assure many different kinds of benefits; the gasoline industry has succeeded often in limiting by constitutional provision the use of income from gasoline taxes. Other special interests protect their place in government by the "earmarking" of certain revenues for special funds to be spent for the particular purpose of the interest.

Such special constitutional provisions do more than give special political status and benefits to particular groups—although that result alone is enough to make them remarkable. They constitute another set of restrictions on governmental power and the ways it can be exercised. Many such provisions were adopted in the distant historical past, yet they remain as constraints on the power of contemporary governments.

DATEDNESS OF STATE CONSTITUTIONS

Most state constitutions suffer one more problem: they are too old. Only a dozen states have substantially revised their constitutions or adopted entirely new ones in the second half of the twentieth century as they assumed more and more policy responsibilities. Old age is not necessarily synonymous with decrepitude for constitutions, of course; the national document is testimony to that. Yet when old age is coupled with much detailed, ordinary law that has been written into a document over many years, it typically is a problem. In general, then, old age and excessive length together mean that a given state constitution is out of date and imposes unnecessary restrictions on the operations of modern government.

In sum, the average state constitution is filled with detailed restrictions on governmental powers carried over from earlier times and with commitments to governing structures better suited to those times. It has been amended piecemeal over and over again, with the same particularistic motivations. And it is unlikely to have been revised systematically in the modern era. Even those few state constitutions that have been recently revised suffer because of the timidity of the changes. Too much of the past structure is generally carried over into the new document.

It is easy to overdramatize these constitutional difficulties. No state government is literally paralyzed in its efforts to respond to modern problems. A few are not subject to most of these concerns because they have short, general constitutions. Yet the flexibility and responsiveness of virtually every state government are limited to some degree for these reasons. And a number of states face formidable constitutional restrictions. Essentially, they must grapple with problems of the late twentieth century employing procedures and institutions from the nineteenth.

CONCLUSION

The political cultures that are prevalent in states and regions affect public preferences about the role of government in society and, therefore, about the appropriateness of many specific governmental activities. They also suggest how the general public is likely to be involved in the processes of governmental decision making. Because of their distinctive political cultures, then, the states will tackle policy challenges in differing ways and with differing emphases. Public participation in state and local government will differ from state to state as well, in accordance with the character of the political culture. To illustrate how these generalizations take specific form, succeeding chapters will explore in more detail the relationships of political culture to institutional patterns, policy priorities, and public participation.

Constitutions, on the other hand, outline the institutional capacities of state and local governments for responding to current policy challenges. These legal documents are themselves largely the products of *past* public and elite preferences concerning governmental power and responsibility. They have been shaped, therefore, by distinctive political-cultural values. Yet the growth of the positive-state ethos illustrates how some common public desires concerning government have evolved in the present century, and there is considerable evidence that the responsiveness of state and local governments to these public desires is weakened by constitutional constraints. These governments are not entirely enfeebled by their constitutions, but their policy efforts are hedged about in a variety of ways. And public expectations for government are at times frustrated for this reason. Since these legal constraints are little appreciated by many citizens, we will describe a number of them in more detail in later chapters.

REFERENCES

Archdeacon, Thomas J. 1983. *Becoming American: An Ethnic History.* New York: Free Press.

Council of State Governments. 1988. *The Book of the States, 1988–89.* Lexington, Ky.: Council of State Governments.

Elazar, Daniel J. 1984. *American Federalism: A View from the States,* 3rd ed. New York: Harper & Row.

Gastil, Raymond D. 1975. *Cultural Regions of the United States.* Seattle: University of Washington Press.

Grad, Frank P. 1970. "The State's Capacity to Respond to Urban Problems: The State Constitution," pp. 27–58 in Alan K. Campbell (ed.), *The States and the Urban Crisis.* Englewood Cliffs, N.J.: Prentice-Hall.

Hill, Kim Quaile. 1988. *Democracies in Crisis: Public Policy Responses to the Great Depression.* Boulder, Colo.: Westview Press.

Lockard, Duane. 1963. *The Politics of State and Local Government.* New York: Macmillan.

Miller, James Nathan. 1968. "Dead Hand of the Past," *National Civic Review* LVII (April): 183–188.

Sturm, Albert L. 1982. "The Development of American State Constitutions," *Publius* 12 (Winter): 57–98.

3

State and Local Governments within the Federal System

The relations between the states and the national government have evolved through American history as both responded to changing socioeconomic conditions and public demands. Periods of intense political controversy and times when governments face especially challenging problems (such as the economic ones described in Chapter 1) have had particular influence on the federal system. The changes brought about in such times have made the ties between the two levels of government so extensive that the operations of either level cannot be understood fully without a consideration of the links between the levels. Furthermore, the question of the appropriate role for the states and the national government has been highly controversial in recent years. To discuss the reasons for this controversy, the prospects for its resolution, or its implications for the policy efforts of the state, we must first assess how the nation got to this point in the first place.

WHAT FEDERALISM IS

Federalism is a system with two distinct levels of government: first, regional entities, called states in this country, and, second, a central government, called (somewhat confusingly) the federal government or the national government. Each of the two levels of government has a set of particular powers, some of which are exclusive and some of which are shared with the other level. Federal systems typically exist in nations with major cultural, social, or political differences that coincide with geographical regions. The independence allowed the regional governments is thus an attempt to allow some autonomy for the expression of distinctive regional traits.

At the time of the American Revolution, the states were, to a considerable degree, separate social and political communities, and they were strongly desirous of maintaining that autonomy. Thus, a federal system was highly appropriate for the United States. The continued importance of distinctive political cultures and cultural regions (discussed in Chapter 2) is evidence for the contemporary appropriateness of this system.

Although Americans take their federal arrangement for granted, such governments are actually in a small minority worldwide. The more common form of government is called a unitary system. In this type of system, regional governmental entities may exist, but they are literally subunits of the national government. In such a system, for example, the leaders of the executive branches of the regional entities, individuals roughly equivalent to governors in the United States, may be appointed by the equivalent of the U.S. President. All state and local government officials might work for the national government. (Even unitary systems may, however, allow some degree of autonomy to local and regional governments.)

You may have recognized that federal systems have a significant problem that unitary ones don't share—how to divide governmental power between the national and the regional entities. To help you understand the resolution of that problem and the working of federalism in this country, we need to answer two questions. First, how was governmental power distributed between the different levels initially? And, second, how has that initial power relationship changed over time?

THE ORIGINAL FEDERAL DESIGN FOR AMERICAN GOVERNMENT

The U.S. Constitution is the source of the original distribution of power in the American federal system.[1] Article I of the Constitution lays out, first, a specific list of powers granted to the national government. These are known as the *delegated powers*. Some of the more important ones are the powers:

1. "to lay and collect taxes; . . ."
2. "to borrow money on the credit of the United States; . . ."
3. "to regulate commerce with foreign nations, and among the several states; . . ."
4. "to coin money [and] regulate the value thereof; . . ."
5. "to declare war; . . ." and
6. "to raise and support armies; . . . ."

At the end of the list of delegated powers there is a catch-all sentence that states that the U.S. Congress has the power "to make all laws which shall be necessary and proper for carrying into execution the foregoing powers." This "necessary and proper" clause has been interpreted very broadly by the U.S. Supreme Court, at least in the twentieth century, to render constitutional many activities of the federal government that extend far beyond the specific list of delegated powers but are somewhat related to one of them.

In addition, the Constitution states in the Tenth Amendment: "The powers not delegated to the United States [government] by the Constitution, nor prohibited by it to the States, are reserved to the States respectively, or to the people." This "residual powers" clause appears to establish quite a prominent role for the states. The central government is, at least in its delegated powers, limited to a very specific list of functions. All else is left to the states. Yet time has brought a considerable evolution of the powers of both levels of government. Both have become far more powerful than they were in 1789, but their relative powers have shifted. An explanation of those changes—and an answer to the second question posed above—can best be framed in terms of a brief survey of the history of American federalism.

THE EVOLUTION OF AMERICAN FEDERALISM

The history of American federalism can be divided into several discrete periods based on changes in the relations between the two principal levels of government. Although there is some disagreement among scholars of federalism concerning the precise dates, names, and features of these periods, there is considerable agreement on the main details. It is generally agreed, for example, that between the ratification of the Constitution in 1789 and the presidential election of 1932 there existed a system called *dual federalism.*

The somewhat ambiguous name "dual federalism" is intended to imply that the two levels of government, the state governments and the national government, each had a distinct set of powers and responsibilities. With only minor exceptions, the relations between the two levels of government between 1789 and 1932 are well described by this definition. The national government was relatively small and largely restricted to carrying out a limited range of functions derived from a narrow interpretation of the powers granted it in Article I of the Constitution. The states were highly independent in their policy activities. The only significant restrictions on the states came as a consequence of the Civil War, which eliminated the possibility of secession from the Union and, in theory, required the states to guarantee the civil rights of all citizens, regardless of their ethnicity.

The states and the federal government responded independently to the major political challenges of the period of dual federalism. For example, efforts to respond to the challenges of industrialization described in Chapter 1 were carried out separately by both levels of government. It should be noted, however, that the states were far more active and responsive to domestic problems than the national government was. The states' efforts during the Progressive era preceded those of the federal government in time and exceeded them in scope.

The economic and social problems created by the Great Depression of the 1930s, however, led to a shift in the character of federal-state relations. That is, a new era in the history of federalism came about because of that economic depression. Most scholars refer to this second era, running from approximately 1932 to 1960, as that of *cooperative federalism.* Cooperative federalism came about largely because of the dire financial straits in which state and local governments found themselves in the 1930s and a widespread tendency to look to Washington for relief.

The period of cooperative federalism witnessed two principal developments. The first of these was the extension of the federal government's regulatory powers over a number of new areas—from monetary and fiscal policy to the banking system, the stock exchange, the agricultural economy, and even labor-management relations. The second development was an extensive amount of joint federal-state policy activity. However, the federal government assumed the initiative for starting these joint efforts, paid the largest portion of their costs, and laid down most of the rules under which they would operate. The actual running of most of these programs was given to the states, who typically also had to contribute some of the money necessary to run them.

What arose in this second era of federalism constituted a dramatic change from the earlier era of dual federalism. The federal government took on many new responsibilities in the areas of social policy and economic regulation. It also forced the states into several policy partnerships, mostly in areas that had been the exclusive responsibility of the states. Yet, as David Walker has pointed out, this was a rather restricted system of partnerships. He observes that only "four programs—highways, old age assistance, aid to dependent children, and employment security—accounted for almost three-quarters of [federal] aid dollars in 1960" (Walker, 1982: 182). Several observers have added that the intent of most of these programs was to help the states achieve their existing goals rather than to impose new goals on them.

Beginning around 1960, however, with the policy efforts of the Kennedy and Johnson administrations, the powers of the national government were greatly expanded at the expense of the states. Thus, a third era of federal-state relations, which Walker (1982) aptly calls *cooptive federalism*, began. (The word "cooptive" refers to the national government's assumption, or cooptation, of powers previously belonging to the states.) This era, which clearly lasted until 1980, featured considerable preemption of state powers by the national government and growing dependence of state and local governments on the national one. Because the era of cooptive federalism led to current controversies over what appropriate federal-state relations are, we will shortly consider that era in some detail. Before doing so, however, we'll bring the story of the general evolution of the federal system up to the present.

A number of ambitious public policy goals lay behind cooptive federalism, and many advocates of those goals still maintain that the changes in government that came about in that era should remain in place. Many even argue for further expansion of federal power in selected policy areas. But cooptive policy efforts always received considerable criticism, too. Many state and local government officials were critical of the federal supervision, the red tape, and what was,

in their view, the inappropriateness of many federal policy requirements. (Yet they were often quite willing to take federal money to
help run their agencies and programs.) Some observers also ques-
tioned the effectiveness of a number of the federal programs created
in the cooptive period and the cost of many others. Political conservatives argued against this broad expansion of federal power at the
expense, in their view, of private individuals as well as the states.

Despite all of those criticisms, cooptive federalism endured at
least until 1980. By then many people inside and outside government
thought that the federal government had become too powerful. Many
more thought that it had become too costly. All of these people agreed
that federal spending should be reduced, and many of them thought
that some power should be returned to the states. The elections of
Ronald Reagan and George Bush, individuals who wanted to reverse
the accumulation of federal power, appeared to signal the start of a
new era in federal-state relations. This era is still too young, however,
to have clearly established its character or to have earned a name,
like those periods of federalism that preceded it.

Throughout this new era, many people, both in and out of government, have wanted to maintain or even extend cooptive federalism. There are many politically powerful groups that want to retain
some particular cooptive federal program. Some of these people hold
such views because they believe the states will not or cannot carry
out the policy or program. Even many state and local government
officials have been, in effect, advocates of cooptive federalism for a
similar reason: they want to continue receiving federal aid. Indeed,
they continue to lobby for more aid, and they are often willing to
accept some of the conditions attached to it. And there are other
advocates of a dominant federal government who might be unex-
pected ones. Many private business leaders, for example, have lobbied for a dominant role of the federal government in business
regulation, because then they would have only one, and not fifty,
policy mandates to follow. Those business leaders also feared that
some states would adopt tougher regulatory policies than the federal
government had. That is, a single, less onerous federal policy might
result from a cooptive federal role in this policy area (Beckman,
1988: 441).

In accord with its conservative views on this subject, in 1981
the Reagan administration proposed a sweeping set of reforms in
federal-state relations, which would have reduced federal cooptation
considerably. The U.S. Congress, however, adopted only bits and

pieces of those proposals. Many state and local officials lobbied against portions of the Reagan package, for it reduced federal aid at the same time as it lowered federal cooptation. And, while Congress was adopting some of the Reagan proposals, it also passed a variety of new cooptive laws, and the federal courts sustained a variety of cooptive rulings on federal-state relations (Beckman, 1986). Even the Reagan administration was inconsistent in this area—calling generally for "devolution" of power to the states but supporting particular cooptive federal laws, such as the 55-mph speed limit (which it supported until 1987), a nationwide minimum age of 21 years for consumption of alcoholic beverages, and extended federal law enforcement powers to aid in the fight against drug dealers.

The Bush administration has been equally ambivalent, pursuing cooptive policies at times but not at others. That fact, coupled with sentiments favoring a strong federal government held by many members of Congress, has meant that the growth of cooptive legislation has continued (Fabricius, 1991). Even the U.S. Supreme Court, which is now dominated by relatively conservative members, had a mixed record in this area in the 1980s and continues to do so in the 1990s. The Court's decisions have both expanded and limited the federal government's powers relative to those of the states, with no clear movement in either direction (Bowman and Pagano, 1990).

The Gramm-Rudman-Hollings Deficit Control Act, passed in 1985, will probably be more important in lessening cooptation than previous, more explicit efforts to do so. That act has led to substantial cuts in federal aid to the states, as one strategy for reducing the federal government's annual deficit. Thus, the financial dependence of the states on the federal government has been reduced, eliminating some of the strings attached to federal aid as well. In the long run, however, the general policy attitudes of the Congress and the President will be equally influential. So far the net effect of both their efforts appears to be a stabilization of the trend toward more cooptation rather than a clear reversal of direction.

By 1980, then, the growth of the federal government's power had become highly controversial, and there were good reasons to anticipate a reduction in its role. At the same time, there remained many powerful advocates of the cooptive federal system, and both sides can point to some successes in the effort to resolve this political controversy. Nonetheless, its ultimate settlement is not yet clear. The long-term trend of federal-state relations in the United States has not yet been determined.

THE ERA OF COOPTIVE FEDERALISM

It is critical that you understand the patterns of state-federal relations that developed in the period 1960–1980, for they remain an important influence on state and local governments. Although those patterns are under sharp criticism and in some flux, much of their effect is still felt. That is, cooptive federalism continues to affect the structure and policies of state and local governments. To understand fully that influence, you must be familiar with more of the specifics of this third era of federal-state relations.

Perhaps the most distinctive aspect of the era of cooptive federalism was that the federal government began to specify the objectives of new programs that affected the states. As James Sundquist (1969: 3) observed, "Before 1960 the typical federal assistance program did not involve an expressly stated *national* purpose. It was instituted, rather, as a means of helping state or local governments accomplish *their* objectives." For the majority of the new federal programs of the cooptive era, on the other hand, the federal government established the objectives as a matter of national policy, specified many of the details of how the programs would be run, provided some of the money, and either required or greatly encouraged the participation of state and local governments. And what made this change even more remarkable was that the federal government began to develop initiatives in a number of policy areas that had previously been wholly or predominantly under the control of the state governments.

EXAMPLES OF THE EXPANSION OF FEDERAL POWER

The extension of federal influence during the era of cooptation was so great that almost every policy concern of *any* level of government in the nation was affected. There were, however, a number of policy areas that were coopted to an especially high degree by the national government; these serve as excellent examples of the extension of federal control during this period.

Social Welfare Policy   The broad area of social welfare offers a particularly good example of federal cooptation of a policy area. Well into the twentieth century, social welfare policy was almost entirely the responsibility of the states. Except for aid to war veterans, the federal government had very modest welfare programs before 1932. The Great Depression, however, as we noted earlier, triggered the creation of a variety of new welfare programs, largely under federal leadership. Direct aid for the needy and the unemployed was extended considerably, and Social Security programs were created to supplement the income of retired workers, widows, the handicapped, and other dependent individuals.

A number of additional social welfare initiatives have also been undertaken by the federal government since the end of World War II, and many of these were created during the so-called War on Poverty of the 1960s. These efforts encompassed a wide range of activities: from direct income programs to ones that provide employment, housing, health care, community development, and many other services. A considerable number of these were entirely federal programs. Many more, however, were initiated and largely paid for by the federal government but were run by state or local governments under federal direction.[2]

As testimony to the extent to which the federal government has coopted the social welfare field, Table 3-1 shows the percentages of total public welfare spending in the United States accounted for by the federal government since 1930. The table documents a remarkable rise in federal responsibility, which has, in effect, left state and local governments as minor participants in what was once their exclusive domain. The figures in the table even underestimate the extent of federal influence, because many of the state-run programs exist and must operate under federal mandate. Thus, much of the

TABLE 3-1
THE PERCENTAGE OF SOCIAL WELFARE SPENDING BORNE BY THE FEDERAL GOVERNMENT, 1930–1987

CATEGORY	YEAR						
	1930	1940	1950	1960	1970	1980	1987
Social insurance	17%	31%	43%	74%	83%	83%	83%
Public aid	0	63	44	52	59	68	63
Health and medical	12	16	29	39	48	47	47
Veterans' programs	100	99	93	98	99	99	99
Education	3	3	2	5	12	11	8
Housing	0	100	100	81	83	92	84
Other	3	9	6	37	55	65	56
Total welfare spending	20	39	45	48	53	62	60

Source: U.S. Bureau of the Census, *U.S. Statistical Abstract,* various years (Washington, D.C.: U.S. Bureau of the Census).

state and local spending exists only because of matching-expenditure requirements of federal programs.

Civil Rights Policy   A second policy area that well illustrates federal cooptation is that of civil rights. When the U.S. Constitution was ratified in 1789, the federal government had a small and circumscribed role in civil rights policy. One of the principal compromises of the Constitutional Convention had been to let the states determine suffrage requirements, that is, establish qualifications for the right to vote. Similarly, state governments played the major role in the protection of all other social and political rights of individuals. As of 1791, the U.S. Constitution did include, it is true, a Bill of Rights ensuring a broad range of individual freedoms. Yet those constitutional provisions only limited the actions of the federal government. They applied neither to the actions of state or local governments nor to those of private individuals who might infringe the rights of others. Thus, state governments had to include their own bills of rights in their constitutions, but the content and enforcement of those provisions varied across the states.

One of the most important civil rights developments of the twentieth century has been the extension of the requirements of the Bill of Rights and other federal constitutional guarantees of civil rights to the states. The foundation for this process was laid in 1868 with the adoption of the Fourteenth Amendment to the U.S. Constitution, the first amendment specifically directed at state and local governments. Written in reaction to the Civil War and the conflict over slavery, that amendment states in part:

> All persons born or naturalized in the United States, and subject to the jurisdiction thereof, are citizens of the United States and of the State wherein they reside. No State shall make or enforce any law which shall abridge the privileges or immunities of citizens of the United States; nor shall any State deprive any person of life, liberty, or property, without due process of law; nor deny to any person within its jurisdiction the equal protection of the laws.

During the twentieth century the Fourteenth Amendment has been applied by the federal courts to one after another of specific policies and practices of state governments. In an incrementally accumulating series of decisions, the U.S. Supreme Court has, in fact, extended the bulk of the Bill of Rights and other civil rights guarantees in the Constitution to cover state and local governments (Cort-

AMERICANS WITH
PHYSICAL HANDICAPS
ARE SOME OF THE
LESS WELL-KNOWN
BENEFICIARIES OF
FEDERAL
COOPTATION OF CIVIL
RIGHTS POLICY
MAKING.

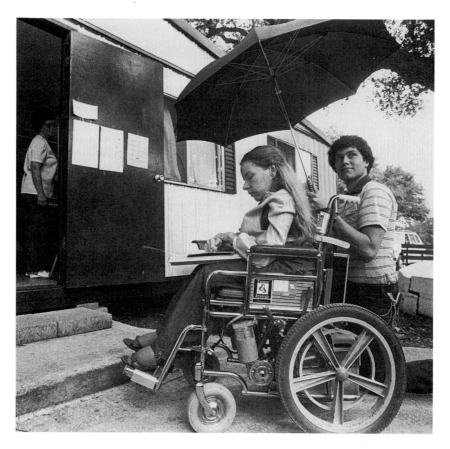

ner, 1981). As constitutional law scholars describe it, the Bill of Rights has thereby been "nationalized." That process has also created for the Supreme Court the role of the major arbiter of civil rights policy for the entire nation. Of this trend, Richard Cortner (1981: 300–301) has observed:

> As a result of the nationalization process the docket of the [Supreme] Court was opened to litigation challenging an almost unlimited array of state and local policies that had previously been insulated from attack on the basis of the Bill of Rights. The result was that the Court was called upon to render more significant interpretations of political and civil liberties than ever before, and in almost every field, from freedom of speech to criminal procedure, a majority of the cases in which the Court rendered decisions on civil and political

liberties were cases challenging state policies under the Fourteenth Amendment.

Through its own evolving interpretation of the Constitution, the Supreme Court has become the overseer of a considerable body of state and local governmental activity. And it is true that many state and local policies—particularly in the areas of the rights of ethnic minorities, of those individuals accused of criminal offenses, and of those convicted of crimes—were at one time quite at variance from the Constitution. The Supreme Court has, then, forced a considerable revolution in policy in requiring the states to operate under the Bill of Rights and the Fourteenth Amendment.

The proliferation of federal statutory law has also been a force extending the power of the U.S. Supreme Court as an overseer of state and local governments. That is the case, of course, because the latter governments must conform to the requirements of federal statutory laws as well as to basic constitutional guarantees. And the federal courts have often been called on to judge the appropriateness of these new laws or of some state policy that falls under their purview.

The role of the federal government in civil rights policy has not been created exclusively, however, by the Supreme Court. The Congress and the President have also produced a sizable body of statutory law in this area. The best-known of these laws are those aimed at ensuring the civil rights of ethnic minorities. The major federal legislation intended to guarantee such rights is encompassed by the Civil Rights Acts of 1957, 1960, and 1964 and the Voting Rights Act of 1965. A considerable regulatory apparatus—supervising, in particular, the activities of state and local governments—was the eventual product of these laws. Beyond its voting rights component, this legislation also prohibited discrimination because of race, color, religion, or national origin in public accommodations such as restaurants, theaters, hotels, motels, and sports facilities. Likewise, discrimination in state or local government programs receiving federal financial aid was prohibited, as was employment discrimination by private employers, membership discrimination by unions, and rental or sales discrimination by the owners of virtually all private housing.

Other federal legislation and court cases prohibited, for example, certain forms of discrimination against the aged, the handicapped, and women desiring abortions. (Concerning the latter, the Supreme Court ruled in 1973 in *Roe* v. *Wade* that a state's law forbidding abortion in the first trimester of pregnancy violated the privacy rights of individuals.) In addition, such diverse matters as the educational rights of minority children who do not speak English, the right to privacy for students' educational records, and the health and safety rights of human subjects of biomedical and behavioral research have been addressed by federal law.

One particular area in which federal cooptation of civil rights policymaking is not fully appreciated is the area of voting rights. Every American probably understands the role the federal government has played in assuring the voting rights of ethnic minorities. But all citizens have been touched by the federal government's actions in this area. The federal government has outlawed the use of such devices as poll taxes, literacy tests, and long residency and annual re-registration requirements, which restricted the voting rights of many Americans besides ethnic minorities. The Supreme Court in the mid-1960s required that state legislatures be regularly redistricted so that all votes would have equal "weight," that is, so that malapportionment of legislative districts would not give some groups of voters disproportionate influence over the legislature.[3] Finally, by the Twenty-sixth Amendment to the U.S. Constitution, adopted in 1971, 18–20-year-olds were given the right to vote in all national, state, and local elections. All of these voting rights policy enactments can be interpreted as reshaping fundamentally the original constitutional bargain that allowed the states to determine suffrage and, therefore, the right to participate in the democratic process. In recent decades the federal government has essentially taken up a good portion of that power and has, in the process, considerably enlarged the number of Americans who enjoy this most basic of democratic rights.

The expansion of federal financial aid to state and local governments also extended the scope of federal civil rights laws. Any program receiving federal assistance must conform to the equal rights requirement of the Civil Rights Act of 1964. Thus, as the federal government began to assist more and more state and local initiatives in the era of cooptive federalism, the reach of its civil rights dictates was also extended.

Environmental and Pollution Control Policy   A third example of the effects of cooptive federalism comes from the field of pollution control policy. Responsibility for dealing with environmental pollution—like most environmental policy—belonged traditionally to state and local governments. As recently as 1948 the U.S. Congress acknowledged in the Water Pollution Control Act of 1948, which provided only research and technical assistance to the states, that "it is hereby declared to be the policy of Congress to recognize, preserve, and protect the primary responsibilities and rights of the states in controlling water pollution."[4] Twenty years after that declaration the roles of the federal government and the states were completely reversed by the growth of cooptive federalism (Advisory Commission on Intergovernmental Relations, 1981). Beginning in the mid-1960s a series of water and air pollution laws were adopted by the federal government; these laws established ambitious *national* goals and dictated the roles that must be played by state and local governments in the pursuit of those goals.

The evolution of this new federal role in pollution policy is summarized in Table 3-2. The table shows the incremental process by which the federal government's role in this policy area evolved from merely providing research assistance to the states to jurisdiction over policy making and definition of both the federal and state governments' responsibilities. Other legislation enacted since 1965 extended the national government's jurisdiction over air and water pollution, solid waste management, noise pollution, chemical hazards, water resources and land use, environmental health and safety, and comprehensive environmental planning (Advisory Commission on Intergovernmental Relations, 1981: 17–40). In all these areas the federal government has taken on a major, if not predominant, policy-making position. Even under Presidents Reagan and Bush, who favor returning more power to the states, federal control of environmental policy has been maintained. As Lester (1988: 406) observes, the states have been allowed "to design and implement their own [environmental] laws, but these laws must meet minimum federal standards and objectives."

Intergovernmental Regulation   In the policy areas discussed above, the federal government directly regulates the activities of state and local governments just as it regulates many activities of private business. Yet there are aspects of this *intergovernmental regulation* that the average citizen probably does not recognize or clearly understand but that are so important that they constitute a fourth example of the results of cooptive federalism (Kettl, 1983).

One dimension of intergovernmental regulation is obvious in the policy examples discussed above. The federal government has often told state and local governments what they can and cannot do. Federal civil rights laws, as just one example, literally ban several

TABLE 3-2
THE NATIONAL-
IZATION OF WATER
AND AIR POLLUTION
POLICY

DATE	TITLE	IMPORTANT PROVISIONS
	Water Pollution Control	
1899	Refuse Act, 30 Stat. 1152	Required permit from Chief of Engineers for discharge of refuse into navigable waters.
1948	Water Pollution Control Act, PL 80–845	Gave the federal government authority for investigations, research, and surveys. Left primary responsibility for pollution control with the states.
1956	Water Pollution Control Act Amendments, PL 84–660	Established federal pollution policy for 1956–1970 period. Provided (1) federal grants for construction of municipal water treatment plants, (2) complex procedure for federal enforcement actions against individual dischargers.
1961	Federal Water Pollution Control Act Amendments, PL 87–88	Strengthened federal enforcement procedure.
1965	Water Quality Act, PL 89–234	Created Federal Water Pollution Control Administration.
1966	Clean Water Restoration Act, PL 89–753	Increased grant authorizations.
1970	Water Quality Improvement Act, PL 91–224	Established liability for owners of vessels that spill oil and created new rules regarding thermal pollution.
1972	Federal Water Pollution Control Act Amendments, PL 92–500	Set federal policy that provided for (1) federal establishment of effluent limits for individual sources of pollution, (2) issuance of discharge permits, (3) large increase in authorized grant funds for municipal waste treatment plants.
1974	Safe Drinking Water Act, PL 93–523	Directed the EPA to set standards, applicable to all public water systems, to protect human health from organic, inorganic, and microbiological contaminants and for turbidity in drinking water.
1977	Federal Water Pollution Control Act Amendments, PL 95–217	Relaxation of some standards under the 1972 amendments, such as industrial antipollution standards on suspended solids, fecal bacteria, and oxygen demand of discharge if it can be shown that the cost of equipment exceeds benefits.

CONTINUED

	DATE	TITLE	IMPORTANT PROVISIONS
TABLE 3-2 CONTINUED			
		Air Pollution Control	
	1955	Air Pollution Control Act, PL 84–159	Authorized a federal program for research, training, and demonstrations relating to air pollution control (extended for four years in 1959).
	1963	Clean Air Act, PL 88–206	Gave the federal government enforcement powers through enforcement conferences similar to the 1956 approach to water pollution control.
	1965	Motor Vehicle Air Pollution Control Act, PL 89–272	Added new authority to the 1963 act, giving HEW power to prescribe emission standards for automobiles as soon as practicable.
	1967	Air Quality Act, PL 90–148	(1) Authorized HEW to oversee state standards for ambient air quality and state implementation plans; (2) set national standards for auto emissions.
	1970	Clean Air Act Amendments, PL 91–604	Greatly expanded the federal role in setting and enforcing standards for ambient air quality, and established stringent new emission standards for automobiles.
	1974	Clean Air Act Amendments, PL 93–319	Technical amendments. Some relaxation of standards.
	1977	Clean Air Act Amendments, PL 95–95	Required states with air-quality nonattainment areas to adopt plans for full compliance by 1982. Deferred further reductions in automobile toxic fumes until 1981.

Source: Advisory Commission on Intergovernmental Relations, *Protecting the Environment: Politics, Pollution, and Federal Policy* (Washington, D.C.: Advisory Commission on Intergovernmental Relations, 1981), pp. 31–32.

forms of racial discrimination previously practiced by state and local governments. The considerable range of intergovernmental regulation is revealed by the list in Table 3-3 of federal statutory laws imposed on the states. When the federal government regulates state

	TITLE	OBJECTIVE	PUBLIC LAW
TABLE 3-3 MAJOR FEDERAL STATUTES REGULATING STATE AND LOCAL GOVERNMENTS	Age Discrimination Act of 1975	Prevent discrimination on the basis of age in federally assisted programs.	94–135
	Age Discrimination in Employment Act (1974)[a]	Prevent discrimination on the basis of age in state and local government employment.	93–259; 90–202
	Architectural Barriers Act of 1968	Make federally occupied and funded buildings, facilities and public conveyances accessible to the physically handicapped.	90–480
	Civil Rights Act of 1964 (Title VI)	Prevent discrimination on the basis of race, color, or national origin in federally assisted programs.	88–352
	Civil Rights Act of 1968 (Title VIII)	Prevent discrimination on the basis of race, color, religion, sex, or national origin in the sale or rental of federally assisted housing.	90–284
	Clean Air Act Amendments of 1970	Establish national air quality and emissions standards.	91–604
	Coastal Zone Management Act of 1972	Assure that federally assisted activities are consistent with federally approved state coastal-zone management programs.	94–370
	Davis-Bacon Act (1931)[b]	Assure that locally prevailing wages are paid to construction workers employed under federal contracts and financial assistance programs.	74–403
	Education Amendments of 1972 (Title IX)	Prevent discrimination on the basis of sex in federally assisted education programs.	92–318
	Education for All Handicapped Children Act (1975)	Provide a free appropriate public education to all handicapped children.	94–142
	Emergency Highway Energy Conservation Act (1974)[c]	Establish a national maximum speed limit of 55 mph.	93–239
	Endangered Species Act of 1973	Protect and conserve endangered and threatened animal species.	93–205

CONTINUED

	TITLE	OBJECTIVE	PUBLIC LAW
TABLE 3-3 CONTINUED			
	Equal Employment Opportunity Act of 1972	Prevent discrimination on the basis of race, color, religion, sex, or national origin in state and local government employment.	92–261
	Fair Labor Standards Act Amendments of 1974	Extend federal minimum wage and overtime pay protections to state and local government employees.	93–259
	Family Educational Rights and Privacy Act of 1974	Provide student and parental access to educational records while restricting access by others.	93–380
	Federal Insecticide, Fungicide, and Rodenticide Act (1972)	Control the use of pesticides that may be harmful to the environment.	92–516
	Federal Water Pollution Control Act Amendments of 1972	Establish federal effluent limitations to control the discharge of pollutants.	92–500
	Flood Disaster Protection Act of 1973	Expand coverage of the national flood insurance program.	93–234
	Hatch Act (1940)	Prohibit public employees from engaging in certain political activities.	76–753
	Highway Beautification Act of 1965	Control and remove outdoor advertising signs along major highways.	89–285
	Marine Protection Research and Sanctuaries Act Amendments of 1977	Prohibit ocean dumping of municipal sludge.	95–153
	National Energy Conservation Policy Act (1978)	Establish residential energy conservation plans.	95–619
	National Environmental Policy Act of 1969	Assure consideration of the environmental impact of major federal actions.	91–190

	TITLE	OBJECTIVE	PUBLIC LAW
TABLE 3-3 CONTINUED	National Health Planning and Resources Development Act of 1974	Establish state and local health planning agencies and procedures.	93–64
	National Historic Preservation Act of 1966	Protect properties of historical, architectural, archeological, and cultural significance.	89–665
	Natural Gas Policy Act of 1978	Implement federal pricing policies for the intrastate sales of natural gas in producing states.	95–621
	Occupational Safety and Health Act (1970)	Eliminate unsafe and unhealthful working conditions.	91–596
	Public Utilities Regulatory Policies Act of 1978	Require consideration of federal standards for the pricing of electricity and natural gas.	95–617
	Rehabilitation Act of 1973 (Section 504)	Prevent discrimination in federally assisted programs against otherwise qualified individuals on the basis of a physical or mental handicap.	93–112
	Resource Conservation and Recovery Act of 1976	Establish standards for the control of hazardous wastes.	94–580
	Safe Drinking Water Act of 1976	Assure drinking water purity.	93–523
	Surface Mining Control and Reclamation Act of 1977	Establish federal standards for the control of surface mining.	95–87
	Uniform Relocation Assistance and Real Properties Acquisition Policies Act of 1970	Set federal policies and reimbursement procedures for property acquisition under federally assisted programs.	91–646
	Water Quality Act (1965)	Establish federal water quality standards for interstate waters.	88–668

CONTINUED

			PUBLIC
TABLE 3-3 CONTINUED	**TITLE**	**OBJECTIVE**	**LAW**
	Wholesome Meat Act (1967)	Establish systems for the inspection of meat sold in intrastate commerce.	90–201
	Wholesome Poultry Products Act of 1968	Establish systems for the inspection of poultry sold in intrastate commerce.	90–492

[a]Coverage of the act, originally adopted in 1967, was extended to state and local government employees in 1974.

[b]Although the Davis-Bacon Act applied initially only to direct federal construction, it has since been extended to some seventy-seven federal assistance programs.

[c]A permanent national 55-mph speed limit was established by the Federal-Aid Highway Amendments of 1974 (PL 93–643), signed into law January 4, 1975.

Source: Advisory Commission on Intergovernmental Relations, *Regulatory Federalism: Policy, Process, Impact, and Reform* (Washington, D.C.: Advisory Commission on Intergovernmental Relations, 1984), pp. 19–21.

and local governments in so many areas—from age discrimination to the wholesomeness of meat and poultry—there is undoubtedly a great body of intergovernmental regulation.

A second form of intergovernmental regulation arises from the strings that are attached to any federal grant program or other joint federal-state initiative. These strings are just as concerned with *how* state and local governments carry out their tasks as with *what* those tasks will be. This is the case, in particular, with the federal government's use of what are known as *cross-cutting requirements* for most of its programs. The majority of federal programs providing financial assistance to the states, that is, now impose a number of requirements on the recipient government that are not directly relevant to the goals of the program at hand. For example, a state or local government receiving federal aid to build a new government building must typically agree that an environmental impact assessment will be completed for the proposed structure, that the contractors hired to construct the building will use equal opportunity hiring practices, that some portion of the work will be accomplished by minority-owned firms, that "locally prevailing wages" will be paid to workers of the contracting firms, that the building will be designed to be accessible to the handicapped, that it will meet federal energy conservation requirements, that various federally approved record-keeping and accounting procedures will be employed in handling the funds, and so on, and so on. The U.S. Office of Management and

The Strings Attached to a Typical Federal Grant

One of the authors of this book recently coauthored a grant proposal for his university requesting fellowship funds for graduate students in public administration who planned careers in the public service. The grant program to which this proposal was submitted, sponsored by the U.S. Department of Education, is subject to a typical set of intergovernmental regulations. All universities applying for these funds have to certify that they will comply with the following federal laws, standards, and regulations:

- The U.S. Intergovernmental Personnel Act of 1970 regarding standards for merit systems as specified by the U.S. Office of Personnel Management's "Standards for a Merit System of Personnel Administration."
- All federal statutes relating to nondiscrimination, including but not limited to (1) Title VI of the Civil Rights Act of 1964, regarding ethnic discrimination, (2) Title IX of the Education Amendments of 1972, regarding gender discrimination, (3) Section 504 of the Rehabilitation Act of 1973, regarding discrimination on the basis of handicaps, (4) the Age Discrimination Act of 1975, (5) the Drug Abuse Office and Treatment Act of 1972, relating to nondiscrimination on the basis of drug abuse, (6) the Comprehensive Alcohol Abuse and Alcoholism Prevention, Treatment, and Rehabilitation Act of 1970, regarding discrimination on the basis of alcohol abuse or alcoholism, (7) the Public Health Service Act of 1912 regarding confidentiality of alcohol and drug abuse patient records, (8) the Civil Rights Act of 1968 regarding discrimination in the sale, rental, or financing of housing, and (9) the "requirements of any other nondiscrimination statute(s) which may apply to the application."
- The Uniform Relocation Assistance and Real Property Acquisition Policies Act of 1970 concerning fair and equitable

CONTINUED

treatment of persons who are displaced or whose property is acquired as a result of federally assisted programs.

■ The Hatch Act, which limits the political activities of employees whose principal employment activities are funded in whole or in part with federal funds.

■ The provisions of the Davis-Bacon Act, the Copeland Act, and the Contract Work Hours and Safety Standards Act regarding labor standards for federally assisted construction subcontracts.

■ The Flood Disaster Protection Act of 1973 regarding flood insurance requirements in flood hazard areas.

■ The environmental standards required by the National Environmental Policy Act of 1969, Coastal Zone Management Act of 1972, the Clean Air Act of 1955, the Safe Drinking Water Act of 1974, the Endangered Species Act of 1973, the Wild and Scenic Rivers Act of 1968, and a number of specific executive orders on this topic.

■ The National Historic Preservation Act of 1966 and the Archaeological and Historic Preservation Act of 1974.

■ Public Law 93–348 regarding the protection of human subjects in research.

■ The Laboratory Animal Welfare Act of 1966 regarding the care, handling, and treatment of warm-blooded animals held for research, teaching, or other activities supported by the particular award of assistance.

Budget identified sixty-eight such cross-cutting requirements in 1985 (Beckman, 1986: 429). Some of these requirements are applicable to all federal programs; others apply to only a handful. The typical federal grant includes at least a dozen of these restrictions. And, once again, these are not just requirements for *what* state and local governments must do; they are a very wide-ranging set of additional requirements for *how* policies are to be implemented and carried out. This is an extraordinary form of intergovernmental regulation that imposes a host of secondary policy requirements on top of the principal ones for any federal program.

- The Lead-Based Paint Poisoning Prevention Act, which prohibits the use of lead-based paint in the construction of residential structures.
- The Single Audit Act of 1984 and its requirements for financial statements concerning the grant funds.
- The Drug-Free Workplace Act of 1988.
- *And* "all applicable requirements of all other federal laws, executive orders, regulations, and policies governing this program."

In addition, the university must certify that it:

- Has the "institutional, managerial, and financial capability to ensure proper planning, management, and completion of the project described in the application."
- Will give "the awarding agency, the Comptroller General of the United States, and if appropriate, the State . . . access to and the right to examine all records, books, papers, or documents" related to the award.
- Will "establish safeguards to prohibit employees from using their positions for a purpose that constitutes or presents the appearance of personal or organizational conflict of interest, or personal gain."

THE METHODS OF FEDERAL COOPTATION

The national government's power was enlarged by several distinct methods during the period of cooptive federalism. The most important of these was the literal usurping of some of the traditional powers of state and local governments. Not only did the federal government take charge of some areas formerly under the control of the states, it also decided on the policy goals *and* procedures that state and local governments must follow in those areas.

Some have called this process *supercession*. James Croy (1975) identified forty-eight federal laws adopted between 1964 and 1973 that superceded, or usurped, a specific power of state or local government. Daniel Elazar (1984: 54–56) extended that count to the period 1965–1982 and identified a total of fifty-eight supercessive statutory laws. Of course, numbers of supercessive laws alone may not fully indicate the present scope of this development. As the discussion above indicates, what the federal government has usurped has included some of the most prominent of the states' policy responsibilities. Clearly, therefore, supercession has been a powerful method of cooptation. It has also led to a redefining of the division of powers between the national government and the states.

A second means by which cooptive federalism has grown has been by the extension of the power of the federal courts over state and local governments. Both the nationalization of the Bill of Rights and the creation of new federal statutory law have promoted this process. The federal courts now have the power to oversee a considerable portion of what state and local governments do. This fact is important for a reason we have not yet mentioned. Some scholars have argued that although the President and some members of the Congress have become interested in reducing federal control of the states, the federal courts have continued to render cooptive judgments in cases involving intergovernmental relations (Madden and Remes, 1983). One might conclude that this is the case because the President and Congress have not actually reformed much cooptive legislation. Thus, the courts must often decide cases on the basis of the considerable body of supercessive and highly regulatory law that is still on the books. Furthermore, some recent efforts of the federal executive branch to lighten the regulatory load on state and local governments have been invalidated by the federal courts because they were in conflict with civil rights legislation or constitutional guarantees.

A final method of federal cooptation, which was referred to above, has been the creation of state and local governments' dependency on federal financial aid. Some of that aid came with a number of strings attached, and some was not welcomed by state and local government officials; yet much of it they did welcome. Indeed, state and local officials often lobbied Washington for more aid of one kind or another during the era of cooptive federalism (Kettl, 1983: 37–38). Over time their governments became dependent in varying degrees on that support. Evidence of this dependency was clear in the considerable outcry from state and local officials over some aspects of President Reagan's reform proposals. They hailed his ideas about reducing federal control but reacted quite negatively to the proposal to reduce federal financial aid at the same time.

Table 3-4 documents the growth of state and local governments' dependency on federal support over the period 1950–1990. The near tripling of that dependency between 1950 and 1980 is quite remarkable. The level of federal grants-in-aid in 1980 also helps explain the anguish of many state and local officials in response to proposals to cut such aid. And the actual decline in aid as a percentage of indigenous revenues since 1980 has made the fears behind that anguish a reality in many places.[5]

Although aid dependency grew in general during the era of cooptive federalism, the states were not affected equally by that increase. There have always been wide variations among the states in the extent to which they have received federal support. Table 3-5 presents that variation for fiscal year 1980–81, when federal aid to the states was near its all-time high. This date was chosen explicitly to illustrate the way the subsequent decline in federal support affected individual states differently. The states' aid dependency on the federal government in 1980–81 ranged from a low of 8 percent for Alaska to a high of 30 percent for Vermont. Most of the states with high aid dependency appear to be poor ones—including Alabama, Arkansas, Kentucky, Maine, Mississippi, North Carolina, South Dakota, Tennessee, Utah, Vermont, and West Virginia. Yet those with low aid dependency—including Alaska, Arizona, Connecticut, New

TABLE 3-4
DEPENDENCY OF STATE AND LOCAL GOVERNMENTS ON FEDERAL AID, 1950–1990

YEAR	FEDERAL GRANTS-IN-AID TO STATE AND LOCAL GOVERNMENTS (MILLIONS)	FEDERAL AID AS A PERCENTAGE OF STATE AND LOCAL GOVERNMENT EXPENDITURES
1950	$ 2,253	10.4%
1955	3,207	10.1
1960	7,019	14.7
1965	10,910	15.3
1970	24,065	19.2
1975	49,791	22.7
1980	91,451	25.8
1985	105,900	20.9
1988	115,300	18.2
1990	133,836 (est.)	n/a

Source: U.S. Office of Management and Budget, *Special Analyses: Budget of the United States Government, Fiscal Year 1990* (Washington, D.C.: OMB, 1989), p. H-22; *Budget of the United States Government: Fiscal Year 1991* (Washington, D.C.: OMB, 1991), p. A-321.

TABLE 3-5
FEDERAL AID AS A
PERCENTAGE OF TO-
TAL STATE AND LO-
CAL GOVERNMENT
REVENUES, BY
STATE, FOR FISCAL
YEAR 1980–81

STATE	PERCENTAGE	STATE	PERCENTAGE
Alabama	24%	Montana	27%
Alaska	8	Nebraska	19
Arizona	18	Nevada	19
Arkansas	29	New Hampshire	25
California	22	New Jersey	17
Colorado	20	New Mexico	20
Connecticut	18	New York	19
Delaware	24	North Carolina	24
Florida	20	North Dakota	20
Georgia	24	Ohio	21
Hawaii	21	Oklahoma	20
Idaho	25	Oregon	22
Illinois	22	Pennsylvania	21
Indiana	21	Rhode Island	25
Iowa	19	South Carolina	24
Kansas	19	South Dakota	28
Kentucky	27	Tennessee	26
Louisiana	22	Texas	18
Maine	28	Utah	25
Maryland	22	Vermont	30
Massachusetts	22	Virginia	27
Michigan	22	Washington	24
Minnesota	21	West Virginia	28
Mississippi	28	Wisconsin	21
Missouri	24	Wyoming	20

Average for all the states 21%

Source: U.S. Bureau of the Census, *Governmental Finances in 1980–81* (Washington, D.C.: U.S. Bureau of the Census, 1982), p. 29.

Jersey, New York, and Texas—are a diverse lot. It is difficult to account for all the reasons behind these variations, but it is clear that widely different hardships have been suffered by the states as a result of the decline in federal aid since the late 1970s.

THE IMPACT OF COOPTIVE FEDERALISM ON STATE AND LOCAL GOVERNMENTS

The original constitutional division of governmental power has been profoundly changed in the twentieth century. Some powers that were once those of the states, such as the exclusive power to regulate environmental pollution, have become those of the national government. But the states have lost more than this or that power. In many instances the federal government has not only taken over the power to make policy decisions, it has also told the states what *their* policies must be. Many contemporary observers see this as a truly unfortunate development. To the extent that any American prizes the independence of the states as well as their right to determine their own policies, he or she must agree with this assessment.

Another criticism of federal policy requirements is that many of them are very costly for state and local governments. Additionally, many argue that these requirements create a red-tape nightmare for those who must comply with them. State and local government officials have pointed out instances in which the benefits of some policies forced on them appear to be slight. In other cases they complain that the costs they had to incur from their own budgets to implement a federal policy were about equal to the federal aid they got to support the program. And the costs of compliance—judged by time, effort, or money—have indeed been high in many instances.

At the same time other observers claim positive benefits from cooptive federalism. First, they argue that many states simply would not have guaranteed the civil rights of their citizens or ensured the social welfare of the poor or addressed the problems of pollution if they had not been forced to do so by the federal government. This argument is, unfortunately, correct for many states. And it means that the costs the states have borne because of cooptive federal policies are offset to some degree, maybe even completely in some instances, by the new policy benefits their citizens enjoy. Federal control of many policy areas has also led to common nationwide policy, which ought, in principle, to be more successful than fifty individual state policies would be. Whether you find these arguments compelling, however, may depend on how much you value the national policies that now exist in civil rights, social welfare, and many other areas over traditional principles of federalism.

Other positive results from cooptive federalism may arise from the impact on state and local governments' capabilities. Because of federal government initiatives, it has been argued, each state must now have a professional welfare agency, professional pollution control agencies, an equal employment agency, and so on. In many instances such agencies are literally required by federal policies. In addition, federal policies typically require the states not only to implement but also to monitor and assess the progress of the policy requirements now imposed on them. Most states have had to develop a host of new agencies and skills as a consequence. Thus, state and local governments have become more competent and professional because of federally imposed requirements. As a result of these changes, they should be better able to address all their responsibilities.

In sum, the era of cooptive federalism led to three distinct kinds of changes: in the constitutional balance between the states and the national government, in the institutional capabilities of both levels of government, and in the policies they pursue both together and separately. Some have argued that the overall results of these changes have been quite important and positive. Others have been generally negative about at least some of them. In any case, conclusions about the wisdom of cooptive federalism ought to be based on a consideration of all three changes.

WHAT ROLE IS LEFT FOR STATE AND LOCAL GOVERNMENTS?

After reading the material in this chapter so far, you might conclude that there is no need to read on. If the federal government has expanded so much, you might ask, what role is left for state and local governments? Is there enough left for them to do to make them worth studying? Do these governments have the power to respond to the contemporary policy challenges described in Chapter 1?

In fact, states and localities still retain considerable and important powers, and there are many reasons to be concerned with *how* their governments operate and *why* they operate as they do. The remainder of this book will address those matters at length, but three important points deserve explication here.

CONTROL OVER MUCH PUBLIC POLICY

First, and in spite of considerable federal cooptation, state and local governments retain control over many important public policy decisions. In particular, state and local governments have taken considerable responsibility for the development of their economies, as described in Chapter 1. They also have predominant responsibility for such functions as public education, public health and health care, policing and other public security measures, the resolution of civil disputes in the courts, the regulation of the professions, and a considerable amount of business regulation, to name only some of the major examples. Local governments are also responsible for the provision of a host of public services, which, though mundane, are critical to the quality of everyday life. Local police, fire, sanitation, welfare, education, transportation, planning and zoning, and other services also constitute the principal means through which most people come in direct contact with government on any regular basis.

In addition, there has existed since 1980 a widespread effort to expand the powers of the states at the expense of the federal government, as described earlier in this chapter. That effort is aimed at moving back toward a system of dual federalism. Any extent to which it succeeds will make the states more important than they were under cooptive federalism.

A familiar example of a state-controlled policy area will illustrate our point. A major service provided by all the states is public higher education—through state colleges and universities. The character and the quality of those educational institutions, and of the education they provide to students, are primarily determined by state governments. To some degree colleges and universities are regulated and even financially supported by the federal government. Their programs must also operate within the confines of several civil rights laws—in particular those relating to ethnic minorities, women, and the handicapped. They must meet federal standards for occupational safety, pollution control, energy conservation, and a variety of other policy goals. They must also abide by a number of strings attached to the many federal financial grants all such institutions seek to support their research or student aid or capital expansion. The essential quality of the service provided by public colleges and universities is shaped by state governments, however. State decisions about funding levels and administrative decisions of college officials—who are themselves state government bureaucrats—about how to use those funds are critical. Decisions about what curricula to offer, what faculty to hire, what students to admit and retain, and what level of excellence to pursue in all these endeavors are made at the state level. Those decisions determine the quality of the public education provided in these institutions and, as we observed in

Chapter 1, education is thought to be critical to the future of individual states as well as individual citizens.

The point we have just made can be applied to state and local government control of a large number of other services and policies. Thus, many important governmental responsibilities in this country are still held by state and local governments.

POLICY INNOVATION AND LEADERSHIP

A second point, somewhat related to the first, is that state governments can play a leadership role in policy making: developing innovative solutions to problems, experimenting with alternative solutions, and stimulating other states and even the federal government to follow their lead. There are important examples of this kind of state leadership. In the area of civil rights policy, New York, Connecticut, and New Jersey have been leaders in the post–World War II era (Dye, 1969: 359). In pollution control and environmental preservation policy, California has been a widely recognized innovator. In more general terms, California, Colorado, Michigan, Minnesota, New York, Ohio, Oregon, and Washington have been found to be among the most innovative states when one considers a wide array of policy areas. At the other extreme, Alabama, Delaware, Georgia, Mississippi, Nevada, and Wyoming have typically been placed among the least innovative (Savage, 1986). You might be wondering just how innovative your state government has been and why. We will satisfy that curiosity in later chapters of this book.

IMPLEMENTATION OF FEDERAL POLICIES

Finally, state and local governments have a role in the shaping of many federally mandated policies, and this role is far more important than a superficial assessment might suggest. Many federal programs, as indicated before, are designed so that a state or local government is responsible for the actual implementation, within federal guidelines and with federal financial support. Yet the ability and the willingness of a given state or local government to take on this responsibility can greatly affect the success of such an initiative. There are a number of good examples—the best of which is school integration—where the resistance of state and local officials to a federal policy delayed implementation for many years and often determined what form it would take. The states, in other words, may have become more dependent on and more regulated by the federal government, but the federal government is also quite dependent on the states for the achievement of many of its goals.

The states also have considerable latitude in carrying out many federal programs. Often the national government only establishes the minimum details of a program along with the broad policy goals, leaving a good deal of discretion to the states in determining the remainder of the details and day-to-day activities. Some states might only carry out what is minimally required of them; others might go far beyond the federal mandate. Some may try to tailor these federal programs to fit their own policy preferences. The character and the success, then, of many federal programs, once they are actually put into the field, owe much to the work, the capabilities, and the interests of state or local governments.

CONCLUSION

Federal-state relations have evolved considerably over time, resulting in a system far different from the one envisioned by the authors of the Constitution. And the federal system's current character is a critical influence on state and local governments. Knowledge of the workings and effects of cooptive federalism and of the efforts since 1980 to weaken that system reveals why state and local governments do some things and not others. Current federal-state relations are highly controversial and in flux. The ultimate resolution of that controversy and the outcome of that flux cannot yet be fully envisioned; however, new opportunities as well as new burdens are developing for state and local governments because of the recent shifts in federal-state relations. These changes, then, have also become a part of the context within which state and local governments must operate.

The ongoing changes indicate the continued dynamism of American federalism. There is no perfect division of powers among the governments in this country. Instead, the practical reality is that changing social, economic, and political problems shape the individual and respective powers of the various levels of government. Even the balance of powers struck by the writers of the Constitution was a product of their own times and political interests. You should not be surprised, therefore, to find that governmental powers have shifted along with changing times, as subsequent political leaders reacted to their own and the public's expectations for governmental action. What is critical, then, is that you understand the contemporary division of powers, how it affects all levels of government today, and in what direction it seems to be moving in response to current problems and controversies.

NOTES

1. As you probably know, the first post-Revolution American government was not a federal system but a confederation, a loose association of the states with a very weak central government. The shortcomings of that system, which only lasted from 1781 to 1788, led to the Constitutional Convention of 1787 and the eventual ratification of the present Constitution.

2. For more details on these social welfare programs, a good source that describes both the federal and state governments' roles is *The Book of the States, 1984–85* (Council of State Governments, 1984: 390–413).

3. In 1964 the Supreme Court ruled on two cases that laid down the "one-man, one-vote" requirement. The court's decision in *Wesberry* v. *Sanders* (376 U.S. 1) required that election districts for the U.S. House of Representatives be apportioned on that basis after each decennial census. Later that same year, in *Reynolds* v. *Sims* (377 U.S. 533) the court ruled that the equal protection clause of the Fourteenth Amendment required similar apportionment in the voting districts for both houses of state legislatures.

4. The Water Pollution Control Act of 1948, PL 80–845 (1948).

5. Federal aid as a percentage of state and local governments' total expenditures actually began to decline in 1979 under the Carter administration. That figure was at its peak in 1978 at 26.8 percent.

REFERENCES

Advisory Commission on Intergovernmental Relations. 1981. *Protecting the Environment: Politics, Pollution, and Federal Policy.* Washington, D.C.: Advisory Commission on Intergovernmental Relations.

Advisory Commission on Intergovernmental Relations. 1984. *Regulatory Federalism: Policy, Process, Impact, and Reform.* Washington, D.C.: Advisory Commission on Intergovernmental Relations.

Beckman, Norman. 1986. "Developments in Federal-State Relations, 1984–85," pp. 426–431 in *The Book of the States, 1986–87.* Lexington, Ky.: Council of State Governments.

Beckman, Norman. 1988. "Developments in Federal-State Relations," pp. 438–443 in *The Book of the States, 1988–89.* Lexington, Ky.: Council of State Governments.

Bowman, Ann O., and Michael A. Pagano. 1990. "The State of American Federalism, 1989–1990," *Publius* 20 (Summer): 1–27.

Cortner, Richard C. 1981. *The Supreme Court and the Second Bill of Rights: The Fourteenth Amendment and the Nationalization of Civil Liberties.* Madison: University of Wisconsin Press.

Council of State Governments. 1984. *The Book of the States, 1984–85.* Lexington, Ky.: Council of State Governments.

Croy, James B. 1975. "Federal Supercession: The Road to Domination," *State Government* XLVIII (Winter): 32–36.

Dye, Thomas R. 1969. *Politics in States and Communities.* Englewood Cliffs, N.J.: Prentice-Hall.

Elazar, Daniel J. 1984. *American Federalism: A View from the States,* 3rd ed. New York: Harper & Row.

Fabricius, Martha. 1991. "More Dictates from the Feds," *State Legislatures* 17 (February): 28–30.

Kettl, Donald F. 1983. *The Regulation of American Federalism.* Baton Rouge: Louisiana State University Press.

Lester, James P. 1988. "Implementation of the Resource Conservation and Recovery Act of 1976: The Role of the States," pp. 406–408 in *The Book of the States, 1988–89.* Lexington, Ky.: Council of State Governments.

Madden, Thomas J., and David H. Remes. 1983. "The Courts and the Administration: Marching to Different Drummers," *Intergovernmental Perspective* 9 (Spring): 23–29.

Savage, Robert L. 1986. "Diffusion Research Traditions and the Spread of Policy Innovations in a Federal System," *Publius* 15 (Fall): 1–27.

Sundquist, James L. 1969. *Making Federalism Work.* Washington, D.C.: Brookings Institution.

U.S. Bureau of the Census. 1982. *Governmental Finances in 1980–81.* Washington, D.C.: U.S. Bureau of the Census.

U.S. Bureau of the Census. 1986. *U.S. Statistical Abstract, 1987.* Washington, D.C.: U.S. Bureau of the Census.

U.S. Office of Management and Budget. 1980. *Managing Federal*

Assistance in the 1980s: Working Papers, Volume I. Washington, D.C.: U.S. Office of Management and Budget.

U.S. Office of Management and Budget. 1989. *Special Analyses: Budget of the United States Government, Fiscal Year 1990.* Washington, D.C.: U.S. Office of Management and Budget.

U.S. Office of Management and Budget. 1990. *Budget of the United States Government: Fiscal Year 1991.* Washington, D.C.: U.S. Office of Management and Budget.

Walker, David B. 1982. "American Federalism–Then and Now," pp. 23–29 in *The Book of the States, 1982–83.* Lexington, Ky.: Council of State Governments.

4

Elections, Political Parties, and Participation in State Politics

We have argued that contemporary economic and social problems will greatly affect the lives and futures of all Americans and that state and local governments will be deeply involved in resolving those problems. Surely, therefore, many Americans will want to influence the policy decisions of those governments. How might they do so? What are the major avenues for public participation in and control over governmental decisions?

The most important avenue for public involvement is the election process. Voting in elections is the easiest way for individual citizens to participate in politics, and it is the only form of such participation that a majority of Americans practice. Elections are, however, limited as means of public control of government. They occur only infrequently, and not all citizens exercise their right to vote. The message voters send to elected officials is often difficult to interpret. Despite these limitations, elections remain the central means of democratic control of government. Therefore, they deserve detailed attention.

In this chapter we explain, first, the institutional setting for state elections: the rules under which they proceed, the major participants, and the role and character of political parties. We then consider the character and amount of public participation in such elections as well as that arising under other circumstances.

How State Elections Work: The Rules

To understand the role citizens can play in the election "game," you must first understand the rules of that game. The procedures by which candidates are nominated, the limits on who can participate in the nomination process, and the rules concerning how election campaigns are carried out all have considerable influence on the public's opportunity to influence governmental activities. Thus, some of these seemingly minor details are of considerable relevance to the democratic process in the states.

NOMINATIONS FOR OFFICE

The overwhelming majority of states use *primary elections* to determine which individuals will be nominated by each party to run for statewide offices in the general election. Thirty-eight states employ this method for all statewide offices. The remaining twelve states use some combination of primary elections and party conventions (Council of State Governments, 1990: 234–235). The employment of primary elections on such a wide scale came about largely because of the Progressive-era movement to democratize the governmental process. Primaries were, however, adopted for other reasons in some states, especially in Southern states during the era of one-party Democratic control early in this century (Jewell, 1984: 3–15). In contrast, the use of party conventions to nominate candidates gives greater influence over the nomination process to party bosses and activists and less influence to average voters.

Eligibility to vote in party primaries is determined in part by meeting a state's requirements for eligibility to vote in its general elections.[1] But each state also has rules that govern in which party's primary a voter may participate. There are, theoretically, two major kinds of primary elections based on such rules: *open primaries* and *closed primaries*. Those voting in closed primaries are only given the ballot for the political party to which they have somehow officially declared their affiliation. Thirty-five states have closed primaries. In open primaries, voters are given the ballots of all the parties, of which they may chose one and cast their vote. The latter system allows voters, of course, to switch parties at whim on the day of the primary.

The differences between the two main types of primary elections are actually more complicated and less clear than the above distinction implies. A number of states that have closed primaries allow voters to declare or change their party affiliation as late as the day of the election, often by simply appearing at their precinct's voting place for the party of their choice. Such closed primaries are effectively open ones. Other states with closed primaries require that declarations or changes of party affiliation be made anywhere from fourteen days to one year before a primary election. Obviously, the longer the required interval, the more restrictive the primary system.

There are also some unusual subtypes among the open primaries. In Alaska and Washington, voters are given the ballots of all the parties and can vote on any or all of these with the only restriction that they vote for only one individual running for any given office. This type of primary, known as a *blanket primary*, is a particularly open form. Louisiana employs another variant of the open primary, in which all candidates, regardless of party affiliation, appear on the same ballot. If one candidate receives over half the votes cast in the primary, he or she is elected to the office in question. If no candidate receives a majority of the primary vote, the race in the general election is between the two top vote getters, again regardless of party. Like the blanket primary, this type of primary is an especially open one.

GENERAL ELECTIONS

The political parties' nominees for statewide offices (the winners of the primary election or convention contest, as appropriate to each state) compete in the *general election* to determine the ultimate winner for each office. Typically, all the seats of the lower house of the state legislature (which usually has two-year terms) will also be filled at a general election, along with some or all of the seats in the upper house (depending on the term of office for those positions). The vast majority of states hold their general elections in November in even-numbered years, coincident with whatever national elections (presidential or off-year congressional) are also being held that year. These elections are officially scheduled on the first Tuesday after the first Monday in November of even-numbered years.

In the last several decades, however, a good many states have shifted the timing of their elections for major state executive offices, such as the governorship, so they do not coincide with presidential elections. Many observers have argued that the intent of such a change is to isolate state elections from the presidential contest so that a popular presidential candidate's coattails can no longer help sweep into office those in the same party who are running for state offices. Over the last few decades, both of the major parties have offered some presidential candidates who proved to be highly attractive to voters and others who were remarkably unsuccessful in that respect. Thus, individuals running for state offices in a presidential election year can never be sure whether their party's ticket or that of the opposing party will be headed by a "sure winner" or a "turkey."

As a result of concerns about such matters, today only fourteen states still hold general elections for major state executive offices at the same time as the presidential race (down from thirty states in the early 1950s). Most of the remaining states hold such elections in off years, with congressional races, and a few have chosen dates entirely separate from any national elections. In addition, voters' increased willingness to split their tickets by voting for candidates from various parties (instead of voting a straight party ticket) has also helped weaken presidential coattails even in those states with combined general elections.

HOW STATE ELECTIONS WORK: THE PARTICIPANTS

Preceding the primary and between the primary and the general election stands, of course, the campaign. During the campaign, candidates try to woo voter support, first for the nomination and then for the general election. To understand the dynamics of campaigning, you need to be familiar with the various players in the election game and the role each of them fills.

THE CANDIDATES

Clearly, the most central participants in a political campaign are the candidates themselves. Thus, the relevance and extensiveness of successful candidates' backgrounds suggest how much professionalization and expertise are typical. And these attributes of successful candidates determine the quality of the leadership and public decision making of state political institutions. Furthermore, successful

candidates' social backgrounds indicate how accessible public office is to citizens of different genders, ethnic groups, and incomes.

As important as these attributes of candidates are, we will delay discussion of them until the chapters on governors, legislatures, judiciaries, and bureaucracies—the institutional sites where various elected state officials function. Because the requirements and expectations for state offices differ so widely, it is more profitable to discuss attributes of successful candidates for and occupants of those offices within the separate contexts of the various governmental institutions.

POLITICAL PARTIES

As recently as the 1950s, political parties seemed to dominate the electoral process in the states. In every state at least one of the two major parties had either a relatively well-developed and electorally successful organization or, at a minimum, a substantial public following that supported its candidates at elections. The party leadership, through its various social ties and its preeminent position in the organization, largely controlled the nomination process in many states. That leadership was also highly instrumental in raising money to cover candidates' election expenses. And the followers—the committed party members who were recruited and organized by local party leaders—provided the time and energy necessary to get out the vote in an age when personal contacts, door-to-door solicitation, and similar direct efforts were the principal means to sway prospective voters.

Because of a variety of changes in campaigns and elections since the 1950s, however, the role of party organizations has changed considerably. The shift from nominating conventions to primary elections has severely weakened the party leaders' influence over who is nominated and, in turn, the nominees' indebtedness to the leadership. In a number of states, prospective candidates virtually nominate themselves, at least for entry into the party primary. The requirements for such nomination may be as minimal as paying a modest filing fee.

Equally important are changes in campaigning style that have reduced the dependence of candidates on both the leadership and the grass-roots membership of the party organizations. Candidates have come to depend more heavily on the wisdom of campaign experts, on the use of sophisticated opinion polls, and on television and other expensive mass-market advertising media. Person-to-person campaigning has largely given way in most places to the widespread application of Madison Avenue techniques. In consequence, candidates no longer need large numbers of party minions to get out the vote. What they have come to need instead—because of their dependence on Madison Avenue techniques—is a considerable amount of money to fund their campaigns.

We will provide some examples of the current cost of state election campaigns later, but the most basic point can be made quite simply: in this media age, campaigning has become a very expensive business indeed. And candidates' needs for money have increased at a time when the party organizations have been declining in power and prominence for the reasons cited above. Thus, most candidates have had to take charge of their own fund-raising efforts, further reducing their dependence on the party organizations.

Although the preceding changes have been widely observed and apply, in general, to all parties and campaigns, their applicability varies somewhat among the states. In many states the political parties are either organizationally weak, as described above, or so internally divided that little in the way of a concerted effort can be mounted for those individuals running for office under a party's banner. In a few states, however, at least one of the major parties is sufficiently well-organized and united to play a significant role in candidate recruitment, fund raising, and campaigning.

Malcolm Jewell and David Olson (1982: 165–166) argue that a state party organization will typically play a strong role when it has considerable internal agreement on its major goals. Jewell and Olson (1982: 58) also indicate that such cohesive parties exist, for the Republicans, in Colorado, Delaware, Indiana, Louisiana, Nevada, New Jersey, Ohio, Rhode Island, Utah, Vermont, Virginia, and West Virginia, and, for the Democrats, only in Colorado, Delaware, Iowa, and North Dakota. That is, only sixteen of the hundred major party organizations in the states conform to this characterization. Their very existence is, however, a reminder that party organizations vary a great deal within the broad outlines suggested above.[2]

CAMPAIGN EXPERTS

Although their reliance on party organizations has declined in the media age, candidates for office have become increasingly dependent on a range of professionals who can market them (Huckshorn, 1984: 133–155). Expertise in political research, in public-opinion polling, in advertising and marketing techniques, in the use of mass media, and in simple organizational management and coordination is required for a serious attempt to win a statewide office today. Even candidates for state legislative seats (whose constituencies are of course geographically limited) and for statewide offices in small, relatively homogenous states need at least some of these skills for effective campaigning. As James Perry (1968: 7) commented, "There are two essential ingredients of the new politics. One is that appeals should be made directly to the voters through the mass media. The other is that the techniques used to make these appeals—polling, computers, television, direct mail—should be sophisticated and scientific."

As a result of how important—and salable—these scientific and professional skills have become, there has literally arisen an industry of campaign experts who will sell such services to political candidates (Sabato, 1981). These experts range from university professors who serve as consultants for a single public-opinion poll to sophisticated campaign management companies that offer complete management services for the entire campaign and all its requirements. The fees for such experts can be quite high. And the costs of research, mass-media advertising, direct mail, and related efforts—Perry's "techniques to make the appeals"—push the overall costs of many campaigns far higher.

HOW STATE ELECTIONS WORK: THE INCREASING IMPORTANCE OF MONEY

We have observed that elections have become increasingly expensive in recent years, and that observation deserves further elaboration and some specific evidence to support it. Some people have always thought that American election campaigns are too expensive and, therefore, too susceptible to influence by those with a good deal of money. Yet statewide and national elections have become particularly costly in the last couple of decades. A few specific examples will illustrate this trend. Because most of the available information on state elections is for gubernatorial races, we will focus on those. The trends observed there, however, are common to all campaigns for elected state positions, although the magnitude of the expenditures required is generally lower for offices other than the governorship.

TYPICAL CAMPAIGN COSTS

Thad Beyle (1990) reports expenditures for gubernatorial campaigns in the late 1980s in all fifty states. The average cost of a successful campaign in that period was over $3 million. The most expensive races—in California and Texas—cost the successful candidates more than $12 million! At the other extreme—in smaller, more rural states such as Georgia, New Hampshire, North Dakota, Vermont, and Wyoming—campaign costs averaged "only" a few hundred thousand dollars. Races for state legislative seats, for statewide offices other than the governorship, and for local government positions are far less expensive than the typical gubernatorial campaign. Yet the costs of virtually all election campaigns have been rising remarkably in recent years.

The principal reason for the increasing costs of political campaigns is the growing use of the technologies mentioned earlier— mass media, direct mail, and so on. But two other factors deserve mention as well. One of these is the fact that in recent years a notable number of very wealthy individuals have sought election to the governorship in their states and have been willing to spend considerable amounts of their own money to win the office. Bill Clements of Texas is one of those individuals. Much of the $33 million he spent during his three campaigns in 1978, 1982, and 1986 was his own money. Another excellent example is Jay Rockefeller, who used more than $11 million of his own money to win reelection to the governorship of West Virginia in 1980. Such big spenders drive up the costs of election campaigns for all the other candidates.

The third reason for the increased costs of elections is the growth in number and importance of *political action committees,* or *PACs.* PACs are "either the separate, segregated campaign fund of a sponsoring labor, business, or trade organization, or the campaign fund of a group formed primarily or solely for the purpose of giving money to candidates" (Sabato, 1984: 7). Organizations like PACs have existed for many years, but the Federal Election Campaign Act of 1971 and its subsequent amendments dramatically enhanced the power and role of these groups (Sabato, 1984: 3–27; Price, 1984: 239–262). Restrictions in this and other federal laws limit how much money individuals and corporations may give to political candidates' campaign funds. Yet the law effectively allows an individual or corporation to give unlimited amounts to PACs (there are limits on how much one may give to a single PAC, but not on the number of PACs to which one may contribute). Federal law also allows unions or corporations to solicit contributions for a PAC they sponsor directly from their members or employees.

Thus, federal laws provide a mechanism by which what was previously done under the table can be accomplished legally—but not entirely openly. Since the PACs contribute the funds to the candidates, the original sources of those funds are obscured, if not entirely hidden. Although these federal laws govern only contributions to candidates for federal offices, they indicate the importance of PACs to all elections. Such organizations have proliferated across the United States since the mid-1970s and have become very active in funding state and local campaigns as well as federal ones. Because most states have some form of regulations on campaign contributions—some of which are modeled after the federal laws—PACs serve the same role in most states as they do at the national level.

At a time when elections are becoming increasingly expensive, PACs provide a legal and attractive means by which those with a lot of money can attempt to influence electoral outcomes. It is very difficult for candidates to fund highly expensive campaigns by accumulating small or even medium-sized contributions of $10 here and $50 there. Today's candidate needs big money, and PACs are a major source of that funding.

DOES SPENDING MORE ENSURE VICTORY?

Before leaving this subject, we must address a question that is surely in the minds of many of you: does big spending ensure election success? Evidently, it does not. Big-spending millionaires, for example, are not always successful. Republican Lewis Lehrman of New York spent almost $4 million of his family's money (and $13.9 million in total) in an unsuccessful bid to defeat Mario Cuomo in 1982 (who had to spend over $5 million to secure the victory). Clayton Williams spent in excess of $8 million of his own money in a losing campaign for the Texas governorship in 1990.

In general, the research on state elections indicates that money is only one important resource, whose influence will depend on the nature of the election and the impact of certain other resources. Jewell and Olson (1982: 192) caution: "In most election campaigns more money is spent by the winning candidates, but this does not prove that greater spending brings victory. Winners are likely to be able to attract more funds because they are expected to win—because they are incumbents, or better known, or represent the dominant party in the district."

Incumbency, name recognition, personal attractiveness, and the general strength of one party over the other are, then, other important candidate resources. To some degree money will help challengers offset the advantages of these other resources, but there are limits on how often and to what degree it will do so. A spending advantage, especially a large one, appears to be most influential in close races and those where neither candidate is an incumbent or a well-known politician.[3] Basically, however, candidates for most statewide offices and for many state legislative seats know that—win or lose—quite a large amount of money is necessary to run a credible campaign today.

REGULATION OF CAMPAIGN SPENDING

Concern about the high cost of campaigning and the possibility that big contributors will gain undue political influence has led most states to regulate the flow and use of money in election campaigns. As Table 4-1 illustrates, states' regulatory efforts have largely taken the form of limits on contributions to candidates. A number of states have also instituted partial public-funding schemes to offset the influence of private contributions. In addition to the regulations summarized in the table, every state has mandated the public disclosure of campaign contributions and expenditures by candidates.

TABLE 4-1
STATE REGULATION
OF CAMPAIGN CON-
TRIBUTIONS AND
EXPENSES

| STATE | LIMITS ON THE CONTRIBUTIONS OF | | | | PARTIAL PUBLIC FUNDING OF CAMPAIGN EXPENSES |
	INDIVID-UALS	CORPO-RATIONS	LABOR UNIONS	PACs	
Alabama	no	yes	no	no	yes
Alaska	yes	yes	yes	yes	no
Arizona	no	yes	yes	yes	no
Arkansas	yes	yes	yes	yes	no
California	no	no	no	no	yes
Colorado	no	no	no	no	no
Connecticut	yes	yes	yes	yes	no
Delaware	yes	yes	yes	yes	no
Florida	yes	yes	yes	yes	no
Georgia	no	no	no	no	no
Hawaii	yes	yes	yes	yes	yes
Idaho	no	no	no	no	yes
Illinois	no	no	no	no	no
Indiana	no	yes	yes	no	yes
Iowa	no	yes	no	no	yes
Kansas	yes	yes	yes	yes	no
Kentucky	yes	yes	no	yes	yes
Louisiana	no	no	no	no	no

CONTINUED

TABLE 4-1
CONTINUED

STATE	LIMITS ON THE CONTRIBUTIONS OF				PARTIAL PUBLIC FUNDING OF CAMPAIGN EXPENSES
	INDIVID-UALS	CORPO-RATIONS	LABOR UNIONS	PACs	
Maine	yes	yes	yes	yes	yes
Maryland	yes	yes	yes	no	yes
Massachusetts	yes	yes	no	no	yes
Michigan	yes	yes	yes	yes	yes
Minnesota	yes	yes	yes	yes	yes
Mississippi	yes	yes	yes	no	no
Missouri	no	no	no	no	no
Montana	yes	yes	yes	yes	yes
Nebraska	no	no	no	no	no
Nevada	no	no	no	no	no
New Hampshire	yes	yes	yes	yes	no
New Jersey	yes	yes	yes	yes	yes
New Mexico	no	no	no	no	no
New York	yes	yes	yes	no	no
North Carolina	yes	yes	yes	yes	yes
North Dakota	no	yes	yes	no	no
Ohio	no	yes	no	no	yes
Oklahoma	yes	yes	yes	yes	yes
Oregon	no	no	no	no	yes
Pennsylvania	no	yes	yes	no	no
Rhode Island	no	no	no	no	yes
South Carolina	no	no	no	no	no
South Dakota	yes	yes	yes	no	no
Tennessee	no	yes	no	no	no
Texas	no	yes	yes	no	no
Utah	no	no	no	no	yes
Vermont	yes	yes	yes	yes	no
Virginia	no	no	no	no	yes
Washington	no	no	no	yes	no
West Virginia	yes	yes	yes	yes	no
Wisconsin	yes	yes	yes	yes	yes
Wyoming	yes	yes	yes	no	no

Source: Council of State Governments, *Book of the States, 1990–91* (Lexington, Ky.: Council of State Governments, 1990), pp. 242–252, 259–260.

However, such laws and the limitations they impose vary enormously from state to state in their scope, restrictiveness, enforcement, and, therefore, effectiveness (Alexander, 1984: 163–184; Huckshorn, 1985).

In sum, the high costs of political campaigns have a number of obvious implications. They affect which individuals can run for office at all, which will have the highest chances of being successful, and how campaigns must be financed and carried out. The high costs of elections also open the possibility that those citizens and private organizations able to contribute large amounts of money to candidates might gain disproportionate political influence.

STATE PARTY SYSTEMS

Although political parties today play a weaker role in elections than they used to, there are ways in which they remain central to state politics. First, the major political parties in this country are not just formal organizations with officers, budgets, and programmatic activities. They are also collections of average Americans who identify with one of these organizations, profess to be Democrats or Republicans, and vote at least some of the time for the candidates associated with their preferred party. In other words, the major parties can also be conceived as being defined by their mass followers, even though those followers are not required to be dues-paying or card-carrying members. The states differ in the extent to which their residents identify with one party over the other. That is, the states have different partisan compositions, which shape distinct political climates and opportunities for the candidates from the competing parties.

Because of both public identification with one or the other of the major parties and public reaction to particular candidates, the states also differ with respect to the competitiveness between the parties for control of the state government. Furthermore, states dominated by one party have very different politics than do ones with two parties that compete on nearly equal footing. Thus, the residents of these two kinds of states have quite different opportunities to shape governmental policies.

MASS PARTISANSHIP AND IDEOLOGY IN THE STATES

If the major parties are thought of as collections of voters who claim some common allegiance to the Democratic or Republican party, then it is possible to assess the relative strengths of those parties in the states in terms of the numbers of their followers. In addition, knowledge of the collective ideological or policy preferences of those voters allows a conclusion about the parties themselves, in terms of ideological or policy preferences. The results of an impressive research project by Gerald Wright, Robert Erikson, and John McIver (1985) assess both party support and ideology in the states in this way. These scholars aggregated public-opinion data from 1976 through 1982 to derive estimates of the distribution of partisan preferences in each state. That is, they estimated the percentage of the adults in each state who identified themselves as Democrats, Republicans, and independents. These scholars also identified the percentage of adults in each state who thought of themselves as liberal, moderate, and conservative.

Based on these estimates, Wright and his colleagues calculated the average partisan and ideological disposition in each state and then graphically displayed the results as shown in Figure 4-1 (only the forty-eight contiguous states were included in this study). On the partisanship scale an average score of 1.0 signifies an entirely Republican population and − 1.0 an entirely Democratic one. Similarly, on the ideology scale 1.0 signifies a totally conservative population and − 1.0 a totally liberal one. In a sense the states cluster within a narrow range on these attributes. The most liberal states are "middle of the road" when the dispositions of their residents are averaged. Yet no state is overwhelmingly conservative by this measure either, and only a few states have an average partisanship that is more Republican than Democratic. However, despite this narrow range of variation, some important differences are evident here. The most heavily Democratic states are, perhaps not surprisingly, in the South. The most Republican ones are found in the West, Midwest, and New England. The most conservative states are in the South and the West. The most liberal states, with the exception of California, lie in the Mid-Atlantic region.

These data indicate that political parties have importance beyond their organizational character. Parties are symbols that attract many Americans and thus enjoy a degree of loyalty and support for their symbolic meaning. And the states differ in the extent to which their populations prefer one major party over the other. At the same time, either party's symbolism and ideological character differs from state to state. Idaho is conservative and Republican; Oklahoma is equally conservative but Democratic. Massachusetts and South Carolina share nearly equivalent degrees of "Democraticness," but they are widely separated in ideology.

FIGURE 4-1
PARTISANSHIP AND
IDEOLOGY IN THE
STATES

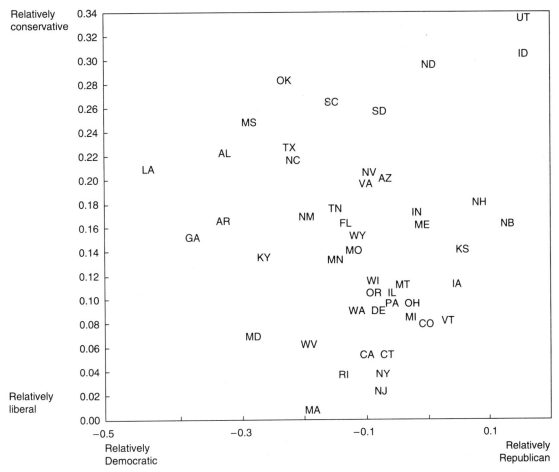

Source: Adapted from Gerald C. Wright, Robert S. Erikson, and John P. McIver, "Measuring State Partisanship and Ideology with Survey Data," *Journal of Politics* 47 (May): 469–489.

ELECTORAL COMPETITION BETWEEN PARTIES

One myth of American politics is that there is, and traditionally has been, two-party competition between groups of leaders who want to govern a state or the nation. Americans even think of two-party competition as essential to democracy. Yet such competition has been more the exception than the rule in state politics. It was common in the first half of the nineteenth century, but the Civil War led to the creation of a number of solidly one-party states. Then the political conflicts arising from the process of industrialization around the beginning of the twentieth century (described in Chapter 1) accelerated the trend toward one-partyism (Burnham, 1981: 176–181; Ladd, 1970).

Most observers argue, however, that two-party competition has increased substantially in the states since 1930. Two explanations for this change have been advanced. First, the motivations for one-partyism arising from the Civil War and the debate over industrial policy in the 1890s have lost salience in a good part of the nation. New political controversies have arisen to take their place. That is, the old reasons that led people to become loyal to one party or another have declined in importance, and new controversies have divided the major parties in new ways.

Second, some observers claim that increased economic and social development is leading to two-party competition in states where it did not already exist. Increased industrialization, urbanization, and modernization should, that is, lead to a greater diversity of political interests and resulting conflicts that cannot be contained within the old single-party systems (Morehouse, 1981: 58–60). Two or even more parties might be necessary to represent all these diverse political interests.

There is considerable evidence to indicate increased two-party competition within states for *national* elections. As late as the 1940s, there was only limited two-party competition at this level in the states. Since the end of World War II, however, virtually every state has seen two-party competitiveness in presidential elections. For *state* politics and elections, however, the evidence is not as clear, and the movement toward two-party competition has been less dramatic. The dispositions concerning partisanship displayed in Figure 4-1 give some evidence on this matter, but they merely indicate people's self-perceptions as to party identification, and not how they actually vote. Those who identify with one party may at times vote for candidates of the other—and for a variety of good reasons.

To assess the actual degree of competitiveness between the two parties in state elections and how it has been changing in the post–World War II period, we can look at competitiveness ratings for two periods, 1946–1952 and 1980–1986, based on (1) the percentage of votes won by each major party in gubernatorial elections, (2) the percentage of seats won in state legislative elections, (3) the length of time for which each party controlled the governorship and legislature, and (4) the proportion of the time that different parties controlled the governorship and the legislature. Classifications based on these ratings are presented in Tables 4-2 and 4-3. The number in parentheses after each state's name is an index of the degree of party competition, where zero represents complete Republican control, 100 represents complete Democratic control, and 50 represents perfect two-party competition. Thus, the greater the numeric score shown for a state in either table, the more Democratic the state was in that period, and conversely.

There have been some interesting changes in party competitiveness in the postwar period, but they have not been entirely in accord with the expectations summarized above. One-party states, both Democratic and Republican, have declined notably in number, and

TABLE 4-2
PARTY COMPETI-
TIVENESS IN STATE
POLITICS, 1946–
1952[a]

ONE-PARTY DEMOCRATIC	MODIFIED DEMOCRATIC	TWO-PARTY COMPETITIVE	MODIFIED REPUBLICAN	ONE-PARTY REPUBLICAN
Georgia (100)	Arizona (80)	Rhode Island (59)	Indiana (37)	South Dakota (15)
Louisiana (100)	Oklahoma (80)	Missouri (56)	Idaho (36)	Vermont (12)
Mississippi (100)	Kentucky (75)	Utah (51)	Michigan (36)	North Dakota (9)
South Carolina (100)	West Virginia (73)	Nevada (50)	Ohio (34)	
Texas (98)	New Mexico (71)	Washington (47)	Wyoming (34)	
Alabama (97)	Maryland (70)	Massachusetts (46)	New York (31)	
Arkansas (96)		Minnesota (42)	Pennsylvania (29)	
Florida (95)		Delaware (41)	New Hampshire (25)	
North Carolina (90)		Montana (41)	New Jersey (25)	
Virginia (89)		Nebraska (40)	California (23)	
Tennessee (87)		Colorado (39)	Wisconsin (20)	
		Connecticut (39)	Iowa (19)	
		Illinois (39)	Oregon (19)	
			Kansas (18)	
			Maine (16)	

[a]The criteria by which states were placed into categories based on party competitiveness conform to those employed by Bibby et al. (1983), which are conventionally employed by scholars of state party systems.

the number of modified (weak) Democratic states has tripled. The number of two-party competitive states has remained virtually unchanged, although there have been some changes in the composition of this category (as is also true of the others).

In either table fewer than half the states are categorized as having true two-party competition. In the remaining states, then, the meaningfulness of mass voting in elections has been limited to varying degrees. In the worst cases, in the strongly one-party Democratic states, it is questionable whether such public participation can have any notable influence on government. The public is not offered a choice between truly competitive parties espousing alternative policy views. And the competition between candidates *within* the dominant party, for nominations, for example, typically focuses more on personality than on policy differences. There can certainly be prob-

TABLE 4-3
PARTY COMPETI-
TIVENESS IN STATE
POLITICS, 1980–
1986[a]

ONE-PARTY DEMOCRATIC	MODIFIED DEMOCRATIC	TWO-PARTY COMPETITIVE	MODIFIED REPUBLICAN	ONE-PARTY REPUBLICAN
Maryland (90)	Alabama (83)	New Mexico (62)	Colorado (37)	
Mississippi (87)	Arkansas (83)	Connecticut (61)	Wyoming (36)	
Georgia (86)	Kentucky (83)	Maine (61)	Arizona (35)	
	Louisiana (83)	Ohio (60)	Kansas (33)	
	Massachusetts (82)	Illinois (56)	New Hampshire (32)	
	South Carolina (81)	New York (55)	Idaho (31)	
	Hawaii (79)	Washington (54)	Indiana (30)	
	North Carolina (77)	Alaska (53)	Utah (26)	
	West Virginia (77)	Montana (53)	South Dakota (23)	
	Rhode Island (76)	New Jersey (53)		
	Virginia (75)	Delaware (51)		
	Oklahoma (74)	Iowa (50)		
	Florida (73)	Nebraska (49)		
	Texas (73)	Vermont (41)		
	Nevada (70)	Pennsylvania (40)		
	Wisconsin (68)	North Dakota (38)		
	Missouri (67)			
	Tennessee (67)			
	Michigan (66)			
	California (65)			
	Oregon (65)			
	Minnesota (64)			

[a]The criteria by which states were placed into categories based on party competitiveness conform to those employed by Bibby et al. (1983), which are conventionally employed by scholars of state party systems.

lems of similar kinds in competitive states, but in those states there is at least the opportunity for voters to choose between candidates and parties offering different policies. Thus, the degree of competitiveness in a state's party system has considerable importance for the meaning of public participation in elections.

PUBLIC PARTICIPATION IN ELECTIONS

Our next concern is with the actual participation of individual citizens in the election process. Opportunities for such participation are wide-ranging. Citizens can choose to ignore elections, that is, to be entirely nonparticipatory. They can participate only in the least arduous of ways—by merely voting. Or they can go so far as to become actively engaged in a campaign by working for a particular candidate and attempting to influence others to vote for that individual. Despite the modest effort required, the most important of these acts is voting itself, for the sum of all individuals' voting choices determines which individuals and parties will control the government and its policies. Thus, voting behavior deserves extended consideration.

MASS VOTING BEHAVIOR

To illustrate recent voter participation in state elections, Table 4-4 presents data on turnout for gubernatorial elections during the period 1980–1986, a time frame chosen to conform with that for the data presented on party competitiveness in Table 4-3. This was also a period when federal civil rights efforts had eradicated most of the restrictive suffrage laws some states had had on the books for as long as a century. Variations in turnout during this period should thus be less affected by differences in registration requirements than would those of earlier times. Turnout during this period should be mostly the product of voters' interest in elections—stimulated by the candidates, parties, issues, and campaigns. The one qualification that should be noted is that thirteen of the states (as indicated in the table) held some of their elections concurrently with national presidential ones during this period. A presidential contest has a stimulative effect on voter turnout, raising it higher than it would be if the state election were being held separately.

TABLE 4-4 VOTER PARTICIPA- TION IN GUBERNA- TORIAL ELECTIONS, 1980–1986	**STATE**	**AVERAGE TURNOUT FOR ALL ELECTIONS**	**STATE**	**AVERAGE TURNOUT FOR ALL ELECTIONS**

STATE	**AVERAGE TURNOUT FOR ALL ELECTIONS**	**STATE**	**AVERAGE TURNOUT FOR ALL ELECTIONS**
Alabama	41%	Montana	64%
Alaska	55	Nebraska	48
Arizona	35	Nevada	37
Arkansas[a]	48	New Hampshire[a]	45
California	44	New Jersey	41
Colorado	43	New Mexico	41
Connecticut	45	New York	38
Delaware[b]	53	North Carolina[b]	46
Florida	37	North Dakota[b]	65
Georgia	28	Ohio	41
Hawaii	46	Oklahoma	38
Idaho[b]	53	Oregon	53
Illinois	42	Pennsylvania	39
Indiana	56	Rhode Island[a]	53
Iowa	46	South Carolina	30
Kansas	45	South Dakota	57
Kentucky	38	Tennessee	35
Louisiana	50	Texas	30
Maine	52	Utah[b]	63
Maryland	35	Vermont[a]	53
Massachusetts	44	Virginia[b]	33
Michigan	42	Washington[b]	60
Minnesota	53	West Virginia[b]	53
Mississippi	41	Wisconsin	44
Missouri[b]	58	Wyoming	48

[a]Governor is elected for two-year term, so every other gubernatorial election is held in a presidential election year.

[b]Some or all gubernatorial elections were held in presidential election years.

The figures in Table 4-4 are not impressive. Voting is, we must emphasize, one of the least demanding of all political acts. It is also the only political activity, other than talking about politics and complaining about the government, that is engaged in regularly by even a sizable minority of citizens. And voting doesn't even require advanced deliberation about candidates or issues. One need only show up at the polling place on election day. Yet nationwide less than half of the population of voting age voted in gubernatorial elections in this period. Only sixteen states had voter participation rates greater

	STATE CLASSIFICATIONS	AVERAGE TURNOUT OF VOTING AGE POPULATION
TABLE 4-5 VOTER TURNOUT FOR GUBERNATORIAL ELECTIONS, 1980–1986, WITH STATES GROUPED BY DEGREE OF PARTY COMPETITIVENESS AND TYPE OF POLITICAL CULTURE	*Degree of Party Competitiveness*	
	Strong one-party	35%
	Weak one-party	45
	Two-party	49
	Dominant Political Culture	
	Traditionalistic	39%
	Individualistic	46
	Moralistic	52

than 50 percent, and no state had as much as 70 percent participation on average.

There are, however, some interesting differences among the states when they are grouped by degree of party competitiveness and type of political culture. Table 4-5 illustrates these differences. The greater the degree of party competitiveness, the higher the voter turnout on average. And, based on their dominant political culture, the states are ranked here precisely as the descriptions in Chapter 2 suggest they should be: moralistic states, where mass participation in politics is culturally encouraged, have the highest turnout; traditionalistic states, whose political culture discourages such participation, have the lowest. Thus, cultural characteristics and party competitiveness help shape the level of mass participation in state elections.

INDIVIDUAL VOTING BEHAVIOR

There is one important qualification that affects the interpretation of data on voter participation presented in Tables 4-4 and 4-5. Those figures indicate *aggregate* turnout for the entire potential electorate in each state. The level of aggregate turnout is influenced by some individual-level attributes of citizens, as well as systemic factors such as political culture and party competitiveness. Research on individual political behavior has identified a number of personal attributes that increase the probability that a given person will vote in any given election. In general, individuals who are older, better educated, or wealthier have higher probabilities of voting. Similarly, WASPs are more likely to vote than ethnic minorities—largely because many ethnics are, on average, poorer and less educated. Thus, these individual-level factors will lower voter participation in a state with many poor, poorly educated, or minority citizens and will boost it in states with greater proportions of white, older, and wealthy citizens.

However, we should not make too much of the individual-level factors just discussed. They probably work jointly with, and not entirely separate from, systematic factors such as political culture and party competitiveness. In the states with high turnouts in Table 4-4, for example, people of all education, income, age, and racial categories likely have relatively high probabilities of voting. Well-educated people would still be more likely to vote than less well-educated ones, but the political culture would boost the turnout within both groups. Alternatively, in states with very low turnouts all groups probably have lower probabilities of participation.

OTHER AVENUES FOR PUBLIC PARTICIPATION

Voting does not, of course, provide the only opportunity for the general public to influence government in the United States. Members of the public can lobby government officials in person, by telephone, or by mail. They can join interest groups that pressure government to adopt their favored policies. And during election campaigns a number of additional modes of participation are available—from contributing financially to a candidate to lobbying one's acquaintances on behalf of that candidate to working actively in his or her organized campaign. Perhaps what is most remarkable about these various opportunities, however, is how seldom they are seized. Only a minority of Americans regularly engage in political activity beyond the simple act of voting.

The range and character of public participation in American politics are clearly delineated by the research of Sidney Verba and Norman H. Nie, summarized in *Participation in America* (1987). This book, which is based on a nationwide survey of involvement at both the local and national level, offers the most comprehensive portrait

ALTHOUGH MASS
POLITICAL
DEMONSTRATIONS
SELDOM INVOLVE A
SIGNIFICANT
PERCENTAGE OF
AMERICANS, THEY
ARE A COLORFUL—
AND SOMETIMES
EFFECTIVE—FORM
OF POLITICAL
PARTICIPATION.

available of Americans' participation in politics. In their research Verba and Nie found that the American public could be stratified into five levels of participation, as portrayed in Figure 4-2.

At the lowest level of Verba and Nie's stratification are about one-fifth of Americans who report virtually no political activity. Another fifth, the *voting specialists*, claim to vote in most elections, but they do no more than that. A tiny percentage goes one step further— besides voting, the *parochial participants* will write, telephone, or personally visit government officials to lobby or complain about a policy matter. This is a narrow and personalized form of participation, but it also requires a notable commitment of time and effort beyond that put forth by the voting specialists.

At the level just above the parochial participants are two groups demonstrating different kinds of participation that are equivalent in the apparent degree of effort required. Besides voting in elections, the *campaigners* will work actively in partisan political campaigns; however, they shun other kinds of organizational efforts. The *communalists* do just the opposite: they vote in elections and stay out of

Figure 4-2
Levels of
Political
Participation in
the United States

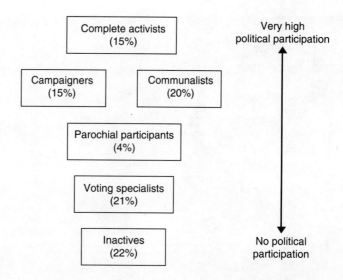

Source: Adapted from Sidney Verba and Norman H. Nie, *Participation in America* (Chicago: University of Chicago Press, 1987), pp. 73–81.

partisan political campaigns, but get involved in nonpartisan organizational efforts to influence governmental policies. Finally, the *complete activists*, making up 15 percent of Verba and Nie's sample, reported regular participation in the full range of voting, personal contacting, campaigning, and communal activities.

In summary, slightly more than half of American adults claim that they participate in politics in ways more difficult than simply voting. However, their claims are subject to several qualifications. Some people surely exaggerate the degree of their participation because the good citizen is encouraged to be politically active in this society. Thus, some people will, in effect, lie about performing such socially desirable acts. But, even if people's claims about their political activities are taken at face value, some of their activities must still be distinguished. Some people vote in only a few, not all, elections. Others belong to community organizations that at times become involved with public policy issues. The actual extent of these individuals' personal involvement with the organizations or the issues and, for that matter, the frequency with which such organizations are concerned with governmental (as opposed to private) matters are unknown. And some people, finally, will be involved with national political issues, organizations, or campaigns but will ignore state and local ones.

The thrust of these remarks is that Figure 4-2 probably gives an accurate picture of the types of participation in state and local politics, but not the real percentages of people who engage in each type. The percentages given in the figure are overestimates by some unknown amounts. It is probably a reasonable guess, however, to say that at least a quarter of Americans never participate in state or local politics. And at least another quarter only vote in major state or local elections. Another 40 to 45 percent may engage in political activities beyond voting, but many of those individuals will only do so quite rarely or with modest degrees of effort or involvement. Perhaps only 5 to 10 percent of Americans can be classed as complete activists in state and local politics.

DIRECT DEMOCRACY

Elections constitute the central mechanism of *representative democracy*. Even in a small state or city, it is impractical for the majority of citizens to make the bulk of governmental policy decisions. Thus, a relatively small number of people are elected to make those decisions for the citizenry and to represent its interests in the process. Several states have provided, however, for certain limited opportunities for *direct democracy* (Cronin, 1989). Those opportunities, by which the general public makes some policy decisions itself, arise with the use of the referendum, the initiative, and the recall.

THE REFERENDUM

A *referendum* is a mechanism of governance that allows the citizenry at large to vote for or against proposed laws or constitutional amendments, usually on general election ballots. Referenda take a number of forms. All the states except Delaware allow their voters to approve amendments to the state constitution by this method. A large number of states also allow for referenda on such matters as municipal incorporations, adoptions and revisions of local government charters, and the issuance of various bonds backed by the state or local government. Several states allow their legislatures to place items voluntarily before the public on referenda, and a number of others allow referenda on the acceptance of laws passed by the legislature if, by the successful use of the initiative, there is a public demand for such an opportunity. The latter form is sometimes called the *popular referendum* (Magleby, 1984).

THE INITIATIVE

An *initiative* allows residents of a state to propose by petition constitutional amendments and statutory laws that are then subjected to a popular vote on adoption via a referendum. The *direct initiative* allows a direct petition-to-referendum process. The *indirect initiative* requires that the petition go initially to the state legislature. If that body does not adopt the requested amendment or law within a specified time, it will then be submitted to the state's voters for approval by referendum.

By 1984 twenty-six states had adopted some combination of the initiative and the referendum; Figure 4-3 shows the state-by-state pattern. There is a clear Western and Midwestern bias toward the provision of these opportunities for direct democracy, which, in contrast, are rare in the South and the Mid-Atlantic states. Their limited use in the South may be attributed to the predominantly traditionalistic political culture of that region and its norm against extensive public influence on government. The pattern of adoption elsewhere, however, is more difficult to explain. The initiative and the popular referendum are largely products of the Progressive era, but a number of states that were pioneers of progressivism (and, for that matter, ones with a moralistic political culture) have not adopted them.

THE RECALL

A *recall* allows the general public to petition to force a public vote on whether a state or local government official should be removed from office before the end of his or her elected term. Fourteen states allow the recall of both state and local officials, and seventeen others allow it only for local ones (Zimmerman, 1986: 175).

UTILIZATION OF THE MECHANISMS FOR DIRECT DEMOCRACY

The initiative and the referendum, in particular, have become increasingly popular in recent years. As Magleby (1984: 43) demon-

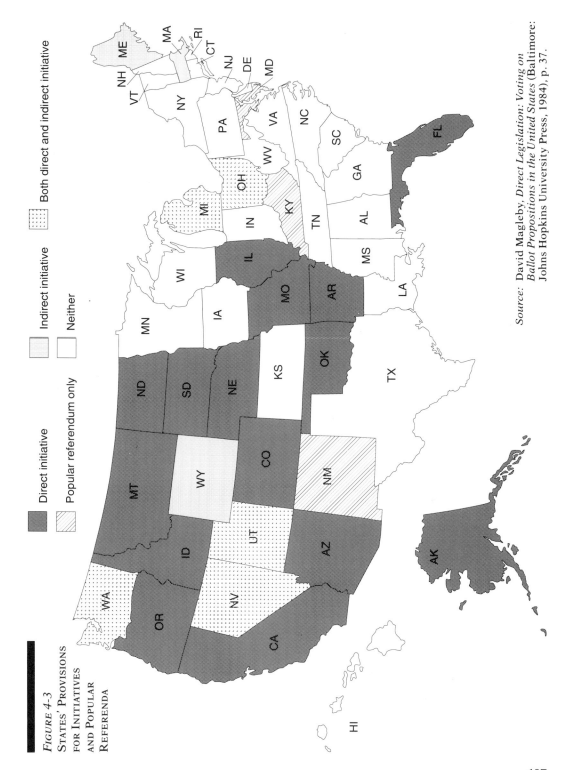

Direct initiative

Popular referendum only

Indirect initiative

Both direct and indirect initiative

Neither

FIGURE 4-3
STATES' PROVISIONS
FOR INITIATIVES
AND POPULAR
REFERENDA

Source: David Magleby, *Direct Legislation: Voting on Ballot Propositions in the United States* (Baltimore: Johns Hopkins University Press, 1984), p. 37.

strates, they have been employed especially frequently in Arizona, Arkansas, California, Colorado, Michigan, Montana, North Dakota, Oklahoma, Oregon, and Washington. The recall, on the other hand, is employed far less frequently in most of the states that provide for it. It is very rarely employed for state-level officials, and only in California, Michigan, and Oregon is it used frequently at the local level. Recalls of local government officials are quite common in those three states.

Despite the popularity of the three devices for direct democracy, there are some notable legal restrictions on their use, which vary widely across the states. These restrictions cover such matters as the subjects allowed for initiative petitions, filing deadlines for petitions, the number of signatures required on petitions, the required voter turnout and the proportion of those voting who approve of measures on referenda, and which particular officials are subject to recall (Cronin, 1989: 125–156; Magleby, 1984: 35–53; Zimmerman, 1986). Thus, the ease of use of these devices also varies considerably among those states that provide for them.

These three devices offer important avenues for public influence over government. Yet they are limited in the breadth of their adoption and by legal strictures on their use in those states that have adopted them. Referenda and recalls are further limited as means of democratic control of government by the extent of public participation in the elections in which they appear on the ballot. Where turnout is high, democratic control is being exercised. Where it is low, only a minority is controlling the decisions made by these mechanisms. Thus, direct democracy in the states is affected by some of the same forces—such as low voter turnout and varying levels of party competitiveness—that limit representative democracy as embodied in general elections.

CONCLUSION

Political parties and elections, the institutional mechanisms of representative democracy, are, no doubt, imperfect means for public control of government. Yet they are essential components of the American system of governance. How these mechanisms function and how actively Americans participate in politics through these means determine the voice they can have in the shaping of governmental policies.

The states differ in both the character of their electoral mechanisms and the extent of public participation in politics. In some states there are well-organized parties; in others there are none. Some states have vigorous two-party competition; in others there is only the appearance of competition in most state and local races. And voter participation in state elections ranges from moderate to embarrassingly low. Thus, the likelihood and extent of public control of government also vary across the states.

NOTES

1. For information on the voter registration requirements of specific states, see *Book of the States, 1990–91* (Council of State Governments, 1990: 261).

2. A number of observers have argued that political party organizations are reviving in strength and importance after suffering a period of decline after the spread of the new modes of campaigning described in this chapter. For discussions of state party revival, see, as examples, Cotter et al. (1984), Gibson et al. (1983), and Rosenthal (1984). Jewell (1984) provides additional details about how party organizations still play important roles in the nomination and election process. Mayhew (1986) offers sketches of the recent histories of party organizations and electoral politics in all fifty states.

3. In some cases the monetary costs of overcoming shortcomings in other campaign resources is staggering. For example, with respect to elections in Texas, Northcutt (1982: 21) observes: "Because of the breadth of the state and the wide distribution of its 14 million population, the only way to get to voters quickly and efficiently is via television and radio in no less than 27 media markets. Austin political consultant John Rogers has a formula for calculating the cost of a name recognition campaign in Texas. He says it takes $15,000 to raise a person's recognition one percentage point for each point between 15 and 75. Once a candidate has 75 percent, the cost per point rises to $25,000. So achieving a 90-percent name recognition should cost a candidate a minimum investment of about $1.5 million." That first $1.5 million is, of course, only for name recognition. Considerably more money would be necessary to familiarize voters with the candidate's per-

sonal abilities and public policy stands. And inflation has been high since 1982, so present-day spending requirements would be far higher.

REFERENCES

Alexander, Herbert E. 1984. *Financing Politics: Money, Elections, and Political Reform.* Washington, D.C.: CQ Press.

Beyle, Thad L. 1990. "The Governors," pp. 50–61 in *The Book of the States, 1990–91.* Lexington, Ky.: Council of State Governments.

Bibby, John F., Cornelius P. Cotter, James L. Gibson, and Robert J. Huckshorn. 1983. "Parties in State Politics," pp. 59–96 in Virginia Gray, Herbert Jacob, and Kenneth N. Vines (eds.), *Politics in the American States.* Boston: Little, Brown.

Burnham, Walter Dean. 1981. "The System of 1896: An Analysis," pp. 147–202 in Paul Kleppner, Walter Dean Burnham, Ronald P. Formisano, Samuel P. Hays, Richard Jensen, and William G. Shade, *The Evolution of American Electoral Systems.* Westport, Conn.: Greenwood Press.

Cotter, Cornelius P., James L. Gibson, John F. Bibby, and Robert J. Huckshorn. 1984. *Party Organizations in American Politics.* New York: Praeger.

Council of State Governments. 1990. *Book of the States, 1990–91.* Lexington, Ky.: Council of State Governments.

Cronin, Thomas E. 1989. *Direct Democracy.* Cambridge: Harvard University Press.

Gibson, James L., Cornelius P. Cotter, John F. Bibby, and Robert J. Huckshorn. 1983. "Assessing Party Organizational Strength," *American Journal of Political Science* 27 (May): 193–222.

Huckshorn, Robert J. 1984. *Political Parties in America,* 2nd edition. Pacific Grove, Calif.: Brooks/Cole.

Huckshorn, Robert J. 1985. "Who Gave It? Who Got It? The Enforcement of Campaign Finance Laws in the States," *Journal of Politics* 47 (August): 773–791.

Jewell, Malcolm E. 1984. *Parties and Primaries.* New York: Praeger.

Jewell, Malcolm E., and David M. Olson. 1982. *American State Political Parties and Elections,* 2nd edition. Pacific Grove, Calif.: Brooks/Cole.

Ladd, Everett Carll, Jr. 1970. *American Political Parties: Social Change and Political Response.* New York: W. W. Norton.

Magleby, David B. 1984. *Direct Legislation: Voting on Ballot Propositions in the United States.* Baltimore: Johns Hopkins University Press.

Mayhew, David R. 1986. *Placing Parties in American Politics.* Princeton, N.J.: Princeton University Press.

Morehouse, Sarah McCally. 1981. *State Politics, Parties, and Policy.* New York: Holt, Rinehart, and Winston.

Northcutt, Kaye. 1982. "Getting Elected," *Mother Jones* VII (November): 16–23.

Perry, James M. 1968. *The New Politics: The Expanding Technology of Political Manipulation.* New York: Clarkson N. Potter.

Price, David E. 1984. *Bringing Back the Parties.* Washington, D.C.: CQ Press.

Ranney, Austin. 1965. "Parties in State Politics," pp. 61–99 in Herbert Jacob and Kenneth N. Vines (eds.), *Politics in the American States.* Boston: Little, Brown.

Ranney, Austin, and Willmoore Kendall. 1956. *Democracy and the American Party System.* New York: Harcourt, Brace.

Rosenthal, Alan. 1984. "If the Party's Over, Where's All that Noise Coming From?" *State Government* 57 (2): 50–54.

Sabato, Larry J. 1981. *The Rise of Political Consultants: New Ways of Winning Elections.* New York: Basic Books.

Sabato, Larry J. 1984. *PAC Power: Inside the World of Political Action Committees.* New York: W. W. Norton.

Verba, Sidney, and Norman H. Nie. 1987. *Participation in America.* Chicago: University of Chicago Press.

Wright, Gerald C., Robert S. Erikson, and John P. McIver. 1985. "Measuring State Partisanship and Ideology with Survey Data," *Journal of Politics* 47 (May): 469–489.

Zimmerman, Joseph F. 1986. "Populism Revived," *State Government* 58 (4): 172–178.

5 Interest Groups in State Politics

Interest groups, like elections, provide an avenue by which citizens can influence the policies of state and local governments. Interest groups have become especially important in American politics in recent years because of substantial growth in their number and activities. But the power of these groups is controversial. Many believe that particular special interests have disproportionate control over government. Representatives of those interests, however, typically disavow such power. To demonstrate the role interest groups can play and to explore this controversy, we will consider the variety of interest groups that operate in state politics, the different political activities they engage in, and the kinds and amounts of influence they exercise.

WHAT INTEREST GROUPS ARE

An *interest group* is a formal association of individuals or organizations that attempts to influence governmental policy. Interest groups are distinguished from political parties in that, unlike parties, they do not run candidates for office under their name or label. Yet interest groups often recruit, endorse, or otherwise associate themselves with candidates who favor their interests. Some interest groups typical of those active in state politics are the Chamber of Commerce, the National Organization for Women, the Sierra Club, and the American Federation of Teachers. These examples also illustrate the considerable variety of such organizations.

Although this chapter will center on groups such as those listed above, you should also be aware of an additional body of special interests. There are many private interests that may be pressed on government, but not by a formally organized group that meets the definition given above. Individual practitioners of a given profession, for example, might lobby the state legislature over proposed legislation relevant to their livelihood, when they have no organized association to do so for them. Or they might lobby individually in addition to the efforts of such an association. Likewise, a single business firm might lobby a government with regard to its particular interests—which might be similar to the interests of other firms— regardless of whether or not an association (or interest group) of such firms exists. Thus, the influence of special interests might be communicated to government through a number of channels, all of which are of some degree of importance.

TYPES OF INTEREST GROUPS

Many different formal organizations attempt at one time or another to influence state and local governments. Some do so on a regular and continuing basis; others will flourish and perish in a period of months. Some attempt to affect governmental policy on a wide variety of issues; others are quite narrow in their concerns. Despite this diversity, we can classify the major interest groups into five types: business groups, occupational groups, agricultural groups, public-interest groups, and single-interest groups. The first three types have been active in state politics for many years. The last two types have grown in number and importance in the last several years.

BUSINESS GROUPS

A number of business groups are closely interested in state and local politics and work regularly to shape state governments' policies. In many cases this kind of interest group arises because those governments have substantial regulatory power over a given industry. The banking, insurance, health care, transportation, alcoholic beverage, hotel, and restaurant industries are some of the most prominent examples for which this situation holds. These industries, along with the real estate and construction industries, are also considerably affected by state and local governments' development policies. That is, such businesses will grow, expand, and profit in direct proportion to governmental efforts to encourage population and economic growth and to provide the public services necessary to support that growth. Furthermore, as you may recall from Chapter 1 many businesses today are particularly concerned with state economic development policies because of the current economic challenges.

Also, some companies do a considerable amount of business directly with the state. State and local governments deposit considerable amounts of money in banking institutions. They purchase insurance and health care for public employees and contract with private firms for large amounts of construction activity, especially for buildings, roads, and highways. Firms in such direct business relationships with government naturally have particular interests in public policy.

Another broad group of businesses that are concerned with state governments' policies are those engaged in the extraction, processing, and sale of natural resources. Such resources are considered, at least in part, public ones, in which a state and its people have some ownership rights. Thus, the crude oil, natural gas, coal, mineral, timber, and similar industries are directly affected by states' policies concerning the extraction, pricing, marketing, and taxing of such natural resources.

These and a good number of other, more specific, business interests are highly concerned with the actions of state and local governments. And most of these interests have developed formal groups that regularly attempt to influence the policies of those governments. Some of these interest groups, such as the Illinois Manufacturers Association and the Mississippi Economic Council, represent the interests of a large and diverse number of business entities. Others, such as California's Bankers Association of America and the Independent (Oil and Gas) Producers and Royalty Owners of Texas, are *single-industry associations*. A few single firms within an industry may even have their own public-affairs staff charged with lobbying government directly, in addition to the representation they get through their interest-group membership.

OCCUPATIONAL GROUPS

Occupational groups are typically motivated by concerns quite similar to those of business groups. Many occupations and professions are either directly regulated or substantially affected by policies of state and local governments. The most typical such circumstance is the state licensing required for entry into a profession. From acupuncturists to veterinarians, more than 800 occupations and professions are licensed by at least one state, and about 60 are licensed by the majority of the states. Accountants, cosmetologists, physicians, plumbers, and undertakers are among the diverse groups included in the latter category.

State governments may set educational and examination requirements for entry into an occupation or profession. They may prescribe standards of practice, pricing, advertising, and ethics and mandate continuing education and periodic retesting of professional competence. Occupational groups, then, are substantially concerned with at least one narrow portion of state governmental policy. And virtually all of these groups have professional organizations that communicate with government about those policies from time to time.

An important occupational group is composed of teachers. The majority of elementary, secondary, and college teachers are employees of a state or local government. Not only do state and local governments prescribe the professional requirements and standards of practice for elementary and secondary teachers, but they also hire, fire, and promote them. And college instructors frequently wish to lobby the state government on pay and related matters. Thus, teachers' professional associations and unions have become quite active as interest groups in state politics.

Finally, there are certain trade unions that have considerable interest in state and local government. In a good number of cities and states, many government employees are unionized. These employees and their unions have concerns with government much like those of teachers. Many other unions have similar interests, too, for state governments have substantial responsibilities for labor policy. They regulate workers' wages and hours, occupational safety and health, workers' compensation rights, and job discrimination based on age, gender, disability, or ethnicity, to name but a few examples. Thus, many union and employee organizations will actively seek to shape a state government's policy making or to protect previous policy victories in certain areas.

AGRICULTURAL GROUPS

The traditional conception of agricultural interests focuses on individual farmers and the broadly based organizations that have sprung up to represent them. Groups such as the American Farm Bureau Federation, the National Farmers Union, and the National Grange are of this type, although they differ in their policy orientations (Schlozman and Tierney, 1986: 43–44). In addition to those organizations, a host of crop-specific ones, for the cotton, tobacco, produce, and cattle industries among others, vary in importance from state to state with the importance of the given crop in that state's agricultural output. Thus, in those states with substantial agricultural economies (discussed briefly in Chapter 1) agricultural groups are particularly important politically.

Furthermore, agriculture has become big business. Therefore, other kinds of business interests beyond those of the farmers are relevant here. The manufacturers of farm equipment and supplies, the chemical industries (on which much of modern agriculture relies for fertilizers, insecticides, pesticides, and related products), marketing organizations, and large retail grocery chains are important agricultural interest groups. And many farms are no longer family-owned and family-run businesses. They are large, multimillion-dollar corporate enterprises. And farm labor organizations such as the United Farm Workers are also active in politics in some states. All of these groups and organizations are important agricultural interest groups,

AGRICULTURE IS AN INDUSTRY IN DECLINE, BUT FARMERS STILL HAVE POLITICAL CLOUT IN A NUMBER OF STATES.

but their character is far more modern and industrial than the average citizen might think.

PUBLIC-INTEREST GROUPS

Of relatively recent prominence (although some of these groups are relatively long-established) is a collection of organizations loosely called public-interest groups. Exemplified by Common Cause and the handful of separate organizations that have developed around Ralph Nader in Washington, D.C., these organizations claim to represent the broad public interest on a host of issues on which narrow interest groups might otherwise prevail. At the state level, the American Civil Liberties Union and the League of Women Voters have long been active as public-interest groups. Some states have, as well, their own chapters of Common Cause or of the Nader-affiliated organizations. These interest groups are distinguished in one significant respect from those described above. Generally speaking, the members of public-interest groups do not anticipate receiving personal material benefits from their groups' efforts (Berry, 1977: 7). They receive, instead, only the personal satisfaction of working to advance causes they believe to be for the common public good.

SINGLE-INTEREST GROUPS

Also of noteworthy prominence in recent years is a number of groups distinguished by a narrow focus on a single policy issue or a closely related set of issues. This category has two subsets, however. The members of some of these organizations do not derive personal material benefits from the activities of their groups. The Sierra Club, anti–nuclear power organizations, pro-choice and anti-abortion groups, and others such as Mothers Against Drunk Driving (MADD) are typical of this subset. Members of such groups would probably argue that their organizations are public-interest groups, but simply ones with a narrow range of interests. Of course, not all members of the public would agree that each of these groups truly works in their interest. Perhaps the most notable of this subset of single-interest groups lately have been pro-choice and anti-abortion rights organizations. Abortion policies have been particularly controversial since the early 1980s, and recent Supreme Court rulings have expanded the power of state governments to set such policies. Thus, the abortion issue has been prominent in many state elections, and groups on both sides of the issue have lobbied state governments especially vigorously.

Many other groups in the single-interest category, on the other hand, work quite specifically for the benefit of their members rather than of the public at large. Senior citizens' groups, gay rights groups, taxpayers' organizations, groups based on members' ethnicity (such as the League of United Latin American Citizens and Jewish Anti-

Defamation League), and a seemingly endless string of other cause-specific organizations populate the political landscape across the states.

We have cast the preceding survey of interest groups in terms of what motivates each type to be concerned with governmental policies. A simple yet important observation about those motivations is that each one appears quite reasonable and legitimate. Anyone who is a businessperson, a teacher, or a member of MADD, the Sierra Club, or the Chamber of Commerce would surely champion the causes and the work of the interest group to which he or she belongs. Yet, in general, people often think of interest groups as bad—as narrowly self-interested and disregarding of the broader public interest. The lesson here, of course, is that people typically think that *their* group is justified in its public policy efforts: its concerns are legitimate; it is only those other groups that are bad. You should resist so slanted a view of interest groups as we attempt to assess evenhandedly their role in state politics.

THE STRATEGIES OF INTEREST GROUPS

How is it that interest groups attempt to press their views on government? In what ways, that is, do they go about their work? Several strategies are common to most such groups.

FINANCIAL AND OTHER ELECTORAL SUPPORT FOR CANDIDATES AND ELECTED OFFICIALS

As Chapter 4 made clear, candidates for public office need publicity, a good deal of money to fund their campaigns, and, eventually, all the votes they can get. They appreciate, as well, the free labor of volunteer workers to reduce the costs of their campaigns. These needs naturally open up a tremendous opportunity for those interest groups that can deliver money, advertising, volunteer time, votes, or other resources to their preferred candidates. Although votes are the ultimately desired resource, money is definitely second in importance to candidates. Money can certainly buy everything else besides votes, and the more money available to a candidate, the greater the likelihood of doing well at the ballot box. Interest groups provide a high proportion of all the funds that flow to candidates in state and local races. They do so by direct contributions, by stimulating their members to contribute individually, and by channeling funds through their affiliated PACs.

Well-funded interest groups can support their favorite candidates in several ways beyond campaign contributions, however. They may disseminate their own advertising in support of such individuals. They may arrange speaking engagements that yield sizable honoraria for favored candidates or public officials. And, where state laws permit, as they often do, special interests may arrange professional or business opportunities for state legislators or their private companies. These opportunities are particularly attractive because, as we will discuss in Chapter 6, only a handful of states pay their legislators full-time salaries. In the bulk of the states, legislators must, of necessity, have another source of income.

Finally, an interest group may recruit someone who is sympathetic to the group's needs and goals to run for political office. Many interest groups attempt such recruitment efforts, but those groups that can promise considerable financial or electoral support to prospective candidates are most likely to be successful. You may have recognized by now that, in their recruitment efforts as well as in their financial support of candidates, interest groups may compete with political parties. Sometimes such competition occurs, but often parties and interest groups work closely together in these and related activities.

LOBBYING THE GOVERNMENT

Lobbying refers to efforts to communicate directly with governmental policy makers in support of or opposition to particular policy goals. Although we will mostly discuss the lobbying of state legislatures, executive-branch agencies are also frequently the targets of lobbyists' efforts. Such agencies make many independent policy decisions and take positions for or against many proposals before the legislature. Thus, some executive-branch agencies develop close ties to particular interest groups.

The word "lobbying" has an unsavory connotation to many people, conjuring up visions of smooth-talking manipulators with suitcases of money and other blandishments lurking in the halls of legislative bodies to buy favors for particular interests. There were certainly days in the not so distant past, particularly in the latter half of the nineteenth century, when that image was quite accurate for lobbyists in many state legislatures in the United States (Thayer, 1973: 37–65). Some of this old-style lobbying still goes on, but the craft has evolved considerably in response to changing public mores, new laws on graft and corruption, and even a changing relationship between policy makers and representatives of interest groups.

The character of present-day lobbying is best exemplified by the work of the full-time, professional lobbyists who are typically employed, of course, by well-funded interest groups. Full-time lobbyists seek regular access to and try to form an established relationship with key legislators or government officials. They may see such officials weekly at a variety of occasions, social as well as strictly business. Through such a relationship the lobbyist hopes for regular opportunities to explain the point of view of the interest group. Additionally, the lobbyist wants to gain the trust of the legislator or public official—so that the information the lobbyist passes along will be considered reliable and useful. Interest groups without full-time lobbyists will also attempt to develop much the same relationship, yet they will be at a considerable disadvantage in doing so. Their representatives are unlikely to be as well-known to public officials. They are not as likely, therefore, to have developed stable, personal ties with very many government officials. And they may simply not be around to present the group's case at all the important times when relevant policy issues are being discussed.

There are still some old-style efforts at persuasion. Lobbyists will indicate the conditions under which their interest group's financial and electoral support will be bestowed or withheld. They may literally make threats about the misfortunes that will befall the official in these and other areas for failure to work for the group's interest. Negative publicity and active support for opposing political candidates are the most likely of the additional sanctions they might suggest. At times, then, the relationship between lobbyist and public official can be highly confrontational. The more typical relationship, however, is of an entirely different character. Professional lobbyists know that they will be most successful in working with public officials already generally favorable to their group's interests. These officials can, in turn, effectively become "inside" lobbyists for the group, working to persuade their colleagues.

Some legislators even want to work closely with certain interest groups and will actively seek those groups' assistance in shaping public policy. There are good reasons, of course, why legislators

Youngsters Get Lobbying Lesson; Massachusetts Gets State Muffin

Sometimes lobbying of the government is considerably removed from its customarily unsavory image, as the following example from Massachusetts suggests.

BOSTON (AP): Thanks to lobbying by a group of fourth-graders, Massachusetts—which has an official bird (chickadee), flower (mayflower), and tree (elm)—now has an official muffin (corn).

Governor Michael S. Dukakis' signature on the corn muffin bill culminated the work of pupils from Brookline's Runkle School, who made the filing and lobbying part of a class project to learn the legislative process.

Their project fired the imagination of Dukakis, who gave them his own corn muffin recipe, and of lawmakers who took up the issue in tongue-in-cheek floor debates.

The pupils watched from the galleries as lawmakers debated whether to make the official state muffin an apple or cranberry [one] instead.

The corn muffin was chosen because it was one of the foods that first sustained the Pilgrims when they settled Massachusetts.

Dukakis, quizzing the children on the legislative process, asked what would happen to the measure if he didn't sign it. One youngster exclaimed, "We'd break down and cry."

Source: Houston Post, May 31, 1986, 7C.

would want to assist certain interest groups. State legislators from agricultural districts, for example, try to be responsive to the needs of their farming constituents. Those from major metropolitan areas will want to work closely with groups from their constituencies, too. And there are other shared policy concerns that can unite legislator and interest group. As just one example, those legislators who want to reduce traffic deaths caused by drunk drivers welcome the analytic

It's Not All Play for Legislators on Annual Ski Junket

One notable form of lobbying the government that average citizens seldom see is known as social lobbying. Social lobbying refers to the plying of legislators with free dinners, receptions, cocktails, travel, and entertainment. In the process lobbyists can develop regular social ties with lawmakers, enjoy particularly hospitable settings for the discussion of their interest group's wishes concerning public policy, and perhaps even develop a feeling of indebtedness among lawmakers. Consider, as an example, the following lobbying effort by the Colorado ski industry to ensure goodwill in that state's legislature.

It's *the* lobbying event of the year for state lawmakers—an all-expense paid weekend of skiing, seminars, and socializing courtesy of Colorado Ski Country USA and the Colorado Association of Ski Towns.

Late this afternoon, a chartered bus will roll up to the Colorado Capitol and 31 lawmakers will climb aboard for the trip—over Loveland Pass—to Breckenridge.

studies and human-interest vignettes offered by MADD. Public official and interest group often stand in mutually dependent roles, then, for what each can offer to the other. And a sympathetic legislator would probably sense no persuasive pressure in such a relationship, but would simply feel that he or she was assisting groups that were legitimate and worthy of government support.

Mass-membership groups also try to "marshal the troops" to aid in their lobbying efforts. They may organize letter-writing campaigns to lawmakers or executive-branch officials, or they may bus large numbers of their members to the state capital to flood the halls of the legislature and demonstrate the voting power and enthusiasm of the interest group. The success of such efforts depends critically on good timing and effective execution. For example, a flood of letters

There, ski industry representatives have scheduled a series of briefings on problems facing Colorado's ski industry and resort towns—where 43,000 Coloradians are employed.

And, of course, there's time set aside for skiing.

"It's the best way we know of to let legislators know what we're all about," said Bob Knons, director of Colorado Ski Country. "It's hard to explain snowmaking when you're down here in Denver."

This is the fifth year the two associations have collaborated on the highly successful trip. In previous years, lawmakers have been whisked to Telluride, Steamboat Springs, and Crested Butte aboard chartered airplanes and taken by train to Winter Park.

"I like to think of it as transcending lobbying," said Jim Bensberg, one of Ski Country's lobbyists.

Now consider the distinct advantages enjoyed by this and other interest groups able to fund such lobbying efforts. Instead of vying for time on the lawmakers' busy office schedule, the Colorado ski industry can make its pitch for beneficial government policies before a roaring fireplace and over hot mulled wine après ski.

Source: Neil Westergard, *The Denver Post*, January 25, 1985, 10A.

copied verbatim from an example given out by a group's leaders will be far less influential than a smaller number of individually written and differently worded expressions of support for a particular policy.

Busloads of members can be influential, but they must be carefully coached in how to approach lawmakers. They must offer good arguments for or against a policy proposal, and they must arrive at the right time during the course of policy deliberation. All too often the timing of such demonstrations is not the best, and, although they indicate something about the numbers of people interested in a given issue, they are seldom a substitute for the long-term established relationship between professional lobbyist and public official described above. Customarily, such busing efforts are also one-shot affairs. The membership is bused in and bused out on the same day. Yet, as the buses drive away from the state capital at the end of the day, the full-time lobbyists of other groups will likely be treating legislators to cocktails or dinner and gently offering their group's point of view—just as they might have done the day before and might well do again the next day.

Ultimately, mass-membership efforts are only as effective as the potential voter support—or rejection—they imply. To be credible and influential, such efforts must clearly indicate that a given interest group can deliver the votes it promises.

LOBBYING THE PUBLIC

An alternative form of lobbying effort is that which attempts to instill in the public at large either a favorable image for a given interest group or support for governmental policies that favor the group's interests. Thus, as Ronald Hrebenar and Ruth Scott (1982: 93–111) point out, such efforts are usually mounted in the mass media to gain goodwill for a particular group or as offensive campaigns for or defensive campaigns against particular government policies. Of course, elaborate mass-media campaigns are expensive and thus beyond the means of many interest groups. Despite this fact, groups of limited means can use the tactic of lobbying the public to some degree. When "right-to-lifers" picket abortion clinics, when environmentalists demonstrate at nuclear power plants, and when public employee unions run charity drives, they are carrying out offensive or goodwill lobbying efforts. Even so humble a medium as the bumper sticker can serve this end, by displaying such slogans as these:

- If you can read this, thank a teacher.
- Oil feeds my family and pays my taxes.
- I smoke and I vote.

BRIBERY

Bribery was a common means of influencing governmental policy in earlier periods of American history. It has declined in frequency since the turn of the century because of changing public mores and tougher legal sanctions. Graft is also less common today because it is not as necessary as in times past. However, crusading public prosecutors and inquisitive news reporters still ferret out juicy examples of these practices in every state. But groups with considerable financial resources can use those resources in many legal ways to influence government policy, as the preceding discussion indicates. And groups with few funds are no more able to pay bribes than to make campaign contributions. Undoubtedly, the bribery of and extortion by public officials still occur regularly, yet they are principally the tools of choice of the unsophisticated and the desperate.

THE POWER OF INDIVIDUAL INTEREST GROUPS

Power means influence, as in causing something to happen or someone to do something they would not otherwise do. It is sometimes difficult, however, to know with certainty when such influence is operating. Consider, as an example of that difficulty, the following situation. Suppose a state legislature adopts a new policy for which one interest group has lobbied but which several others opposed. Three possible explanations might account for this new policy: (1) the interest favored by this new policy was so prominent and important in the state that the legislature would have adopted the policy even if the interest group had not lobbied for it; (2) the group persuaded—that is, had power over—the legislature, to adopt the policy when it would not otherwise have done so; (3) the legislature came, by way of open-minded deliberation of all points of view, to the independent conclusion that the policy should be adopted.

On many occasions it is difficult to determine which of these three possibilities is correct. One reason for this difficulty is that even when interest-group power is responsible (the second possibility), both the interest group and many legislators talk as if it were otherwise. Powerful interest groups often discount their power, and both interest groups and legislators prefer to describe their actions as being motivated by the public interest rather than private interests. That posture, by the way, is every bit as likely to be adopted by environmentalists, anti-abortionists, or the Moral Majority as by the oil lobby or the real estate lobby or the insurance lobby.

The difficulty of assessing interest-group power is also aggravated by the behind-the-scenes character of much lobbying activity. Neither citizens nor scholars can often observe what interest group representatives say or promise to public officials or know with what unfortunate consequences those officials may be threatened. In part, this circumstance arises because of the bad public image in which lobbying and other activities of interest groups are held. Thus, lobbyists often try to keep their efforts private, and they understate the effects of those efforts.

Yet another reason why assessing interest-group power is difficult is because an interest group's lobbying effort can be highly dispersed. That is, the total effort may be the sum of so much in campaign contributions, so much in advertising of various kinds, so much time spent with a number of public officials, and so much activity by group members in letter writing and related mass-membership lobbying. When interest groups apply their efforts so broadly, it is difficult to assess or compare the totality of each group's efforts. Thus, it is also difficult to quantify the two sides of the power equation: to determine how much persuasive effort was expended on each side and to what effect.

Despite these difficulties, the subject of interest-group power is too important to ignore or dismiss. In some cases unambiguous judgments may be made, but only very cautiously. Also to be taken with a grain of salt are other people's assessments of these matters, whether they be muckraking journalists out to expose instances of special-interest domination or the representatives of particular groups making quiet protestations of their own weakness. There are some clear and relatively unambiguous instances of (and circumstances that promote) interest-group power. Those groups with greater political resources will, quite obviously, be more influential than those with fewer. And the most important political resources of interest groups can be inferred from their strategies.

VOTES

Those groups that can promise—and deliver—large numbers of votes to candidates at elections will obviously be far more influential than those that cannot. The key, however, is the ability to deliver the votes. Many groups, such as labor unions, have large numbers of members. Yet the members are often politically heterogeneous; they differ among themselves and from the union's leaders on a variety of public-policy issues. Thus, such a group may stand together politically only occasionally and on highly specific issues.

MONEY

As we noted above, votes are the best of political resources, but money is surely the second best. Those groups with considerable financial resources can more effectively utilize virtually all of the strategies discussed earlier.

EXPERTISE AND INFORMATION

Governmental policy making often proceeds under conditions of limited information, imperfect analysis of the available information, and, therefore, a good deal of uncertainty. Thus, those who can bring relevant information and compelling analysis to policy debates will be especially influential. Some interest groups are particularly well-prepared to do this. They are capable, that is, because of their organization, professional skills, and money, of marshaling a considerable research effort.

STATUS

Some groups clearly have another resource that, to a great extent, money can't buy. This is high status in the eyes of or respect from government officials and, perhaps, even the public at large. Some groups have such status with regard to only a limited range of policy issues. Physicians are accorded considerable political status with regard to certain health-care issues. Lawyers get similar status when they address legal controversies. (Lawyers are probably aided here because many state legislators are themselves lawyers.) There are also some interest-groups that clearly have low status in most states. Gay rights groups, prison reform groups, and others who represent unpopular or "deviant" causes are good examples.

In addition to the exemplary high-status groups mentioned above, business and businesspeople are widely acknowledged to have a high position in American society and politics. The status of business in this society is in part a product of Americans' reverence for free enterprise and those who typify it in operation. Business also benefits, as Edwin Epstein (1969: 208–212) and others have observed, because of the argument that business enterprise is so central to the economic and social health of any state or even the entire nation.

Thus, business interests, it is further argued, deserve special attention from government.

Charles E. Lindblom (1977: 172) stated this argument most succinctly by saying that "businessmen generally and corporate executives in particular take on a privileged role in government that is, it seems reasonable to say, unmatched by any leadership group other than government officials themselves." Lindblom (1977: 175) went on to add, with particular relevance to our concerns here:

> In the eyes of government officials, therefore, businessmen do not appear simply as the representatives of a special interest, as representatives of interest groups do. They appear as functionaries performing functions that government officials regard as indispensable. When a government official asks himself whether business needs a tax reduction, he knows he is asking a question about the welfare of the whole society and not simply about a favor to a segment of the population, which is what is typically at stake when he asks himself whether he should respond to an interest group.

And, because many officials in state and local governments come from business careers, they are particularly sympathetic to the position of business.

ACCESS

A final political resource, arising as a product of an interest group's successful use of one or more of the others, is access to governmental decision makers. Those groups that have considerable clout in terms of the preceding four resources will be accorded good access to public officials. They will have frequent and extended opportunities to explain their points of view, and, consequently, they will be highly successful in influencing government policies.

THE COLLECTIVE POWER OF INTEREST GROUPS

The preceding section delineated the resources that distinguish powerful individual interest groups. An additional concern we must raise is with the collective or overall power of interest groups in any given

state, how that power is shared by competing groups, and how it is
or is not moderated by other forces.

AN EXTREME EXAMPLE: COMPANY STATES

One particularly instructive instance of the power of interest groups
has been termed the company state (Phelan and Posen, 1973). A *company state* is one whose economy and politics are dominated by a
single business firm. We will also include under this label a few states
in which a small number of dominant industries or firms are alleged
to control state politics. In the late nineteenth and early twentieth
centuries, a good number of states could have been described in this
way. Subsequent economic development and diversification have
weakened the once dominant interests in most company states, yet
until quite recently a few choice examples still existed, although in
somewhat weakened form. Even if company states are passing from
the political scene, they do provide an excellent example of high
interest-group power in state politics.

One state that existed for a long time as a company state is
Delaware. Consider Mark Green's (1973: 50–51) remarks about the
role of the DuPont family and corporation there in the early 1970s:

> DuPont in Delaware is the best (but not the only) example of a "com-
> pany state." The firm employs 11 percent of the state work force and
> generates 21 percent of the state's gross product. The DuPont family
> controls the DuPont company through board membership and the
> Christiana Securities, the family's holding company, which owns
> the company that publishes the state's two biggest newspapers, the
> *Morning News* and the *Evening Journal.* . . . In the city-county com-
> plex in Wilmington works the county executive, a former DuPont
> lawyer, and Wilmington's mayor, whose father was a prominent
> DuPont executive. The state's one congressman is Pierre S. DuPont
> IV; another family member is attorney general; the governor, Russell
> Peterson, is a former DuPont research director. DuPont firm or fam-
> ily-connected members comprise a fourth of the state legislature, a
> third of its committee heads, the president pro tempore of the Sen-
> ate, and the majority leader of the Delaware house. Twenty-two of
> the twenty-six Delaware campaign donations of five hundred dollars
> or more in 1969 were given by DuPont family members or employees,
> and all the contributions went to Republicans.

Other states reputed to be company states in relatively recent times include Montana, said to be dominated by the Anaconda

Company, the major mining interest in the state (Payne, 1961); Texas, whose politics have long been heavily influenced by oil interests (Stilwell, 1949); Oregon, considered to be dominated by lumber interests; and Maine, dominated by a triumvirate of lumbering, electric power, and manufacturing interests (Lockard, 1959: 79).

L. Harmon Zeigler and Hendrik van Dalen (1976: 101–103) have warned, however, against presuming too much about the power of the dominant interests in company states. Such a presumption risks confusing the reputation and the reality of power. At one time, and perhaps still today in some instances, dominant companies or industries may have controlled several states' politics. Because of continuing economic development and diversification, however, they are now more likely to be only one of several prominent, and at times conflicting, interests in their states. Although they may still be highly influential with respect to some policy-making efforts of state and local governments, the range of policies they influence is likely to be narrower and more closely identified with their specific economic concerns.

HOW MANY GROUPS?

The example of company states suggests one way to make a more general assessment of interest-group power in the states. The dominant firm or industry is so powerful in a company state because it dominates the entire economy. The economies of such states are, in other words, highly homogenous. States with heterogenous economies, on the other hand, have a considerable number of important interest groups. Some of these groups represent competing economic sectors, and many of them represent the variety of social and cultural groups that also proliferate in more developed economic settings. There are more of the latter kind of group because states with heterogeneous economies typically have, in addition to greater economic diversification, greater urbanization, more developed class, ethnic, union, and professional groups, and larger numbers of the social, cultural, economic, and political organizations that spring from such interests.

Thus, those states with heavily agricultural economies, those with economies based largely on the extraction of a few natural resources, and even some of those having a narrow and exclusive industrial base are the ones that have only a few prominent interest groups. Those states with diverse economies and with highly advanced industrial economies have many active interest groups.

HOW POWERFUL ARE INTEREST GROUPS?

There is a second dimension to the pattern of interest politics in the states. It is not simply the number of interest groups and, therefore, the potential competition among them that determine their power in state politics. Other factors also shape that power. For example, in some states in which interest groups are numerous, such groups *in general* have unusually high influence over state politics. Zeigler and van Dalen (1976: 105–109) refer to this pattern of interest-group power as the "triumph of many interests." Yet there are other economically advanced states that have many important interest groups, but in which those groups are generally less powerful. These differences are the result, in part, of the states' distinctive political histories. Unique events and developments, in other words, explain some of these state-to-state differences in interest-group power.

In addition, several systemic political characteristics of states have been linked to the general power of interest groups and may explain some state-to-state differences. One of the most important of these is the character of the political party system. States with organizationally weak parties and those with only one strong party (which is usually weak as an organization for it can get away with being so in the absence of a strong second party) generally have especially powerful interest groups (Zeigler, 1983). Organizationally powerful parties can, in other words, moderate interest-group power. Such parties can function as brokers, negotiating directly with selected interest groups and assuming part of the representational load of conveying those groups' points of view to government. Similarly, the presence of two competitive parties in a state should help ensure that a greater range of political interests will get some kind of representation and that there will be a greater probability of competition among those interests for control of government.

A second important systemic characteristic is the political culture of the state. Recall from Chapter 2 that in individualistic and traditionalistic cultures it is accepted that certain (different) individual interests will be legitimately pressed on government. In moralistic cultures, on the other hand, there is a cultural bias that the public interest is more important than any individual or group interests. Thus, the climate for and the acceptance of efforts by interest groups to influence government should differ from culture to culture. In moralistic states, interest groups should *in general* be weakest. In traditionalistic states, establishment groups associated with the social elite and its economic interests should be especially powerful. And in individualistic states, it is possible that a wide variety of self-interested groups will be powerful.

Finally, the degree of professionalization of a state's government is also associated with the general level of interest-group power. As one example, in states with highly professionalized legislatures (whose members have at least quasi-professional commitment to their elected positions, are paid full-time salaries, and have access to substantial research and technical assistance), legislators are better able to make independent political judgments. They are in better positions, that is, to resist interest groups' lobbying efforts. Likewise, state bureaucratic agencies that are professionalized, well staffed, and organizationally highly developed are also better able to make policy decisions independently of interest-group pressure.

The collective power enjoyed by the interest groups in a given state is, then, a result of a number of factors. The number of such groups, their economic and social status in the state, the power of political parties, the political culture, and the professionalization of state (and local) government all work to shape this power. And each state's individual political history has determined the particular way in which these forces have produced the current pattern of interest-group power. Thus, such patterns are the product of complex, interconnected forces and events. And those patterns are undoubtedly still evolving because of equally complex contemporary forces.

Having explained why the collective power of interest groups varies from state to state, we would ideally like to characterize each state in these terms. We would like, that is, to indicate explicitly which states have especially weak interest groups and which have especially strong ones. Such characterizations are always controversial, largely because of the difficulties of assessing interest-group power, explained earlier. Because it is possible to *conceive* of such a thing as the collective power of interest groups but difficult to *measure* that power unambiguously, efforts to do so have always generated disagreement. Yet political scientists have frequently made valiant and commendable attempts at such measurement, and the results of a recent such effort are useful to the present discussion.

Clive Thomas and Ronald Hrebenar (1990) report the results of an ambitious research effort in which political scientists who were experts on the politics of the fifty states were asked to rate the collective power of interest groups in each state on a common scale. That scale distinguishes the states with respect to whether interest groups are (1) the dominant influence over state policy in comparison to such other actors as the political parties, legislature, governor, and so on, (2) somewhat dominant and somewhat complementary in their power relative to those other actors, (3) complementary with those other actors, (4) somewhat complementary with and somewhat subordinate to those other actors, or (5) entirely subordinate to those other actors.

Table 5-1 reports the results of Thomas and Hrebenar's scholarly effort. In nine states interest groups are classified as the dominant political actors, and in another eighteen states they are very powerful but somewhat weaker (dominant/complementary). Thus, in over half the states interest groups are judged to be powerful political organizations. Furthermore, interest groups are rated as subordinate in no states and as complementary/subordinate in only five. These ratings testify, then, to some diversity of interest-group power among the states but also to the generally powerful political role such groups enjoy in most states. Despite the difficulty of rating

TABLE 5-1
THE COLLECTIVE
POWER OF INTEREST
GROUPS

STATES WHERE THE OVERALL IMPACT OF INTEREST GROUPS IS:				
DOMINANT (9)	**DOMINANT/ COMPLEMENTARY** (18)	**COMPLEMENTARY** (18)	**COMPLEMENTARY/ SUBORDINATE** (5)	**SUBORDINATE** (0)
Alabama	Arizona	Colorado	Connecticut	
Alaska	Arkansas	Illinois	Delaware	
Florida	California	Indiana	Minnesota	
Louisiana	Hawaii	Iowa	Rhode Island	
Mississippi	Georgia	Kansas	Vermont	
New Mexico	Idaho	Maine		
South Carolina	Kentucky	Maryland		
Tennessee	Montana	Massachusetts		
West Virginia	Nebraska	Michigan		
	Nevada	Missouri		
	Ohio	New Jersey		
	Oklahoma	New Hampshire		
	Oregon	New York		
	Texas	North Carolina		
	Utah	North Dakota		
	Virginia	Pennsylvania		
	Washington	South Dakota		
	Wyoming	Wisconsin		

Source: Clive S. Thomas and Ronald J. Hrebenar, "Interest Groups in the States," in Virginia Gray, Herbert Jacob, and Robert B. Albritton (eds.), *Politics in the American States*, 5th edition (Glenview, Ill.: Scott, Foresman, 1990), pp. 123–158.

interest-group power, Thomas and Hrebenar's scholarly team produced ratings that are in generally high agreement with those developed entirely independently by Morehouse (1981: 95–141). Thus, there is some general scholarly consensus about variations in collective interest-group power across the states.

THE BIAS OF THE INTEREST GROUP SYSTEM

A final point about the number and power of interest groups concerns what L. Harmon Zeigler (1983: 99) calls the "bias of the interest group system." Zeigler observes, as have a number of other scholars, that in every state the largest *number* of active interest groups represents business interests. Furthermore, he cites a variety of evidence to indicate that business groups are always among the *most powerful* in every state.

These observations provide empirical evidence for Epstein's (1969) and Lindblom's (1977) view that business enjoys a special status in American politics. And that special status is easy to understand if you recall some of the earlier observations in this chapter. Business interests have high status because of their presumed importance to the health of the economy. They are also typically well-equipped with other political resources. They have organizational skill and the ability to produce information and research relevant to their policy interests. Most are also financially well-off and are thus able to use money as another political resource. And the great number and power of business groups produce a bias in their favor within the interest-group system.

CONCLUSION

A great variety of interest groups attempt to influence state and local governments. In fact, their numbers and activities have both grown considerably in recent decades. All of these groups attempt to use a number of persuasive strategies, yet some of them have distinct advantages in the form of status, expertise, financial resources, and/or vote-getting power. Business groups, in particular, are especially prominent in all the states for this reason. Many occupational and agricultural groups are highly influential in particular states, where their business is prominent in the economy.

We suspect that almost all the other kinds of groups discussed here are generally less powerful. Some may be highly influential for a time or on a single issue. Others, such as some of the public-interest groups, may be long-time political activists, constantly biting at the heels of government to encourage it to take the "right" path. None of these groups, however, has the status, the resources, the staying power, or the breadth of interests that business groups do. Furthermore, the economic uncertainties of the current times redound to the advantage of business interests. As explained in Chapter 1, most state and local government officials believe they are in active competition with other states and localities to attract new business enterprises. These officials also want to fashion policies that will enhance economic development generally, and they typically turn to business leaders for advice on how to do so. Thus, business interests are receiving especially high attention today, and their potential influence over governmental policy making is enhanced beyond what it would have otherwise been.

The possibility exists that business groups will be more concerned with their own narrow economic interests than with the broader public interest. And in today's increasingly internationalized economy, with more and more multinational firms, many people have come to question the kind of thinking expressed along the line of "what's good for General Motors is good for the government" (Reich, 1988). Thus, citizens should be concerned generally with whether interest groups have disproportionate influence over their governments and, in particular, whether business groups are especially favored in this regard.

We have reviewed both the bad news and the good news in scholarship on interest-group power. In over half the states, interest groups are thought to be collectively quite influential in politics. In only a handful are they considered by political scientists to be relatively weak. They must, then, play a very important role in state politics, as we suggested at the beginning of this chapter. The character of that role is suggested by the fact that interest groups are strongest where the value placed on the public interest is lowest (in traditionalistic and individualistic political cultures) and where governmental institutions and political parties are weakest. These observations indicate that strong interest groups are a threat to democracy. And if one accepts the argument about the special prominence of business interests, then the threat to democratic control of government comes from the economically most powerful segment of society.

Fortunately, the power of interest groups can be moderated by other features of a state's political system—such as a number of competing interest groups, high mass participation in politics, and strong two-party competition. In states with these characteristics, interest groups may play a useful and legitimate role in politics. They facilitate communication by like-minded citizens with government, but their power is moderated by other aspects of the democratic process. In states without these offsetting forces, powerful interest groups, especially ones concerned with their own economic interests, have disproportionate control over government's agenda and policies.

REFERENCES

Berry, Jeffery M. 1977. *Lobbying for the People: The Political Behavior of Public Interest Groups.* Princeton, N.J.: Princeton University Press.

Epstein, Edwin M. 1969. *The Corporation in American Politics.* Englewood Cliffs, N.J.: Prentice-Hall.

Green, Mark J. 1973. "The Corporation and the Community," pp. 42–66 in Ralph Nader and Mark J. Green (eds.), *Corporate Power in America.* New York: Grossman.

Hrebenar, Ronald J., and Ruth K. Scott. 1982. *Interest Group Politics in America.* Englewood Cliffs, N.J.: Prentice-Hall.

Lindblom, Charles E. 1977. *Politics and Markets: The World's Political-Economic Systems.* New York: Basic Books.

Lockard, Duane. 1959. *New England State Politics.* Princeton, N.J.: Princeton University Press.

Payne, Thomas. 1961. "Under the Copper Dome: Politics in Montana," pp. 181–206 in Frank H. Jonas (ed.), *Western Politics.* Salt Lake City: University of Utah Press.

Phelan, James, and Robert Posen. 1973. *The Company State: Ralph Nader's Study Group Report on DuPont in Delaware.* New York: Grossman.

Reich, Robert B. 1988. "Corporation and Nation," *The Atlantic* 261 (May): 76–81.

Schlozman, Kay Lehman, and John T. Tierney. 1986. *Organized Interests and American Democracy.* New York: Harper & Row.

Stilwell, Hart. 1949. "Texas: Owned by Oil and Interlocking Directorates," pp. 314–344 in Robert S. Allen (ed.), *Our Sovereign State.* New York: Vanguard Press.

Thayer, George. 1973. *Who Shakes the Money Tree? American Campaign Financing Practices from 1789 to the Present.* New York: Simon and Schuster.

Thomas, Clive S., and Ronald J. Hrebenar. 1990. "Interest Groups in the States," pp. 123–158 in Virginia Gray, Herbert Jacob, and Robert B. Albritton (eds.), *Politics in the American States,* 5th edition. Glenview, Ill.: Scott, Foresman.

Zeigler, L. Harmon. 1983. "Interest Groups in the States," pp. 97–132 in Virginia Gray, Herbert Jacob, and Kenneth N. Vines (eds.), *Politics in the American States: A Comparative Analysis,* 4th edition. Boston: Little, Brown.

Zeigler, L. Harmon, and Hendrik van Dalen. 1976. "Interest Groups in State Politics," pp. 93–138 in Herbert Jacob and Kenneth N. Vines (eds.), *Politics in the American States: A Comparative Analysis,* 3rd edition. Boston: Little, Brown.

6 *State Legislatures*

Legislatures are, in a sense, the heart of American government. The democratic linkage between citizen and government is given its most direct expression in legislatures. And government policies are created there. Thus, these institutions are at the center of the governmental process in the states. And, because of their centrality, legislatures are subject to especially heavy pressures from environmental forces, partisan political forces, and interest groups. For these reasons, these institutions are also where the impact of changes in the political economy is felt most immediately. And the major policy decisions about how to respond to the challenges discussed in Chapter 1 will be made in state legislatures. Thus, the material of all the preceding chapters is relevant to the operations of these bodies.

WHAT LEGISLATURES DO

As every schoolchild knows, legislatures are composed of publicly elected individuals expected to represent the interests of those who elected them while making governmental policy. It is easy, however, to underestimate the complexity of the individual legislator's tasks, as well as those of the entire legislature, by failing to consider just what that simple statement means. It implies, first of all, two separate legislative functions.

The first of these is the function of *representation*. The men and women elected to a state legislature are in some sense supposed to represent those who elected them—either to do as those citizens wish them to in making policy decisions or to act in their best interests. But even in theory the representation function is complex. Should a legislator be simply an "errand boy," following mindlessly the will of his or her constituents? Or should the legislator try to be a leader of public opinion and shape the political ideas of those constituents? And is it legitimate for a legislator to make policy decisions that his or her constituents would apparently *not* prefer but that the legislator believes are in their best interests? There is no single philosophy of how elected representatives ought to resolve these questions or any single, commonly accepted answer to any of them. This philosophical difficulty is mirrored in the everyday practice of representation. Research on how legislators actually carry out this function indicates that they differ widely in how they perceive it, how they attempt to perform it, and how they justify their actions toward that end. The reasons for the difficulty of this task and for why individual legislators might pursue it in different ways will be explored in this chapter.

The second function embodied in the commonplace definition of what legislatures do is that of *lawmaking* (or *policy making*). With some participation by governors, state legislators make all state laws and enact all revisions of those laws. The fact that this is a major task of legislatures is widely recognized, but its complexity is seriously underestimated. That complexity can best be indicated by reiterating some of the major points about state government and the challenges it faces today that were made in earlier chapters.

State and local governments assumed a wide range of new responsibilities in the twentieth century. Many of those responsibilities developed in response to widespread changes in social and economic conditions, such as the spread of industrialization, the concentration of substantial economic power in the hands of private corporations, and the growth of big cities. That is, large-scale changes in the economy and the society forced new items onto the agenda of government. And today's economic challenge is creating more problems for state and local governments.

The federal government has also shaped the current responsibilities of state and local governments in two ways. First, during the era of cooptive federalism (1960–1980), the federal government forced the states to expand their activities and functions to pursue policy goals that it established for them. Then, in the 1980s, the federal government began to give more of the responsibility for these programs to the states while, at the same time, providing fewer funds to assist in paying for them.

And what is the significance of these several changes? State governments have taken on a long list of goals for which their legislatures must make policy. States are attempting to regulate and stimulate the development of their economies, to provide for the welfare and security needs of their populations, to serve the needs of their cities, to maintain their physical environments, and so on, down a very long list. The lawmaking function is, then, much more difficult today than in the past. It is more difficult, in part, because legislatures must tackle far more problems than in times past. But it is also more difficult because many of these problems are quite complex ones about which even the experts disagree. How state governments can best promote economic development and how they can most satisfactorily reform their educational systems to prepare children for the high-tech future are just two examples of matters that are widely debated, even among professional economists and educators.

The rise of such extensive responsibilities for state governments also complicates the task of representation. When government was less ambitious, there were fewer matters about which citizens and legislators might have to communicate. That is, the representational dialogue and public policy debates were conducted over fewer issues. There were also fewer occasions when government touched the life of the average citizen. Today, of course, government profoundly affects the character and quality of citizens' lives, and the breadth of that influence further complicates citizens' evaluations of government and the citizen-legislator dialogue.

There is one final point to be made about the implications of "big government" for state legislatures. A derivative task of lawmaking has always been *oversight*, or the legislature's efforts to monitor the work of the executive branch to ensure that laws and policies are being implemented as the legislature intended. In the past, when the agenda and therefore the executive branch of state government were relatively small, oversight was a relatively easy task. Today, however, state bureaucracies are not only larger; they are far more active. Local governments, which fall under the lawmaking authority of state legislatures, are also numerous, often quite sizable, and highly active. Simply put, there is now a great deal more to oversee. And the ambitiousness of some of the goals of government—along with the technical nature of many governmental programs designed to pursue those goals—makes this task still harder.

THE MECHANICS OF REPRESENTATION

How is it, specifically, that representation is difficult? How do legislators go about accomplishing this task? There are three ways in which a legislator can represent some of the interests of his or her constituents: *policy representation* (following the constituency's preferences in decisions about new policy proposals), *constituency service* (assisting individual constituents in their dealings with government), and *pork barrel politics* (seeking material benefits for part or all of the constituency). Each of these three avenues of representation poses distinctive problems for the legislator. And legislators believe they must spend time on all three of these activities if they are to be successful—and if they are to ensure their reelection.

POLICY REPRESENTATION

Carrying out policy representation necessitates a three-step process for the state legislator. First, the legislator must decide *which* constituency is the relevant one for a given policy proposal or, for that matter, for all such proposals on which he or she must vote in the legislature. Is the relevant constituency the legislator's entire geographic district? Is it some subset of the district, perhaps just members of the legislator's own political party? Is it only the people from the district who have actively communicated with the legislator about a given proposal? Might a particular interest group in the district be *the* constituency for a given issue? And there is one more possible constituency. Some legislators might seek to represent the people at large in the state in carrying out this form of representation.

Research on state legislators has generally found that they claim a strong interest in representing their individual district *in general* (Jewell, 1982: 78–102; Wahlke et al., 1962: 287–310). When a policy proposal is perceived as highly salient to their constituency, most legislators will try most of the time to follow what they believe to be the general districtwide view (Rosenthal, 1981: 98). However, legislators often make decisions on policy proposals that they perceive as having little impact on their district or as provoking little interest among their constituents. The considerable number of such issues gives legislators a good deal of discretion in their decision making. On such issues they may adopt the views of special constituencies (such as their political party or a particular interest group), or they may consider a variety of points of view and then make an independent decision.

Once the legislator has chosen the constituency to represent on a given issue, he or she must carry out the second step of policy representation: learning the opinions of that particular group on that issue. If the group is an interest group, this task is fairly easy—for the reasons explored in Chapter 5 concerning the abilities and efforts of such groups to communicate their points of view. For the district at large, however, this task is far more difficult. The legislator must rely on a variety of typically unrepresentative sources of information when attempting to gauge the general preferences of his or her district.

Election returns may indicate something about how well a legislator—or, perhaps, his or her policy position—is accepted by those in the district who cared to vote. Those returns will seldom, however, indicate how much public agreement there is with the legislator's position on any single issue. Mail from constituents is another source of information concerning their preferences; yet it will arrive only erratically with respect to most issues. And letters to legislators are generally written by those unrepresentative people who care enough about a policy issue to take the effort to write. (These are principally the parochial participants discussed in Chapter 4.) Alternatively, when mail comes in a great volume on a single issue, it is usually the product of an interest group's public lobbying effort—and most lawmakers will discount it to some degree in recognition of that fact.

All of a legislator's information sources—election returns, mail, polls of constituents, even efforts to "hang out" with the folks back home to learn their opinions—share the problem of being unrepresentative. Yet such are the available sources with which the legislator must estimate district preferences. The conscientious legislator will have a variety of impressions and several bits and pieces of hard evidence about the constituency's policy views from these sources. That information will, on some occasions, indicate a clear district-wide preference. On a good many other occasions, the legislator may—rightly or wrongly—believe that he or she has a "feel" for the district's general view, even though there is little hard evidence to substantiate that belief. And on a number of issues, the honest legislator is forced to conclude there is no majority preference in the district or, even worse, not enough people there know or care sufficiently about the issue to hold a preference.

The third step in the process of policy representation is deciding whether to follow the apparent constituency preference or to work instead for what the legislator believes is in the best interest of the constituents—even if that conflicts with their apparent preference. If the legislator believes there is no majority preference on a subject or if the constituents have no knowledge or interest in the subject, then this dilemma does not arise. The legislator can try to work for what he or she believes is in the best interest of the constituency. At other times, however, this step has both philosophical and practical aspects. Philosophically, this last step is affected by how a legislator envisions his or her responsibility. Some see themselves as mere delegates bound to follow their constituency's preferences. Others see themselves as leaders chosen for their wisdom, who must at times do what is "right" even if it is not what is popular. Practically, a legislator's decision here will influence his or her prospects for reelection. Some issues may be so salient to the constituency, as noted above, that the legislator must follow the majority preference. Others may provoke so little interest that the legislator is free to act on his or her independent judgment. Thus, every legislator must consider both the philosophical and the practical implications of his or her efforts to carry out policy representation.

CONSTITUENCY SERVICE

Constituency service, also known as *casework*, is the second, and more straightforward, way in which the legislator can represent the district. This task consists of handling specific requests from individual constituents concerning problems they have encountered with state or local governments. For example, a constituent seeking a state government job may desire the legislator's assistance or presumed influence. Another constituent may be having trouble getting some benefit he or she is claiming from a state agency, such as unemployment compensation or a worker's compensation settlement. Yet another constituent seeking help might be a businessperson having a problem with the red tape of some state agency.

Some have argued that constituency service has grown considerably more important in the last several decades (Jewell, 1982: 159; Rosenthal, 1981: 102–107). We should not be surprised by that observation. As state and local governments have grown, there are simply more occasions and more reasons why individual citizens might get ensnarled in the tentacles of one of those big governments and then turn to their legislator for assistance. As further evidence of how much demand there is for constituency service, Alan Rosenthal (1981: 104) estimates that somewhere between one-third and two-thirds of all state legislators think this is their most important job. Likewise, in his research on representation in state legislatures, Malcolm Jewell (1982: 141) interviewed many legislators for whom half of their and their staff's time was devoted to casework.

Some legislators are also simply more interested in casework than others. For some, it is a way they can see direct, individual consequences for their work, and thus they are highly attracted to it. Futhermore, some legislators are in a better position than others to handle constituents' requests. The better the staff support provided for individual legislators, for example, the better their resources for handling such requests. Some legislators even delegate constituency service entirely to their staff, reserving their own time for lawmaking. Whether or not they are personally attracted to this kind of work and regardless of how extensive their staff resources are, all legislators see casework as a very important part of their job. And they recognize that they may benefit from it as much as their constituents do. They hope, of course, that every constituent individually assisted through casework is a vote (or more) earned for the next election.

PORK BARREL POLITICS

A final way in which lawmakers can represent their districts is by "bringing home the pork." "Pork" and "pork barrel," venerable terms in American politics, describe the efforts of legislators to secure specific material benefits for their districts.[1] Road construction contracts, new hospitals, parks, or government office buildings, and new colleges or the expansion of existing ones are examples of the pork that state legislators can bring to their districts—to be paid for by the state's taxpayers at large. Such prizes create new jobs, increase the level of public services or amenities, and may even generate a permanent flow of state money into the district. Even a state-supported program of college scholarships can be handled as pork, as Rosenthal (1981: 100) indicates with an example from Pennsylvania:

> One noteworthy example was the senatorial scholarship program, which every year allowed each of the 50 members of the senate to award 100 or more scholarships, each worth about $600, to Pennsylvania colleges. . . . Pennsylvania's 5400 senatorial scholarships cost over $3 million. Apparently no conventional criteria—neither achievement nor financial need—were used in selecting among the applicants, but awards seemed to be based mainly on how close a student's parents were to a state senator or how much clout they had. The program came under scathing attack by the press, and was abolished in 1978, having been in effect a few years short of a century.

THE MECHANICS OF LAWMAKING

Many textbooks discuss lawmaking in terms of "how a bill becomes a law." That is, they describe the organizational steps within the legislature through which a proposed new law must pass to be approved. You remember from high school civics classes: "the bill goes in the hopper, then it goes to committee, then it goes to the floor of the House or Senate for debate," and so on. Simple as these steps are, you can't take them entirely for granted. Each of them is important in certain ways, and each can be a critical hurdle for the political supporters and opponents of new laws. And crafty politicians know how to manipulate the rules and procedures to their best advantage.

The most meaningful way to consider the institutional process of lawmaking is by examining how each step in the process can contribute to the rational *and* political analysis of proposed new laws. Consider, then, Figure 6-1, which shows the steps in how a bill becomes a law in New Jersey. Some of the minor details given in the figure are unique to New Jersey (such as the specifics of the first, second, and third readings and of the governor's veto powers). The

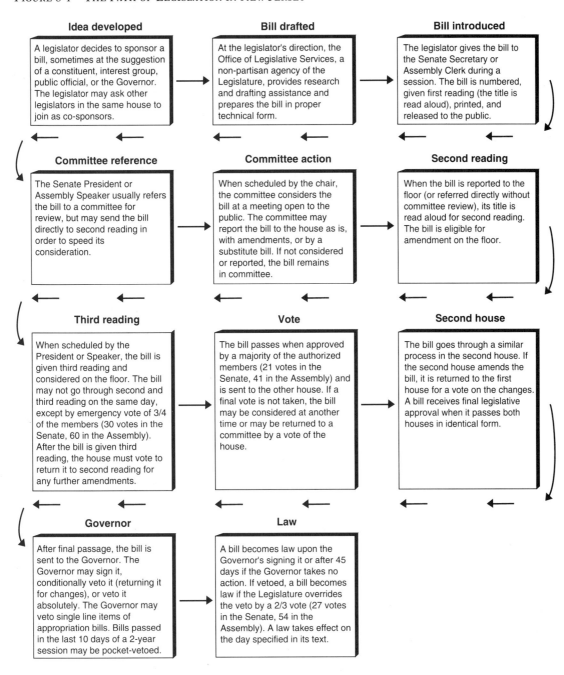

FIGURE 6-1 THE PATH OF LEGISLATION IN NEW JERSEY

Idea developed

A legislator decides to sponsor a bill, sometimes at the suggestion of a constituent, interest group, public official, or the Governor. The legislator may ask other legislators in the same house to join as co-sponsors.

Bill drafted

At the legislator's direction, the Office of Legislative Services, a non-partisan agency of the Legislature, provides research and drafting assistance and prepares the bill in proper technical form.

Bill introduced

The legislator gives the bill to the Senate Secretary or Assembly Clerk during a session. The bill is numbered, given first reading (the title is read aloud), printed, and released to the public.

Committee reference

The Senate President or Assembly Speaker usually refers the bill to a committee for review, but may send the bill directly to second reading in order to speed its consideration.

Committee action

When scheduled by the chair, the committee considers the bill at a meeting open to the public. The committee may report the bill to the house as is, with amendments, or by a substitute bill. If not considered or reported, the bill remains in committee.

Second reading

When the bill is reported to the floor (or referred directly without committee review), its title is read aloud for second reading. The bill is eligible for amendment on the floor.

Third reading

When scheduled by the President or Speaker, the bill is given third reading and considered on the floor. The bill may not go through second and third reading on the same day, except by emergency vote of 3/4 of the members (30 votes in the Senate, 60 in the Assembly). After the bill is given third reading, the house must vote to return it to second reading for any further amendments.

Vote

The bill passes when approved by a majority of the authorized members (21 votes in the Senate, 41 in the Assembly) and is sent to the other house. If a final vote is not taken, the bill may be considered at another time or may be returned to a committee by a vote of the house.

Second house

The bill goes through a similar process in the second house. If the second house amends the bill, it is returned to the first house for a vote on the changes. A bill receives final legislative approval when it passes both houses in identical form.

Governor

After final passage, the bill is sent to the Governor. The Governor may sign it, conditionally veto it (returning it for changes), or veto it absolutely. The Governor may veto single line items of appropriation bills. Bills passed in the last 10 days of a 2-year session may be pocket-vetoed.

Law

A bill becomes law upon the Governor's signing it or after 45 days if the Governor takes no action. If vetoed, a bill becomes law if the Legislature overrides the veto by a 2/3 vote (27 votes in the Senate, 54 in the Assembly). A law takes effect on the day specified in its text.

Source: Adapted from Karen A. West, *New Jersey: Spotlight on Government,* 5th edition (New Brunswick, N.J.: Rutgers University Press, 1985), pp. 62–63.

general process, however, is applicable to all the states except Nebraska, which has a single-house legislature and thus lacks the step labeled "Second house" in the figure. Once the idea for a new law has arisen, the following steps are the key ones: drafting of the bill, committee review, debate and vote by either or both houses of the legislature, and approval or veto by the governor.

DRAFTING THE BILL

Bills introduced in the legislature are proposed new laws. As such, they must be written in technically appropriate form. Their common-sensical or policy-specific intent must, that is, be expressed in the correct language of the law. And a bill must be written to minimize the possibility of later challenges to its legality (for example, with respect to constitutionality or a conflict with other, preexisting laws).

Good bill drafting requires, then, the skills of a lawyer trained in that field. Because many state legislators are not lawyers or, even if they are, do not have expertise in that particular legal field, many states have, like New Jersey, employed a staff of lawyers in a bill-drafting agency of the legislature to assist in this process. The importance of good drafting is illustrated by the example of the Texas legislator who in 1985, working without professional assistance on drafting, introduced an antipornography bill that, if adopted into law, would have inadvertently legalized sexual relations with animals.

COMMITTEE REVIEW

After a bill is introduced, it is referred to the appropriate subject-matter committee of the house in which it was introduced. A typical array of legislative committees, again for New Jersey, is presented in Table 6-1. Each house in a legislature has an array of subject-matter committees, which are referred to as reference committees in New Jersey. In addition, legislatures often have a number of other committees that handle administrative, short-lived policy issues, or matters that must be resolved by joint and simultaneous action of both houses. The administrative, select, and joint committees of the New Jersey Legislature are examples of these types.

The subject-matter committees are the most important ones for the lawmaking function. It is in these committees that proposed bills typically receive their most detailed and critical review. Bills judged by the committee to be unimportant, technically or otherwise

TABLE 6-1
COMMITTEES IN THE
NEW JERSEY LEGIS-
LATURE, 1986

SENATE COMMITTEES	GENERAL ASSEMBLY COMMITTEES	JOINT COMMITTEES
Standing Reference (Policy) Committees	*Standing Reference (Policy) Committees*	Ethical Standards
County and Municipal Government	Appropriations	State Library
Education	County Government	Legislative Oversight
Energy and Environment	Economic Development and Agriculture	
Institutions, Health, and Welfare	Education	
Judiciary	Energy and Natural Resources	
Labor, Industry, and Professions	Environmental Quality	
Law, Public Safety, and Defense	Financial Institutions	
Resources and Agriculture	Health and Human Resources	
Revenue, Finance, and Appropriations	Higher Education and Regulated Professions	
State Government and Federal and Interstate Relations and Veterans Affairs	Housing	
Transportation and Communications	Independent and Regional Authorities	
	Insurance	
Standing Administrative Committees	Judiciary	
Intergovernmental Relations	Labor	
Rules and Order	Law, Public Safety, Defense, and Corrections	
Ways and Means	Municipal Government	
	Regulatory Efficiency and Oversight	
	Senior Citizens	
	State Government	
	Transportation, Communications, and High Technology	
	Urban Policy and Waterfront Development	
	Standing Select Committees	
	Division of Motor Vehicles	
	Solid Waste Disposal	
	Tourism	
	Veterans Affairs	

Source: State of New Jersey, *Manual of the Legislature of New Jersey* (Trenton, N.J.: Edward J. Mullin, 1986), 327, 366–367.

weak, or lacking significant public or political support will be quickly voted down and will receive no further legislative attention. Those considered to have merit will, on the other hand, get extensive consideration.

Typically, legislative committees hold public hearings on important bills. Members of the public may testify before the committee in support of or against a bill that is the subject of such a hearing. More likely to testify, however, are such individuals as the legislative sponsor of the bill, representatives of any interest groups that will be most affected by the bill, and executive-branch officials from those state agencies that are likely to be charged with implementing the policies envisioned in the bill. The hearing stage is, then, an opportunity for the legislative committee to get technical and policy critiques of a proposed bill from a number of perspectives. It is also a chance to test the political waters and determine just how strong support for or opposition to the bill is.

The committee members themselves play an especially important role here. If they have served on a given subject-matter committee for a long period, they should have developed some expertise in this policy area. They should know the state's existing policies in this field and the strengths, weaknesses, and continuing problems of those policies. The extent to which committee members have developed such expertise and to which members are assigned to committees for which they have relevant expertise will have a considerable influence on the quality of the legislature's decision making.

After the public hearing, the committee will review the bill again. At this point the committee may kill the bill and thus end its consideration by the legislature, or it may pass the bill on to the full house in original or revised form. If the bill is passed on, any original technical or policy deficiencies should have been corrected, and the bill should have at least substantial, if not overwhelming, political support.

DEBATE AND VOTE BY THE LEGISLATURE

This stage is of considerable policy and political importance to the fate of the bill, because the subject-matter interests and expertise of the full house are not likely to match those of the committee. Some committees may be made up of ideologues who wish to fashion extremely liberal or conservative policies for education, economic development, or whatever is the subject-matter specialty of the

VOTING ON LEGISLATION IN THE NEW YORK ASSEMBLY IS THE FINAL STEP IN A LONG SERIES OF POLICY DELIBERATIONS.

committee. The full house, on the other hand, might have a different, if only more moderate, disposition. There may be, then, political support or opposition in the full body that does match that in the committee. Likewise, in the full house there may be technical knowledge relevant to a bill that is not available on the committee. In many state legislatures committee members do not, in fact, have much real subject-matter expertise. This can be the case for a number of reasons. If the turnover of membership from election to election is high, the typical member will not have been in the legislature long enough to gain much knowledge. The failure of many legislatures to assign members to committees based on their expertise and the practice of frequently rotating members among committees further weaken the degree of expertise (Oxendale, 1981).

Finally, the full house has to weigh a bill's merits against those of a number of other ones. If the education committee wants more funds to support remedial programs, that request must be considered in the context of many other bills seeking increased funding for health care, highways, business regulation, and so on. The subject-matter committee has the luxury of trying to craft good education policy divorced from such considerations. But the full house must attempt to balance all of the state's needs.

Senate Should End Calendar Trickery

Tourists briefly visiting Senate sessions this year may leave with the idea that creating a Texas-flag flower bed at the Capitol is the Senate's next item of business.

Right there at the top of the Senate calendar, printed daily in a little green booklet, is Senate Bill 123, by Sen. Roy Blake of Nacogdoches, "relating to the creation and maintenance on the grounds of the State Capitol a permanent flower bed depicting through appropriate design and flower selection the Texas flag."

Blake is chairman of the powerful Senate Administration Committee, so his bill—up there first in line to be considered by the full Senate—ought to move fast, right?

Wrong.

His bill is not going anywhere. By agreement with Lt. Gov. Bill Hobby, Blake will never try to pass it.

SB123 is just a serious joke, the session's blocking bill. Its whole purpose is to ensure that the calendar, which is officially the "regular order of business," or ROB, is never followed. Since Blake will not try to pass it, no bill beneath it on the calendar can be considered by the Senate unless its author has rounded up an extraordinary majority of votes to suspend the ROB.

A sponsor may have 16 or 18 votes committed for his very good bill—enough to pass it in the 31-member Senate—but it won't ever be passed unless he can muster a two-thirds majority of those present to suspend the ROB so it can be brought to the simple-majority passage vote. The two-thirds-of-those-present majority is 21 votes if there's a full house.

First the sponsor must get recognized by the presiding officer (the lieutenant governor) to make a motion to suspend the ROB. If he is recognized and wins the two-thirds majority for his motion, his bill is brought up, explained, debated, possibly amended, and tentatively approved. Then, if the author can muster a four-fifths majority of the membership (25 votes) to suspend a constitutional rule requiring final passage on another day, the bill may be finally passed and sent to the House the same day.

If the four-fifths majority can't be achieved, then on another day the sponsor must get the ROB suspended again by a two-thirds majority, after which the bill may be passed by a simple-majority vote.

If you ask me, it's terribly undemocratic and the Senate should have a better way to regulate traffic. But this has been the Senate system for as long as anybody there can remember. Lieutenant governors and most senators like it. It enhances a lieutenant governor's control and helps senators obscure their stands on hot-potato bills. It "works both ways," preventing passage of bad bills as well as good ones, its admirers say.

But if a bill has simple-majority support, as long as it is not shown to be unconstitutional, it should become law. Merit, not tricky rules, should determine whether it is passed; this should not have to wait for years until the majority support has grown bigger.

Senate bill traffic could be regulated instead by having committees, which already study bills closely, decide which have enough merit to be voted on at all by the full Senate.

Blake, who seems fond of flower bills, used the same flower-bed bill to block the calendar in the regular legislative session in 1983. The State Purchasing and General Services Commission even wanted to help pass it—until Blake explained.

In 1981, he introduced a bill to prohibit importation of diseased camellias. But whatever dangers foreign camellias threatened us with, Texas evidently remains unprotected from them, because that was just the 1981 calendar-blocking bill.

Cute, eh? But such a system has a profound effect on our law.

Source: Felton West, *Houston Post,* 1985.

The Role of the Second House If a bill is accepted by one house of the legislature, it must, in every state except Nebraska, go through the same process in the second house. The rationale for two-house legislatures in the states originally rested on a shaky analogy with the U.S. Congress. In the Congress the Senate has always represented states per se, but the House is organized on the principle of proportional representation for the states' population (states with more people get more members in the House). Until the mid-1960s state legislatures were similarly structured, with senatorial districts based purely on geographic areas within the states and house districts based on population. It is in the design of senate districts that the analogy with Congress breaks down, of course, for counties or multicounty units do not have the autonomous political role within states that the states have within the federal system. The whole analogy was effectively eliminated, however, when the Supreme Court declared in a series of cases in the 1960s that both houses of state legislatures must be apportioned on the basis of population.[2]

It is possible to conclude, then, that forty-nine of the states have two-house legislatures because they have always had them, not because such a structure serves a technically or politically useful purpose. The existence of two houses has one clear effect on the lawmaking process, however. It makes the process of passing new legislation more difficult because of the additional number of hurdles. Furthermore, a good case can be made that these additional hurdles particularly inhibit the passage of legislation that is innovative or that threatens the status quo.

The Manipulation of Parliamentary Procedures The fate of a bill in a legislature can often be determined by the clever manipulation of the parliamentary rules. The leader of the house or senate usually has some influence (and sometimes complete control) over which committee will review a bill. A knowledge of the ideological composition of the committees combined with a strategic choice of which one will get to consider a given bill can often determine the bill's fate automatically. Similarly, the fate of a bill can hinge on such seemingly mundane matters as when it is scheduled for debate by the full house, whether amendments will be allowed from the full house, and who will serve on the conference committee if differences must be reconciled with the other house's version of the bill. Of course, it is not just the leaders who might use the rules to their own advantage, but they have the best opportunities to do so because of their various formal and informal powers.

One case of clever manipulation of the parliamentary rules is described in the editorial on the scheduling of debate on bills in the Texas Senate. In each legislative session there, a new, and equally unimportant, blocking bill is first on the calendar. The control of this seemingly mundane administrative matter significantly enhances the power of the lieutenant governor, the presiding officer of the senate. It allows the lieutenant governor and his (or her) supporters significant control over what the senate will debate and, therefore, what will and will not become law. This may be an extreme example of manipulation of the rules, but every state legislature is to some degree vulnerable to such tactics.

THE GOVERNOR'S APPROVAL OR VETO

Governors also play a role in the lawmaking process that is more important than the simple diagram of Figure 6-1 suggests. Governors are active, powerful participants in the lawmaking process. They can propose new laws for legislative consideration. They can lobby actively for or against particular bills being considered by the legislature. And, in all states except North Carolina, governors can veto bills passed by the legislature (although there is the possibility that the legislature will subsequently override the veto by an extraordinary majority vote). The full scope and importance of the governor's lawmaking role can be best understood, however, in the context of the other powers of that office. Thus, we will discuss that role more fully in Chapter 7.

THE ERA OF STATE LEGISLATIVE REFORM

The expansion of state governments' responsibilities and, therefore, those of the state legislatures has been particularly rapid since the end of World War II. And as legislative responsibilities burgeoned in the 1950s, there developed an increasing awareness that state legislatures were ill-equipped to handle their increasing responsibilities. State governments and legislatures have responded to these challenges in dramatic ways.

As recently as the early 1950s, the typical state legislature was something of an amateur body. It met for short sessions, usually just once every two years. The individual legislators were paid, at best, a very modest annual salary or, at worst, only a daily expense allowance while the legislature was in session. Only in about a half dozen states did legislators have as high an annual salary as the average office secretary. In consequence, legislators had to have another full-time job or source of income, and their legislative work could only be a part-time endeavor. In general, states provided few resources or perquisites to their legislators, and for these and related reasons the turnover of membership in state legislatures was typically high. Similarly, in the early 1950s the typical state legislature had quite limited capabilities for information gathering and analytic and technical decision making. Professional and clerical staff were limited in number, information and research resources were poor, and time for the deliberation of policy questions was inadequate because of the short periods for which most legislatures were in session.

Many outside observers, as well as many legislators, quickly recognized these problems as the work of state legislative bodies became more complex. And the most common response was to argue that legislatures should become more professionalized. That is, they should develop a variety of more modern and sophisticated decision-making practices. They should hire more staff, meet more often and for longer periods, and pay higher salaries so that their members could devote more time to their legislative work. More specifically, the legislative reform movement sought nine goals (Rosenthal, 1971: 3–4):

1. Elimination of many constitutional limitations on the authority of state legislatures
2. Increase in the frequency and length of legislative sessions
3. Reduction in the size of legislative bodies, so that they are no larger than fair representation requires
4. Increase in compensation and related benefits for legislators
5. The adoption of more rigorous standards of conduct, by means of codes of ethics and conflict of interest, disclosure, and lobbying legislation
6. Provision of adequate space and facilities for committees and individual members, including electronic data processing and roll-call voting equipment

7. Improvement of legislative operations, to ensure efficiency in the consideration of bills and the widespread dissemination of procedural and substantive information
8. Strengthening of standing committees
9. Increasing the number and competence of legislative staff

The arguments of this reform movement have been especially influential since the early 1970s. Many states have made dramatic improvements in these nine areas since that time. And every state's legislature has shared, at least in part, in this reform movement (Pound, 1986). Some states have, however, progressed considerably further than others, and some lag far behind the average.

On the other hand, some people have not been entirely convinced of the need for professionalization. Some have argued, instead, that legislatures should retain their amateur character because that keeps them "closer to the people." Amateur legislatures, that is, are seen as *citizen legislatures*, allowing for wide representation of a state's different kinds of citizens, many opportunities for the infusion of new ideas because of high turnover, and less likelihood of being controlled by professional politicians. This line of argument has an intuitive appeal, but there are two problems with it. First, professionalization has, in fact, improved the competence of state legislatures (Thompson, 1986). Second, it is not clear that amateur legislatures are truly citizen legislatures. In many states, citizen legislatures have been dominated by special-interest groups and the few experienced and powerful members who formed the leadership of the legislature (Mladenka and Hill, 1986: 104–135). The amateur members of those bodies typically have quite short careers there and have little influence.

STATE LEGISLATURES TODAY

What have been the results of the legislative reform movement? Which states have advanced the most toward professionalism, and which have remained committed to a citizen legislature? To answer these questions, we will stratify state legislatures in terms of the extent of their progress toward professionalization. Because of the complexity of the nine reform goals, it is not possible to take account of every state's adoption of every possible reform that is directed toward any one of them. But there is general agreement among scholars about the most essential traits of professionalized legislatures, and we will develop our ranking system on those traits.

As Jewell (1982: 7) observes, the principal distinguishing attribute of highly professional legislatures is that they meet annually in long, usually year-round, sessions. And to sustain such a demanding time commitment from the elected members, full-time professional salaries are necessary. Similarly, legislative staff and other internal administrative resources must be considerably enlarged to fulfill this year-round schedule. Legislatures that move toward full-time schedules must, that is, make progress toward several of the other reform goals at the same time.

It is certainly true that even a citizen legislator's job entails year-round responsibilities. Constituency service, as described above, is one of those, since constitutents encounter problems that they want their legislator to solve all year long. Nonetheless, a full-year schedule of regular sessions inevitably imposes higher demands on legislators. And legislatures that do not meet year-round may have to meet periodically in special sessions to settle pressing matters of state business that arise between regular sessions. Thus, they may be in session for longer than is indicated by noting their regular sessions alone. However, special sessions are hurried affairs when legislative deliberations are particularly compromised by the press of time and the limits on careful analysis of issues. In consequence, the length of just the regular session is a better indicator of the professionalization of a given legislature.

Based on these ideas, the legislatures of the various states can be categorized into four groups:

■ Professional legislatures, which meet annually for between nine and twelve months and pay their members annual salaries of at least $30,000 a year (usually with an allowance for personal and office expenses added on top of this salary).[3]

■ Quasi-professional legislatures, which meet annually in regular session for between five and eight months on average and pay their members at least $17,500 in annual salaries.

A QUESTION OF
LEGISLATIVE
PROCEDURE RESULTS
IN A TENSE AND
PROTRACTED DEBATE
WITH THE PRESIDING
OFFICER IN THE
TEXAS SENATE.

■ Citizen, or nonprofessional, legislatures that meet annually in regular session for only two to six months a year. Only a few of these bodies pay their members as much as $15,000 a year in salary, and 14 of the 25 states in this group actually pay annual salaries of $10,000 or less.

■ Citizen, or nonprofessional, legislatures that meet biennially (once every two years) in regular session, typically for from four to five months. Three of the seven states in this group pay no legislative salaries, and the highest salary paid here is less than $12,000 a year.

Table 6-2 classifies the legislatures of all fifty states into these four types. In addition, the table gives the annual salaries paid to legislators in 1990 (in parentheses). Although progress toward professionalism may have been made everywhere, as noted earlier, the extent of that progress is still debatable. Only nine state legislatures can be labeled professional using these criteria, and thirty-five fall into one of the two categories of citizen legislature. And Table 6-2 may make some legislatures appear more professional than they really are. The states of Florida and Maryland, for example, pay moderately high salaries to their legislators, but legislative sessions there have not been appreciably longer than those of some of the citizen legislatures that meet annually.

TABLE 6-2
THE PROFESSIONALI-
ZATION OF STATE
LEGISLATURES
(WITH 1990 ANNUAL
SALARIES OF
LEGISLATORS)[a]

PROFESSIONAL LEGISLATURES	QUASI-PROFESSIONAL LEGISLATURES	CITIZEN LEGISLATURES MEETING ANNUALLY	CITIZEN LEGISLATURES MEETING BIENNIALLY
California ($40,816)	Alaska ($22,140)	Alabama (0)	Arkansas ($7,500)
Illinois ($35,661)	Delaware ($23,282)	Arizona ($15,000)	Kentucky (0)
Massachusetts ($30,000)	Florida ($21,684)	Colorado ($17,500)	Montana (0)
Michigan ($45,450)	Maryland ($25,000)	Connecticut ($16,760)	Nevada (0)
New Jersey ($35,000)	Minnesota ($26,395)	Georgia ($10,376)	North Dakota (0)
New York ($57,500)	Missouri ($22,414)	Hawaii ($27,000)	Oregon ($11,686)
Ohio ($34,905)		Idaho (0)	Texas ($7,200)
Pennsylvania ($47,000)		Indiana ($11,600)	
Wisconsin ($32,239)		Iowa ($16,600)	
		Kansas (0)	
		Louisiana ($16,800)	
		Maine ($6,600)	
		Mississippi ($10,000)	
		Nebraska ($12,000)	
		New Hampshire ($100)	
		New Mexico (0)	
		North Carolina ($11,124)	
		Oklahoma ($32,000)	
		Rhode Island (0)	
		South Carolina ($10,000)	
		South Dakota ($4,267)	
		Tennessee ($16,500)	
		Utah (0)	
		Vermont ($6,750)	
		Virginia ($18,000)	
		Washington ($17,900)	
		West Virginia ($6,500)	
		Wyoming (0)	

[a]The categorization of the states by the extent of legislative professionalization is based on the criteria described in the text. The annual salaries come from Council of State Governments, *The Book of the States, 1990–91* (Lexington, Ky.: Council of State Governments, 1990).

STATE LEGISLATORS TODAY

The most typical state legislator is a white middle-aged male who is either an attorney or a businessman. About 85 percent of state legislators were male in 1986, and, although precise data on their ethnicities are not available, probably over 90 percent are white (National Conference on State Legislatures, 1987; Patterson, 1983: 153–155). However, even though the numbers of women and ethnic minorities are small, they have increased substantially in recent decades. Women constituted, for example, less than 5 percent of all state legislators as recently as 1960.

Regardless of their gender or ethnicity, legislators are typically far better-educated and far more likely than their constituents to come from business, professional, or other relatively high-status occupational groups. Blue-collar and clerical occupations are especially underrepresented compared to their proportions in the general population. Farmers constitute the only notable exception to these generalizations, being well represented in Southern, Midwestern, and other heavily agricultural regions.

Nationwide, about 16 percent of state legislators are attorneys, and 20 percent list their principal occupation as business owner or manager (14 percent and 6 percent, respectively). Yet these groups have been declining in recent years as the demands of legislative work increase and thus impose further limitations on a legislator's other career. In the same period the number of individuals who give their profession as "full-time legislator" has grown, and 11 percent nationwide so designated their occupations in 1986. This number probably underestimates the proportion of those who, whatever their principal occupation, wish to maintain a legislative career once in office.

There is significant variation in the demographic composition of legislatures across regions as well as in the levels of professionalization of those bodies themselves. Lawyers have always been especially numerous in Southern legislatures. They still comprise over a third of the legislators in that region—and even constituted 45 percent of the Virginia Legislature in 1986. Those giving their occupation as full-time legislator, on the other hand, are most numerous in states with professional legislatures. In New York, for example, 60 percent of the legislators so designated themselves in 1986 (National Conference of State Legislatures, 1987).

WHY DO THEY RUN FOR OFFICE?

Why would anyone want to run for the state legislature? The job is, after all, not highly attractive at first glance. Only a handful of states provide anything like a full-time salary. Furthermore, the job also requires that one suffer through the better part of a year's electioneering—kissing babies, begging for campaign contributions, making promises, and excoriating one's opponent. Then the successful candidate gets the privilege of leaving home, family, and job for anywhere from two months to a full year to live in the state capital and tackle the job of lawmaking. And a conscientious individual— whether a member of a citizen or a professional legislature—can easily make this position a full-time, six-or-seven-days-a-week activity. Clearly, many personal sacrifices and hardships are required, and the apparent benefits are modest.

However, many people seek the position, in spite of the costs. Some of the attractions of the job are also readily apparent. It is a position of some status. It is also one in which a person can indeed serve the public interest—which may not, however, be a goal of all candidates. And it is one from which an ambitious person might launch or further a political career intended to reach far greater heights. There are, then, clear costs and benefits. Yet not all the benefits will be compelling to everyone; some of them are of interest only to those with long-term political ambitions.

Why, again, do candidates run? Perhaps the most useful answer to this question is provided by James David Barber (1965) in a study of the motivations of Connecticut legislators. Barber found four types of individuals serving in that state:

1. *Spectators*—who were low in political ambition and activity and who literally behaved more as onlookers than as active participants in the legislative process. These people typically ran for a seat in the legislature because they were coerced into doing so by the local party organization or because they saw the post more as an honor than as a responsibility. While in the legislature, they enjoyed the "show" but participated little in the actual work of the institution.

2. *Reluctants*—who served, somewhat unwillingly, in the legislature to fulfill a civic obligation others had imposed on them. They were usually recruited, that is, by a political party or interest group and accepted the task only because of the social pressure or their own sense of civic duty.

3. *Advertisers*—who actively sought their legislative position and who worked aggressively at certain aspects of the job, but whose principal motivation was to further their occupational career. These might be, for example, young professionals in law, real estate, insurance, or other business pursuits who saw in legislative service an opportunity to gain friendships, publicity, or skills useful for their private careers.

4. *Lawmakers*—who actively sought their legislative post with the primary intention of having an effect on legislation and, therefore, public policy. Such individuals were motivated by a desire either to serve the public interest or to pursue a particular ideological or policy agenda of their own.

All four of these types are probably found in every state legislature, but the first three are especially common in citizen and quasi-professional legislatures. As legislative bodies become more professionalized, they become more attractive to the fourth type, lawmakers. They then also offer more inducements for such individuals to seek long legislative careers. But professionalized legislatures, despite their higher salaries, may be especially *unattractive* for the other three types of legislators. Elections for such bodies are particularly competitive and costly, imposing, in effect, especially high burdens on spectators, reluctants, and advertisers in light of their motivations to enter the legislature in the first place. On top of that, such individuals would find the full-time regular sessions of professional legislatures taxing.

Because most state legislatures are not highly professionalized, however, many of the first three types of legislators identified by Barber are in office across the nation. In those states with citizen legislatures, there may be only a small percentage of legislators who qualify as lawmakers by Barber's criteria. Other research has offered support for Barber's motivation-based typology and has also suggested some other common characteristics of state legislators. A large proportion of legislators come from politically active families and report an early interest in politics (Wahlke et al., 1962: 77–94). Many of them claim a desire to serve the public interest—although it is likely that some of those say this because it is the socially desirable response. And an increasing percentage of legislators—mostly

Legislative Furniture

One can easily imagine that spectators, reluctants, and advertisers will be quickly recognized by other legislators and close observers of the legislative scene. In Texas, many of these people have earned the nickname "furniture," as the magazine Texas Monthly *reports.*

The term "furniture" first came into use around the Legislature to describe members who, by virtue of their indifference or ineffectiveness, were indistinguishable from their desks, chairs, and spittoons. It is now used, casually and more generally, to identify the most inconsequential members.

Source: Texas Monthly, July 1985, p. 122.

Barber's lawmakers, one must suspect—express an interest in a long-term political career.

Other research in this field has indicated some important impediments to fulfillment of legislative ambitions. Campaign costs remain relatively modest in some states and districts, especially in rural areas and small towns. But those costs are on the rise everywhere (discussed in Chapter 4) and have reached quite high levels in the largest states and in most urbanized areas. Thus, candidates must have good prospects of raising the necessary election funds—whether from ties to a well-funded political party, interest group, or PAC or from their personal wealth or their own "arm twisting" efforts.

Even if the legislative hopeful can raise the necessary money, there remain other constraints on fulfilling his or her ambition. One of these is simply the availability of an opportunity. And the opportunity itself is shaped by several factors. Most wise prospective candidates are, for example, unwilling to challenge an incumbent legislator of their own party. Incumbents are usually too well placed, both in the party and with respect to their reelection prospects. This fact limits opportunity because, in any given election year, a very high percentage of incumbents will seek reelection.

Even if the incumbent is a member of another party, many prospective candidates will still not run for the office. They know that most incumbents running for reelection are kept in office by the voters. In an analysis of state legislative elections in twenty-nine states between 1966 and 1976, Jerry Calvert (1979) found that about 90 percent of incumbents running for reelection were successful. More recent evidence suggests that the number of incumbents desiring to be reelected has increased and the advantage of incumbency has remained very high (Patterson, 1983: 150–153; Rosenthal, 1981: 22–26).

Finally, the opportunity to run for office is limited in some states by the party organizations. Where political parties are well organized, they have significant control over the recruitment of prospective candidates. Those who run for office are those who are chosen by a party. Elsewhere, recruitment efforts may be shared by leaders of parties and interest groups, and in the states with the very weakest party organizations, many candidates are self-recruited. That is, they may even be "political nobodies" with no prior activity in or tie to the party under whose banner they wish to run. (It is the case, however, that a high percentage of legislators nationwide report activity in their party prior to the time they first sought election.)

Admittedly, candidates who can't spend much sometimes whip well-funded ones. Incumbents are at times defeated, and political nobodies occasionally score dramatic election victories. Wise prospective candidates, however, know the favorable odds associated with money, incumbency, and party ties. They groom themselves so that they will be at the right place at the right time knowing the right people. Yet for many of those hopefuls, that situation never arises.

WHY DO THEY LEAVE OFFICE?

Why do most legislators eventually leave their positions? The increasing interest of incumbents in seeking reelection—as well as their high success in doing so—is a somewhat recent phenomenon. In the 1940s, a period that preceded the efforts to professionalize legislatures, the average turnover of members of state legislatures for any given election was 51 percent in lower houses and 43 percent in senates (Shin and Jackson, 1979: 99). That is, after any election slightly over half of the members of the average lower house were newly elected "freshmen." Both those percentages have been declining, however, over the rest of the twentieth century. Richard Niemi and Laura Winsky (1987) report that by the 1980s those percentages had fallen to 28 percent turnover for lower houses and 24 percent for senates.

Variation in the turnover rates is apparent across professional, quasi-professional, and citizen legislatures. Table 6-3 reports such figures for two time periods since 1970. Furthermore, Table 6-4 reports the percentages of incumbents who were defeated in their reelection efforts and who did not seek reelection in the period 1966–1976 (the most recent data available for such an analysis). Not surprisingly, turnover is higher in the less professionalized legisla-

TABLE 6-3
LEVELS OF TURN-
OVER IN STATE
LEGISLATURES

TYPE OF LEGISLATURE	TOTAL TURNOVER 1971–1976[a]		TOTAL TURNOVER 1971–1980[b]	
	SENATE	HOUSE	SENATE	HOUSE
Professional	27%	29%	26%	24%
Quasi-professional	30	39	27	33
Citizen, meeting annually	37	38	31	35
Citizen, meeting biennially	30	40	23	32

[a]Calculated with data for all fifty states from Shin and Jackson (1979).
[b]Calculated with data for all fifty states from Niemi and Winsky (1987).

TABLE 6-4
REASONS FOR TURN-
OVER IN STATE
LEGISLATURES,
1966–1976[a]

TYPE OF LEGISLATURE	PERCENTAGE OF LEGISLATIVE POSITIONS WHERE INCUMBENTS LOST REELECTION BIDS		PERCENTAGE OF LEGISLATORS WHO DID NOT SEEK REELECTION	
	SENATE	HOUSE	SENATE	HOUSE
Professional	11%	6%	22%	14%
Quasi-professional	14	11	27	25
Citizen, meeting annually	12	10	30	24
Citizen, meeting biennially	16	11	34	34

[a]Calculated from Calvert (1979), who provides data on twenty-nine states, five with professional legislatures, six with quasi-professional ones, fifteen with citizen ones that meet annually, and three with citizen ones that meet biennially.

tures, although the differences across the types of legislatures have declined since the early 1970s. The rates of incumbents' defeat and retirement (choosing not to run) are also higher in the less profession-alized legislatures. These differences are the result of the character-istics of both the different types of legislatures and the kinds of people they attract. Professional legislatures attract more of Barber's law-makers, who wish to remain in office for longer periods than do the considerable numbers of spectators, reluctants, and advertisers who populate less professionalized bodies. Professional legislatures also offer more institutional resources to their members who wish to seek reelection. Higher salaries, more staff and related resources, and full-time efforts allow professional legislators to achieve higher public visibility and public awareness of their legislative accomplishments. Those resources create advantages, then, that enhance the prospects of being reelected.

As we observed earlier, all state legislatures have become more professionalized to some degree in recent decades. That is probably another part of the explanation for the general decline in turnover of members. But, as we also noted, the members of professional legis-latures have important advantages that probably account for their lower turnover. Incumbents in those institutions are better equipped to campaign for reelection, and fewer of them choose voluntarily to retire. Of course, some of the retirees from state legislatures leave to run for higher office. And one would expect to find an especially large number of legislators with such ambitions in professional bodies.

The preceding remarks about the amount of turnover have hinted at the reasons behind it. First, some portion of turnover is accounted for by the losses of incumbents in their bids for reelection. But incumbents are mostly successful in those efforts, and a variety of evidence summarized by Francis and Baker (1986) suggests that reelection losses account for only about one-third of total turnover nationwide. The remaining two-thirds is voluntary turnover as a re-sult of incumbents not seeking reelection.

Some members leave voluntarily because they have accom-plished their goals, others because they have been frustrated in their goals, and others because they have found the costs of legislative service too high relative to the rewards. Some of each of Barber's types of legislators might be included in all three of these categories. Reluctants, advertisers, and spectators might quickly accomplish what they hoped to achieve by way of doing their civic duty, gaining experience or exposure for their private-sector occupation, or enjoy-ing the show. Lawmakers, too, can reach a point where they have accomplished their public-policy agenda. If their original list of policy interests was short, they might quickly accomplish—or fail entirely to accomplish—everything on it. Alternatively, some lawmakers have ambitions for higher public office, such as the governorship or a congressional seat, where they might seek to accomplish other policy goals. Thus, some incumbents will retire from the state legislature to satisfy higher ambitions rather than because all of their ambitions have been fulfilled. In either case, however, they will have accomplished what they desired while in the legislature.

The group of legislators most likely to be frustrated in the pursuit of specific policy goals is Barber's lawmakers. Some of these individuals will be largely unsuccessful in their efforts. They may not be sufficiently skillful, they may be hampered in their efforts by more powerful adversaries, or they may be constrained by being a member of a minority party that is too small to win many legislative battles. Other types of legislators may suffer frustration while serving in the legislature, but it is likely to be different from that arising in the pursuit of explicit policy goals. Many will simply find the costs of the job too high and the rewards too small. The demands on one's time, the effort required, and the separation from one's family will finally wear down many legislators. And the hectic pace and conflictual nature of political life will finish off a good many more. Even many individuals who might endure these difficulties under some conditions, however, will not do so for long for the salaries and benefits provided by most legislatures.

POLITICAL INFLUENCES ON THE LEGISLATURE

To this point, we have concentrated on the technical, professional, and institutional aspects of legislatures, focusing on how they have or have not responded to the growth of the responsibilities of state governments. A preoccupation with these matters, however, could tend to obscure the fact that legislatures are political bodies. Their members and many of the individuals and groups who attempt to influence those members' decisions are driven by a variety of political motives. Political parties and interest groups, in particular, are important sources of some of the political influences on state legislatures.

POLITICAL PARTIES

Those members of a state legislature from the same political party may organize into highly cohesive groups that act together to pursue common policy interests—or they may not. There is considerable variation across the states with respect to this kind of party-based behavior, but political scientists have made only limited progress in unraveling the causes of that variation. Some states where party cohesion is notably high are Connecticut, Massachusetts, and New York (Patterson, 1983: 168). Perhaps not surprisingly, parties are especially fragmented and uncohesive in one-party states, such as many of those in the South. That is, where there is no significant rival party, the members of the dominant party often divide along lines of ideology, personal political interests, or urban-rural differences that distinguish their constituencies.

In general, it has been found that party cohesion is high—though not universal—in relatively urbanized and economically advanced states where legislators of different parties represent sharply different constituencies (Jewell, 1982: 15–16). In such states, that is, Democrats might typically represent working-class and lower-class areas, and Republicans might typically represent small-town, upper-class, or professional areas. Additionally, party cohesion is high where party organizations are strong, where they play an active role in recruiting candidates for office, and where they attempt to marshal strong organizational efforts within the legislature. As you may recall from Chapter 4, however, there are not very many states today in which the party organizations are truly strong in these terms.

Where parties are strong and cohesive, their leaders and even other partisan colleagues become important influences on the individual legislator's behavior. There are strong pressures to go along with the party when voting on proposed legislation. Of course, to the extent that a given party is homogeneous in terms of the constituencies it represents, there should be a high degree of unanimity on many policy questions. Party leaders in states where parties are not strong or cohesive will also attempt to influence members' behavior in similar ways, but they will generally be less successful.

INTEREST GROUPS

Representatives of interest groups have a significant influence on the behavior of all state legislatures. Chapter 5 revealed that a wide variety of such groups are active in state politics and that they pursue a variety of strategies to influence legislators: campaign assistance, direct lobbying, provision of research material on policy issues, lobbying the public, and occasionally even bribery. Many groups, then, will vie for the lawmaker's support using a range of techniques.

Although there is the potential for conflictual relations between lawmakers, and lobbyists, the typical relationship is more likely to be cordial and constructive. Most lawmakers are willing to work closely with some interest groups, those with a direct tie to the legislator's district or to one of his or her personal policy interests, as explained in Chapter 5. Thus, most of the time it is those groups with which legislators will meet and "do business."

The level of professionalization of the legislature, however, has a significant influence on the character of legislator-lobbyist relations. In citizen legislatures the average member is at a substantial disadvantage in dealing with the professional lobbyist. The legislator is likely to be a relative newcomer to the political scene, while the lobbyist will have been on the job for several years. The legislator may know but the barest of details about current state policy, while the lobbyist will be an expert in the policy fields in which he or she works. The legislator will have few research resources available for performing independent analysis of policy issues; the lobbyist, on the other hand, may have considerable information and research resources. The situation is entirely different, and therefore more balanced, in the more professionalized legislatures. Legislators here welcome hearing the points of view and policy arguments of some lobbyists. But they are also in a far better position to critique those points of view or even to develop substantial opposing arguments should they choose.

GOVERNORS

Governors also exert political pressures on legislatures to influence the lawmaking function. Despite the appearance of separation of powers, a governor in fact shares the lawmaking function with the legislature. As we mentioned earlier, governors can propose new laws. They lobby for and against particular bills a legislature is considering and can use the threat or the reality of a veto to increase their lawmaking power. Furthermore, governors often try to use their political party ties with legislators to develop cohesive party support for their own policy proposals. Governors exert, then, important political influence on the actions of most state legislators. We will discuss the governor's lawmaking role and the factors that can enhance or weaken it in more detail in Chapter 7.

CONCLUSION

State legislatures are at the heart of governmental efforts to respond to changing social and economic problems and to do so in accord with the public will. These institutions' abilities to fulfill their role have been considerably compromised, however, in the last generation or so. The agenda of state government has expanded dramatically, as has the complexity of the problems on that agenda. Many observers have argued that state legislatures must adapt as the complexity of their work increases. They should become more professional and should rely more heavily on systematic and scientific knowledge. All fifty state legislatures have moved in that direction since the early 1970s, but some have advanced much farther than others.

Professional legislatures certainly have their own shortcomings. They are very expensive, and they encourage the proliferation of full-time politicians—a species widely disliked by average Americans. Nonetheless, the quality of any state legislature's lawmaking, representation, and oversight is shaped by the extent of its professionalization. Furthermore, even the political context of legislative work is affected by the degree of professionalization. Citizen legislatures are more likely than professional legislatures to be dominated by economically powerful interest groups. Thus, if you know how professionalized the legislature of your own state is, then you have a clear indication of both the technical and the political character of its work.

NOTES

1. *Safire's Political Dictionary* (Safire, 1978: 553) defines "pork barrel" as "the state or national treasury, into which politicians and government officials dip for 'pork,' or funds for local projects."

2. In 1962 in *Baker* v. *Carr* and in 1964 in *Reynolds* v. *Sims*, the U.S. Supreme Court ruled that both houses of state legislatures had

to be regularly apportioned on the basis of population and that the populations of individual districts for either house had to be as equal as possible in size. Those requirements have been dubbed "one man, one vote" rules in light of the basis of representation they mandate.

3. The good-government group the Citizens Conference on State Legislatures recommended a minimum salary for state legislators of $10,000 a year in 1971. According to calculations by the Advisory Commission on Intergovernmental Relations (1985: 87), that salary would have been equal to $23,422 in 1981 if inflation in the intervening years was taken into account. The $30,000 salary cutoff for the legislatures we identify as professional is very close to that standard.

REFERENCES

Advisory Commission on Intergovernmental Relations. 1985. *The Question of State Government Capability.* Washington, D.C.: Advisory Commission on Intergovernmental Relations.

Barber, James David. 1965. *The Lawmakers: Recruitment and Adaptation to Legislative Life.* New Haven, Conn.: Yale University Press.

Calvert, Jerry. 1979. "Revolving Doors: Volunteerism in State Legislatures," *State Government* 51 (Autumn): 174–181.

Francis, Wayne L., and John R. Baker. 1986. "Why Do U.S. State Legislators Vacate Their Seats?" *Legislative Studies Quarterly* XI (February): 119–126.

Jewell, Malcolm E. 1982. *Representation in State Legislatures.* Lexington, Ky.: University of Kentucky Press.

Mladenka, Kenneth R., and Kim Quaile Hill. 1986. *Texas Government: Its Politics and Economics.* Pacific Grove, Calif.: Brooks/Cole.

National Conference of State Legislatures. 1987. *State Legislators' Occupations: A Decade of Change.* Denver, Colo.: National Conference of State Legislatures.

Niemi, Richard G., and Laura R. Winsky. 1987. "Membership Turnover in U.S. State Legislatures: Trends and Effects of Redistricting," *Legislative Studies Quarterly* XII (February): 115–124.

Oxendale, James R. 1981. "Membership Stability on Standing Committees in Legislative Lower Chambers," *State Government* 54 (4): 126–129.

Patterson, Samuel C. 1983. "Legislators and Legislatures in the American States," pp. 135–179 in Virginia Gray, Herbert Jacob, and Kenneth N. Vines (eds.), *Politics in the American States.* Boston: Little, Brown.

Pound, William T. 1986. "The State Legislatures," pp. 76–144 in *The Book of the States, 1986–87*. Lexington, Ky.: Council of State Governments.

Rosenthal, Alan. 1971. "The Scope of Legislative Reform: An Introduction," pp. 3–13 in Donald G. Herzberg and Alan Rosenthal (eds.), *Strengthening the States*. Garden City, N.Y.: Doubleday.

Rosenthal, Alan. 1981. *Legislative Life: People, Process, and Performance in the States*. New York: Harper & Row.

Safire, William. 1978. *Safire's Political Dictionary*. New York: Random House.

Shin, Kwang S., and John S. Jackson III. 1979. "Membership Turnover in U.S. State Legislatures: 1931–1976," *Legislative Studies Quarterly* IV (February): 95–104.

State of New Jersey. 1986. *Manual of the Legislature of New Jersey*. Trenton, N.J.: Edward J. Mullin.

Thompson, Joel A. 1986. "State Legislative Reform: Another Look, One More Time, Again," *Polity* XIX (Fall): 27–41.

Wahlke, John C., Heinz Eulau, William Buchanan, and LeRoy C. Ferguson. 1962. *The Legislative System*. New York: Wiley.

West, Karen A. 1985. *New Jersey: Spotlight on Government*. New Brunswick, N.J.: Rutgers University Press.

7 *Governors and State Executive Branches*

The growth in the size and responsibilities of state and local governments, which we described in earlier chapters, has posed substantial new problems of leadership and management in the executive branch of state government. That branch is, of course, charged with implementing the expanded agenda of state government. That branch is also where the greatest growth in size has occurred, and where the need for coordinating the responsibilities and activities of government is greatest.

Americans typically assume that the governor of their state can and should provide this coordination. The governor, that is, is expected to be the chief executive officer for the state. After all, isn't that what a governor is elected to do? Did not all the candidates for the office at the last election promise to do so? Some governors attempt to fulfill these public expectations. Some do not make much of an effort, and many fail even though they make a good try. Some, finally, cannot live up to these expectations because of the limitations of their office. To explain why this is the case, we must first consider how the role of the governor has evolved throughout this nation's history.

A HISTORY OF THE OFFICE OF GOVERNOR

Americans have not always expected political and administrative leadership from their state governors. In the early years of the United States, just the opposite was true. Then Americans remembered with distaste the arbitrary power that colonial governors exercised as they acted for the British crown. In consequence, Americans feared strong public executives, and they sharply limited the powers of governors after the Revolution. Herbert Kaufman (1956: 1058) has observed of the original thirteen states:

> The governors were reduced to figureheads with little influence in the making of governmental decisions. In ten of the states, the governors were elected by the legislatures, most of them for only one-year terms; in just one state did the governor have a veto, and even that was limited by present-day standards. Governors had few powers of appointment and removal, or of administrative supervision and control. They did not function as legislative leaders. Lacking in status and in constitutional and administrative strength, governors had no source of political strength, and they therefore remained subordinate to the legislatures in every respect.

Governors were weakened further in the 1830s and 1840s during the flowering of democratic government. The right to vote was extended widely in this period—at least to free white males. The semi-aristocratic elite that had governed the United States since before the Revolution was giving way to "men of the people," such as Andrew Jackson. And more ways were sought to increase public control of government. One of the ways in which public control was increased was by letting the voters elect more and more government officials. What could be more democratic? Why not elect every state officer from governor to sheriff? One consequence of this movement toward what has been termed the *long ballot* was that the executive power in state government became highly fragmented. The governor was only one of a large number of separately elected, relatively independent officers of the executive branch. Central authority was compromised in trying to realize this conception of democracy.

To make matters even worse, a second wave of governmental reform beginning in the 1870s further weakened the office of governor. State governments were beginning to take on a number of new functions in this period, as a result of the activities of the Populists and then the Progressives (described in Chapter 1). Two distinct motivations, however, shaped the manner in which government took on these functions. First, there was a widespread desire to minimize corruption among the government officials charged with these new tasks, as well as unfair influence over them by special interests. In this period Americans had witnessed extensive corruption and machine politics intended to accrue political spoils rather than to serve the public interest. Thus, many reformers sought a means to cleanse government of these influences. Second, it was believed that governmental decisions should be based as much as possible on technical and rational criteria. The social sciences were beginning to come of age in this period. Similarly, systematic theories of management were being developed for the growing business sector. Why not apply that knowledge and those theories to government? It was also believed that reliance on technical decision making would minimize partisan and special-interest influence on government.

One result of these developments was the structuring of new executive branch agencies as independent commissions. Typically, these were headed by a multimember board, of which each member was appointed by the governor with the approval of the legislature. Expertise in the matters that came under the board's supervision was often a requirement for appointment. Once appointed, the members of the board were highly independent of the governor and the legislature. The agency's budget was approved by the legislators, as were its general duties under state law. But the board would have wide discretion in the way it implemented the law and with regard to the day-to-day operations of the agency. In addition, board members served overlapping terms longer than that of the governor, so rarely could a single governor appoint a majority of the members. Nor could governors remove board members at will.

The implications of this second period of reform should be obvious. State government expanded dramatically in the period 1880–1920. Many new agencies were created; many new goals were established. Nobody, however, was in charge—or, more accurately, no single chief executive was empowered to coordinate and manage the state's executive branch. Power was highly fragmented. Many officials in the executive branch were beyond the direct control of the governor, the legislature, and, therefore, the electorate. Dissatisfaction with these problems did arise early in this century in some states, and a variety of reforms were implemented to strengthen the governor's role. Other states began to follow this lead in the 1930s and 1940s, after the Great Depression gave further evidence of the weaknesses of fragmented government. Then, when state and local governments began to expand very rapidly after 1950, all the states moved to some degree in this direction.

Since the 1950s, many governors' terms of office have been extended, and many of these officials have been allowed two or even an unlimited number of terms. The number of other officials who are popularly elected has been reduced in many states, and governors have been given greater authority over the executive branch. Enhanced budgetary power, control of policy implementation, and the staff necessary to carry out these responsibilities have been provided to many governors. Along with these institutional changes have come increased public expectations for governors. More and more, citizens expect candidates for the office to be strong leaders and aggressive chief executives. Legislatures in many states, at least, have developed similar expectations.

Unfortunately, the states have not participated equally in this movement toward stronger governorships. Some have advanced quite far and have established a formidable array of powers for their chief executives. Others lag far behind and still have governors with powers much like those of their nineteenth-century forerunners. Public expectations—both before a given candidate is elected and, very importantly, when he or she might run for reelection—are not as high in some states as in others. Thus, the caliber of gubernatorial candidates varies across the nation, as do public expectations about the performance of governors once they are in office. The trend, nonetheless, is toward strong and active individuals who will use the powers of the office aggressively.

THE ROLES OF THE MODERN GOVERNOR

What exactly do we mean when we say that more is expected of governors today? What, that is, are the specific tasks of the modern governor? Those tasks can be classified under five principal guber-

ACTING IN HIS ROLE OF CEREMONIAL LEADER, GOVERNOR DOUGLAS WILDER OF VIRGINIA ATTENDS A STATE DINNER ACCOMPANIED BY HIS DAUGHTER.

natorial roles: policy leader, legislative leader, chief executive officer, ceremonial leader, and party leader.

POLICY LEADER

The general public and the legislature increasingly expect governors to lead in the development of new state policies. Governors are expected to tackle the most pressing problems of their states when they take office, to prepare an agenda of proposed policies to address those problems, and to take on new problems as they arise. And candidates for the office typically reinforce these expectations with their laundry lists of promises about what they will do if elected.

LEGISLATIVE LEADER

Growing out of the role of policy leader is the necessity that the governor play an active part in the making of new law. Although state constitutions, just like the federal one, give the appearance of creating a strict division of powers among the legislative, executive, and judicial branches, that appearance is misleading. Governors have an important role in the lawmaking process. They are expected to propose new laws for the legislature to consider. Such proposals arise as a matter of course out of the policy agenda that most governors bring with them into office. In most states, governors also propose the budget of the executive branch for legislative consideration. They must lobby the legislature to get the bills they favor passed, and they typically use their party ties to help accomplish this. The veto power, finally, is the governor's ultimate bargaining tool and weapon in this process.

CHIEF EXECUTIVE OFFICER

It is also expected that the governor will be the chief executive officer, or boss of the executive branch. Most state constitutions imply that such should be the case, although the long ballot and the widespread use of board and commission agencies have often prevented it. Under reformed executive-branch systems and in line with contemporary public expectations, however, the governor can play this role. And it is a critically important one. Despite the fact that executive agencies are restricted by their legislative mandate, they typically have considerable discretion concerning how they carry out their tasks. Furthermore, new problems frequently arise that were not anticipated in the legislative design of agencies and programs. In their role as chief executives, governors can help ensure that agencies work in accord with both the spirit and the letter of the law as they employ their discretion and confront unanticipated problems.

It is important not to underestimate the difficulty of the role of chief executive officer. A governor who wishes to impose his or her ideas on a state's executive branch will encounter a number of hurdles that are created by the typical character of public-sector organizations. Lynn Muchmore (1981: 74) has observed:

> The governor will realize after only a few months in office that the executive branch, however it is organized, obeys no coherent set of goals or objectives. The responsibilities assigned to government are not the single product of one well-organized mind. They are the cumulative debris of legislative battles, court compromises, interest group demands, bureaucratic tradition, and federal mandate that has arrived from different perspectives, for different reasons, and at different points in time. Each one has an organizational counterpart, and each organization or suborganization has its own constituency. Few of these are as concerned about the overall architecture of government as they are with the narrow sliver of the public interest they believe they represent. All respect the governorship in the abstract and all treat the governor with deference, but none rely upon the governor to furnish them with an agenda.

Muchmore's observations testify to more than the difficulty of imposing the governor's will on any single agency. They also suggest the problems of providing central coordination across the variety of public agencies and programs in a state. Those difficulties are largely due to the size of state government today. Even the smallest state governments have over 10,000 employees, and the largest states employ over 300,000. And state budgets range from about $2 billion a year to over $80 billion. Big government has come to the states as well as the nation, and it necessitates a true chief executive to provide central coordination and control.

CEREMONIAL LEADER

Governors also have to kiss a lot of babies and shake a lot of hands—even after the election campaign is over. Citizens expect governors to do such things and would be dissatisfied if they did not. More is encompassed in this role, of course, than pressing flesh. At the most elevated level, governors represent the power and authority of the state on official and ceremonial occasions. They speak for the state on such occasions: a visit from foreign dignitaries or high federal officials, a celebration of a major state event, or a memorial service for victims of a disaster.

Despite the prosaic aspects of this role, it is an important one for the state and for the governor personally. The governor can bestow some of the symbolism and power of the office on the individuals, groups, or causes represented at any occasion he attends. And assuming ceremonial duties provides the governor with a free opportunity to improve public relations and a chance to emphasize the apparent power of his or her office.

PARTY LEADER

Finally, governors must try to lead their political parties. They attempt to sustain the support of their partisan colleagues in the legislature and of that part of the electorate that might vote for the party's nominees in the next election. All governors pursue these goals, because of the traditional importance of political parties in marshaling support for policy proposals (discussed in Chapter 4). The nature and importance of the role of party leader depend, however, on the partisan composition of the state government and the relative strength of the governor's party.

Governors in states where two-party competitiveness is the order of the day must be especially attentive to intraparty unity, because the threat from the other party is so substantial. Such governors should work diligently, then, at filling the role of party leader. The support of other members of the party in the state legislature is especially important in this situation for the success of the governor's policy agenda.

A governor whose party holds a lopsided numerical advantage over the opposition, on the other hand, will likely approach this role quite differently. Such governors may find party unity easy to maintain on some decisions and of only secondary importance on others. If a dominant party is large enough, it can withstand a relatively high level of internal disagreement and still remain successful. But the largest party in one-party states is often divided internally along ideological or sectional lines, and the governor has to bargain with one or more factions to maintain unity. These kinds of internal divisions may be far more important than the common party label under which the groups function. They may also mean that a workable consensus within a party is nearly impossible to achieve on some important issues.

Finally, a governor from a minority party must try not only to maintain the support of fellow partisans but to attract some from the rival party. Such a governor must make appeals, that is, to state legislators to rise above party considerations and support his or her policies.

THE DEMANDS OF THE GOVERNOR'S OFFICE

Our summary of the roles and responsibilities of the modern governor indicates that this is a highly demanding job. Vivid testimony to the accuracy of that conclusion is found in the reminiscences of former governors. Consider, as just two examples, the following remarks:

> Serving as governor of North Carolina is a job for three men. One man is needed to answer the mail and to carry on the detailed work of the office. A second one is needed to get out, make speeches, and travel around the state. The third man is needed for work with special projects . . . and to plan many things necessary to insure a good future for our state.
>
> Luther H. Hodges,
> governor of North Carolina, 1954–1958
> (Hodges, 1962: 298)

> From the moment of the oath of office to his supersession, death, resignation, incapacitation, or impeachment, [the governor] must resolve important issues almost hourly. No special session of the legislature will be called except by him. No convict will be pardoned or paroled unless he approves. No man or woman will be appointed to a state board, no vacancies in office filled, and no special elections called except at his direction. . . . Martial law will not be declared unless he declares it. The militia will not be called out unless he calls it. Only he can veto legislative acts, sign proclamations, and permit fugitives to be extradited. These are ordinary, almost routine prerogatives of the governor. The shock he feels upon assuming them does not derive from surprise but rather from the realization that all of these responsibilities and many more have descended upon him at once. There is no "warmup" period for the governor.
>
> Allan Shivers,
> governor of Texas, 1949–1957
> (Gantt et al., 1974: 197–198)

This testimony is all the more compelling because it comes from governors who were in office more than thirty years ago *and* served in states where the powers of the governor's office were relatively quite weak (we will compare gubernatorial powers later). The governorship in all the states is a considerably more demanding job today than when these two men served their terms in office.

A Day in the Life of a Governor

To suggest to newly elected governors how busy and hectic their job will be, the National Governors' Association prepared an account of a typical day in the life of a hypothetical governor. The complete diary for that one day is nine pages long, but even the briefer version presented here reveals how demanding this post is.

8:00–9:00 A.M.   The governor begins the day with office time set aside to read newspapers, mail, and telegrams. Dictates several letters and memoranda in response.

9:00   Receives a delegation of legislators and local officials who wish to lobby the governor over a highway project. At the end of the lobbying session has a pow-wow with one of the legislators over political party matters.

10:00   Participates in a ceremonial function—an awards ceremony and photo session to initiate National Cancer Week. At the end of the ceremony one person lobbies the governor to help with a problem his son is having with the U.S. Army. The governor pleads lack of jurisdiction, but passes the problem on to an aide.

10:30   Begins to return telephone calls but is interrupted by the press secretary for a statement for the news media about announced layoffs in the state TB hospital. Postpones two meetings originally scheduled for later in the morning to handle the telephone calls. Confers by phone with the heads of two state agencies, one of his own legislative aides, two state legislators, the budget director, and even his wife—all of whom press for certain policy changes or decisions from the governor. Must leave several other

	phone messages unanswered or calls unreturned.
12:00	Meets with budget director and state transportation officials over a highway funding problem. Confers with press secretary again over news reports about layoffs at the TB hospital. Gives an interview to a reporter about a fight in the governor's party over a mayoral campaign. Has secretary cancel his appearance at a highway ribbon-cutting ceremony scheduled for 1:00. Eats a quick and late lunch in his office.
1:15 P.M.	Talks to health director about TB hospital problems. Hears from a secretary that he has several calls protesting the firings. Decides to hold a meeting later in the day to pursue the matter further. Is briefed by secretary about several calls on different pending decisions.
1:45	Returns some calls, and puts off several aides waiting to see him.
2:12	Has extended meeting over TB hospital problem. Takes a call in the middle of the meeting from federal relations aide in Washington over another matter. Leaves meeting to confer with legal aide about a welfare rights lawsuit against the state.
3:20	Returns to TB hospital meeting, which finally concludes with a short-term solution. Instructs a press aide in how to communicate the decision to the press and state legislators.
3:35	Is briefed by a secretary on a long list of new calls, messages, and requests for meetings or returned calls—all of great urgency to the people requesting them. Meets with insurance commissioner—for a session that has been postponed twice before because of other pressing business. Even today, the meeting must be limited to a

CONTINUED

	few minutes instead of the two hours the commissioner desires. Meets with political advisor over three separate matters.
4:30	Calls the mayor who requested his presence at the highway ribbon cutting to apologize for missing it. Gets a request to handle yet another problem, which must be delegated to the state highway commissioner.
4:45	Has a meeting to resolve a controversy over the allocation of office space to state agencies. Leaves the meeting in progress to attend to other matters.
5:00	Handles more messages, makes phone calls, instructs secretary how to handle some problems, and then briefly reviews a short speech he will make at a dinner that evening with prominent businesspersons.
5:30	Attends meeting with his staff to schedule future political and administrative meetings and events. The list of items to be included is a long one.
6:00	Leaves for home accompanied by an aide who briefs him on problems in the state's community colleges *en route*.
6:40	Appears in receiving line to greet business lead-

FORMAL SOURCES OF GUBERNATORIAL POWER

If governors are to don a Superman suit and accomplish all the tasks described in the section on their roles, they must have the tools and powers to do so. They must, that is, be empowered in law to carry out their tasks. Scholars of the office of governor have identified several sources of such power (Beyle, 1982; Ransone, 1982: 27–47; Schlesinger, 1965).

	ers arriving for dinner. Discusses various state policy issues over and after dinner.
9:45	Retires to family quarters in the governor's mansion. Reads memoranda from his staff and signs letters.
10:15	Quits work for the day, leaving a number of items on the day's agenda unresolved.

This day's schedule vividly attests to the demands imposed on a governor. All those public officials, legislators, and lobbying citizens expect the governor to solve their problems. The National Governors' Association also observed the following about this schedule, which indicates that immediate pressures and unanticipated problems can push aside long-term plans and policies.

[It] cover[s] a quiet time without a major crisis (prison riot, natural disaster) or having the legislature in session. It suggests a governor's constant need to make choices in the use of his [or her] own time and, more important, to avoid becoming a captive of the pressures on him [or her]. In a day such as the one described, it is hard to imagine the governor contemplating, much less doing much about, his [or her] broad strategies for government leadership and public affairs.

> *Source:* Adapted from National Governors' Association, *Governing the American States: A Handbook for New Governors* (Washington, D.C.: Center for Policy Research, 1978), 10–20.

TENURE POTENTIAL

Scholars have come to use the rather awkward term *tenure potential* to describe one of the most elementary, but critical, sources of gubernatorial power: the opportunity to stay in office. Under the heavy nineteenth-century restrictions on their powers, governors typically served only two-year terms. And many states disallowed running for reelection. Such limits on the term of office made it difficult for governors to develop and carry out even a modestly ambitious policy agenda. There was little time for them to learn the ropes of the office, and frequent elections meant that they had to spend an inordinate amount of time campaigning instead of running the government.

Twentieth-century reformers have sought an extension of the term of office to four years, with few, if any, restrictions on the number of times a person might run for reelection. By 1989, forty-seven of the states had adopted a four-year term of office, but twenty-five states limit the governor to two terms and three others prohibit successive terms. Thus, considerable progress has been made nationwide in expanding governors' tenure potential. Getting to remain in the governor's mansion a long time is, of course, merely a prerequisite to fulfilling the roles outlined earlier. More substantial powers must be available for a governor to succeed at the jobs associated with the office today.

THE UNIFIED EXECUTIVE

Reformers have argued that state executive systems ought to be modeled after that of the federal government, where the president and vice-president are elected as a team and the president has the power to appoint the principal officials who will run the government. State governments have traditionally deviated considerably from this standard in their use of the long ballot and of board and commission agencies. Only modest progress has been made toward this goal in recent decades. Twenty-three states have adopted team elections for the governor and lieutenant governor. The overwhelming majority of states, however, and even many of those twenty-three, still have plural, relatively independent executives. Most states still require the separate election of a number of key officials such as the secretary of state, the attorney general, and the state treasurer. Some even allow the legislature to elect one or more of these executive-branch officials. Only Alaska, Hawaii, New Jersey, and New York approximate a unified executive in which the governor has the power to fill such principal state offices by appointment.

Better progress has been made with respect to the governor's power to appoint the heads of state agencies. As we observed earlier, state governments have considerably expanded their functions, and thus the number and variety of their executive agencies, in recent decades. In those states where there was a desire for a strong chief executive, governors have been given the power to hire and fire the heads of many agencies. Beyle and Dalton (1981) calculated, for example, that the average governor in 1980 could appoint 47 percent of the principal administrative officials in forty-eight key functional areas of government. Yet the range around that average was quite wide. The strongest governor in these terms was that of New York, who could appoint 87 percent of the principal administrative officials. At the other extreme, the governor of South Carolina could appoint only 21 percent of them.

ORGANIZATIONAL CONTROL OF THE EXECUTIVE BRANCH

Closely related to achieving a unified executive is strengthening the governor's general administrative control over the executive branch. A number of specific powers might be granted to the governor to enhance this control. These include increasing the number of agencies reporting directly to the governor, reducing the number of state agencies so as to consolidate and streamline the entire executive branch under closer gubernatorial control, and granting the governor the power to reorganize all or a portion of the executive branch structure (Beyle, 1982). Many of these reforms might be implemented regardless of how unified the executive branch is, as discussed in the preceding subsection. And, as H. Edward Flentje (1981: 78–79) has observed,

> the administrative power of organization—the power to create and abolish offices and to assign and reassign purposes, authorities, and duties to these offices—is critical to the governor as manager, for it may be used to confer organizational status and give certain programs, purposes, and constituencies higher priority and easier access than others.

The ultimate form of organizational control is, then, the power to reorganize the agencies of the executive branch to suit one's policy and administrative goals as governor. Twenty-four of the nation's governors have this power today (Council of State Governments, 1990: 67–68). Table 7-1 indicates which governors are empowered through the existence of a unified executive and through organizational control of the executive branch by presenting state-by-state comparisons on four indicators of these two traits. On the basis of these comparisons, the governors of Massachusetts, New Hampshire, New Jersey, New York, Pennsylvania, and Virginia are especially powerful. At the other extreme, those of Georgia, Mississippi, South Carolina, and Texas are especially weak in these terms.

TABLE 7-1
THE UNIFIED EXEC-
UTIVE AND ORGANI-
ZATIONAL CONTROL
POWERS OF THE
GOVERNORS

STATE	TEAM ELECTION WITH LIEUTENANT GOVERNOR	NUMBER OF OTHER EXECUTIVE BRANCH ELECTED OFFICIALS	PERCENTAGE OF MAJOR EXECUTIVE POSITIONS GOVERNOR APPOINTS	POWER TO REORGANIZE EXECUTIVE BRANCH
Alabama	no	17	46%	no
Alaska	yes	1	40	yes
Arizona	a	8	45	no
Arkansas	no	6	44	no
California	no	6	47	yes
Colorado	yes	4	49	no
Connecticut	yes	5	57	no
Delaware	no	5	39	yes
Florida	yes	6	37	yes
Georgia	no	12	32	yes
Hawaii	yes	14	44	no
Idaho	no	6	53	no
Illinois	yes	14	67	yes
Indiana	yes	6	50	no
Iowa	yes	6	61	no
Kansas	yes	15	48	yes
Kentucky	no	7	48	yes
Louisiana	no	21	68	yes
Maine	a	0	54	no
Maryland	yes	3	51	yes
Massachusetts	yes	5	64	yes
Michigan	yes	35	45	yes
Minnesota	yes	5	46	yes
Mississippi	no	13	26	yes
Missouri	no	5	36	yes
Montana	yes	10	36	yes
Nebraska	yes	26	45	no
Nevada	no	23	45	no
New Hampshire	a	5	60	no
New Jersey	a	0	56	no

TABLE 7-1
CONTINUED

STATE	TEAM ELECTION WITH LIEUTENANT GOVERNOR	NUMBER OF OTHER EXECUTIVE BRANCH ELECTED OFFICIALS	PERCENTAGE OF MAJOR EXECUTIVE POSITIONS GOVERNOR APPOINTS	POWER TO REORGANIZE EXECUTIVE BRANCH
New Mexico	yes	8	50%	yes
New York	yes	3	92	no
North Carolina	no	9	50	yes
North Dakota	yes	13	40	no
Ohio	yes	28	53	no
Oklahoma	no	9	37	yes
Oregon	a	5	30	no
Pennsylvania	yes	4	62	no
Rhode Island	no	4	41	no
South Carolina	no	8	16	no
South Dakota	yes	9	38	yes
Tennessee	no	3	45	no
Texas	no	29	28	no
Utah	yes	14	42	no
Vermont	no	5	54	yes
Virginia	no	2	74	yes
Washington	no	8	45	no
West Virginia	a	5	46	yes
Wisconsin	yes	5	35	no
Wyoming	a	4	56	no

[a]No lieutenant governor.

Source: Council of State Governments, *Book of the States, 1990–91* (Lexington, Ky.: Council of State Governments, 1990), pp. 242–252, 259–260.

BUDGETARY POWER

The majority of states have given the governor the power to prepare a proposed state budget for the consideration of the legislature. Reformers interested in strengthening the chief executive have long recognized the importance of budgetary power for developing policy and controlling executive agencies. Today the governors of forty-two states—all except Colorado, Kentucky, Louisiana, Mississippi, New Mexico, North Carolina, South Carolina, and Texas—have this power. In those other eight states, the power is shared with the legislature.

LEGISLATIVE POWERS

Either through law or by custom, all fifty governors have acquired a number of powers in the legislative process. All of them can make specific recommendations about new laws to the legislature. Many are either required by law or expected by custom to make periodic "state of the state" addresses to the legislature proposing new policy initiatives. Governors can also call the legislature into special session, and most of them can set at least part of the agenda to be considered in a special session. Finally, all but one of the governors, that of North Carolina, have veto powers over bills passed by the legislature.

The ability to veto bills passed by the legislature is both a tool and a bargaining device for the governor with regard to his or her participation in the lawmaking process. The veto power has always been limited; in some states it did not even exist before the reforms of this century. The simplest form of the veto allows the governor to reject a given bill in its entirety, thereby necessitating an extraordinary overriding vote by the legislature (in which a majority, three-fifths, or two-thirds, as examples, of the legislators vote to override the veto) for the bill to become law. Additional forms of the veto have also been developed: with an *item veto* a governor rejects only a portion—or a single line item—in a budget bill, and with an *amendatory veto* a governor returns a bill to the legislature with specific recommendations for revision, which, if enacted, will forestall his or her vetoing of the bill.

All the states except North Carolina allow the governor at least the simplest form of veto. Forty-three allow some form of the item veto, and four have enacted some version of the amendatory veto. Gerald Benjamin (1982: 104) argues, however, that the latter form of veto has developed in a number of other states by custom. Finally, we should note that the veto is a truly formidable power because of the infrequency with which it is overridden in most states. Charles Wiggins (1980) has shown that, on average, governors' vetoes are overridden only about 6 percent of the time.

POWERS ASSOCIATED WITH INTERGOVERNMENTAL RELATIONS

Governors have always been seen as a principal voice for the state in dealings with the federal government. This role of spokesperson arises more out of convenience and public expectation, however, than law. The governor will, however, receive and send many of the formal communications that pass between these two levels of government. Governors often lobby Congress or particular federal agencies, as well, for policies of interest to their states.

Under federal law governors have been accorded some more substantial powers in this area. Some cooperative federal-state programs require that the governor designate the state agency that will actually implement the program's activities. Some federal grants require that the governor review and sign all requests for funds made by state agencies. Other federal programs, such as those that designate local disaster areas, require that the governor initiate a state's request for federal assistance or other policy action. These federal laws and programs, then, make the governor a central actor in a number of policy areas.

As testimony to the importance of governors' activities in this area, a survey of governors who served in the period 1960–1980 revealed that they devoted about one workday a week, on average, to concerns associated with relations with the federal government (Grady, 1984). Furthermore, almost half of the governors responding to the survey indicated that they would advise newly elected governors to spend even more time on such matters.

SIZE OF THE GOVERNOR'S STAFF

Recognizing the complexity of the governor's duties, all the states provide for professional and clerical staff support in the governor's office. Typically included among the professional members of a governor's office are policy advisors, administrative assistants, public relations specialists, budget specialists, and liaison staff to communicate with the state legislature and the federal government. A sizable professional staff can be a source of considerable power for a governor. A large staff can extend the breadth of the governor's information-gathering, decision-making, and organizational powers. However, the size of the governor's staff and, therefore, the extent to

The Organizational and Staff Structure of the New York Governor's Office

EXECUTIVE DEPARTMENT

THE GOVERNOR

Mario M. Cuomo became Governor January 1, 1983, reelected on November 4, 1986, term expires December 31, 1990. Salary $130,000.

GOVERNOR'S STAFF

Secretary of the Governor	Gerald C. Crotty
Counsel to the Governor	Evan A. Davis
Special Counsel to the Governor	Fabrian G. Palomino
Director of State Operations and Policy Management	Henrik N. Dullea
Counselor and Press Secretary to the Governor	Gary G. Fryer
Director of Criminal Justice	John J. Poklemba
Director of Economic Development	Vincent Tese
Director and Washington Counsel to the Governor	Brad C. Johnson
Assistant to the Governor for Management and Productivity	Thea Hoeth
Executive Assistants to the Governor	Pamela U. Broughton
	Mary A. Tragale
Deputy Press Secretary to the Governor	Anne W. Crowley
Deputy Director of State Operations and Policy Management	Mary Ann Crotty

which it can provide policy, administrative, or other support to the governor varies widely among the states.

The organization and functions of the governor's staff also vary across the states, making direct comparisons somewhat difficult. Yet the formal organization of the governor's office—as it is reported in the official records of the individual states—is probably a good general indication of how generous the support provided to the governor is. The Council of State Governments reports that the average gov-

First Assistant Counsel to the Governor   Patricia K. Bucklin
Assistant Counsels to the Governor Patrick E. Brown, Lise Gelernter
              Nancy G. Groenwegen, Hermes A. Fernandez
              Harold N. Iselin, Phyllis Taylor, Ben Wiles
Deputy Secretaries to the Governor
    Senior Deputy Secretary to the Governor   Andrew J. Zambelli
    Deputy Secretary to the
        Governor   Francis J. Murray, Jr., Michael J. Dowling
Director of Administration   Ellen E. Conovitz
Director, Correspondence Control   Vincent A. Scalzo
Director, New York City Office   Mary A. Tragale
Director of Research   Robert J. Sullivan
Director, Scheduling   Howard B. Glaser

Divisions and Commissions

Adirondack Park Agency   Herman F. Cole, Jr.—Chairman
Advocate for the Disabled,
    Office of the   Frances G. Berko—Advocate
Aging, Office for the   Jane G. Gould—Acting Director
Alcoholic and Beverage Control,
    Division of   Thomas A. Duffy, Jr.—Chairman
Alcoholism and Alcohol Abuse,
    Division of   Marguerite T. Saunders—Director
Arts, Council on the   Kitty Carlisle Hart—Chairperson
Black Affairs, Advisory Committee for   Bernard Charles—Chairman
Budget, Division of the   Dall W. Forsythe—Director
Business Permits and Regulatory Assistance,
    Office of   Ruth S. Walters—Director
Cable Television, Commission on   William B. Finneran—Chairman

CONTINUED

ernor's staff numbered 51 in 1990. The largest was that of New York with 216 positions; that of Wyoming ranked last with a mere 8 staff positions (Council of State Governments, 1990: 65).

To illustrate how substantial these staff resources can be, the box on the New York governor's office presents the staff and organizational support associated with that office. The governor of New York heads the Executive Department, one of twenty departmental divisions of the executive branch of that state's government. Those

Children and Families,
      Council on   Joseph J. Cocozza, Ph.D.—Director
Consumer Protection Board,
      State   Richard M. Kessel—Chairman and Executive Director
Correction, State Commission of   William G. McMahon—Chairman
Crime Control Planning Board   Richard L. Gelb—Chairman
Crime Victims Board   Catherine M. Abate—Chairperson
Criminal Justice Services,
      Division of   John J. Poklemba—Commissioner
Developmental Disabilities Planning
      Council   Isabel T. Mills—Executive Director
Emergency Management Office, State   Donald A. DeVito—Director
Employee Relations, Office of   Elizabeth D. Moore—Director
Energy Office, State   William D. Cotter—Commissioner
Equalization and Assessment,
      Division of   David H. Gaskell—Director
Financial Control Board,
      New York State   Philip R. Michael—Executive Director
General Services, Office of   John C. Egan—Commissioner
Hispanic Affairs, Office of   Shirley Rodriguez-Remeneski—Director
Housing and Community Renewal,
      Division of   Richard L. Higgins—Commissioner
Human Rights, Division of   Douglas H. White—Commissioner
Interdepartmental Traffic Safety
      Committee   Patricia B. Adduci—Commissioner
Lottery, Division of the   Russell V. Gladieux—Acting Director
Military and Naval Affairs,
      Division of   Major General Lawrence P. Flynn
Minority and Women's Business Development,
      Office of   Stephanie M. Brown—Director

individuals listed as the Governor's Staff in the box provide the most direct support to the governor. Those listed under Divisions and Commissions advise the governor on specialized policy concerns and implement a variety of programs housed in the Executive Department. Clearly, the governor of New York presides over an office that encompasses a great breadth of planning, policy-making, and administrative expertise.

Parks, Recreation and Historic Preservation,
    Office of   Orin Lehman—Commissioner
Parole, State Board of   Ramon J. Rodriguez—Chairman
Probation, Division of   Edmund B. Wutzer—Director
Quality of Care for the Mentally Disabled,
    State Commission on   Clarence J. Sundram—Chairman
Racing and Wagering Board,
    New York State   Richard F. Corbisiero, Jr.—Chairman
Rural Affairs, Office of   Joseph Gerace—Director
St. Lawrence–Eastern Ontario
    Commission   Daniel J. Palm—Director
State Police, Division of   Thomas A. Constantine—Superintendent
Substance Abuse Services, Division of   Julio A. Martinez—Director
Veterans' Affairs, Division of   Thomas Lewis—Director
Voluntary Service, Office for   Joyce M. Black—Director
Women's Division   Judith I. Avner—Director
Youth, Division for   Leonard G. Dunston—Director

The Governor's Military Staff

The staff of the Governor consists of the Chief of Staff to the Governor and not more than eighteen aides, sixteen being detailed by the Governor from the commissioned officers of the National Guard or Naval Militia, and two from officers on the National Guard reserve or State reserve list. Officers so detailed shall not be relieved from their ordinary duties except when actually on duty with the Governor.

    The Adjutant General—Major General Lawrence P. Flynn
    Deputy Adjutant General—Major General Martin E. Lind

Source: New York Red Book, 1989–90 (Albany, N.Y.: Williams Press, 1989), pp. 462–463.

INTERSTATE COMPARISON OF GOVERNORS' FORMAL POWERS

To provide a summary measure of the relative formal powers of the fifty governors, Beyle (1990) developed a power index based on assessments of tenure potential, appointive power, budget-making power, budget-changing power, veto power, and the strength of the governor's party in the legislature. Although the index does not encompass all the areas of formal power discussed above, it is useful for comparing the governors.

Table 7-2 reproduces the separate and composite scores derived by Beyle. The separate components are scored on a range of 1–5 or 1–7, with higher scores indicating greater formal power in that area. The composite score (total index) derived from summing the compo-

TABLE 7-2
A SUMMARY ASSESS-
MENT OF THE GOV-
ERNORS' FORMAL
POWERS

STATE	TENURE POTENTIAL	APPOINT-IVE POWER	BUDGET-MAKING POWER	BUDGET-CHANGING POWER	VETO POWER	POLITICAL STRENGTH IN LEGISLATURE	TOTAL INDEX
Alabama	4	4	5	1	4	1	19
Alaska	4	5	5	1	5	3	23
Arizona	5	3	5	1	5	2	21
Arkansas	4	5	5	1	4	5	24
California	5	4	5	1	5	2	22
Colorado	5	5	4	1	5	2	22
Connecticut	5	4	5	1	5	4	24
Delaware	4	5	5	1	5	3	23
Florida	4	4	5	1	5	2	21
Georgia	4	2	5	1	5	5	22
Hawaii	4	4	5	1	5	5	24
Idaho	5	3	5	1	5	2	21
Illinois	5	5	5	1	5	2	23
Indiana	4	6	5	1	1	3	20
Iowa	5	5	5	1	5	2	23
Kansas	4	5	5	1	5	4	24
Kentucky	3	5	4	1	4	4	21
Louisiana	4	4	4	1	5	5	23
Maine	4	5	5	1	2	2	19
Maryland	4	5	5	5	5	5	29
Massachusetts	5	6	5	1	5	5	27
Michigan	5	4	5	1	5	3	23
Minnesota	5	5	5	1	5	4	25
Mississippi	4	2	5	1	5	5	22
Missouri	4	4	5	1	5	2	21
Montana	5	3	5	1	5	3	22
Nebraska	4	3	5	4	5	3	24

nent ones has a possible range of 6–32. No governor has a perfect score on Beyle's index, but the governors of Maryland, Massachusetts, New York, and West Virginia rate quite highly. At the other extreme, the governors of North Carolina, Rhode Island, and Texas have relatively limited powers. Thus, Beyle's index provides ample additional evidence for the wide differences in the governors' formal powers and, hence, their opportunities to fulfill the demands of their office.

TABLE 7-2
CONTINUED

STATE	TENURE POTENTIAL	APPOINTIVE POWER	BUDGET-MAKING POWER	BUDGET-CHANGING POWER	VETO POWER	POLITICAL STRENGTH IN LEGISLATURE	TOTAL INDEX
Nevada	4	4	5	1	2	3	19
New Hampshire	2	4	5	1	2	4	18
New Jersey	4	5	5	1	5	4	24
New Mexico	3	4	4	1	5	2	19
New York	5	5	5	3	5	3	26
North Carolina	4	5	5	1	0	2	17
North Dakota	5	4	5	1	5	3	23
Ohio	4	5	5	1	5	3	23
Oklahoma	4	2	5	1	5	2	19
Oregon	4	5	5	1	5	4	24
Pennsylvania	4	5	5	1	5	3	23
Rhode Island	2	4	5	1	2	1	15
South Carolina	4	2	4	1	5	2	18
South Dakota	4	4	5	1	5	4	23
Tennessee	4	6	5	1	4	4	24
Texas	5	2	1	1	5	2	16
Utah	5	4	5	1	5	4	24
Vermont	2	5	5	1	2	3	18
Virginia	3	5	5	1	5	4	23
Washington	5	3	5	1	5	3	22
West Virginia	4	4	5	5	4	5	27
Wisconsin	5	4	5	1	5	2	22
Wyoming	5	4	5	1	5	2	22
Average Score	4.2	4.2	4.8	1.3	4.4	3.1	22.0

Source: Thad L. Beyle, "Governors," pp. 201–251 in Virginia Gray, Herbert Jacob, and Robert B. Albritton (eds.), *Politics in the American States*, 5th ed. (Glenview, Ill.: Scott, Foresman, 1990).

INFORMAL SOURCES OF GUBERNATORIAL POWER

The formal powers described above—those derived from law and organizational authority—are an important, but not the exclusive, reason for gubernatorial success. Another quite important source of that success includes what can be called informal powers. These are not based in law but arise instead out of custom, opportunity, or individual skill.

PUBLIC EXPECTATIONS FOR THE OFFICE

The informal gubernatorial powers are important mainly because of public expectations as to what governors should do. Because many Americans *think* their governor is powerful, *assume* that the governor should fill the roles we described earlier, and *evaluate* candidates for the office based on such criteria, governors can draw on these public expectations as a source of power. Governors can argue to the legislature, for example, that they have been elected to assume policy and administrative leadership and to participate as a coequal in the lawmaking process. They can make the same argument to other elected state officials and to the heads of executive agencies over whom they might otherwise have little or no control. Not all governors have been successful in turning public expectations to their advantage, however, and the extent to which they can do so depends on how skillful they are as political leaders.

PERSONAL POLITICAL SKILLS

A broad grant of formal powers presents only an opportunity and not a guarantee of power to a governor. Similarly, although very limited formal powers will surely restrict a governor's ability to fill the range of roles described earlier, personal political skills will help some individuals minimize that obstacle. In short, any governor's success will be contingent to some degree on his or her political skills: the power of persuasion, the ability to bargain successfully and to create support for policy proposals, and the extent to which he or she has that hard-to-define quality of leadership.

Politically skillful governors take maximum advantage of their formal powers. Whether those powers are substantial or scanty, in other words, some governors will push them to, and even beyond, their apparent limits. In addition, skillful governors use two other opportunities to enhance their power, arising out of their ceremonial and party roles.

THE SYMBOLISM OF THE ROLE OF CHIEF OF STATE

As we observed earlier, every governor must be a ribbon cutter, an honorary proclamation declarer, and a baby kisser. Some carry out these duties with indifference or even disgust; some prize them as an escape from the more serious work of their job. But the sophisticated ones know how important these symbolic duties are for maintaining public support and increasing gubernatorial power.

Such duties are, first, opportunities for free public relations and advertising for the governor. They keep the governor in the public eye and indicate his or her interest in the concerns of many groups of citizens. Additionally, carrying out these duties reinforces the image of the governor as the most important officer of the state and gives the governor the *appearance* of power and authority. Skillful politicians, once again, try to use these opportunities to build and maintain high public support for their role and power as governor.

OPPORTUNITIES FOR PARTY LEADERSHIP

The fact that the governor is accorded at least the ceremonial leadership of his or her political party within the state offers another opportunity to enhance gubernatorial power. Typically, governors have only informal power here, for most state political parties are highly decentralized and have only a loose leadership structure. Because campaign styles have changed (as described in Chapter 4, candidates now tend to fashion their own campaigns separate from the work of the party organization), the power the governor can acquire by being the leader of the formal party apparatus is limited. Nonetheless, governors can draw on their leadership position in the party, even if it is only a symbolic one, and those who are particularly skillful will use this resource to great advantage.

CHARACTERISTICS OF TODAY'S GOVERNORS

The likelihood that governors will fill the roles expected of them today is conditioned by the character of the individuals who seek this office. Their preparation for the job, their administrative and political skills, and their ambition are all relevant to their ultimate records in office. Even the motivations that lead them to run for public office—and to depart from it—may be important here. A consideration of some of the personal characteristics of governors, then, is important to a complete understanding of what they can achieve.

A PROFILE OF THE CONTEMPORARY GOVERNOR

The typical governor is a middle-aged male with a professional background in law or business who served in another elected state office before winning election to the governorship. An investigation of governors' backgrounds in 1984 indicated that thirty-one claimed their profession to be law and twelve referred to themselves as businessmen. No other occupational background was claimed by more than two governors. The large number of lawyers suggests the relatively high educational status of governors. Virtually all of them have a college degree, and many, including the lawyers, hold advanced degrees of some kind. Of those forty-four governors for whom sufficient information was available to trace their pregubernatorial careers, twenty-six had served previously in another statewide elected office. Among the remainder, seven had come to the governorship from the state legislature, three from the federal bureaucracy, two from Congress, and one from local government (Council of State Governments, 1984: 49–50).

You should also recall that getting elected governor is an expensive undertaking. As we noted in Chapter 4, the average campaign expenditure reported by successful candidates in recent gubernatorial elections was over $3 million, and in quite a number of states the cost was much higher than that average. Thus, to be competitive in their campaigns, candidates must marshal considerable financial resources.

A candidate who is successful in a bid for the governorship will step into a position that generally has a number of perks. Contemporary governors enjoy a variety of benefits and resources, which suggests that the office is one of high status and power. Table 7-3 summarizes the salary, staff, and transportation resources enjoyed by all fifty governors, as well as indicating whether each state provides an official residence. Although these perks vary across the states, as do the formal powers of the governor discussed earlier, they are typically rather generous.

TABLE 7-3
THE PERKS OF THE
GOVERNOR'S OFFICE

STATE	GOVERNOR'S SALARY	SIZE OF GOVERNOR'S STAFF	STATE-PROVIDED TRANSPORTATION			OFFICIAL RESIDENCE
			AUTO	PLANE	HELICOPTER	
Alabama	$ 70,223	22	yes	yes	yes	yes
Alaska	81,648	67	yes	yes	yes	yes
Arizona	75,000	50	yes	yes	yes	no
Arkansas	35,000	48	yes	no	no	yes
California	85,000	86	yes	no	no	yes
Colorado	70,000	42	yes	yes	no	yes
Connecticut	78,000	38	yes	no	no	yes
Delaware	80,000	22	yes	no	yes	yes
Florida	100,883	129	yes	yes	no	yes
Georgia	88,872	55	yes	yes	yes	yes
Hawaii	94,780	28	yes	no	no	yes
Idaho	55,000	16	yes	yes	no	yes
Illinois	93,266	173	yes	yes	yes	yes
Indiana	77,200	34	yes	yes	yes	yes
Iowa	72,500	10	yes	yes	no	yes
Kansas	73,137	22	yes	yes	no	yes
Kentucky	69,731	78	yes	yes	yes	yes
Louisiana	66,060	46	yes	yes	yes	yes
Maine	70,000	21	yes	yes	no	yes
Maryland	85,000	104	yes	yes	yes	yes
Massachusetts	75,000	81	yes	yes	yes	no
Michigan	106,690	45	yes	yes	yes	yes
Minnesota	103,860	30	yes	yes	yes	yes
Mississippi	75,600	39	yes	yes	yes	yes
Missouri	88,541	34	yes	yes	no	yes

CONTINUED

TABLE 7-3
CONTINUED

STATE	GOVERNOR'S SALARY	SIZE OF GOVERNOR'S STAFF	STATE-PROVIDED TRANSPORTATION			OFFICIAL RESIDENCE
			AUTO	PLANE	HELICOPTER	
Montana	$ 51,713	24	yes	yes	yes	yes
Nebraska	58,000	16	yes	yes	yes	yes
Nevada	70,857	17	yes	no	no	yes
New Hampshire	75,753	27	yes	no	no	yes
New Jersey	85,000	60	yes	no	yes	yes
New Mexico	90,000	38	yes	yes	yes	yes
New York	130,000	216	yes	yes	yes	yes
North Carolina	123,000	86	yes	yes	yes	yes
North Dakota	65,196	19	yes	yes	no	yes
Ohio	65,000	60	yes	yes	yes	yes
Oklahoma	70,000	34	yes	yes	no	yes
Oregon	77,500	44	yes	no	no	yes
Pennsylvania	85,000	60	yes	yes	no	yes
Rhode Island	69,000	47	yes	yes	yes	yes
South Carolina	84,897	30	yes	yes	yes	yes
South Dakota	60,819	26	yes	yes	no	yes
Tennessee	85,000	40	yes	yes	yes	yes
Texas	93,432	178	no	yes	yes	yes
Utah	69,992	18	yes	yes	no	yes
Vermont	75,800	21	yes	no	no	no
Virginia	85,000	36	yes	yes	yes	yes
Washington	96,700	37	yes	yes	no	yes
West Virginia	72,000	30	yes	yes	yes	yes
Wisconsin	86,149	38	yes	yes	no	yes
Wyoming	70,000	8	yes	yes	no	yes

Source: Council of State Governments, *Book of the States, 1990–91* (Lexington, Ky.: Council of State Governments, 1990), pp. 65–66.

The preceding discussion suggests that the typical contemporary governor is a mature individual who is well educated, professionally and politically experienced, has substantial material resources for carrying out his or her job, and therefore ought to be well prepared for the office in many ways. More is required, however, than maturity, education, experience in business or government, and material resources to be a successful governor. A good bit of luck may be helpful, and the candidate can bring other important traits to the job. Unappealing as it may sound to some, we suspect a critical one of those traits is ambition: what the newly elected governor wishes to achieve while he or she is in office.

GUBERNATORIAL AMBITIONS

As recently as the 1950s, governors were widely criticized as a group for being of limited ability and ambition. Thinking of leaders of state governments in general, the newspaper columnist James Reston commented in 1962 that "the state capitols are over their heads in problems and up to their knees in midgets." Although there were, of course, exceptions, governors were frequently among the "shortest" of state officials. Even today the office of governor in some states suffers from the reputation—and sometimes the reality—of having limited power. Thus, many ambitious individuals seeking public careers believe that they can achieve more elsewhere: in the state legislature, in Congress, or even in local government. Many of the potentially best candidates, then, have avoided the governorship and pursued more attractive alternatives.

The governorship has therefore often been a modest prize fought over by "midgets." The office has also often been filled by aging politicians who have long, if not necessarily admirably, served their state in the legislature or some other elected post. Being governor is a tribute or reward rather than a challenge to such individuals. Many governors prize the job, then, for its ceremonial significance and give proportionately less attention to its policy-making and leadership functions. By the time such individuals are elected to the governorship they have used up most of the ambition they had when they first entered politics. Such people do not *want* to achieve much as governor, in other words. Individuals of this kind who enter an office widely perceived to be a weak one will not be successful in fulfilling the demanding expectations we outlined earlier. Even when the office has substantial formal powers, the limited ambitions of many of those elected to it are such that those powers may be little used.

It is widely argued, however, that most contemporary governors are quite different from the midgets of old. Larry Sabato (1983) has made this argument most forcefully, pointing out that contemporary governors are more ambitious and activist. They see the office not as an end in itself, but as an opportunity to do great things. Many of them also see it as a steppingstone to higher public office. There is, Sabato says, a new breed of governors in the United States.

Jimmy Carter and Ronald Reagan are examples of this new breed of governors. Both had ambitious political agendas that carried them, first, to the governor's mansion in their respective states and then to the White House. (It is notable that the last state governor to become President before Jimmy Carter won the office in 1976 was Franklin Delano Roosevelt in 1932.) Many current governors appear interested in sustaining this new political prominence for their office. A number of governors were active candidates for the presidency in 1988, and Michael Dukakis of Massachusetts was, of course, the presidential nominee for the Democrats.

Although there are many ambitious, energetic, and highly capable governors today, not all of the current officeholders can be said to merit that description. Some governors are limited by either their talent or their ambitions. Some will be content to end their political careers with a successful record of policy and administrative achievements as governor. Others may even be satisfied with only a fair record in that office. Many governors, too, will have indifferent or even unfortunate tenures because of poor luck or their own limited abilities. Furthermore, the majority of contemporary governors will never hold any other governmental post after they leave the governorship. There are, then, still some governors of the old breed in office, and there may always be. Even some of the new breed may not prove to be as clever and capable as they imagined or as they promised during their campaigns for office. However, these ambitious governors are, at least, seeking to fulfill public expectations for the office.

Several factors ultimately determine whether a given governor is capable of filling the "big shoes" of the office. Individual traits such as education level, professional and political experience, and interpersonal and political skills are important. Perseverance may be critical, as well, and luck can be a factor in the careers of many. But ambition—what a governor wants to achieve in office—is an especially important trait. The past history of the office of governor might seem to indicate that the governorship has been of modest importance mainly when people of modest ambitions filled it. Because more ambitious individuals seek the post today, it is becoming a truly important and powerful position.

THE STATES' EXECUTIVE BRANCHES

We have alluded several times to state agencies in the executive branch below the governor and, in particular, to the governor's ability (or inability) to control those agencies. Further discussion of the executive branch at this point will serve to illustrate its importance to both contemporary state government and the governor's efforts to direct policy initiatives.

THE CHARACTER OF THE MODERN EXECUTIVE BRANCH

The growth of the positive state during the twentieth century has meant the proliferation of executive-branch agencies charged with new policy responsibilities. Older, more traditional, agencies have also expanded in size and function in this process. New agencies and programs have been established by state governments in such diverse fields as social welfare, business regulation, environmental control, civil rights, and economic development. One result of these changes has been remarkable growth in the size of state and local governments. In 1950 state and local governments employed a total of about 4.3 million people; today they employ about 14 million. The populations served by those governments have grown too, but government has grown faster. In 1950 there were 70 state employees for every 10,000 Americans; today there are about 170 state employees for every 10,000 Americans.

Thus, the executive branches of state governments have become dramatically larger since 1950. And the governor is supposed to manage and lead this branch. Larger size alone makes this task more difficult. Coordinating the activities of the entire executive branch is also made harder by the larger number and greater diversity of programs and activities now carried on there. But executive agencies are not only more numerous and diverse, they are also increasingly staffed with highly trained and specialized professionals, who attempt to use their expertise to shape those agencies' policies and administration. Economists, accountants, engineers, lawyers, physicians, and professional educators populate the executive branches of state governments. In fact, every public agency and function have experienced increased professionalization. Even a sanitary engineer, who was once a jokester's target, is now likely to have a specialized college degree, membership in a professional society or organization, and advanced training.

Professionalization is certainly laudable. If American government is to achieve its current ambitious goals, it will need the most advanced and systematic knowledge available. But the trend toward professionalization does have certain political consequences. Bureaucrats with professional training have goals and criteria for their work that arise out of that training. They resist control of their work by laypersons and especially by politicians. Consider, for example, a professor teaching a college course in a public university for which this book is required reading. That person is an employee of a state government who is delivering a public service, but who undoubtedly considers himself or herself a professional who knows how the course should be designed and taught. That professor is very likely to resist efforts by elected political leaders, and even by bureaucrats in the university itself, to change the content, methods, or grading standards for the course. The vast majority of public-sector employees, from police officers to social workers, have been imbued with such attitudes.

Of course, American governments operate under the assumption that elected officials and the general public will indeed control government employees and agencies. Americans want government to be guided by the best minds and the most up-to-date and sophisticated knowledge, but they also want public control of government. Not surprisingly, these competing desires generate tension between professional public servants and their agencies and the elected officials who are supposed to supervise and oversee them. Neither the general public nor its elected leaders can always appreciate the professional values and the expert knowledge of these public servants. Furthermore, those individuals may lobby for goals and programs that the public and its elected officials cannot fully appreciate or endorse.

To complicate this problem, elected officials such as governors must force state agencies to compromise on their goals. No government can afford to subsidize the wish lists of all those agencies—to fulfill all the grand goals they can envision. And the activities of some agencies must be limited so that they will be compatible with those of others. Thus, the tension between governors and bureaucrats arises in part because of their different values and goals and in part because of the coordination governors and other elected officials attempt to impose on state agencies, restricting their desired independence and resources. (In Chapter 13 we explore these problems and the role of bureaucracies in state and local government in more detail.)

THE GOVERNOR AND THE EXECUTIVE BRANCH

The size, diversity, and professionalization of the states' executive branches make the governor's job more difficult today than in the past. For this reason, the governor's formal powers for leadership of the executive branch are especially important. We described those powers earlier, but here we will underscore why governors who are strong in those terms (as indicated in Tables 7-1 and 7-2) have considerable advantages in supervising the modern state bureaucratic system.

We can illustrate the importance of the governor's formal powers by considering a state whose governor has only a few of them. The governor of Nevada is ranked as one of the weaker ones in the nation (see our earlier discussion). And one reason for this weakness is apparent in Figure 7-1, a simplified organizational chart of the executive branch of Nevada's state government.

Note, first, that Nevada has a plural executive: the governor is only one of a host of separately elected officials, and none of the others reports to the governor. Thus, some of the state's most prominent officials and departments are independent of gubernatorial control.

Second, many of Nevada's state agencies are relatively independent of the governor. These agencies, labeled "Agencies headed by boards or commissions appointed by the Governor" in the figure, have multimember boards that are supposed to function largely on the basis of professional criteria free from political control. The intent is that they will be politically neutral and professionally competent. The governor is able to nominate the members of these boards, but this appointive power is limited by the fact that their terms of office are staggered and are longer than that of the governor. And, once in office, these officials are beyond the governor's direct control.

The governor of Nevada does appoint the heads of, and thus control the activities of, some agencies, which are labeled "Agencies headed by directors appointed by the Governor" in Figure 7-1. But it is clear from the figure that the governor controls only a minority of the executive-branch agencies in this way. In sum, in Nevada the

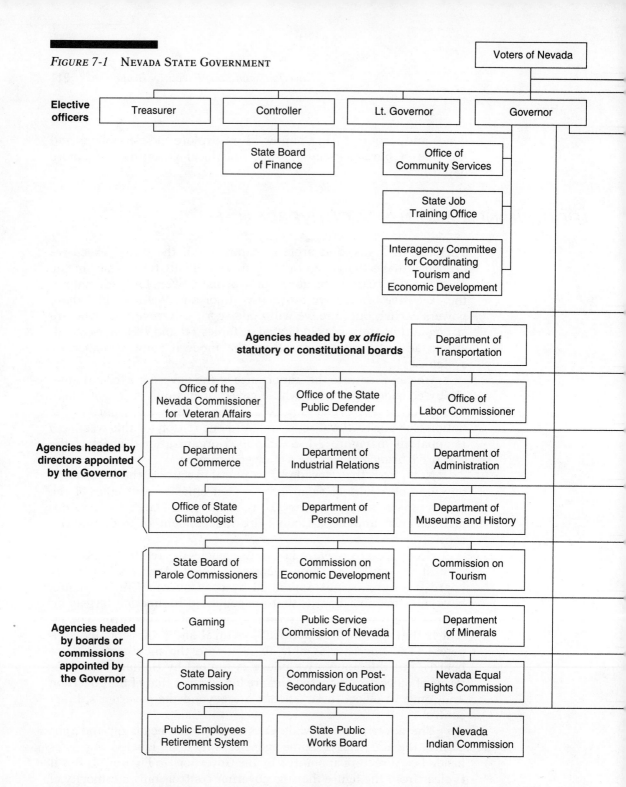

FIGURE 7-1 NEVADA STATE GOVERNMENT

Voters of Nevada

Elective officers

Treasurer

Controller

Lt. Governor

Governor

State Board of Finance

Office of Community Services

State Job Training Office

Interagency Committee for Coordinating Tourism and Economic Development

Agencies headed by *ex officio* statutory or constitutional boards

Department of Transportation

Agencies headed by directors appointed by the Governor

Office of the Nevada Commissioner for Veteran Affairs

Office of the State Public Defender

Office of Labor Commissioner

Department of Commerce

Department of Industrial Relations

Department of Administration

Office of State Climatologist

Department of Personnel

Department of Museums and History

Agencies headed by boards or commissions appointed by the Governor

State Board of Parole Commissioners

Commission on Economic Development

Commission on Tourism

Gaming

Public Service Commission of Nevada

Department of Minerals

State Dairy Commission

Commission on Post-Secondary Education

Nevada Equal Rights Commission

Public Employees Retirement System

State Public Works Board

Nevada Indian Commission

Source: Nevada Legislative Council Bureau, *Legislative Manual* (Carson City, Nev.: State of Nevada, 1991).

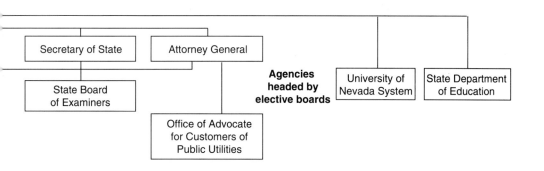

Secretary of State	Attorney General		**Agencies headed by elective boards**	University of Nevada System	State Department of Education
State Board of Examiners					
	Office of Advocate for Customers of Public Utilities				

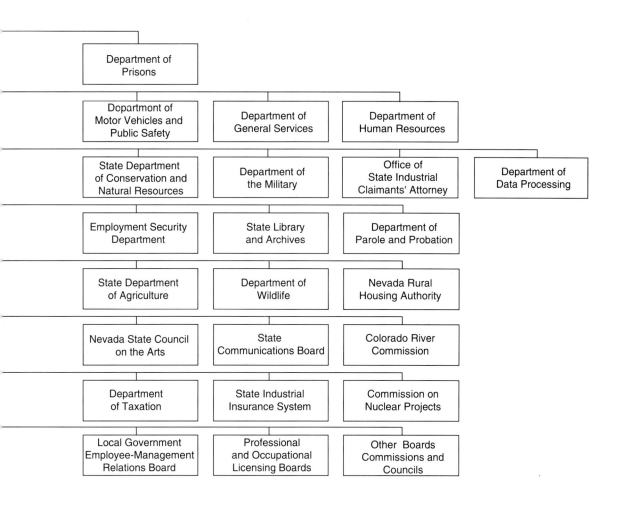

Department of Prisons			
Department of Motor Vehicles and Public Safety	Department of General Services	Department of Human Resources	
State Department of Conservation and Natural Resources	Department of the Military	Office of State Industrial Claimants' Attorney	Department of Data Processing
Employment Security Department	State Library and Archives	Department of Parole and Probation	
State Department of Agriculture	Department of Wildlife	Nevada Rural Housing Authority	
Nevada State Council on the Arts	State Communications Board	Colorado River Commission	
Department of Taxation	State Industrial Insurance System	Commission on Nuclear Projects	
Local Government Employee-Management Relations Board	Professional and Occupational Licensing Boards	Other Boards Commissions and Councils	

organization of the executive branch limits the powers of the governor, giving that official few resources with which to try to overcome the resistance to central control inherent in modern bureaucracies.

The governors of several other states face restrictions similar to those limiting the power of Nevada's governor. Some governors do have strong organizational powers, but even they can have difficulty leading and managing the executive branch. And this problem arises because of the size, diversity, and professionalization of state bureaucracies. Thus, the way in which the executive branch of state government has evolved under the positive-state ethos emphasizes the importance of the various gubernatorial powers we discussed earlier.

CONCLUSION

The contemporary office of governor has been shaped by the confluence of several twentieth-century trends: changing public expectations, evolving formal powers, and the rise of more ambitious candidates. The executive branch of state government also grew enormously during this century. The need for central executive leadership of this branch has become, then, an additional force favoring the extension of gubernatorial power. The governors of all the states have been affected to some degree by these trends. The formal powers of their office are considerably greater today than they were even a decade ago. We suspect that the general caliber of candidates for the office is higher in all states, too.

There are, however, great differences among the states in the formal and informal powers accorded to their governors. This has occurred because individual states have differed considerably in the timing and extent to which they have sought to empower the governor as a true chief executive. Some of the holders of the office are equipped to play the roles of a modern governor. Others are given but the barest essentials for that task.

Furthermore, the abilities and ambitions of candidates for the office are still variable and unpredictable. Many impressive candidates will prove to be lackluster or inept governors. Some seemingly ordinary candidates will fashion quite credible records in office. We suspect that each gubernatorial career is a unique product of individual ability and effort, formal powers, and luck. It may not, therefore, be possible to predict in advance the course of any governor's career. But it is possible to assess the formal powers available to the governor in each state and to anticipate the kinds of personal resources candidates must bring to the office to enhance the likelihood of success.

REFERENCES

Benjamin, Gerald. 1982. "The Diffusion of the Governor's Veto Power," *State Government* 55 (3): 99–105.

Beyle, Thad L. 1982. "The Governor's Power of Organization," *State Government* 55 (3): 79–87.

Beyle, Thad L. 1990. "Governors," pp. 201–251 in Virginia Gray, Herbert Jacob, and Robert B. Albritton (eds.), *Politics in the American States*, 5th edition. Glenview, Ill.: Scott, Foresman.

Beyle, Thad L., and Robert Dalton. 1981. "The Appointment Power: Does It Belong to the Governor?" *State Government* 54 (1): 2–13.

Council of State Governments. *Book of the States, 1984–85*. 1984. Lexington, Ky.: Council of State Governments.

Council of State Governments. *Book of the States, 1988–89*. 1988. Lexington, Ky.: Council of State Governments.

Council of State Governments. *Book of the States, 1990–91*. 1990. Lexington, Ky.: Council of State Governments.

Flentje, H. Edward. 1981. "The Governor as Manager: A Political Assessment," *State Government* 54 (3): 76–81.

Gantt, Fred, Irving O. Dawson, and Luther G. Hagard. 1974. *Governing Texas: Documents and Readings*, 3rd edition. New York: Thomas Y. Crowell.

Grady, Dennis O. 1984. "American Governors and State-Federal Relations: Attitudes and Activities, 1960–1980," *State Government* 57 (3): 106–112.

Gray, Virginia, Herbert Jacob, and Kenneth N. Vines (eds.). 1983. *Politics in the American States*, 4th edition. Boston: Little, Brown.

Hodges, Luther H. 1962. *Businessman in the Statehouse*. Chapel Hill: University of North Carolina Press.

Kaufman, Herbert. 1956. "Emerging Conflicts in the Doctrines of Public Administration," *American Political Science Review* 50 (December): 1057–1073.

Muchmore, Lynn. 1981. "The Governor as Manager," *State Government* 54 (3): 71–75.

National Governors' Association. 1978. *Governing the American States: A Handbook for New Governors.* Washington, D.C.: Center for Policy Research.

Nevada Legislative Council Bureau. 1991. *Legislative Manual.* Carson City, Nev.: State of Nevada.

New York Red Book, 1989–1990. 1989. Albany, N.Y.: Williams Press.

Ransone, Coleman B., Jr. 1982. *The American Governorship.* Westport, Conn.: Greenwood Press.

Sabato, Larry. 1983. *Goodbye to Good-time Charlie,* 2nd edition. Washington, D.C.: CQ Press.

Schlesinger, Joseph A. 1965. "The Politics of the Executive," pp. 207–237 in Herbert Jacob and Kenneth N. Vines (eds.), *Politics in the American States.* Boston: Little, Brown.

Wiggins, Charles W. 1980. "Executive Vetoes and Legislative Overrides in the American States," *Journal of Politics* 42 (November): 1110–1117.

8 *The Judicial Branch*

The growth of the positive state in the twentieth century has resulted in the creation of many new laws regulating individual and corporate behavior. Furthermore, many public programs dispense a host of goods and services to individual citizens. This expanded role of government has meant that more and more citizens find themselves caught in the web of governmental regulation or seek to ensure their access to the publicly provided goods and services. In either case, citizens often end up in the court system, where disputes about law, policy, and individual rights are settled.

The likelihood that an individual citizen will become involved in the court system has also been increased by the expansion of guarantees of individual rights, such as the nationalization of the Fourteenth Amendment. As we discussed in Chapter 3, the Fourteenth Amendment and the bulk of the U.S. Constitution's guarantees of individual rights were extended to the states in the twentieth century. Many states had previously not honored those guarantees, and state governments and officials were subsequently the target of many lawsuits over such matters.

Thus, the expanded scope of state and local governments' regulatory and policy activity, coupled with these new legal guarantees of equal treatment, has heightened the importance of the judicial branch for all citizens. Yet this branch of government is one about which Americans are particularly ill-informed. We will therefore consider it in some detail to reveal its typical modes of operation and its relevance to the rest of the American system of government.

WHAT COURTS DO

The judicial branch is responsible for three interrelated tasks. First, the court system is charged with settling disputes that arise under existing law. Most of these are *civil cases*, disagreements between individual citizens, between individuals and private institutions such as business firms, or between individuals and government agencies. Civil cases range from divorce proceedings to multimillion dollar disputes between business corporations over such matters as contractual disagreements, bankruptcy proceedings, and takeover attempts. The courts also handle *criminal cases*, in which individuals or companies have been charged by the government with behavior that is proscribed by law. Here, too, the range of cases—of proscribed behavior—is quite broad. Crimes of violence and passion are more often reported in the media, but far more numerous are the less exciting transgressions: traffic offenses, violations of city ordinances, burglary, and white-collar crimes such as embezzlement and fraud.

Implicit in this dispute-settling task is what Herbert Jacob (1978: 23–31) refers to as *norm enforcement*, the responsibility of the judicial branch for enforcing a good many societal rules. A number of societal preferences for individual and collective behavior are embodied in civil and criminal laws. The regular enforcement of those laws helps ensure the compliance of other members of society beyond those charged with the offense or involved in the litigation. Furthermore, a widespread sense that such enforcement is carried out promptly and equitably enhances public support for government in general.

Second, the courts process a variety of social and business transactions to ensure that they are carried out in conformance with the law. In civil proceedings concerned with divorce, probate, or bankruptcy, for example, there is often no literal dispute between the parties involved. Yet there is a relevant part of the legal code that prescribes how the action should be settled to ensure that the rights of all those parties will be protected.

As their third task, the courts have the power to determine what the law is when there is uncertainty or disagreement about that matter. In other words, courts settle disputes *about* law as well as disputes *under* law. This third responsibility is especially controversial. Many critics allege that courts often make law and policy independently, and these critics see this activity as an undesirable usurpation of legislative power. There are, however, many instances when courts must appear, at least, to make law: at times two or more laws are seemingly in conflict; individual laws may be ambiguous in certain respects; and the applicability of a given law to a particular set of circumstances may be in question. In these kinds of instances, the judicial branch must resolve the conflict, ambiguity, or uncertainty. And, in doing so, the courts decide what the law actually is.

In carrying out these three responsibilities, state and local courts are far more important than you might initially guess. The federal judicial branch—especially the U.S. Supreme Court—gets the most intensive media coverage and may, in some senses, be more important. But state and local courts process the vast majority of judicial proceedings in this country. Approximately 300,000 new cases have been initiated in the federal courts annually in recent years. State and local courts, on the other hand, take on over 80 million new cases each year! About three-quarters of these involve traffic offenses, but well over 10 million other civil cases *and* 10 million criminal cases are filed annually in state courts (Flango and Ito, 1984). Not only do most court cases begin in the state courts, they also end there. Thus, the overwhelming majority of Americans who are involved in court proceedings depend on state or local courts for justice.

In recent years state courts have also become more important for ensuring individuals' civil rights. Ronald Reagan's appointees to the Supreme Court made the decisions of that body fundamentally more conservative in the 1980s and 1990s. Thus, individuals pursuing civil rights claims have increasingly—and often successfully—sought redress of their grievances in state courts under state civil rights guarantees.

PUBLIC UNDERSTANDING OF COURTS AND LAW

Despite how important the courts are, public knowledge of this branch of government is very low compared to that of the executive and legislative ones. Furthermore, Americans' perceptions of their courts and what they do are highly influenced by the mass media's portrayals, which emphasize only selected aspects of the judicial system. Thus, the problem of limited public knowledge is further aggravated by the persistence of a number of misconceptions about how the courts work.

Widespread public misunderstanding of law and of the court system has been revealed by a number of opinion polls in recent years. A common example of this problem, which has been demonstrated by many polls, concerns knowledge of constitutional law. Many in the general public have dramatic misconceptions about what the U.S. Constitution does and does not say. For example, a nationwide poll revealed that substantial majorities of Americans believe that the Constitution establishes English as the national language and that it guarantees a free public education (United Press International, 1987). Many other surveys have found that a majority of respondents cannot recognize—and often disagree with—the guarantees of individual liberty found in the Bill of Rights.

Similarly limited knowledge about the court system in general has also been demonstrated. A nationwide survey in 1983, for example, found that only a small minority of Americans believed that they were well informed about the court system (Bennack, 1983). Large numbers of those polled, at times even substantial majorities, entirely misunderstood a number of fundamental aspects concerning how the courts and the justice system operate. Half of the respondents in this poll, for example, did not understand that criminal defendants are presumed innocent until proven guilty. Even half of those respondents who had once served on a jury—and, therefore, had been instructed in the law on this point—did not understand this.

More than for any other branch of government, Americans are exposed to images of the judicial branch in the mass media. News reports on television and radio and in the press typically cover only the most sensational court proceedings. Thus, criminal cases get far greater media attention than civil ones do, almost in reverse proportion to their relative numbers. Cases in the appeals courts, especially in the Supreme Court, also get more attention than the substantially greater numbers of lower-court cases do. The mass media, especially television, also shape Americans' images of the courts through dramatic portrayals of the criminal justice system. *L.A. Law* and other similar shows may be just as important as news programming in molding public understanding of the court system. Yet, once again, it is the sensational and the unusual that is typically emphasized in dramatic series on television. Even *People's Court,* which presents routine civil disputes, reinforces the common but inaccurate perception that all court cases are settled by a trial before a judge or jury.

COURTS AS POLITICAL INSTITUTIONS

One common misconception of the judicial branch is that courts and judges are above politics. Many people see courts as politically neutral institutions for arbitrating disputes and perceive judges as professional referees of the legality and fairness of the proceedings. There is some truth in this view, for courts and judges must and generally do strive to operate in this fashion. But the judicial branch is closely linked to everyday politics and to partisan arguments about what public policy should be.

Several characteristics of the courts reveal their political ties. First, in all the states there is at least some partisan politics involved in the selection of judges. In twelve states judges run for election to their positions on partisan ballots—just like governors and legislators. Although candidates for such judgeships mostly try to avoid the more common elements of election campaigning, they must work within their political party to get the nomination, twist arms and perhaps make promises to acquire campaign funds, and face the possibility of partisan criticism during the campaign itself.

Because judges have the opportunity to interpret the law and to settle disputes about what it actually is, they are recognized by other elected officials as playing a significant role in the making of public policy. Other officials attempt to influence the selection of judges to ensure that candidates with the "right" judicial and political philosophies will be chosen. Presidential efforts to get ideologically like-minded individuals onto the federal bench are mirrored in all the states in which elected officials can in any way affect the selection of judges. Some observers have argued that this concern for judges' ideological and policy views is greater today than in the past. As Henry Glick and Craig Emmert (1986: 107) observe,

> In years past . . . party loyalty and patronage were the most important concerns, and presidents, governors and party leaders worried little about specific judicial attitudes. Today, however, where judges

stand on abortion, the rights of criminal defendants, and other civil liberties issues is a major consideration in the judicial selection process.

Furthermore, state and local judgeships have often been used for political patronage—as rewards to individuals who have served their political party long and faithfully. Thus, those who are nominated and supported for election to these posts are often chosen not for their legal skills but for their partisan activities. And, once elected or appointed to a judgeship, an individual has opportunities to dispense patronage to other members of the party. Judges often have a hand in awarding lucrative business to individual lawyers and law firms. In some cases, such as probate proceedings, judges may be able to dispense business to banks and other financial institutions. In other cases, they will appoint legal or financial guardians, private investigators, or special masters to oversee the activities of defendants; all of these individuals receive fees, of course. Many judges can also fill a number of paid positions in their court and office. Thus, state and local judgeships can be at the center of a network of partisan and patronage ties.

The growth of big government in the states—the expansion of state and local governments' policy responsibilities—has made state courts more prominent and controversial actors in the political process than they were in earlier times. State courts today must settle disputes under a wide array of laws that regulate individual, group, and corporate behavior, that distribute substantial benefits to millions of Americans, that impose significant costs and burdens on millions more, and that are intended to achieve a host of ambitious social and economic goals. Many of these laws and their goals are controversial. Some state laws have vital consequences for individual citizens—such as laws concerning abortion, capital punishment, and access to publicly funded health care. Business regulations concerning corporate acquisitions and mergers, fair trade, labor-management relations, and environmental preservation, to name but a few examples, can create multimillion-dollar opportunities, or costs, for private firms. We could cite further examples, but the point should be clear already. Because of their power to arbitrate disputes about such consequential matters, state courts have increasingly been drawn into the political arena.

Political ideologues, representatives of political parties, interest groups, and private citizens whose interests are at risk under state laws have become intensely concerned about the role, activities, and general functioning of the courts. Judicial elections (and, where they are used, other selection methods to be described later) have become spirited affairs with significant partisan and policy content. Courts are literally lobbied by special interests when they address many controversial topics. And court decisions frequently generate intense political controversy. Thus, state courts have become regular participants in day-to-day state politics. In fact, judicial politics is often barely distinguishable from legislative or gubernatorial politics.

THE ORGANIZATION OF STATE AND LOCAL COURTS

To understand how state and local courts carry out their responsibilities, you first need to know how they are organized as institutions. The majority of states have four hierarchical levels of courts, with distinct functions. The courts at each level have different names in different states, but their responsibilities are generally similar. Figure 8-1 shows the hierarchical structure of the California court system, which is typical of such arrangements.

FIGURE 8-1
THE ORGANIZATION
OF THE CALIFORNIA
COURT SYSTEM

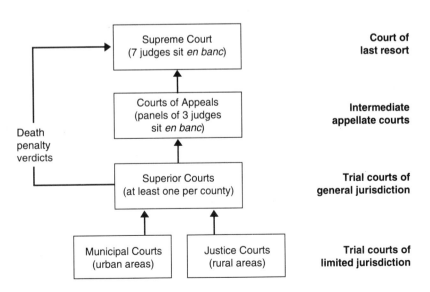

TRIAL COURTS

At the lowest level are *trial courts of limited jurisdiction.* These may be called police courts, municipal courts, justice of the peace courts, or courts of common pleas, as examples. Many of these are run by local government jurisdictions, such as cities. In California, the Municipal Courts serve cities, and the Justice Courts serve rural areas.

Courts of limited jurisdiction are trial courts, which means that they hear original cases. However, they are limited to the less serious ones of both the criminal and civil types. Typically, their criminal jurisdiction is limited to those offenses for which the punishment upon conviction is relatively modest: a monetary fine less than some fixed, limited sum or incarceration for only a short period of time. The civil jurisdiction of these courts is similarly circumscribed, often to include only those cases where the dollar value of the claim or dispute is relatively small. Typical criminal cases heard at this level concern traffic violations, public intoxication, driving while intoxicated, simple assault, and bad check offenses. The civil cases coming before courts of limited jurisdiction include those involving violations of local government ordinances, such as for noise, zoning, and public health. These courts may also hear divorce, probate, personal injury, and unpaid debt cases, usually depending, once again, on the dollar amount of the claim.

In a number of states, certain courts at the lowest level are designated as *small claims courts.* In California both the Municipal Courts and the Justice Courts are so designated. Small claims courts hear disputes between individuals over modest amounts of money in relatively informal proceedings where lawyers are not required. Instead, the parties to the suit argue their own cases in lay terms.

Because trial courts of limited jurisdiction hear relatively minor cases, it is easy to underestimate their importance. But they carry out a very large proportion of all state and local judicial proceedings. Just the traffic cases filed in these courts account for about three-fourths of all state and local court actions. Furthermore, many of the cases heard at this level, although perhaps of minor importance to the judicial system, are of great significance to the parties involved.

The second level of state courts consists of what are called *trial courts of general jurisdiction.* These courts, which might be known as circuit courts, superior courts, or district courts, hear the more serious original cases. Felony criminal cases, for example, are mostly tried at this level. The civil dockets of these courts are heavily weighted with divorce, personal injury, tax, and business claims cases. In California, courts at this level are called Superior Courts, and at least one exists in every county in the state. This, too, is a typical arrangement, for trial courts always serve specific geographic areas.

APPELLATE COURTS

The third level of state courts is composed of *intermediate appellate courts*. These are not trial courts and do not hear original cases. Instead, they decide appeals of decisions made in lower courts. Any individual or organization who loses a case in a trial court is guaranteed at least one rehearing of the case in a higher court if that person or organization desires—and can afford—to sustain the appeal. These appellate courts also have a variety of names. In California they are the Courts of Appeal.

Intermediate appellate courts usually sit *en banc*, as panels of three judges who hear each case together. After one of these courts hears a case, the panel of judges will reach a decision based on a majority vote. The judges do not reconsider the facts of the case that were determined in the trial court. Instead, they review whether the relevant laws were properly interpreted and applied. Appellate courts are heavily concerned, therefore, with issues of constitutionality and due process. The findings of these courts are especially important because they stand as precedents that must be followed by all lower courts in similar cases.

At the highest level in each state is the *court of last resort*, known in most states—as in California—as the Supreme Court. These courts, typically with five to nine judges, sit as panels to hear selected cases appealed from the intermediate appellate level. Judges in courts of last resort have discretion, that is, in deciding which cases to hear. They will look over the cases appealed from the lower appellate courts and vote among themselves as to which to consider. Undoubtedly, they accept some cases because they suspect justice may not have been served by the earlier decision. More typically, however, they accept those cases that pose a substantial unsettled question about what the law is. Courts of last resort, then, are particularly likely to settle controversies about the law itself and to make law and public policy in the process.

EXCEPTIONS TO THE TYPICAL ORGANIZATIONAL STRUCTURE OF STATE COURT SYSTEMS

A JUSTICE OF THE PEACE OFFICE IN A RURAL AREA EVOKES A SPIRIT OF LAW AND JUSTICE FROM ANOTHER ERA.

There are a few notable deviations from the four-tier hierarchical structure of court systems discussed above. Six states—Idaho, Illinois, Iowa, Massachusetts, Missouri, and South Dakota—have only one level of trial courts. Thus, the trial courts in these states hear all kinds of cases. And twelve states do not have intermediate appellate courts. Appeals are heard in these states by the court of last resort. (These are Delaware, Maine, Mississippi, Montana, Nebraska, Nevada, New Hampshire, Rhode Island, South Dakota, Vermont, West Virginia, and Wyoming—mostly states with relatively small populations, where, in consequence, the number of original and appeals cases is not as large as in more populous states.) Finally, Arkansas, Texas, and Oklahoma have not one but two courts of last resort: one for civil and one for criminal cases.

More important than the preceding exceptions is an elaboration of the four-tier structure that is found in a large number of states, including the most populous ones. Many states have created trial courts specialized by subject matter, which will hear only criminal, civil, probate, family law, or juvenile cases, as examples. The judges of such courts can specialize, too, so they are better able to be truly expert in the legal matters that come before them. This specialization of trial courts has an obvious rationale, yet it can also lead to the existence of an almost bewildering array of courts in a single jurisdiction. This problem is aggravated by the fact that trial courts serve limited geographic areas. There might be, then, many courts of original jurisdiction in a given county or metropolitan area.

Figure 8-2 illustrates this kind of situation by displaying the state and local courts located in Harris County, Texas, the center of the Houston metropolitan area. Two circuits of intermediate appellate courts operate here, as well as a host of general and limited jurisdiction trial courts. Even so mundane an offense as a traffic citation could require a Harris County resident to appear before any of

FIGURE 8-2
THE COURTS OF
HARRIS COUNTY,
TEXAS

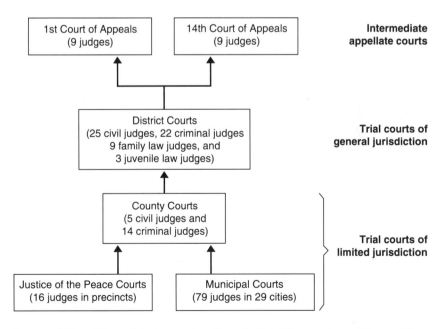

Source: Office of Court Administration, *Texas Judicial System, Annual Report, Fiscal Year 1986* (Austin, Tex.: Office of Court Administration, 1986).

109 municipal, justice of the peace, or county criminal judges (who are located in various offices spread throughout the county). Furthermore, all of the courts shown in the figure have jurisdictions narrowly defined by state law. This proliferation of courts makes it easy to appreciate why the average citizen contemplating or faced with a legal action needs the services of an attorney. Otherwise, simply finding the proper court—much less presenting the case—could be a formidable task.

THE WORK OF STATE AND LOCAL COURTS

To appreciate the functioning of state and local courts, you need to know something about the character and volume of the work they do. An examination of the number and variety of cases processed by the state and local courts in Texas in a recent year will illustrate several typical aspects of court business.

COURTS OF LIMITED JURISDICTION

Texas has several different courts of limited jurisdiction, but their caseload activity may be combined for purposes of this examination of court business. In the fiscal year ending August 31, 1986, there were over 9.5 million cases filed in courts at this level. Of these cases, about 2.6 million concerned parking citations, and almost 4.9 million were for other traffic violations. The remaining approximately 2 million cases ranged from divorces and suits over debts on the civil docket to minor theft and bad check charges on the criminal docket. On a per capita basis, there was more than one case filed in these courts for every two Texans. Excluding the parking and traffic cases, there was one case filed for every eight Texans.

Finally, all the courts at this level settled fewer cases than were filed during the year. And they all started the year with substantial numbers of pending cases. Thus, they reached the end of the fiscal year with even larger case backlogs. This situation is common among trial courts at all levels in the United States. Caseloads have expanded rapidly since the 1960s, and every state has found it difficult to add sufficient new judges and courts to keep up with the growing volume of business.

COURTS OF GENERAL JURISDICTION

The Texas courts of general jurisdiction are the District Courts, in which there are 374 judges, some of whom specialize in either civil or criminal matters. Table 8-1 illustrates the volume and flow of cases in these courts for 1986.[1] The most remarkable numbers implied by this table are for the average number of cases per judge. On average, each District Court judge disposed of 1,625 cases annually. Assuming a five-day-a-week, fifty-week work year, the average judge had to dispose of 6.5 cases per workday to attain this figure. The logical conclusion from these figures is that Texan justice is exceedingly swift or that the vast majority of cases consume very little court time.

The real explanation for the high number of cases disposed of per judge, which is true of all the nation's trial courts, is that most cases require little court time. The data in Table 8-1 show how this is so. Barely half of the criminal cases disposed of in the Texas District Courts, for example, required a trial. Furthermore, in most of the cases where there was a trial, the proceedings hardly seem worthy of the designation. Over 90 percent of the defendants in these cases chose to plead guilty and accept immediate sentencing, thereby using up only a modest amount of court time.[2] Furthermore, those criminal cases settled without any trial were disposed of by dismissal or related legal actions that terminate a case without prosecution. They, too, required little court time.

A further notable fact about the disposition of the criminal cases in Table 8-1 is that only about one defendant in five who pleaded "not guilty" was acquitted. This means that over 98 percent of *all* criminal defendants who went through any form of a trial were convicted. In addition, some of those defendants whose cases were dismissed were to be retried later or had been convicted in other cases. Justice, therefore, appears sure as well as swift in these courts (at least once cases get before a judge or jury).

Table 8-1 also reveals that it was the rare *civil* proceeding that required extensive legal action in the Texas District Courts. Only 29 percent of civil cases were settled by trials. The largest number of the remainder were dismissed, often because of out-of-court settlements between the litigants. Summary, agreed, and default judgments and other nontrial settlements account for the balance of the cases.

The backlog of unresolved cases in the Texas District Courts is also of note. Despite the fact that the backlog was reduced over the year 1986, there was still about a year's worth of cases pending at the end of the year (based on the earlier calculation of average number of dispositions per judge). This observation suggests that cases move

	CATEGORY	NUMBER OF CASES
TABLE 8-1 **CASES IN TEXAS DISTRICT COURTS, 1986**	*Criminal Cases*	
	Pending at beginning of year	86,649
	Added to docket	152,306
	Disposed by:	
	Conviction by guilty plea	62,361
	Conviction by bench trial	942
	Conviction by jury trial	3,365
	Acquittal by bench trial	705
	Acquittal by jury trial	612
	Dismissal[a]	29,204
	Placed on deferred adjudication	14,171
	Other[b]	27,905
	Total disposed	139,265
	Pending at year end	99,690
	Civil Cases	
	Cases pending at beginning of year	539,414
	Added to docket	416,219
	Disposed by:	
	Bench trial	129,484
	Jury trial	3,709
	Dismissal	166,572
	Default judgment	33,345
	Agreed judgment	39,342
	Summary judgments	6,600
	Show-cause motions	49,824
	Other	26,973
	Total disposed	455,849
	Pending at year end	499,784

[a]Almost half of these cases were either refiled for later trial or dropped because the defendant had been convicted in another case.

[b]These include changes of venue, shock probation, transfers to other courts, and acceptance or denial of motions to revoke.

Source: Office of Court Administration, *Texas Judicial System, Annual Report, Fiscal Year 1986* (Austin, Tex.: Office of Court Administration, 1986).

slowly through the court system, even though many are settled without trials. Other data illustrate the slowness of case processing more clearly. The median criminal case settled by these courts had been on the docket for more than ninety days. Forty percent of criminal cases were over four months old when they were settled.[3] On the civil docket, the median case had been filed for over a year before it was settled, and one-third of the civil cases were on the docket for more than eighteen months before they were settled. Such figures, which are typical throughout the states, raise a question posed by many critics of the courts: is not justice delayed, justice denied?

Finally, we should point out that caseload data do not fully describe the duties of trial court judges. Judges in both limited and general jurisdiction courts must handle a variety of other legal matters. They may have to hold a number of kinds of hearings, some concerning upcoming trials and others concerning completed trials, especially in civil cases where one of the parties allegedly has not lived up to the settlement. Trial judges must also devote time to the issuing of a variety of legal instruments: writs of habeas corpus, search or arrest warrants, and injunctions against parties in a case under litigation, among others. Some judges perform weddings, and some even serve as coroners in rural areas. In the midst of these activities and their efforts to dispose of as many cases as possible, judges must study new legal precedents and changing statutory law to maintain their expertise and stay up-to-date in their field.

INTERMEDIATE APPELLATE COURTS

The Courts of Appeals occupy the intermediate appellate level in Texas, and three-judge panels there hear appeals of cases from the lower courts. The jurisdiction of these courts includes essentially all first-time appeals except for those involving death-penalty convictions (which go directly to the Court of Criminal Appeals, the court of last resort in Texas for criminal cases).

The Courts of Appeals began fiscal year 1986 with 5,684 pending cases held over from the prior year. These courts disposed of 8,161 cases during that year and ended the year with 5,355 unsettled ones. Thus, their backlog was modestly reduced, but it was still nearly as large as the number of new cases filed during the year.

What is most remarkable about the caseload of these courts is the small number of cases that are appealed from lower courts. The 7,832 new cases added to the Courts of Appeals dockets in fiscal 1986 represent less than 1 percent of the lower court cases settled the prior year that, theoretically, could be appealed to this level. Americans are conditioned by the mass media's coverage of sensational and unusual cases to believe that a high percentage of original court decisions is appealed; yet just the reverse is true. A major reason for the small percentage of cases appealed is the manner in which cases are typically settled in the trial courts. Criminal defendants who plead guilty forfeit almost all possible bases of appeal. Civil litigants who settle out of court do so as well. Many others who lose a case in the lower courts, of course, believe that they have no sufficient basis to appeal the decision. Others do not have the money to pay for further legal efforts, or they think that the costs of an appeal in time, money, and effort are likely to be higher than would be justified by its uncertain and distant outcome.

COURTS OF LAST RESORT

Texas has two courts of last resort: the Supreme Court for civil cases and the Court of Criminal Appeals for criminal ones. These two courts received appeals for review of a total of 2,404 lower court decisions in 1986. In addition, over 4,300 other writs and motions were filed with these two courts. Most of the latter were writs of habeas corpus and motions for one of these courts to reconsider a case it had previously rejected. Together, Texas's two courts of last resort accepted only 314 new cases for review in 1986, and they disposed of 549 cases. The cases appealed to these courts of last resort constitute about 30 percent of the cases settled in the intermediate appellate courts the prior year. Furthermore, through their power of discretionary review, these courts of last resort accepted only about 13 percent of the cases appealed to them.

MAJOR PARTICIPANTS IN THE COURT SYSTEM

Information on caseloads and disposition of cases indicates the flow of business through the courts but gives very little sense of how that business is actually transacted. Who appears in the courts? Who shapes the decisions of those bodies? And, perhaps even more important, what individuals and circumstances have the most influence on the outcomes of particular cases?

JUDGES

Judges are the most visible and prominent of the regular participants in the settling of legal disputes. They are, in some senses, technical experts charged with refereeing such disputes to ensure that they are fairly settled—to ensure, that is, that they are settled in accordance with the law. This view of judges' role is a commonplace one that also fits some of the stereotypes about the court system we discussed earlier. Yet it is not as accurate as it might seem. The prominence of judges suggests that they are the most important actors in the courtroom, but the information on case disposition given in the preceding section indicates that this is not true for the majority of cases. Judges may have some, but usually only modest, influence over civil cases settled out of court and over criminal cases where the defendant pleads guilty. Because plea bargaining with the prosecuting attorney occurs in a large proportion of criminal cases, that official is typically more important than the judge in determining verdicts and sentences. Judges are certainly influential in those cases that go to trial and in some of the instances of pretrial bargaining that may occur among the litigants. For the majority of cases, however, they are distant and only peripheral actors, who only become important if the litigants are unable to reach a settlement before going to trial.

The notion of judges as technical experts is also subject to some question. Many judges are indeed quite knowledgeable in the law, and most strive to achieve a record free of errors that might be sustained in appellate rehearings of their cases. However, the extent of judicial expertise should be scrutinized closely for several reasons. In no state are applicants formally trained for the judicial role. Practic-

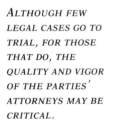

ALTHOUGH FEW LEGAL CASES GO TO TRIAL, FOR THOSE THAT DO, THE QUALITY AND VIGOR OF THE PARTIES' ATTORNEYS MAY BE CRITICAL.

ing lawyers obviously have much of the appropriate technical knowledge, but many of them have also specialized in quite narrow legal fields. And it is the rare attorney in private practice who knows the full range of judicial responsibilities as well as *how* they are to be carried out. Thus, new judges often go through a period of "apprenticeship" while they learn many of their duties through "on the job training" (Ryan et al., 1980: 135–137).

Furthermore, many states do not require all of their judges to be formally trained as lawyers. Customarily, such training is required of judges of appellate courts and courts of general jurisdiction. Many judges in courts of limited jurisdiction, however, are poorly trained, or completely untrained, in the law (Provine, 1986). Fortunately, those judges are allowed to settle only minor legal disputes. As we observed earlier, though, many of those disputes are of considerable importance to the parties involved, and so, therefore, is the quality of the judicial decision making.

Finally, the processes by which judges are selected and retained in office seldom focus explicitly on the technical or professional expertise of the candidates. As we will discuss in some detail below, even the best of these procedures share this problem to some degree.

TRIAL JURIES

Those individuals accused of crimes and those who are parties to civil disputes are constitutionally guaranteed the right to a trial by a jury should they desire it. Some exercise this option; others prefer a *bench trial*, in which a judge alone determines the verdict and sentence or settlement. The choice between a bench trial and a jury trial is a strategic one, made by the litigant and his or her lawyer based on their expectations as to which alternative is most likely to produce a favorable decision.

Jury trials are a central element of the American legal system. As V. Hale Starr and Mark McCormick (1985: 47–48) have observed, that fact is remarkable:

> The United States is unique in its adherence to the system of trial by jury in civil and criminal cases. Approximately ninety-eight percent of the world's civil jury trials and ninety percent of the criminal jury trials are conducted in this country. The use of juries in civil cases has virtually gone into eclipse in the rest of the world. They are used in some Canadian provinces and Australian states. In England they are used only in the trial of personal torts like libel and slander.

Although juries were used for trying major crimes in many European countries in the nineteenth century, today they are used in only a handful of countries outside the English-speaking world.

Jury trials are, however, relatively rare even in the United States. They account for less than 10 percent of all cases handled by the courts in any given year, although they are more common for certain kinds of cases (such as personal injury) than others. For cases where lay jurors might be especially sympathetic to a defendant or plaintiff or where there is a history of generous jury findings, attorneys are more likely to recommend that their clients opt for a jury trial. For other cases the factual or technical nature of the case or the law under which it falls suggests that a bench trial would be preferable.

In spite of the infrequency of its use, trial by jury is central to American justice. As Hans Zeisel, an eminent authority on the jury system in the United States, has observed, that system affects all cases and settlements through "the expectation of what a jury is likely to do in a particular case that informs the decisions as to whether or not to settle or plead guilty, or whether or not to waive a jury" (Starr and McCormick, 1985: 47).

Finally, although the U.S. Constitution ensures the right to a jury trial, it does not specify the details of how juries are to be composed or employed. As a result, state laws vary widely with respect to such particulars. Some states require twelve-member juries that must reach unanimous decisions. Other states allow as few as eight out of twelve jurors to render a verdict. And, for less serious cases, many states employ six-member juries that must reach unanimous verdicts (Hastie, Penrod, and Pennington, 1983: 2).

PROSECUTING ATTORNEYS

The most important actors in the settling of criminal cases are prosecuting attorneys. Also known as district attorneys, county attorneys, or state's attorneys, these are elected officials in the vast majority of states (Neubauer, 1984: 104–107). Within counties or other limited geographic areas, they are responsible for determining which individuals to charge with criminal offenses and for carrying out the actual prosecution of those individuals. In small counties, prosecutors may be part-time officials who head offices composed of only one or two assistants. In large metropolitan areas, they lead large prose-

The Modern Art and Science of Jury Fixing

The term jury fixing *refers to illegal efforts by lawyers or litigants to obtain a jury that is disposed to favor their side of a case. Today, however, lawyers' use of techniques from the social sciences constitutes a new and legal means by which to select a panel of jurors who might be especially sympathetic to one's case as well as to decide how best to present the case. The following account explains this practice.*

In June of 1980, after 15 weeks of testimony, a federal jury deciding an antitrust suit awarded M.C.I. Communications Corporation $600 million, to be paid by the American Telephone and Telegraph Company. Antitrust awards are automatically tripled for punitive purposes, which meant that M.C.I. was to receive the largest antitrust judgment ever—the stunning amount of $1.8 billion. Although the attorneys for the winning side were jubilant, they were not really surprised by the decision. Before the trial, they had engaged jury researchers who used sophisticated social science techniques to determine which jurors would be most favorable to M.C.I., and to predict how jurors would react to the evidence.

A Chicago research firm conducted a telephone poll of local residents and supplemented it by personal interviews. In their interviews they asked questions designed to reveal whether the respon-

cutorial agencies, often having several hundred assistant prosecutors, who are the ones who actually represent the state in the trials of criminal defendants.

Prosecutors are important because of the considerable power and wide discretion they have for shaping the criminal justice process. Abraham Goldstein (1981: 3–4) has discussed the broad role of these officials:

The public prosecutor is the central figure in the administration of American criminal justice. It is he who chooses, from a mass of over-

dents, if they were jurors, would be likely to side with M.C.I. or with A.T.&T. They also obtained the demographic characteristics of these individuals. With computer analyses of these responses, the researchers developed demographic profiles of people who were favorable and unfavorable to M.C.I.'s case, knowledge that would later be of benefit in selecting jurors for the trial.

Next, the firm paid individuals of varying sympathy toward M.C.I. to meet on three successive evenings. On each evening, a mock jury composed of eight of these individuals listened to M.C.I.'s attorneys present abbreviated versions of both M.C.I.'s and A.T.&T.'s sides of the dispute in a minitrial. The researchers and attorneys then watched the mock jurors deliberate on the case through a one-way mirror. What they learned from behind the one-way mirror affected how the attorneys presented their side before the real jury. . . .

Thus, from the community surveys and the mock juries, the M.C.I. attorneys learned what kinds of jurors to look for and to eliminate during the [jury] selection process. They also obtained tactical clues about how to present their case to different types of individuals. . . . [Yet] the M.C.I. team may have been *too* successful. The jury award was judged to be excessive and on appeal it was overturned. A second jury evaluating the damages awarded M.C.I. only $37.8 million.

Source: Valerie P. Hans and Neil Vidmar, *Judging the Jury* (New York: Plenum Press, 1986), pp. 79–80.

lapping and redundant criminal statutes, which of them best fits the facts presented by the police. And he is the one who decides how many offenses to charge and whether the evidence will support a conviction. . . . In short, the prosecutor establishes enforcement priorities and accommodates conflicting statutory, correctional, and constitutional objectives. At the same time, he individualizes justice, induces cooperation, and mitigates the severity of criminal law. His instruments for achieving these remarkably diverse objectives are his exclusive authority to initiate a criminal charge, his power to dismiss or reduce charges, and his overwhelmingly dominant role in plea bargaining.

The prosecutor's control of the plea-bargaining process is especially important because of the considerable number of criminal cases settled by this means, as we indicated earlier. For these cases, judges and juries are either peripheral or entirely irrelevant, and prosecutors determine the character and standards of justice.

Another notable fact about prosecutors is that most of them are elected officials. This fact means, first, that they must sustain (or appear to) a record of aggressive and successful prosecution of accused criminals in order to maximize their chances for reelection. In a sense, prosecutors arc politicians, who must, like all incumbent politicians, run for reelection on their record in office. Second, many incumbents of the prosecutor's office hope to attain higher elected positions. They may thus be led to shape much of their prosecutorial work to political ends, either by establishing a high-visibility anti-crime record or by leading a crusade against well-known crime figures in their state. In several ways, then, prosecuting attorneys must be seen as political figures operating in the court systems.

PRIVATE ATTORNEYS

Attorneys are those individuals who have met the prerequisites for and then passed a state bar examination. Having done so, they are admitted to the bar in that state, meaning that they have the privilege of practicing law there or of "appearing before the bar" in its courts. Today, all states require that one graduate from law school before taking the bar exam. Thus, attorneys are highly educated professionals. Two other distinctive traits of attorneys, however, are also important. First, they are in business to sell a service for a fee. Second, they are regular participants in the day-to-day routines of the judicial system, whereas many of their clients will enter the court system once or quite rarely. Both these traits have important implications for the relationships attorneys have with their clients and the quality of the legal representation those clients will receive.

As businesspeople, attorneys have their own interests as well as those of their clients to serve. They must carefully consider the potential economic return likely to accrue from the legal problems of each prospective client, and they must regiment the amount of time they spend on each case they take on. Some clients—those with complicated problems and plenty of money to pay for legal services—will receive a good deal of a lawyer's attention. Such cases offer the prospect of many billable hours to be charged to the client. Other clients—because of their limited finances or the modestness of the settlement likely to be awarded them—will get cursory attention at best. In almost all instances, however, attorneys are better served by keeping their clients' problems out of court. Court proceedings are the slowest and most deliberate actions associated with any legal dispute, and they also move at a pace over which the individual attorney has little control. Court time, then, is highly costly to the attorney.

In the United States criminal defendants unable to afford lawyers are represented by public defenders or court-appointed private attorneys. There are pressures on these lawyers, too, to minimize their efforts on individual cases. Public defenders' offices usually have large backlogs of cases in which they are to appear. And court-appointed attorneys are typically paid relatively modest hourly rates or flat fees for their work. Therefore, it is in those attorneys' best interests, economically, to speed the processing of each case (Albert-Goldberg and Hartman, 1983).

Because of the large number of indigent criminal defendants and the widespread use of plea bargaining, the role of the criminal attorney in representing his or her client has been transformed in recent years. As Jerome Corsi (1984: 224) observes,

> No longer is the criminal lawyer strictly an advocate for the defendant, a trained alter ego charged with presenting his client's best case in the adversarial forum of the courtroom. Rather, the professional role of the criminal lawyer has come to resemble more closely that of a broker. The lawyer stands between his client and the prosecutor in the attempt to match his client's needs for minimum punishment with the prosecutor's demand for justice.

As regular participants in the legal process, lawyers also know both the formal and informal "rules of the game" far better than their clients do. They know more than just the law itself, that is. They are aware, for example, of what kinds of plea bargains can be arranged with particular prosecutors in particular criminal cases and of how sympathetic juries are likely to be toward certain personal injury claims. Lawyers' decisions about which cases to pursue and how vigorously to do so are shaped by this kind of knowledge.

The contemporary role of attorneys has led some observers to fear they are too closely associated with the decision routines of the courts to represent all their clients as well as they could. Because criminal lawyers negotiate pleas with prosecuting attorneys so regularly, some fear that this process has become a routine procedure for them, in which guilt is automatically assumed and the rapid processing of cases is the highest priority. Even in many civil cases (especially insurance and personal injury claims) there is evidence that the legal representation afforded clients by their attorneys is often brief, circumscribed, and motivated by a desire for a quick settlement rather than the best outcome for the client (Corsi, 1984: 218–222).

LITIGANTS

At one time or another most Americans will be either a defendant or a litigant in a court proceeding. For the vast majority, however, the reasons for such an appearance will be minor criminal charges such as for traffic violations or routine civil matters concerning divorce, probate, or family law. Some Americans, of course, will be caught up in legal cases of momentous importance, where personal integrity, wealth, business, freedom, or even life might be at stake. Two particular characteristics of litigants in eventful cases significantly shape the legal outcomes they receive.

The first of these characteristics is familiarity with the court system and its processes. Some litigants, especially among those involved in civil cases, are fairly regular court actors themselves. A large proportion of civil cases involve disputes over business transactions: debt claims, contract disputes, foreclosures, evictions, and so forth. Furthermore, many of these cases pit a commercial entity such as a bank, a loan company, or real estate holding company against an individual (Glick, 1983: 129–132; Jacob, 1983: 232–235). The corporate entities in such disputes are likely to have extensive knowledge of both the law and the court routines relevant to such cases, because such litigation is a regular part of their business. The individuals involved, on the other hand, are likely to be engaged in a court case for the first time. Knowledge of the law and of how the courts process particular kinds of cases turns out to be a significant advantage for ensuring a favorable outcome.

A second characteristic of litigants that affects the outcomes of their cases is, unfortunately, the private financial resources they can marshal to pursue litigation. Wealth can be critical to getting the legal settlement one prefers—because it allows one to hire a more capable (more expensive) lawyer or to pay for more of a lawyer's time and attention. More money can, therefore, ensure better legal representation.

The advantages of having a good lawyer are evident outside the courtroom as well as in it. Because so many cases are disposed by some kind of negotiated settlement (such as plea bargains in criminal cases and out-of-court settlements in civil ones), a lawyer's planning, research, and bargaining skills can be crucial. A good lawyer can present a case in the best possible light—even before the trial. He or she can also move the negotiations rapidly or slowly, whichever seems more likely to encourage the other parties to bargain and to lower their demands. Because legal cases are seldom settled in an all-or-nothing fashion and, therefore, bargaining is so critical to outcomes, the value of a good attorney is heightened.

The ability to hire good legal counsel can also offset a litigant's personal unfamiliarity with the law and courtroom routines. Thus, a wealthy individual can match the advantages that corporate entities typically have in civil cases. The corporate litigant, on the other hand, is often well served by a lawyer of average quality who specializes in the kind of case at issue (and who will typically face unknowledgeable individuals on the opposing side).

Compelling criticisms of the importance of wealth to outcomes in the criminal justice system have been made. For example, Herbert Jacob (1978: 185–186) argues as follows:

> All the evidence available indicates that the criminal courts are fundamentally courts against the poor. The crimes that attract the notice of the police are those committed by poor people much more frequently than by rich. Those few defendants who are not poor can often escape the worst consequences of their involvement, provided they are not caught in a spectacular crime. They can afford bail and thus avoid pretrial detention. They can obtain a private attorney who specializes in criminal work. They can usually obtain delays that help weaken the prosecution case. They can compensate victims where it helps them escape punishment. They can enroll in diversion programs by seeking private psychiatric treatment or other medical assistance. They can keep their jobs and maintain their family relationships and, therefore, qualify as good probation risks. They can appeal their conviction (if, indeed, they are convicted) and delay serving their sentence. However, it is essential to note that all these advantages accrue to only a tiny portion of all criminal defendants. Most of them are welfare poor or working poor and cannot utilize this array of tactics.

A virtually identical argument can be made for the importance of wealth in many civil disputes. Justice is not always reckoned on the basis of litigants' bank balances. However, as we observed earlier, more money can ensure significantly better legal representation, and there is abundant evidence that litigants with little money get, on average, mediocre representation.

METHODS FOR JUDICIAL SELECTION

One of the most controversial aspects of state court systems concerns how judges are chosen for the bench as well as whether and how their performance is subsequently reviewed. This controversy focuses on several different matters related to judicial selection and qualifications. One of these is the technical competence of judges, their knowledge of the law and the care with which they apply it to particular cases. Some judicial selection methods have been touted for alleged superiority in ensuring judicial competence. (The best-known of these is the so-called merit selection method, which is described below.) Another concern has been with judges' independence from undue political influence and, for that matter, from any unsavory, immoral, or illegal pressure. Once again, some judicial selection methods have been promoted, and others criticized, for how well they ensure that this concern is addressed. Finally, some have argued that judges, like legislators and chief executives, should be subject to some degree of popular control. Various electoral systems for choosing judges have been advanced to answer this third concern.

These concerns have been of varying importance over the history of this nation, but the evolution of judicial selection methods has closely followed that identified by Herbert Kaufman (1956) for the selection of executive branch officials (described in Chapter 7). Early in U.S. history, state and local judges were typically chosen by the legislature or governor. The judicial branch was, then, highly dependent on one or both of the other branches. The Jacksonian era, however, led many states to embrace popular election of judges, often on partisan ballots. The preeminent concern of that reformist period, as Kaufman argued, was with maximizing the democratic accountability, or *representativeness*, of judges. The Progressive era in the early twentieth century brought new concerns for technical competence and nonpartisanship, for *neutral competence*, according to Kaufman. New selection methods, particularly nonpartisan elections, were developed in many states early in the twentieth century to further this last goal.

During most of the twentieth century, there has been considerable concern for the technical competence of judges. The *merit selection method* has been promoted by those who see such competence as an important goal. Some version of this method, which is often referred to as the Missouri plan after the first state to adopt it in 1940, has been implemented for all, or at least the most prominent, judicial posts in twenty states. Under the merit selection method a nonpartisan panel, usually consisting of lawyers and lay members, composes a list of supposedly technically qualified candidates for any judicial vacancy. The governor then chooses one of these candidates to fill the position. Typically, after one or more years in office, each judge is listed unopposed on an election ballot for a nonpartisan retention vote. Voters simply vote "yes" or "no" on whether to retain the judge, presumably basing their choice on an evaluation of his or her performance in office. Retained judges will periodically face new retention votes; rejected ones will be replaced through the merit appointment system.

Despite the spread of new judicial selection systems such as the Missouri plan, many states still use methods adopted in earlier times. The result is that judicial selection methods vary considerably across the states and even to a notable degree within states. Table 8-2 lists the states that employ each of the principal methods. The merit selection method is used in almost half the states, but partisan or nonpartisan elections are employed in more than half. The remaining two alternatives are used relatively rarely, but note that appointment by the governor, a holdover from the early days of the nation, is especially popular in New England.[4]

Somewhat surprisingly, especially in light of how much scholarly attention the methods for judicial selection have received, there is little consensus on their relative merits. All of these methods have been shown to be affected by partisan and other kinds of political influence. The election procedures are adversely affected by low public interest, low turnout, and only casual and superficial scrutiny of candidates by voters—whether in partisan, nonpartisan, or retention elections. And the concept of judicial competence has proved so difficult to define precisely that it has not been possible to substantiate that any system is superior to the others in ensuring a technically competent bench (Dubois, 1980: 3–35; Glick and Emmert, 1987).

The lack of proof that any selection method succeeds in ensuring judicial competency is an especially compelling point. As Philip Dubois (1980: 13–14) observes, even the legal community of lawyers and sitting judges—presumably experts in the subject—has been unable to articulate clear and concise professional criteria by which poten-

Council of State Governments, 1990), pp. 210–212.

████████████

TABLE 8-2
CLASSIFICATION OF
THE STATES BY
THEIR PRINCIPAL
METHOD OF SELECT-
ING JUDGES

tial judges might be scrutinized. In the absence of such criteria, there is no satisfactory means by which to compare the judges chosen by different methods. And it is not just scholars who are affected by this lack. Voters in popular elections for judges *and* selection panels and governors in states that use merit selection methods are also affected adversely. Thus, superficial criteria and ones based on partisan or policy preferences are likely to be especially influential.

PARTISAN ELECTIONS	NONPARTISAN ELECTIONS	MERIT SELECTION	GUBERNATORIAL APPOINTMENT	LEGISLATIVE ELECTION
Alabama	Georgia	Alaska	Maine	South Carolina
Arkansas	Idaho	Arizona	New Hampshire	Virginia
Illinois	Kentucky	California	New Jersey	
Indiana[a]	Louisiana	Colorado	Rhode Island[j]	
Mississippi	Michigan	Connecticut[e]		
New York	Minnesota	Delaware		
North Carolina	Montana	Florida[f]		
Pennsylvania[b]	Nevada	Hawaii		
Tennessee	North Dakota	Indiana		
Texas	Ohio	Iowa		
West Virginia	Oklahoma[c]	Kansas[g]		
	Oregon	Maryland		
	South Dakota[d]	Massachusetts		
	Washington	Missouri[h]		
	Wisconsin	Nebraska		
		New Mexico		
		Oklahoma[i]		
		South Dakota[i]		
		Utah		
		Vermont		
		Wyoming		

[a]Mostly below the appellate level.
[b]Reelection by nonpartisan election.
[c]Intermediate appellate and general jurisdiction courts.
[d]Circuit courts.
[e]Legislative appointment from list submitted by governor.
[f]Appellate levels.
[g]District judges chosen by nonpartisan commission.
[h]Circuit courts and higher.
[i]Courts of last resort only.
[j]Supreme court judges chosen by legislature.

Source: Dixie K. Knoebel, "The State of the Judiciary," in *Book of the States, 1990–91* (Lexington, Ky.: Council of State Governments, 1990), pp. 210–212.

CHARACTERISTICS OF JUDGES

There are some remarkable commonalities that cut across all state judiciaries regardless of the method used in selecting judges. A nationwide survey of the states' general jurisdiction trial courts found, for example, that 96 percent of the judges in those courts were white and 98 percent were male![5] The few female and minority judges were heavily concentrated in large metropolitan areas, usually outside the South (Ryan et al., 1980: 124–130). The average age of the judges at the time of the survey was 53, and their average age on attaining the bench was 46. Furthermore, a more recent study of state courts of last resort found that only 3 percent of the judges at that level were women, that less than 1 percent were nonwhite, and that the average judge reached the bench at age 53 (Glick and Emmert, 1986).

Just as important as the preceding demographic information, but more difficult to document precisely, are the occupational and social backgrounds of judges. The available research suggests, however, that something over half of all trial judges come out of private practice, usually having practiced alone or in small, general-practice firms. Smaller but notable percentages come from prosecutors' offices or from other appointed or elected public posts. And the majority of judges on both trial and appellate courts are "local boys," who attended law school in their home state, have close ties to the community, and have been active in partisan politics.

Most notable about these patterns is the selectivity they suggest may characterize the recruitment and selection procedures for judicial positions. Only certain kinds of individuals—distinctive in their social, occupational, and political backgrounds—are typical of the bench. As Jerome Corsi (1984: 115) observes, this phenomenon may result as much from self-selection as from the operations of local politics and the mechanics of the formal selection procedures. Whatever the source, however, the result has been a relatively homogeneous and distinctive collection of judges.

Considerably less is known, it should be observed, about the characteristics of judges in courts of limited jurisdiction. The selection procedures for those judges vary even more than the ones for judges at higher levels and are often determined by local (city or county) rules. Many of the judges in courts of limited jurisdiction are elected in one fashion or another; many are appointed. To some observers, the most remarkable fact about these judgeships is that many of them are held by individuals who are not attorneys. The precise number of such judges nationwide is not available, but Linda Silberman (1981) observed that forty states allow them in at least certain levels of courts, twenty-nine states allow them to hold judgeships with substantial if limited jurisdiction, and, nationwide, nonattorneys outnumber attorneys in those courts where they are allowed to serve.

Many critics, especially within the ranks of attorneys, lament the existence of any judges not formally trained in the law. Their existence certainly defies, as well, the public notion that judges are technical experts. It may even challenge the assumption that they *should* all be experts. Doris Provine (1986), for example, has presented evidence from a study in New York that suggests that judges who are not lawyers carry out their duties about as well as those who are, in comparable courts. However, the existence of nonattorney judges remains controversial.

Another characteristic of judges that is worth considering is the financial remuneration they receive. In 1990 the average salary for a judge serving in a state court of last resort was about $82,000. The best-paid judges in courts of last resort were those of California and New York, who earned over $90,000 a year. The average salary for a judge in a trial court of general jurisdiction was about $70,000 (Knoebel, 1990).

What is most interesting about judicial salaries is how they compare to the financial remuneration that is possible in private legal practice. It has been widely observed that the most successful lawyers, particularly those in large corporate firms, earn far more than judges. And even many lawyers who practice alone or in a small firm earn quite substantial incomes. Thus, many lawyers, regardless of the form or extent of their practice, can earn far better incomes in private practice than on the bench. Evidence on the relationship of private-practice incomes to judicial salaries is provided by Table 8-3, which presents the average salary of partners in law firms in selected cities along with the base salary for judges in general-jurisdiction trial courts in the same state.

Some precautions are in order about how to interpret these comparisons. First, the salaries given for lawyers are for *partners*, typically those who have practiced at least six years in a firm and have been accepted as permanent members. This means, of course, that they are experienced and successful—appropriate characteris-

	AVERAGE SALARY OF LAW PARTNER (ROUNDED)	BASE SALARY OF GENERAL-JURISDICTION TRIAL JUDGE
TABLE 8-3 COMPARISON OF THE SALARIES OF PART-NERS IN PRIVATE PRACTICE FIRMS AND JUDGES IN GENERAL JURISDICTION TRIAL COURTS / **CITY AND STATE**		
Atlanta, Georgia	$165,000	$68,838
Boston, Massachusetts	170,000	80,360
Chicago, Illinois	173,000	75,113
Denver, Colorado	130,000	63,000
Detroit, Michigan	175,000	58,633
Houston, Texas	230,000	76,309
Los Angeles, California	220,000	94,344
Milwaukee, Wisconsin	186,000	73,003
New York, New York	279,000	95,000
Philadelphia, Pennsylvania	238,000	80,000

Sources: Student Lawyer, "The Wages of Time. The 15th Annual Salary Survey" 18 (November 1989): 27–31; Dixie K. Knoebel, "The State of the Judiciary," in *Book of the States, 1990–1991* (Lexington, Ky.: Council of State Governments, 1990), pp. 221–222.

tics for judges if they were expected to be technical experts in the law. The lawyers' salaries in Table 8-3 do not include bonuses, however, which can elevate their total incomes substantially and make the contrasts even more striking. Furthermore, they are the *average* salaries of law partners in those cities; many of the highest such salaries in each city are far above the average.

Nonetheless, the contrast in Table 8-3 is striking. The trial judges' salaries range from about one-third to one-half of the law partners' salaries. In no state are the two close. Although it may not be realistic to expect the judiciary to attract the very ablest of lawyers, it seems reasonable to hope for at least ones of average capabilities. If the average salary levels in private practice are any indication, no state can expect to compete for capable individuals on the basis of income alone. If the status of being a judge and the prospects of serving the public interest offset the income differential, then there are surely many judges drawn from the best of the legal profession. If those factors are not generally compelling, then state judiciaries may be populated with many lawyers of mediocre talent and professional prospects.

CONCLUSION

Court systems are linked to the politics and policies of state and local governments in several ways. Most notably, the decisions of several key actors in the judicial system shape public policy and legal outcomes. Public policy thus becomes not just the laws "on the books" but the laws as interpreted and affected by the decisions of these actors. Lower court judges' sentencing decisions, for example, determine the extent to which laws will be strictly or harshly applied to individual cases. Appellate judges' decisions shape law and policy for all future cases of a given kind. Appellate courts also resolve many inconsistencies in and contradictions between law and policy. Prosecuting attorneys largely determine the severity of criminal sanctions. Even private attorneys' business decisions about which cases to pursue and how vigorously to do so affect broad classes of legal outcomes.

The court system is not, then, simply a technical and politically neutral arena for the settling of legal disputes. It is intimately linked to the partisan and ideological politics of the larger system of governance. It is also fundamentally affected by the private business practices of attorneys. However, the judicial arena is quite distinctive from other governmental ones in terms of the actors who participate there and the roles they assume. Furthermore, much of the business of the courts is conducted in ways the average citizen may little understand. Widely held beliefs about how legal disputes are resolved are quite unlike the reality. Even Americans' common notions about the most important actors in the courts—about the roles of judges and juries, that is—are subject to considerable qualification.

It is crucial that you appreciate the political functions of courts *and* the manner in which their business is actually conducted. Because of the growth of the positive state and the nationalization of federal civil rights guarantees, courts play an increasingly prominent role in the settling of public policy disputes. The widened scope of governmental efforts has generated considerable disagreement concerning the appropriateness of many governmental goals and the means to achieve them. Thus, the courts are increasingly drawn into disputes about what public policy and law should be. They are competing with the executive and legislative branches in the shaping of public policy to a greater degree today than at any time in American history.

Courts have also become more important in the lives of individual citizens for similar reasons. In this era of the positive state, it is increasingly likely that individual citizens will be personally affected by particular court decisions of great substance. Thus, you should know the courts better to understand both their role in the larger governmental system and their potential influence on your life.

NOTES

1. The Texas District Courts also disposed of over 17,000 juvenile cases in 1986, which are not included in Table 8-1.

2. One study of judicial supervision of the plea-bargaining process in six states revealed fascinating data on the length of trials in such cases. All six of the courts studied were ones in which some explicit judicial procedure had been introduced to ensure the fairness of the plea-bargaining process. These procedures typically amounted to extended questioning of the defendant by the judge before the latter official accepted a guilty plea. These procedures, therefore, should have had the effect of lengthening the average time for trials relative to whatever was the prior practice. Despite that fact, the average plea-bargained felony case in these courts was disposed of in only 9.9 minutes! The average misdemeanor case took 5.2 minutes (McDonald, 1987).

3. A breakdown of the disposition of serious criminal cases in New York in 1980 demonstrated similarly slow judicial processes. The average plea-bargained criminal conviction required 202 days from arrest to conviction; the average conviction attained in a trial before a judge or jury took 362 days (Nelson A. Rockefeller Institute of Government, 1983: 383).

4. Many states, using various judicial selection methods at the appellate and general jurisdiction levels, allow local government officials to appoint judges of limited jurisdiction courts such as municipal, police, county, and similar courts.

5. The small number of female judges is largely due to the traditional male dominance of the legal profession. As recently as 1970, fewer than 3 percent of all lawyers in the United States were women. An upsurge of female law students in the intervening years increased that figure to about 14 percent by 1986 (Curran, 1986). Obviously,

women are still rare in this profession, and most of them are concentrated among the youngest and least experienced of its members. Thus, it is likely to be many more years before women make significant inroads within the judiciary.

REFERENCES

Albert-Goldberg, Nancy, and Marshall J. Hartman. 1983. "The Public Defender in America," pp. 67–102 in William F. McDonald (ed.), *The Defense Counsel*. Beverly Hills, Calif.: Sage Publications.

Bennack, Frank A., Jr. 1983. "The Public, the Media, and the Judicial System," *State Court Journal* 7 (Fall): 4–13.

Corsi, Jerome R. 1984. *Judicial Politics: An Introduction*. Englewood Cliffs, N.J.: Prentice-Hall.

Curran, Barbara A. 1986. "American Lawyers in the 1980s: A Profession in Transition," *Law & Society Review* 20 (1): 7–18.

Dubois, Philip L. 1980. *From Ballot to Bench: Judicial Elections and the Quest for Accountability*. Austin: University of Texas Press.

Flango, Victor E., and Jeanne A. Ito. 1984. "Advance Caseload Report, 1983," *State Court Journal* 8 (Fall): 8–15.

Glick, Henry R. 1983. *Courts, Politics, and Justice*. New York: McGraw-Hill.

Glick, Henry R., and Craig F. Emmert. 1986. "Stability and Change: Characteristics of State Supreme Court Judges," *Judicature* 70 (August/September): 107–112.

Glick, Henry R., and Craig F. Emmert. 1987. "Selection Systems and Judicial Characteristics: The Recruitment of State Supreme Court Judges," *Judicature* 70 (December/January): 228–235.

Goldstein, Abraham S. 1981. *The Passive Judiciary: Prosecutorial Discretion and the Guilty Plea*. Baton Rouge: Louisiana State University Press.

Hans, Valerie P., and Neil Vidmar. 1986. *Judging the Jury*. New York: Plenum Press.

Hastie, Reid, Steven D. Penrod, and Nancy Pennington. 1983. *Inside the Jury*. Cambridge, Mass.: Harvard University Press.

Jacob, Herbert. 1978. *Justice in America: Courts, Lawyers, and the Judicial Process*, 3rd edition. Boston: Little, Brown.

Jacob, Herbert. 1983. "Courts," pp. 222–243 in Virginia Gray, Herbert Jacob, and Kenneth N. Vines (eds.), *Politics in the American States*, 4th edition. Boston: Little, Brown.

Kaufman, Herbert. 1956. "Emerging Conflicts in the Doctrines of Public Administration," *American Political Science Review* 50 (December): 1057–1073.

Knoebel, Dixie K. 1990. "The State of the Judiciary," pp. 194–223 in *The Book of the States, 1990–91.* Lexington, Ky.: Council of State Governments.

McDonald, William F. 1987. "Judicial Supervision of the Guilty Plea Process: A Study of Six Jurisdictions," *Judicature* 70 (December/ January): 203–215.

Nelson A. Rockefeller Institute of Government. 1983. *New York State Statistical Yearbook, 1983–84.* Albany: Nelson A. Rockefeller Institute of Government, State University of New York.

Neubauer, David W. 1984. *America's Courts and the Criminal Justice System,* 2nd edition. Pacific Grove, Calif.: Brooks/Cole.

Office of Court Administration. 1986. *Texas Judicial System Annual Report, Fiscal Year 1986.* Austin, Tex.: Office of Court Administration.

Provine, Doris Marie. 1986. *Judging Credentials: Nonlawyer Judges and the Politics of Professionalism.* Chicago: University of Chicago Press.

Ryan, John Paul, Allan Ashman, Bruce D. Sales, and Sandra Shane-DuBow. 1980. *American Trial Judges: Their Work Styles and Performance.* New York: Free Press.

Silberman, Linda. 1981. "Non-attorney Justice," pp. 253–262 in Fannie J. Klein (ed.), *The Improvement of the Administration of Justice.* Chicago: American Bar Association.

Starr, V. Hale, and Mark McCormick. 1985. *Jury Selection.* Boston: Little, Brown.

Student Lawyer. 1989. "The Wages of Time: 15th Annual Salary Survey," *Student Lawyer* 8 (November).

United Press International. 1987. "Most Americans Lack Constitution Knowledge," *Houston Post* (February 14): 11F.

9

The Politics and Economics of Urban Life in the United States

The United States is a remarkably urbanized nation. Over three-quarters of the U.S. population lives in a metropolitan area, and almost half of all Americans live in metropolitan areas with 1 million or more residents. These percentages have grown steadily throughout the twentieth century. And they offer vivid testimony as to how the lives of the majority of Americans are intimately associated with the fortunes of cities: with the kinds of social and economic opportunities they offer, how they evolve and change, and how they are governed.

Furthermore, the governments in metropolitan areas—including cities, counties, and a host of special-purpose jurisdictions—face remarkable challenges because of the nature of urban life. It is in these areas that the problems of poverty, crime, drugs, pollution, transportation, and public health—as just a few of many examples—are their worst. Besides having to respond to those problems, local governments are also called on to deliver the most fundamental public services, including such activities as policing, collecting garbage, maintaining streets, roads, and sewers, and enforcing building, sanitation, and health codes. These municipal services may seem mundane, but they are essential to the quality of Americans' daily lives. And the success of local governments in meeting their policy challenges and providing public services is shaped by the character of metropolitan life and how it is changing, just as are the lives of urban residents.

The residents of metropolitan areas also face unusual problems as they attempt to influence the policies of their local governments. In several earlier chapters we described the general means by which Amereicans influence their governments: through interest groups, political parties, and various modes of individual political participation, including voting in elections. However, these means of participation often work quite differently when used to influence local governments as opposed to state and federal governments. And some powerful and unusual other means of political participation are available to urban residents. Thus, public participation in politics takes on a special character in large metropolitan areas.

You need to understand the character of modern American cities, how they are evolving, and the problems and opportunities faced by both their residents and governments in order to understand local governments in and of themselves. But such understanding is also critical for seeing how state and local governments together might respond to the broader social and economic challenges described in Chapter 1. The problems of urban areas we describe in this chapter have arisen in part because of the evolution of the national economy from an industrial to a postindustrial one. And those urban problems offer concrete and immediate examples of how governments in the United States must grapple with the consequences of that economic transition.

THE FRAGMENTATION OF GOVERNMENT AUTHORITY IN METROPOLITAN AREAS

When you think of an urban area, what probably comes to mind is the central city. However, the central city accounts for only part of the population in a metropolitan area. For example, of the several million people who live in the Chicago metropolitan area, only a few million reside within the boundaries of the city of Chicago. The millions of others live in surrounding jurisdictions that are separate and independent from the central city.

The U.S. Census Bureau designates metropolitan regions *Metropolitan Statistical Areas (MSA)*. To be classified as an MSA, an area must include a city with a population of at least 50,000 or an urbanized area of at least 50,000 with a total metropolitan population of at least 100,000. An MSA is basically a large population nucleus together with adjacent communities that have a high degree of social and economic integration with that nucleus. Central cities are the cores of MSAs. Suburban cities are the other cities, towns, and incorporated places within MSAs. Central cities account for only a few hundred of the several tens of thousands of local units of governments. As you can see in Table 9-1, there are also counties, townships and towns, school districts, and special districts (which include port, housing, transit, and urban renewal authorities; zoning, conservation, and land use commissions; and flood, drainage, mosquito control, utility, water, sewer, and sanitation districts). Many of these local governments are fully independent. They can levy taxes and raise revenues, incur long-term debts, condemn private property through eminent domain, and pass laws and regulate the behavior of citizens within their jurisdiction. Thus, they have direct and important impacts on people's lives.

One of the most fundamental characteristics of local government in the United States today is the tremendous fragmentation and decentralization of authority that prevails. Power is fragmented at the local level because each of the dozens or even hundreds of governments in a single metropolitan area exercise independent authority. Some MSAs contain more separate governments than there are nation-states in the world! Power is therefore splintered and divided up. No single government has responsibility for housing, police and fire protection, education, transportation, health, welfare, zon-

TABLE 9-1
NUMBERS OF LOCAL GOVERNMENTS IN THE UNITED STATES, 1942–1987

TYPE	YEAR					
	1942	1952	1962	1972	1982	1987
Municipalities	16,220	16,778	18,000	18,517	19,083	19,200
Counties	3,050	3,049	3,043	3,044	3,041	3,042
Townships and towns	18,919	17,202	17,142	16,991	16,748	16,691
School districts	108,579	67,346	34,678	15,781	15,032	14,721
Special districts	8,299	12,319	18,323	23,885	28,733	29,532
Totals	155,067	116,694	91,186	78,218	82,637	83,186

Source: U.S. Bureau of the Census, *Census of Government: 1987* (Washington, D.C.: U.S. Government Printing Office, 1990).

The Nation's Largest Metropolitan Areas

Listed below are the fifteen largest metropolitan areas in the United States, as defined by the U.S. Bureau of the Census, along with their populations in 1988. Even the names given these areas indicate that they include a large number of separate cities and counties—that they are highly fragmented in terms of the division of public authorities attempting to govern in each area. Some of them even occupy portions of two or more states! Equally notable, however, is their size. About *35 percent* of *all* Americans live in these fifteen areas. This fact is remarkable testimony to the importance of urban life and the problems of governing large metropolitan areas today.

New York–New Jersey–Long Island	18,120,000
Los Angeles–Anaheim–Riverside	13,770,000
Chicago–Gary–Lake County	8,181,000
San Francisco–Oakland–San Jose	6,042,000
Philadelphia–Wilmington–Trenton	5,963,000
Detroit–Ann Arbor	4,620,000
Boston–Lawrence–Salem–Lowell–Brockton	4,110,000
Dallas–Ft. Worth	3,766,000
Washington, D.C.–Maryland–Northern Virginia	3,734,000
Houston–Galveston–Brazoria	3,641,000
Miami–Ft. Lauderdale	3,001,000
Cleveland–Akron–Lorain	2,769,000
Atlanta	2,737,000
St. Louis	2,467,000
Seattle–Tacoma	2,421,000

Source: U.S. Bureau of the Census, *Statistical Abstract of the United States, 1990* (Washington, D.C.: U.S. Government Printing Office, 1990), pp. 29–31.

ing, planning, crime, pollution, water, sanitation, and recreation services.

FRAGMENTATION AND SELF-INTEREST

It is probably fairly safe to assume that most people are motivated most of the time by narrow self-interest. We want more rather than less—more money, a better job, a better house, prestige, status, power. Some of us are more altruistic than others. We may give to charity or do volunteer work in the local hospital or retirement home. But most of us find our greatest rewards in the pursuit of narrowly self-interested goals. Our altruism doesn't extend much beyond our hopes for our children—an extension of our own dreams and aspirations. We also need to belong, to have a sense of community with fellow human beings. However, we largely prefer a certain type of community, the community of those who are much like us or better than us. We want to be surrounded by people with similar or better incomes, housing, education, occupation, and status. We go to great lengths to exclude the undesirables, those who look, behave, and live differently than we do. We cluster together based on a variety of status-related characteristics, and we use local government to preserve and enhance those differences. There are occasional exceptions to this pattern, but they are as few and far between as the person who spends his leisure time emptying bedpans in the local charity hospital.

The result of this vigorous pursuit of individual self-interest is tremendous segregation at the local level on the basis of race and wealth. The rich live with the rich, the poor with the poor, the white with the white. The splintering of political power and authority at the local government level provides a perfect environment in which citizens can maximize their pursuit of their narrow self-interests. Fragmented government does not *cause* self-interested behavior. It does, however, encourage the pursuit of class-based goals and penalize cooperative action. Political life at the local level would be vastly different if governmental authority were not so fragmented. As it stands, some citizens win, and some lose.

THE PROS AND CONS OF FRAGMENTATION

Is the fragmentation and decentralization of political power and authority at the local level in the individual's best interests? That depends on who that individual is. If he or she is economically well-off or hopes to be, then definitely yes. If the individual is poor and looking to government to improve his or her life, then certainly not. A variety of arguments have been marshaled both for and against the fragmentation of metropolitan governments.

FREEDOM OF CHOICE

The advocates of fragmentation see nothing but benefits to be derived from the present structural arrangement of local governments, advantages that allegedly accrue to all citizens, regardless of race or class. First, they maintain that fragmentation is at the heart of the American system of government. It makes the notion of freedom of choice meaningful. Without it, the idea of local self-government would have little substance. Americans are free to pick and choose where they wish to live. Fragmentation gives substance to the meaning of individual freedom.

Imagine the following scenario. A certain family lives in the central city. Its members like the metropolitan area, their jobs, and the cultural and social opportunities urban life provides. They don't want to move to another city. However, they are displeased with the city government. Taxes are too high, they don't want their kids to attend inferior inner-city schools, they don't want them bused, and they are upset about the high crime rate. What can they do about the situation?

The urban family in question has three options. First, it can do nothing. But this particular family is not apathetic. It refuses to sit by and watch the situation deteriorate. The family's second option is to take political action. However, family members are convinced that political participation is not worth the effort. They joined a neighborhood organization to work for better schools, but nothing changed. They have always voted, but their candidate never wins. Besides, many of the important political issues, such as busing, aren't decided by local elected officials but by appointed federal judges. Political participation is a waste of time and money. However, the family has a third option. Move—not to another city but to a nearby suburb. The dissatisfied family can escape high taxes, high crime, inferior schools, and busing but keep its jobs and continue to take advantage of the cultural opportunities provided by the city.

Thus, fragmentation gives Americans freedom of choice. It prevents an unresponsive government from enforcing its will on them permanently. It is democracy at work. Intensely dissatisfied with the actions of government, individuals can seek redress by moving to another jurisdiction that is responsive to their needs. Fragmentation greatly enhances each citizen's political options. If a single government (rather than several dozen or even several hundred) exercised control over an entire metropolitan area, such individual freedom of choice would be severely limited.

THE HEALTHY EFFECTS OF COMPETITION

Fragmentation is also alleged to make local governments more efficient, effective, and responsive. According to this point of view, families are assumed to be rational consumers of public goods. They give the same effort and attention to the selection of a jurisdiction in which to live as they give to the purchase of a new car. They carefully shop among the variety of governments available within a metropolitan area until they find one that offers the best mix of public goods and services at the lowest cost. Consequently, governments are forced into competition with each other in an effort to attract desirable residents and exclude undesirable ones. The elected manager of the political supermarket is required to stock the shopping aisles with good products (attractively packaged) at low costs. He may even throw in a special (such as quality schools) to entice the discerning shopper. However, only preferred customers will be allowed to purchase the merchandise. No suburban government can afford to antagonize its valuable clientele (middle- and upper-class consumers) by allowing access to bargain-basement shoppers.

This competition among metropolitan governments for preferred residents forces them to provide better services, lower taxes, and more efficient management. The unresponsive and inefficient government will lose out to another jurisdiction. Fragmentation ensures that the operation of the political sector will resemble that of the private sector. The citizen is the winner in this process because competition is better than monopoly. Governments have a powerful incentive to improve their performance in a fragmented system.

THE DISPARITY BETWEEN NEEDS AND RESOURCES

The critics of fragmentation are vehement in their attacks on the prevailing structural arrangement of urban government in the United States. First, it is argued that fragmentation has produced a tremendous disparity between needs and resources. Needs are concentrated in the central city, and the vast wealth and political energies necessary to address those needs are just out of reach in the suburbs. Those who have the least need for public services are those who are most able to afford them. Upset with what it perceives to be an unresponsive city government (declining services, high taxes, too many welfare programs, high crime rates), the better-off family can sell its home and move to an exclusive, wealthy suburb. The residents of such a suburban community have much less need for government services than do the poor people who remain in the central city. Crime rates are lower in wealthy areas, so there is less need for police, courts, prosecutors, and correctional institutions. The typical home is carefully constructed and designed, well-maintained, located on a large lot, and equipped with a fire alarm and sprinkler system. The probability of fire and its spread is much lower than in deteriorating, multifamily, slum housing in the central city, where trash may be piled in the hallways, several families may share cooking facilities, and heating is often provided by space heaters. Consequently, fire-fighting expenditures are lower in the suburbs.

Residents of the exclusive suburban jurisdiction also have less need for public recreational facilities. They have spacious backyards with a swimming pool and a variety of play and gymnastic equipment, and their houses have elaborate game rooms. The husband and wife belong to an exclusive racquet club, and they may have a place in the country. They go skiing in the winter, and they rent a condo at the beach in the summer. Consequently, these residents place few demands on their government to provide public parks and recreational facilities. Public welfare and health needs are virtually nonexistent.

Since wealthy families demand fewer public services, taxes in suburban jurisdictions tend to be lower. There is one exception. The upper class insists on quality education for its children. Schools must be the best to prepare those children for college. The importance of education to suburban whites is demonstrated by the fact that governments frequently advertise the quality of their schools in an effort to attract residents.

This pattern of low services, low taxes, and great wealth stands in stark contrast to that found in central cities. Poor families have high service needs. High urban crime rates require more police. Dilapidated wooden structures and inadequate cooking and heating facilities result in greater expenditures on fire protection. High unemployment, inferior housing, and poverty lead to demands for public housing, public transportation, and a variety of social-welfare programs. The inner-city poor look to government rather than to their backyards, racquet clubs, condos at the beach, and places in the country for their recreational needs. They turn to government for protection from criminals; they can't rely on trained guard dogs, burglar alarm systems, and private security forces.

As a result of these differences, taxes in the central city tend to be higher. When all services are considered, expenditures per capita are considerably higher in central cities than in suburbs. When expenditures on education are excluded, expenditures per person are even higher in the city. The high taxes and greater service needs, however, have been part of the cause of the flight of both jobs and people from the central cities. The result has been a deterioration and erosion of the tax base. Service needs and problems are disproportionately concentrated in the central city. The vast wealth of the metropolitan area has found a safe haven in the suburbs.

RACIAL AND CLASS SEGREGATION

The critics of fragmented governmental power and authority also maintain that one of the most damaging consequences is intense segregation on the basis of race and class. Table 9-2 indicates the

TABLE 9-2
CHARACTERISTICS OF
URBAN GROUPS BY
RACE, 1987

CHARACTERISTIC	BLACK	HISPANIC	ASIAN	WHITE
Median family income	$17,604	$19,995	not available	$30,809
Percent below the poverty line	31.1%	27.3%	10.3%	11.0%
Unemployment rate	13.0%	8.8%	4.6%	5.3%
Percentage who have completed high school (25 years and older)	37.1%	29.0%	75.3%	39.2%
Percentage who have completed college (25 years and older)	10.7%	not available	34.3%	25.5%

Source: U.S. Bureau of the Census, *Statistical Abstract of the United States, 1989* (Washington, D.C.: U.S. Government Printing Office, 1989).

disparities in income, education, and employment among urban blacks, Hispanics, Asians, and whites in the United States. Even within suburban areas, communities are highly differentiated with respect to housing and income. And Table 9-3 reveals that residential segregation greatly contributes to segregation in the educational system.

TABLE 9-3
SEGREGATION
LEVELS FOR BLACK
STUDENTS IN LARGE
CITY SCHOOL DIS-
TRICTS, 1986–1987

DISTRICT	PERCENTAGE OF BLACKS IN SCHOOLS WITH A MAJORITY OF WHITES	PERCENTAGE OF BLACKS IN SCHOOLS WITH MORE THAN 90 PERCENT NONWHITES
Albuquerque	51.8	2.5
Akron	48.5	27.1
Anchorage	90.0	0
Atlanta	1.6	90.8
Austin	21.8	6.9
Baltimore	5.1	68.3
Birmingham	5.0	74.9
Boston	4.0	13.3
Brownsville	0	84.8
Chicago	2.4	81.3
Cincinnati	15.8	21.2
Cleveland	0.9	5.2
Colorado Springs	88.6	0
Columbus	5.13	0
Corpus Christi	6.9	51.2
Dade (Miami)	8.2	59.2
Dallas	4.6	65.7
Dayton	12.6	0
Denver	19.0	0
Des Moines	95.5	0
Detroit	0.6	76.1
El Paso	9.8	3.1
Flint	11.8	48.7
Fort Wayne	67.2	13.9
Fort Worth	22.1	36.4
Fresno	23.7	25.7
Gary	0	97.3
Houston	3.4	69.6
Indianapolis	44.6	0
Jackson	9.9	73.2
Jersey City	0.3	79.1
Kansas City, Mo.	9.6	53.3
Los Angeles	4.9	70.0

	PERCENTAGE OF BLACKS IN SCHOOLS WITH A MAJORITY OF WHITES	PERCENTAGE OF BLACKS IN SCHOOLS WITH MORE THAN 90 PERCENT NONWHITES
TABLE 9-3 CONTINUED		
DISTRICT		
Memphis	12.0	66.0
Milwaukee	11.8	23.6
Minneapolis	57.2	0.3
Montgomery	29.4	37.8
Newark	1.0	96.6
New Orleans	0.7	84.2
New York City	6.8	74.1
Norfolk	13.4	16.8
Oakland	1.5	83.7
Oklahoma City	27.9	18.9
Omaha	72.0	0
Philadelphia	10.6	73.7
Portland	47.7	0
Richmond	0.1	56.6
Rochester	9.5	23.3
Sacramento	12.1	0
St. Louis	6.8	64.5
San Antonio	0	81.3
San Diego	26.5	8.5
San Francisco	0	49.3
San Jose	67.6	0
Seattle	25.8	4.5
Toledo	34.2	39.0
Tucson	63.0	1.4
Tulsa	37.0	29.2
Washington D.C.	0.5	94.1
Wichita	91.2	0

Source: Gary Orfield and Franklin Montfort, "Change in the Racial Composition and Segregation of Large School Districts, 1967–1986," a report to the National School Boards Association, June 1988, p. 29–30.

Obviously, segregation wouldn't disappear if a single government exercised jurisdiction over an entire metropolitan area. However, it is almost certainly the case that the extent and intensity of such segregation would decline. The isolation of the poor, the old, and the black from the larger society around them cannot be a healthy development for society as a whole. Crowded into the central city and cut off from the opportunities around them, the inner-city poor are denied the development of their full human potential (Lucy,

1975; Newton, 1975). Some have compared the decaying inner city to a reservation where this society consigns its losers. Indian agents periodically pass out shoddy merchandise (government services) to calm the occasionally restless natives. Another student of the city has likened the situation to a sandbox, populated by adults who are treated as children, who perform little useful function in this society, and who are kept occupied by the occasional new toy or gimmick (government program) thrown into their midst.

The segregation of the American population affects poor whites and the elderly as well as blacks. Many elderly people are terrified at the prospect of being robbed or mugged, struggling to survive on a fixed income, and embittered over the decay and possible death of their once lively, close-knit neighborhoods. They are as firmly trapped in the inner city as any ghetto black. Their neighborhoods will continue to deteriorate despite anything they might do to try to reverse the process. The suburbs are a powerful magnet, draining off wealth, the young, the middle and upper classes, and political energies and leaving the wreckage of once stable, thriving neighborhoods.

THE LIMITED MOBILITY OF THE POOR

One of the most disastrous consequences of fragmentation is the tremendous disruption it causes in people's lives. For many, life takes meaning from a closely knit community of friends, neighbors, extended family, place of worship, and school. Although fragmentation does not by itself destroy those neighborhood relationships and institutions, it can be a major contributing factor because it fundamentally alters the nature of political participation. Confronted with serious problems (high taxes, declining services, busing, racial strife), it is in the best interests of many to simply move away from those problems. There is little incentive to stay and fight. However, as a problem-solving strategy, mobility is limited to those who can afford it. The poor, and increasingly even the middle class, are excluded from many suburban jurisdictions. The cost of housing keeps many families out of the market. The argument that citizens are rational consumers who shop and choose among competing jurisdictions in the metropolitan area can be applied only to those who can afford to play the game. Wealth is the key to intense segregation within urban areas. We have already noted that suburban jurisdictions compete to attract desirable consumers and exclude undesirable ones. The price of housing is crucial to an understanding of how this goal is accomplished. The inner-city poor cannot afford an expensive home in the suburbs. They are as effectively excluded from those jurisdictions as though there were a law that prohibited them from living among the rich.

Housing and the Exclusion of the Undesirable   Suburban jurisdictions need a more precise tool than the housing market to exclude the poor and their problems. What is to prevent a developer from building multifamily, low-income housing on a tract of land squarely in the midst of an exclusive, wealthy suburb? If that happens, the exclusivity of the suburb disintegrates. If the poor and the black are not denied access to a suburb, the wealthy will surely avoid it. The devices that are employed by suburban jurisdictions to accomplish the task of excluding the lower classes are zoning ordinances, deed restrictions, and building codes. These tools of government are applauded by some as crucial to maintaining the principle and practice of local self-government and freedom of choice. Without them, the middle and upper classes would be powerless against the onslaught of the poor and the black, hordes of service demanders who would invade the community, drive up the crime and tax rates and drive down property values. The problems of the inner city would quickly spread to the suburbs. No place would qualify as a safe haven. In the absence of zoning ordinances and deed restrictions, the proud owners of the expensive, well-maintained, single-family homes might wake up one morning to discover workers breaking ground next door for a multifamily, low-income housing project. Zoning protects such a family from the unthinkable.

To its critics, however, zoning is an instrument of oppression wielded by the middle and upper classes against the disadvantaged. Exclusionary zoning does more than prevent the poor from being the neighbors of the rich. It consigns them to an isolated environment characterized by high crime, inferior housing, and inadequate education and denies them the jobs available in the suburbs. It allows and perpetuates the problems that inevitably arise in a society distinguished by intense racial and class segregation. According to this view, little progress can be made toward a more humane and progressive society until exclusionary zoning, the bulwark of narrow self-interest, is abolished. Separatism, isolation, exclusion, discrimination, segregation, and the consequent huge disparities between overwhelming need on the one hand and vast wealth on the other are the natural outcomes of exclusionary zoning.

Whether zoning ordinances and deed restrictions are devices to guarantee local self-government or instruments of class oppression, one thing is certain. They are among the most important actions that government at *any* level in this country can take. The mechanics of these ordinances are relatively simple. They specify that any residential structure built in a particular area must meet certain requirements that specify lot size, square footage of living space, and number of families residing there. For example, the government of a wealthy suburb may require that all new homes be single-family residences, with a minimum of 3,000 square feet of living space and located on a lot measuring at least half an acre.

At first glance, zoning regulations appear harmless. Shouldn't governments and their citizens have the right to control new construction within their jurisdictions? Who wants run-down wooden shacks scattered about among nicely maintained middle-class houses? Closer examination reveals, however, that the apparent simplicity of zoning ordinances conceals consequences of vast importance. Single-family, 3,000 square feet, and half-acre lot requirements guarantee that a suburb will remain essentially all white and all rich. The only poor people entering the area will be those driving through, delivery persons making their daily rounds, and cleaners and other menial laborers on their way to work. A bit of quick computation readily demonstrates why. Assuming a cost of only $60 per square foot for a new construction and a lot price of only $25,000 yields a conservative figure of $205,000 for the cost of a new home in a suburb. This figure may be considerably higher depending on construction costs, land values, and building code requirements with respect to construction materials and techniques. In any case, $205,000 is a mighty deterrent to entry into the suburb. Even if the prospective buyer can afford the down payment of $30,000 to $35,000 and the required points (a fee of from 1 to 7 percent of the loan charged by the lender), the monthly mortgage payment for 30 years could easily exceed $2,000 per month. Thus, all but upper-class families are excluded from many suburbs. The exclusionary impact of zoning ordinances is further demonstrated by the fact that frequently these laws prohibit all but single-family residences constructed on individual lots. Consequently, multifamily structures (public housing projects, apartment buildings) as well as townhouses and condominiums are excluded.

Fragmentation within metropolitan areas, more than any other characteristic of urban life, allows the powerful play of narrow self-interest. It both reflects and reveals certain fundamental facts about human nature. People want more rather than less. They desire to live with their own kind. They are willing to assume little or no responsibility for those less well-off than themselves. Many do not see zoning ordinances as instruments of class and racial oppression that generate and perpetuate vast inequalities of wealth, security, and opportunity. Instead, they view them as absolutely essential if the fruits and benefits of their hard work and self-sacrifice are to be protected.

The Constitutionality of Zoning   It is legitimate to ask if exclusionary zoning violates constitutional guarantees. The answer is no. The courts have consistently upheld the right of local governments to regulate the use of property, even though that right denies others the right to live where they choose. How can it be constitutional for citizens living in one jurisdiction to exclude others because they can't afford to buy or build a house that meets certain arbitrary requirements? The answer is simple. Discrimination on the basis of income does not violate constitutional protections. If you are discriminated against simply because you are poor, then the constitution provides you with no remedy, no way to redress your grievance.

However, all the poor must be discriminated against equally. If you are poor and black and can demonstrate that a discriminatory practice occurred because of race rather than income, then a constitutional remedy is available. Pursuant to its interpretation of the equal protection clause of the Fourteenth Amendment, the U.S. Supreme Court has established the concept of *suspect classifications*. Race, religious preference, and national origin are included in this category. If a citizen alleges that he or she was discriminated against (with respect to housing, a job, an education) because of membership in a suspect classification, the court will apply its doctrine of *close scrutiny* and order a remedy if the facts of the case support the allegations. A person who is black, a Jew, or of Polish origin cannot be treated differently by government *because* he or she is black, a Jew, or a Pole.

A problem arises, however, when a citizen who alleges discrimination is *both* black and poor. A Federal District Court addressed this issue in 1969 in the case of *Hawkins* v. *Town of Shaw*. The town of Shaw, Mississippi, was charged with discriminating against black neighborhoods in the provision of basic public services (police and fire protection, water supply, and so forth). The court ordered the local government to take action to eliminate the differences because it was obvious that services were much better in the white part of town than in the black. The court further held that since these differences were so clearly associated with the residents' race, the evidence was sufficient to support the charge of racial discrimination. *Outcome* on the basis of race rather than *intent* on the basis of race was the standard employed by the court to decide *Hawkins* v. *Town of*

Shaw. That is, if the negative impacts of a particular policy disproportionately affect blacks, the plaintiffs do not also have to demonstrate that public officials *intended* to discriminate against blacks.
The facts speak for themselves.

This issue as it affects zoning was further addressed in a case in
1977, *Metropolitan Housing* v. *Arlington Heights.* Arlington Heights, a
suburb of Chicago, was sued by the Metropolitan Housing Development Corporation because the town government refused to allow the
corporation to build a number of low-income townhouses within its
boundaries. The town invoked the classic defense against this proposed intrusion upon its turf by undesirables—zoning. It simply argued that its zoning ordinances prohibited the construction of low-
income housing. Since discrimination on the basis of income does
not violate the Constitution, the town anticipated no additional trouble. However, the development corporation brought the charge of
racial discrimination. Look at the effects of zoning, charged the plaintiffs. Only 200 of the town's 70,000 citizens were black. It must certainly be the case that zoning has a disproportionate impact on
blacks. If the Court employed the same line of reasoning used in
Hawkins v. *Town of Shaw,* it would be bound to overturn the constitutionality of local zoning ordinances. It would be a decision of vast
importance, since zoning is the heart and soul of local government.

However, the Court decided in favor of zoning. In essence, unlike
the reasoning in *Hawkins* v. *Shaw,* the justices decided that racially
discriminatory *impacts* were not sufficient to support the charge of
denial of constitutional guarantees under the equal protection clause
of the Fourteenth Amendment. Instead the Court held that, hence-
forth, the plaintiffs would have to show *intent* to discriminate on the
basis of race. Such intent is extraordinarily difficult to demonstrate
since it involves the conscious, deliberative behavior of public officials. Local governments can defend zoning by arguing that it dis-
criminates against *all* poor people and is essentially color-blind. This
is a powerful argument. Exclusionary zoning continues to receive
constitutional blessing.

FRAGMENTATION AND LACK OF INTERGOVERNMENTAL
COOPERATION

The critics of fragmented local government also maintain that one of
its worst long-term consequences is that it contributes to a lack of
cooperation among separate jurisdictions with respect to areawide
problems. There is little incentive for many to insist on solutions to

a variety of urban ills. Instead of working to reduce inner-city crime rates, they find it in their narrow self-interest to move away from the problem and then devote their energies to excluding those people and situations associated with crime. If you want low crime rates, simply move to the suburbs and then erect barriers (zoning) to keep out poor, underemployed, and unemployed persons. You can do much more to prevent crime by prohibiting the construction of a public housing project in your neighborhood than you can by insisting on more and better-trained police. More police officers will cost more money and result in higher taxes and may not have much impact on crime rates. Excluding the poor is an easier and less costly solution to the problem.

Both the advocates and critics of fragmentation agree that it produces competition among governments. The advocates believe such competition is a good thing because it forces governments to become more responsive and efficient in their efforts to attract desirable consumers (the middle and upper classes). To critics of fragmentaton, the resulting competition is bad because it encourages narrow, self-interested, and class-based solutions to urban problems. In the short run, such self-interested behavior works to the advantage of the better-off. In the long run, however, even the wealthy residents of the metropolitan area are losers. If every problem is solved by moving away from it, then real solutions will never be found. And, eventually, society as a whole must pay the bill. Unemployment means more crime, and higher crime rates mean that there must be more police, more prosecutors, more judges, and more jails. If a separate, isolated, dependent welfare population is effectively confined to the inner city, a variety of social-welfare programs will be required to support these dependent poor. And if the costs of these expensive programs are not paid by local governments, they must be assumed by the state and national governments. Individual citizens will eventually and inevitably pay higher taxes, whether they are levied by local, state, or national governments. In the short run, wealthy suburban residents can escape responsibility for devising solutions to common urban problems. They cannot, however, escape the costs of these problems.

FRAGMENTATION—GOOD OR BAD?

Is fragmentation a bad thing? Would this be a better society if city governments exercised jurisdiction over their entire metropolitan regions? Would it be better if the various state legislatures abolished the hundreds of competing governments in urban areas and consolidated political power and authority under a single jurisdiction? Would Americans be better off if zoning ordinances, deed restrictions, and building code regulations were declared unconstitutional? The answers to those questions revolve around another one: better for whom? Every political decision and policy produces winners and losers. Fragmentation is good for some and bad for others. There is no doubt that a fragmented system operates in the best interests of some. They can keep their jobs in the city, drive to work on a federally financed freeway system, pay no taxes for the variety of city services they use during the day, and drive home in the evening to a wealthy, homogeneous, safe neighborhood. They don't have to worry that local government will tax them to support welfare programs for the poor. Others, of course, are not so fortunate, and they bear the burdens of the fragmentation of the urban area.

We do not mean to imply that the structure of metropolitan government—the tremendous fragmentation and decentralization of political power and authority—is the only cause of American cities' problems. Certainly a variety of other factors are also at work. Nor do we intend to suggest that there would be little class and racial segregation if city governments exercised jurisdiction over their entire urban areas. Zoning ordinances are used to exclude the undesirable *within* cities as well as within metropolitan regions. Neighborhoods within individual cities are highly segregated on the basis of race and wealth. What we do want to emphasize is that the basic structural condition of fragmentation greatly increases individual choice for members of some select groups, severely limits the ability of public officials in the central city to effectively deal with major problems, profoundly limits the utility of political action, and makes the city a captive of events and policies far beyond its control. Within a fragmented system of local government, the city does not control its own destiny.

CAUSES OF SUBURBANIZATION

Fragmentation of political power and authority has always been a possibility in urban America. In theory, at least, citizens have always had the opportunity to leave the central city, relocate in suburban areas, create new governmental jurisdictions, and use zoning ordinances, deed restrictions, and building codes to protect their homogeneity and exclude undesirables. In practice, however, the mass exodus to the suburbs, the splintering of urban political power and governmental authority, and the intensive and extensive segregation of the urban population based on race and income have been relatively recent developments. What has accounted for these fundamental and enduring changes? Certainly, the migration of huge numbers of rural Southern blacks to Northeastern and Midwestern cities in the twentieth century had an impact. Although the impact of this migration on the decisions of millions of urban whites to exit the city can't be gauged with any degree of precision, it is likely that it was considerable. In addition, the black migration coincided with rising taxes and crime rates, increased social-welfare programs, integration of the public school system, busing, and a perceived decline in the quality of public services.

Since fragmentation increases the value of exit as a problem-solving mechanism (and weakens the utility of such political strategies as voting, contacting, protesting, and interest group activity), the white flight to the suburbs should have been predictable. For the middle and upper classes, moving away from problems became a widespread, economical, and rational strategy. Just as the wealth, opportunities, and high service levels in the cities served to attract millions of poor people from the hinterlands, the flight of better-off whites to the suburbs served to sap that wealth and those resources. The homogeneity and security of the suburbs, just out of reach of the poor but within easy striking distance of the city's jobs and cultural opportunities, was an irresistible lure to those wealthy enough to afford to pull up stakes. However, the central city did not begin to decline simply because blacks began to move in. The process of decline was aided and abetted by other factors. These include federal housing policy, practices of the housing industry, and federal highway policy.

FEDERAL HOUSING POLICY

Housing has always been crucial to the growth, change, and decay of cities, and the activities of the national government with respect to urban housing have had major and enduring impacts on the lives of individual Americans. To understand those profound impacts, you need to know something about the history of the federal role in housing policy.

There was a huge demand for single-family housing in the years immediately following World War II. However, this demand could not be met by the private sector. To minimize their risks, banks and savings and loan associations imposed unacceptable requirements on prospective home buyers. Huge down payments and short repayment periods were required to qualify for a mortgage. Most families could not buy a home because they could not come up with enough cash to make the down payment and their incomes were not sufficient to afford the high monthly mortgage payments. The situation was characterized by a huge pent-up demand for single-family housing on the one hand and the inadequacy of private-sector financing mechanisms on the other. The federal government entered the picture and helped millions of families realize the American dream of owning one's own home. Without that intervention, there can be little doubt that U.S. cities would look vastly different than they do today.

Two federal agencies were instrumental in reshaping the American city. The first, the Federal Housing Administration (FHA), was created under the National Housing Act of 1934 to revive the depressed housing industry. The Veterans Administration (VA) was also established to administer a variety of programs for those who had served in the armed forces. The housing policies followed by these two agencies were similar. Both used federal funds to guarantee a portion of a mortgage loan. Although the prospective home buyer still had to find a bank or savings and loan to provide a mortgage, the chances of doing so were greatly improved. The federal guarantees vastly reduced the risks facing lending institutions. If the buyer failed to make the monthly mortgage payments, the bank or savings and loan was essentially insured against risk. In fact, these financial institutions were the direct and immediate beneficiaries of the changes in federal housing policy. The entire housing industry— builders, developers, banks, savings and loans, and realtors—received a great boost from the creation of the FHA and the VA. In essence, their activities were subsidized and made almost risk-free by the federal government. Since they incurred little risk, lenders began to make loans with little down payment required (5 percent for FHA mortgages and no down payment for VA ones). In addition, the period of repayment was extended from only a few years to 30 years.

The impact was vast. The FHA alone guaranteed the mortgages on over 11 million homes between 1935 and 1974. However, the impact of federal housing policy was not limited to dramatically increasing the level of home ownership in the United States. It also made a significant contribution to the segregation of the metropolitan population and to the decline of the central city. The FHA pursued a distinctly segregationist policy. In its *Underwriting Manual,* it specified those areas that did not qualify for federally guaranteed home loans. Such areas included racially integrated neighborhoods. Even prospective home buyers seeking to purchase a home in an all-white neighborhood were denied loans if the area happened to be located next to a black neighborhood. The FHA would consider such loans only if the two neighborhoods were separated by physical barriers or if a racially restrictive covenant was in effect (contracts that stipulated that a home in the area could not be sold to blacks). The use of redlining (the actual drawing of a red line on a map of an area to indicate those residential areas that did not qualify for loan approval) had particularly negative consequences for the central city. Racially integrated neighborhoods and white neighborhoods located next to black neighborhoods were not found in the suburbs. Little new federally subsidized single-family housing was built in the central city because the FHA refused to encourage a mixing of the races that it considered to be detrimental to property values. Consequently, most FHA and VA loans were for new homes built in the suburbs for white people.

Federal housing policy was not the sole cause of suburbanization. Suburban areas were attractive to developers because of the greater availability and lower cost of land. Home builders could realize economies of scale as a result. However, there can be little doubt that the great difficulty in securing a federally guaranteed loan for a home in the central city was a major factor in the cities' decline. When residential neighborhoods cannot obtain adequate financing for home construction, they eventually begin to deteriorate. When such loans are readily available for new housing in the suburbs, the pattern of growth and the corresponding pattern of decline are both predictable. The FHA and VA did not *intend* federal housing policy to contribute to the decay of the central city. It was an unanticipated impact. Their primary purpose was to stimulate the housing industry and increase the level of single-family home ownership, and they were successful with respect to that goal. That millions left behind in the central city would suffer hardship as a result of the process of decay did not occur to them.

Given the background of the bureaucrats who staffed the FHA and made the key decisions about who qualified for a loan and who was rejected, their racial biases are not difficult to understand. Many of them were recruited from the housing industry itself and from that part of the financial community involved with arranging home financing. They took to their new jobs a powerful ideology that emphasized "sound" investment practices. It was not good business to make loans in racially integrated neighborhoods (or in those that had the potential for integration) because it was believed that property values would decline in such neighborhoods. Thus, those bureaucrats and their sound investment strategy did much to hasten the process of decline and decay in the cities of the United States.

PRACTICES OF THE HOUSING INDUSTRY

The private housing industry, as well as federal housing agencies, made a major contribution to suburban growth and central city decline. Again, the availability of home financing provides the key to understanding this process of deterioration. Because of the advantages to be realized from economies of scale, home builders prefer to construct several dozen or even hundreds of homes at one time in one place, rather than a few. The scale of development favors suburban growth and expansion at the expense of the central city because of the greater availability and lower cost of land in fringe areas. However, another force is also at work. The construction of large housing projects requires vast sums in financing. Traditionally, such financing has been provided by local banks and savings and loan associations. Increasingly, however, the scale of residential development outpaced the capacity of local financial institutions to respond to the needs of the housing construction industry. Those institutions lacked adequate investment capital. In addition, state banking regulations limit the amount of funds that a bank or savings and loan can invest in a particular project. As a result, residential development corporations have turned to the national financial market. Mighty institutions such as major insurance companies now play a major role in providing the funds necessary to support large-scale housing development.

Again, however, there is a catch that works to the disadvantage of the city and to the benefit of the suburbs. Once more sound investment strategy prevails and has significant impact. Large financial institutions operate under the assumption that investments in the suburbs are less risky and more profitable than those in the central city. It is their conclusion that the suburbs will continue to grow and the city will continue to decay. The future is with the suburbs; the cities are dead or dying. Why pour good money after bad? Consequently, large-scale residential development projects in the suburbs are much more likely to attract adequate financial backing than are those proposed in the city. The belief that the city is in the throes of irreversible decay is, in part, a self-fulfilling prophecy. If central city neighborhoods cannot secure investment capital, then they will inevitably decay. Ironically, they will decay because they are thought to be unsalvageable. No financing, decay; decay, no financing. It is a no-win situation.

Even banks and savings and loan associations in declining neighborhoods frequently invest the funds of their local depositors in wealthy parts of the city or in the suburbs. Residents have contributed (thought certainly not knowingly) to the deterioration of their own neighborhoods. If citizens deposit their savings in a local institution that subsequently refuses to make loans for construction, repair, and rehabilitation projects in the neighborhood, the area will inevitably decline. No government social-welfare program can repair the immense damage caused by inadequate investment capital. Boarded-up stores, abandoned homes, and declining populations are the results of a self-fulfilling prophecy that assumes continued suburban growth and prosperity and inevitable inner-city decline.

The pursuit of narrow self-interest is rational for the owners and managers of financial institutions. Given the nature of the capitalistic economic system, it would be unrealistic to expect them to behave any differently. They do not consciously intend that their investment decisions should play havoc with the social and economic stability of countless inner-city neighborhoods. Their goals are narrowly self-interested ones: career success, maximization of profits, higher incomes. When such impersonal investment choices are duplicated thousands of times in hundreds of cities over dozens of years, however, the impacts are vast and profound. Millions of citizens will win and millions of others will lose. Most will not understand the powerful forces that have altered their lives for better or worse.

FEDERAL HIGHWAY POLICY

Still another national policy has operated to sap the strength and vitality of the inner city. In 1956, the federal government enacted the National Defense Highway Act. The birth of the interstate highway system greatly enhanced the ability of wealthier persons to escape the problems of the central city. Prior to the construction of the 41,000-mile system (most of which was paid for with federal funds), exit to the suburbs was not a particularly effective strategy. The inadequacy of the urban road network imposed unacceptable commuting costs. Forced to live in neighborhoods located near their places of work, people were essentially stuck in the city. The national government's decision to pick up the tab for construction of a massive freeway system changed all that. The middle and upper classes could keep their jobs in the inner city and live in homogeneous and well-protected suburbs located several or even dozens of miles from their places of work. Although complaints about traffic jams are incessant, the urban freeway network in fact was and is a highly effective means of moving millions of wealthier citizens into and out of the city each day. Without it, the process of suburbanization would never have happened. The average suburbanite would, quite simply, have been unable to get to work in the morning and unable to get home in the evening. In the absence of the freeways, most suburbanites would have no choice but to live in the city. And the nature of urban politics and conflict would be vastly different.

BUMPER-TO-BUMPER RUSH-HOUR TRAFFIC ON A FREEWAY IN BOSTON IS BOTH A RESULT OF AND A CONTRIBUTOR TO THE EXODUS TO THE SUBURBS AND URBAN FRAGMENTATION.

The freeway provided an escape route and millions of better-off Americans eagerly took advantage of the opportunity. Aided and abetted by the FHA and the VA and by the financial and investment practices of the private housing industry, huge residential housing projects soon surrounded every city. Closely guarded by zoning ordinances, deed restrictions and building codes, these segregated neighborhoods siphoned off much of the vitality and wealth of the city. Every change experienced by the central city (increasing number of blacks, higher crime rates, more taxes, busing, school integration) simply served to enhance the attraction of the homogeneous suburbs. The pursuit of narrow self-interest won the day.

ATTEMPTS TO COMBAT FRAGMENTATION

The fragmentation of power and authority within metropolitan areas clearly presents a number of problems. For example, the duplication of public services across several separate governments results in the needless waste of resources. Why should dozens of different jurisdictions in an urban area each maintain a separate police department? One of the arguments advanced in favor of governmental consolidation is that common services such as police and fire protection could be more efficiently and effectively delivered if they were centralized under a single public authority. Elimination of the duplication of effort would benefit everyone.

Another argument made on behalf of consolidation is that fragmentation works against cooperative action. Governments are forced into competition with each other. However, many problems of urban areas do not respect interjurisdictional boundaries. Crime, transportation problems, and air pollution have scope and impact that are areawide. Such problems cannot be solved when government action is piecemeal and taken in isolation from neighboring jurisdictions. Consolidation would permit a coordinated and comprehensive effort to solve shared problems. Consolidation of governments would also permit an equalization of the financial imbalance. Frequently, commuters pay little or nothing for their daily use of the services provided by the central city. Their consumption of these services imposes a serious fiscal strain on the city. Suburban jurisdictions would be more likely to bear their fair share of the financial burden under metropolitan consolidation.

A variety of attempts have been made to consolidate urban areas to lessen the impact of fragmentation. These include annexation, the creation of special districts, voluntary agreements, and councils of governments.

ANNEXATION

Some states give their cities liberal annexation powers. Consequently, cities in these states can lessen the impact of fragmentation by annexing suburban areas before they have the chance to incorporate and form separate, independent jurisdictions. Liberal authority to annex represents a major power for a city. No city can prevent the flight of middle- and upper-class citizens to the suburbs. If a city possesses sufficient annexation power, however, it can take over new residential development on its fringe and prevent the escape of wealth that these new communities represent. The disparity between inner-city needs and suburban resources is thereby lessened. Many central cities, however, are denied the annexation weapon in their fight against fragmentation. Many state governments simply do not provide their central cities with the authority to annex new suburban areas. In addition, many older central cities are already ringed by independent, incorporated jurisdictions. Such a city could not annex these separate units of government even if it possessed liberal annexation powers. Hemmed in by competing governmental jurisdictions, the city's growth is choked off. Escape from the problems of the inner city can be accomplished simply by buying a house in a nearby suburban community. The city is powerless to react to the impacts of white flight. It must make do with the people and resources that remain within its boundaries. Increasingly, those who are left are those who are too poor to leave.

One of the major factors limiting the effectiveness of annexation is the bitterness with which suburban areas frequently resist such efforts. Such opposition is to be expected. Suburban residents are motivated to fight a nearby city's takeover attempt for the same reasons that prompted their flight to the suburbs in the first place. They see little gain and much cost in becoming part of the city. Not surprisingly, the degree of income and racial differences between the suburbs and the central city is the best determinant of whether annexation efforts will be successful. Central cities with heavily black and low-income populations can expect vigorous, bitter, and effective opposition when they attempt to annex their wealthy, white suburbs.

SPECIAL DISTRICTS

Other, more limited approaches have also been used to deal with the fragmentation of power and authority in metropolitan areas. Special districts are an example. These districts are created to deliver a particular service for the entire urban area: flood control, sanitation, water, sewerage, parks and recreation, or mass transit. In essence, special districts are separate, independent units of government. They have the power to tax, spend, and borrow. Since they are independent units of government, they compound rather than alleviate the problems of fragmentation. They simply become one of several dozen or even hundreds of competing jurisdictions in a metropolitan area. Power and authority are further fragmented rather than consolidated.

VOLUNTARY AGREEMENTS

Voluntary agreements are another organizational device employed to enhance cooperation among governments in metropolitan areas. These arrangements can take a variety of forms, ranging from the sale of a service (water, police) by one government to another to joint responsibility among jurisdictions for the provision of a particular service. Since these agreements are completely voluntary and generally limited to only a few services, their impact on fragmentation is slight.

COUNCILS OF GOVERNMENTS

Councils of governments (COGs) constitute a final organizational structure that has developed to deal with the problem of fragmentation. COGs are associations whose members are the governments in a metropolitan area. Since they cannot force individual governments to follow their recommendations, these associations have, in general, degenerated into planning, study, and advisory commissions. Although COGs may well serve useful functions of planning and information sharing, they lack the clout to alter the existing balance of power. They can do nothing about tax and service differentials, the disparity between needs and resources, segregation, and exclusionary zoning. Consequently, they can do nothing about fragmentation and its impact.

It is highly unlikely that these various structural devices employed to reduce the negative consequences of fragmentation will ever be anything more than feeble attempts to deal with a fundamental problem. The primary motivating forces behind suburbanization and fragmentation were narrow self-interest and the pursuit of homogeneity. The goal of the better-off is to put as much distance as possible between themselves and the poor and black. Any proposal that reduces the effectiveness of this exclusionary strategy is doomed to failure.

POLITICAL PARTICIPATION IN METROPOLITAN AREAS

Many Americans are concerned about the problems of urban areas that we have discussed so far in this chapter. How might they influence the efforts of local governments to respond to those problems? How successful can they be in doing so? As we argued at the beginning of this chapter, the opportunities for individual citizens to influence their local governments are quite different from those available for influencing other levels of government. The traditional means of political participation often work differently at the local level, and some unusual means are available that have remarkable consequences for how cities evolve.

There are a number of ways in which people participate in the governance of a metropolitan area. In this section we will discuss six of the most important ones: voting, contacting, group activity, nonviolent protest, violence, and exit. We will analyze the limitations of these various modes of participation, comment on differences in their effectiveness, and conclude with observations about the significance of political participation in the lives of individual citizens.

Voting is the best known and most widespread form of political participation. We will also argue later that, for many, it is also one of the least effective.

A citizen can also participate by contacting a government official with respect to a specific problem. When an individual calls or writes an elected official or city bureaucrat to complain about a huge pothole, a missed garbage pickup, a broken or clogged water or sewer line, an obstructed drainage ditch, an overgrown vacant lot, trash and debris on the street, stray animals, drugs in the schools, the need for a stop sign at a busy intersection, the high crime rate, violations of the zoning ordinance, a landlord who won't repair the leaky roof or provide adequate heat in winter, a dirty park, a street gang terrorizing the neighborhood, a loud party next door, pornographic material, high taxes, or any of hundreds of other possible grievances, that person is engaging in political participation. He or she is demanding that the political authorities take action and commit resources to solve a problem. Contacting is a widespread, important, and underestimated form of participation in local politics.

In addition to voting and contacting, some citizens participate by joining groups that pursue political goals. Membership in a political party or labor union is an example of such group activity. A variety of other groups also have political objectives. Some churches support candidates and take positions on political issues. Neighborhood organizations and a variety of civic associations are frequently active in monitoring, evaluating, and calling attention to changes in zoning ordinances, budget appropriations, tax rates, and school board decisions. Business organizations such as local chambers of commerce are among the most powerful of these groups. Effective group activity requires organization and money. It is no surprise, therefore, that the most active and effective political groups represent upper-class and business interests.

Voting, contacting, and group activity are conventional forms of political participation. They are widely accepted as legitimate ways in which citizens can put pressure on government authorities to achieve political goals. No one will be taken aback if you go to the polls with the express purpose of voting against an unpopular mayor, if you complain to a public official about city services, or if you join a group to lobby for changes in local policy. Although many people never vote, contact, or join a group with political goals, these participatory opportunities are widely recognized as available and legitimate. However, there are other participatory options that are unconventional, unorthodox, or even illegal. If you use them, you may receive strange and hostile looks. Some may call you a troublemaker and attempt to interfere with your effort to participate in this fashion. You may be criticized, attacked, injured, arrested, or even killed. However, the costs of engaging in these types of participation have not prevented great numbers of citizens from relying on them throughout the history of the United States. Those people believe that the more conventional methods of political participation are ineffective.

One of these unconventional means of political participation is nonviolent protest. Strikes, sit-ins, demonstrations, and marches are examples of this participatory mode. Nonviolent protest is one of the many strategies used by political groups to achieve their goals. Groups can rely on nonviolent protest to further their objectives just as they employ voting and contacting. From the perspective of the individual citizen, however, membership in a group such as a labor union or a neighborhood association differs considerably from participation in a nonviolent protest activity. The differences in cost, risk, effort, and prospects are significant.

Another unconventional and extremely dangerous form of political participation is violent protest. Protests that start out as peaceful sometimes become violent ones. The riots in American cities during the 1960s are an example of violent protest behavior. Some observers have argued that those riots were not really political protests. They were not motivated by anger and bitterness over racial discrimination, poverty, police brutality, slum housing, bad schools, or unemployment. Instead, they were spontaneous explosions that simply provided an opportunity for the participants to pillage, loot, and burn. It is certainly very difficult to determine whether the participants in some violent protests initially intended to use violence, were motivated by intense political grievances, or wanted to rip off a television or jewelry or liquor store. However, it is plausible to assume that some citizens some of the time consciously and deliberately intend to use violence to achieve their political goals.

Exit is a final form of political participation that is generally not even recognized as such. Many citizens move from the city to the suburbs or from one metropolitan area to another for reasons that have little or nothing to do with politics. For example, many employees have to relocate simply because they are transferred by their companies. Millions of others, however, base such decisions at least in part on political factors. Discontentment about high taxes and crime rates, inadequate educational facilities, poor city services, busing, and integration of the schools has played a prominent role in white flight to the suburbs. In fact, exit has been the most important form of political participation at the local level in metropolitan areas during the past few decades. It has done more to shape and fashion the American city than any other form of political expression. Often overlooked and underestimated as a participatory mechanism, it has achieved its vast impact without the fanfare surrounding voting and elections, in the absence of the scholarly attention devoted to group behavior, and without the media attention given to mass protests. Rather than try and change the politics of government through voting, contacting, group activity, and/or violent or nonviolent protest, millions of Americans simply decided to solve their problems by moving away from them. Exit is a highly effective form of political participation, and the fact that its use is essentially denied to the poor makes it more effective for those who can afford to exercise this option.

VOTING

The vote does not transmit citizens' preferences with a great degree of precision. In fact, one of the problems with voting as a form of political participation is that it's difficult to know what the results mean. Is the incumbent mayor voted out of office because the voters are dissatisfied with specific policies (if so, which ones?), because they agree with the proposed policies of the challenger (if so, which ones?), because they like the challenger's image (nice smile, good looks), or because they think it's time for a change? Once elected, the public official doesn't have clear guidelines as to what the voters want him or her to do. Preferences aren't always expressed. It is difficult for the elected official to be responsive when he or she doesn't know what the citizens expect.

Although voting is a major form of political participation, not many citizens vote in local elections. Even though voter turnout in presidential elections in the United States is low (50 to 60 percent of those eligible to vote) in comparison to turnout in other countries, a much larger percentage of eligible voters participate in presidential elections than in local ones. In the mid-1970s, there was an average turnout of only 31 percent of those eligible to vote in city elections. By the mid-1980s, average turnout had declined to 27 percent of those 18 years old and older (Karnig and Walter, 1989). In some local elections, only 10 to 15 percent of those eligible to cast a vote do so. Why is turnout so low? Several factors appear to be important.

First, the absence of competitiveness between political parties in many cities depresses voter turnout. Turnout is higher in highly partisan cities (36 percent) than in nonpartisan ones (27 percent) (Alford and Lee, 1968). The activities of political parties stimulate participation because they mobilize voters, publicize issues, generate debate and controversy, heighten interest, and raise the salience of elections. When parties are not active, interest declines.

A factor that accounts for the much higher level of turnout in presidential elections is the extensive media coverage of those campaigns. Americans are bombarded throughout a national election year by television, radio, and newspaper coverage. Voter awareness and interest are raised as a result. There is much less media attention to local campaigns.

Turnout is also lower in local elections because labor unions are generally inactive in city politics. Labor leaders perceive that their vital interests lie elsewhere. Important labor legislation and policies (right-to-work laws, minimum wage, collective bargaining) are determined not by mayors and city council members but by state and national officials. Consequently, labor unions are very unlikely to spend time and money to mobilize the rank and file to participate in local political campaigns. This inactivity of unions depresses voter turnout (Hamilton, 1971).

Another factor that operates to reduce turnout is that many potential voters simply do not think that local elections are particularly important. It's much easier to get excited about presidential elections that involve "significant" issues: questions of war and peace, national defense, energy, inflation, unemployment, welfare programs, and national leadership. What's politically significant about local elections? How can the average voter get interested in (much less excited about) garbage collection, water and sewer systems, street repair, and public libraries? Many citizens simply don't see local governments as political institutions. Instead, they are viewed as service-providing mechanisms. The primary function of local government is seen as a housekeeping one: clean the streets, pick up the trash, catch the criminals, and maintain the parks. Keeping house is administrative and routine. Housekeepers should emphasize efficiency and effectiveness; they don't have to be concerned about wider political issues. When seen from that perspective, there's little incentive for the potential voter to participate in selecting among competing housekeepers. That's particularly true in cities that are run by a city manager, where power is in the hands of an appointed, highly trained, professional "housekeeper." This widely held view of the nature and function of local government accounts, in part, for the lower level of voter turnout.

However, local government is distinctly political. There *is* a Republican way and a Democratic way to pave the streets. City politics is about winners and losers. Some citizens get more and others get less because of the policy choices that local public officials make. Local governments deal with fundamental issues and human values. Their influence extends to vital service areas, such as education, police and fire protection, health, welfare, and transportation. Their impact on the quality of the individual's life is, in many respects, more significant, more continuous, and more direct than that exerted by the national government. But many citizens simply don't perceive it that way. The absence of partisanship in many cities, the relatively lower level of mass media coverage, the inactivity of labor unions, and the perception that local governments are housekeeping rather than political institutions all operate to reduce the perceived importance of local elections.

It would not matter that voter turnout in local elections is low if that fact had little effect on governmental policies. However, there is evidence to suggest that the low level of turnout may influence what government does. Not only is turnout much lower in local elections than in presidential elections, but the *composition* of the electorate also differs. The electorate in local elections tends to be dominated by better educated, wealthier, and more conservative voters. Lower-income persons are less likely to participate in local elections for the same reasons that account for the differences in turnout rates (Hamilton, 1971).

The absence of competitive political parties has a particularly depressing effect on the participation rates of lower-income citizens. The party designation of candidates on the ballot is more likely to serve as a clue to voting for poorer persons than for wealthier ones. The party identification of a candidate as Republican or Democrat conveys a wealth of information about his or her political philosophies. In nonpartisan cities, the poorer citizen is less likely to know what the candidates stand for. The resulting confusion and frustration discourage such citizens from voting. Political parties' activities and media coverage serve to increase the awareness and interest of lower-status voters because wealthier, better-educated citizens rely on a variety of additional sources (interpersonal communication, for example) to obtain political information. Consequently, the inactivity of parties and the media is most likely to exert a negative impact on the turnout of lower-income voters. And labor unions are most likely to mobilize working-class citizens.

We have seen that the absence of active political parties, the reduced level of media coverage, the inactivity of labor unions, and the low salience of city politics operate to depress turnout in local elections. These influences have an especially severe effect on poorly educated, low-income voters. There is also evidence that local public officials are most responsive to the most intense participators. Since this group is dominated by well-educated, high-income voters, local public policy is likely to be more conservative than would ordinarily be the case.

Will voting get the average citizen what he or she wants? Is voting an effective form of political participation? The answer to these questions is a very qualified maybe. Since citizens often expect voting to accomplish so much and since it so frequently doesn't deliver, we need to carefully consider the serious limitations on voting as an effective means of political action. In order for the vote to get citizens what they want, the following conditions have to be met:

1. Citizens have to actually get out and vote.
2. Elected officials have to know the citizens' policy preferences.
3. The candidate who is elected must agree with the citizens' policy preferences.
4. Elected officials must have the power and authority to implement the policies the citizens want.
5. Elected officials must feel compelled to implement the policies the citizens want.

Frequently, none of these conditions are met. As we have already discussed, a large majority of citizens don't vote in local elections. In addition, the vote seldom expresses specific policy preferences. Furthermore, many who vote in nonpartisan elections (where political parties aren't active and where the candidates aren't identified by party labels) won't know the candidates' stand on issues. Those voters are more likely to cast their votes on the basis of name identification and familiarity than on the basis of policy position. Also, elected officials frequently don't have the power to translate citizens' preferences into policy. Many cities are beset by fiscal difficulties. The financial resources necessary to do what the voters want may well not be available. Elected officials often have little control or jurisdiction over major policy areas such as education, welfare, and transportation. The power of the municipal bureaucracy often limits the ability of elected officials to translate voters' preferences (assuming, of course, that they know what those preferences are) into policy. Finally, one of the few controls that voters have over elected officials is that they can vote them out of office. How effective is such a threat, however, when many elected officials may not be particularly concerned with remaining in office?

Evidence reveals that many city council members serve out of a sense of civic duty and responsibility. They are not motivated by career ambitions. This volunteerism makes them immune from voters' retaliation (Prewitt, 1970). Elected officials who hold office to serve the public interest, rather than to advance their own narrow self-interest, are less likely to be responsive to voters' preferences. In addition, a large majority of council members who leave office quit simply because they get tired of the job. Few are defeated for reelection. How can voting get citizens what they want when those who are supposed to champion their claims on government can't be punished for inadequate performance? Public officials who don't have political ambitions and who voluntarily leave office can't be held accountable.

Scholars know a great deal more about who votes and why they vote than about the impact of voting on policy. Although we have just discussed several serious limitations on the effectiveness of the vote, we must admit that no one knows whether the vote works. Local policy is probably more conservative than it would otherwise be because of the low level of voter turnout and the domination of the electorate by middle- and upper-class voters. Also, the higher the level of participation, the greater the agreement between leaders and citizens with respect to their perceptions of community problems. And some studies have found that increased voting by blacks has led to more city jobs and better municipal services (Keech, 1968). It should be noted, however, that still other research found no relationship between the vote for an incumbent mayor and the level of services provided to neighborhoods (Mladenka, 1980).

CONTACTING

Contacting is an immensely important form of political participation for individual citizens. Frequently, it involves a matter of some significance to them and their families. Elections are held only once or twice every year. In contrast, tens of thousands of citizens complain to local government officials every day about personal problems that have a direct and immediate impact on their lives. They seek help in recovering stolen property or getting an overdue welfare check, a traffic light at a busy school intersection, action against a landlord who won't fix the plumbing, repair of huge potholes in the street or clogged sewer lines, or more police. The list of citizen complaints is almost endless. They phone; they write; they demand that governmental action be prompt and effective. Contacting is one of the most widespread forms of political participation and, therefore, deserves close attention.

It is possible that contact with government officials may be the most frequently used form of political participation. In some cities the number of citizens who complain to political authorities each year about personal problems may exceed the number who vote. One study revealed that several hundred thousand contacts with the mayor's office in Chicago are recorded each year (Mladenka, 1981). This figure does not include the thousands of other complaints, requests, and demands made to bureaucrats, aldermen, and ward committeemen. Therefore, it is conceivable and perhaps even probable that the number of citizens who initiate a contact with government officials at the local level is greater than the number who go to the polls. It is certainly true that more people engage in contacting as a form of political participation than join interest groups. Relatively few people participate in violent or nonviolent protests. And, although exit from the city is a widespread form of political participation that is extremely important for both the individual family and the city as a whole, on a day-to-day basis more citizens rely on contacting to further their goals.

Contacting is also a unique form of political participation because it involves a direct interaction between the individual citizen and a public official. Voting does not involve the same direct, personal communication; nor does it convey much information. What does a single vote mean? How is it to be interpreted? A citizen may cast a vote against an incumbent or for a challenger because he or she thinks that taxes are too high, services are inadequate, there is too much crime, it's time for a change, or for a variety of other unarticulated reasons. The contact, on the other hand, communicates a great deal of precise information about an individual personal problem to a local official. The public official may or may not respond to the demand, but at least he or she knows what the problem is and what the citizen wants done about it. The same cannot be said for the vote.

Who contacts government? The evidence on political participation at the local level suggests that it is strongly class-based. Those who vote, participate in political campaigns, join interest groups, and leave the city for the suburbs are disproportionately middle- and upper-class citizens. There is also some evidence to suggest that con-tacting exhibits this same class bias. One study argued that middle- and upper-class citizens are more likely to contact bureaucrats because these better-educated individuals possess the skills and knowledge necessary to deal effectively with government (Verba and Nie, 1972). They understand the rules of the game and know how to manipulate the governmental machinery. Poor persons, on the other hand, are easily frustrated by the bureaucratic labyrinth and are less likely to express their demands. Another study found that blacks are less likely to contact a governmental official about a personal prob-lem (even though they have a greater need for public services), be-cause contacts with white public officials involve the crossing of a color barrier (Sjoberg, 1966). Apparently, black citizens may be in-hibited by the requirement that they communicate with a white per-son in order to solve a problem.

How responsive is local government to individuals' demands? Are most citizen complaints ignored? Do wealthy white citizens re-ceive preferential treatment? Does contacting as a form of political participation work? Various studies reveal that the relationship of citizen demands and government response is a complex one. First, some cities are more responsive to individual service complaints than others. Chicago successfully resolves a larger percentage of its citizens' demands than Houston does. This is probably because the city of Chicago spends considerably more per capita on urban ser-vices than Houston does (Mladenka, 1981). Second, there is no evi-dence that local governments discriminate against black and low-income citizens in responding to individuals' demands. In fact, just the opposite is sometimes the case. In Chicago, there is actually a slight tendency for complaints from minority neighborhoods to re-ceive a faster or more effective response than complaints from white areas. In Houston, calls for police assistance originating in black neighborhoods got a faster response than calls from white districts (Mladenka and Hill, 1978). In Boston, housing complaints from poor and working-class neighborhoods were more effectively handled than ones from middle-class areas (Nivola, 1978).

However, it should be emphasized that many citizen demands for service receive no response. The evidence suggests that the failure of governments to effectively respond to many citizen demands can-not be dismissed by attributing it to governmental inefficiency, in-competence, and disdain for the needs of the citizen. Instead, studies of contacting activity reveal that the extent of governmental respon-siveness is determined by the level of resources required to resolve the problem. How much money will it cost to respond as the citizen requests? Demands that do not involve a vast outlay of resources—such as complaints about missed garbage pickups, stray animals, or trash on the streets—are frequently handled. Those problems that require a lot of money to solve are often dismissed. There is never enough money to effectively deal with all citizen demands. Therefore, public officials make selective judgments about which problems will receive attention.

GROUP ACTIVITY

One of the advantages of contacting as political participation is that it provides public officials with a great deal of precise information about citizen grievances. Government knows exactly what is expected of it: fix the streets, pick up the garbage, kill the rats. A major disadvantage of contacting is that it doesn't exert much pressure on government. If a government official chooses to ignore your individual complaint (as frequently happens), there isn't much you can do about it. The vote, on the other hand, is somewhat more powerful. Elected officials can be removed from office by a negative decision at the polls. However, the vote doesn't convey much information about citizens' preferences.

Interest groups attempt to rectify these limitations on political participation. There is strength in numbers. If you want government to fix the streets, lower taxes, or do something about crime, it makes sense to join with other like-minded citizens in an effort to accomplish these goals. Government is more likely to listen to hundreds or thousands of complaining citizens than to a single voice. Members of groups pool money, time, and energy to enhance the effectiveness of their claims on government. They attempt to avoid the shortcomings of voting and contacting by maintaining high pressure on government without sacrificing the clear expression of their preferences.

However, several things about interest groups ensure that they will be most effective as instruments of the upper classes. First, wealthier persons are much more likely than poorer people to join interest groups. One study found that 25 percent of upper-class citizens belonged to local political organizations, but only 6 percent of the lowest social class did. Poor citizens have less time to spend on political issues, are less interested in politics, and are less likely to believe that their efforts will produce results (Verba and Nie, 1972).

Another characteristic of interest groups is that money determines their success. The most effective groups tend to be those with the most resources, as we explained in Chapter 5. Groups derive their strength largely from organizational structure, and it requires money to organize. Computerized mailing lists, telephone banks, office space and equipment, and a research and clerical staff cost a great deal of money. In addition, groups attempt to influence citizens' opinions and public policy through public-relations campaigns. The molding of opinion is accomplished through mass mailings, telephone campaigns, newspaper advertisements, and radio and television spots. Successful campaigns are very expensive. Groups also attempt to influence policy by contributing money to political campaigns and by mobilizing the vote on behalf of favored candidates. They also organize information, conduct research, and hire lobbyists to press their claims on government. Again, to be successful, these activities require large amounts of money. Thus, wealthy groups have a pronounced advantage.

There is another reason why groups that represent upper-class interests are more likely to influence public policy. Public officials are simply more apt to identify with the goals of wealthier groups. Frequently, these officials are themselves upper-class in terms of income, status, and background. They look, dress, talk, and behave like upper-class citizens. Similar environments tend to produce similar values. Representatives of lower-class groups differ from the officials with whom they interact in terms of dress, appearance, manners, and values. They are less likely to understand and appreciate the rules of the game. Although the influence of different backgrounds on policy is a subtle and poorly understood one, we think it has a significant impact on the way in which policy is made.

Public officials are also predisposed to identify with the goals of upper-class groups because those citizens are perceived as revenue providers. Poor people are seen as service demanders. Upper-class groups represent stability, order, low taxes, and high employment. They contribute to a solid tax base and a balanced budget and enhance the image and business climate of the city. Lower-class groups, on the other hand, are associated in the minds of public officials with high taxes, demands for expensive services, social-welfare programs, decaying tax bases, white flight, and deteriorating neighborhoods. These powerful images (growth and fiscal strength versus decline and decay) operate to the disadvantage of lower-class groups (Stone, 1980).

Business Groups   Although it is exceedingly difficult to measure
the effectiveness of various groups in influencing local government,
we are probably on safe ground in assuming that business organizations are among the most powerful (for several reasons, as explained
in Chapter 5). Who can doubt that the local chamber of commerce
wields clout? The problem with determining the actual power of
business groups is that they may not have to rely on traditional forms
of political participation to achieve their goals. Less well-financed
and well-organized groups may have to bring considerable pressure
to bear through voting, campaigning, protesting, and lobbying before
their voices are heard. Not only are business organizations better
equipped to engage in these political activities because of their command of resources, they have another powerful weapon at their disposal. The business community is synonymous with jobs, high
employment, and economic growth. It is difficult, if not impossible,
for public officials to separate the public interest from business interests. This perceived commonality of interests is enhanced by the fact
that many elected officials come from business backgrounds.

We do not mean to imply that business groups always get their
way on every issue. As a matter of fact, they probably don't even care
about a number of issues that are of concern to other groups. But
when business groups do want something, they may not even have to
fight to get it. They may not even have to voice their demand. The
notion of *anticipated reactions* conveys the idea that political authorities sometimes choose one course of action over another not because
the economic elite has actually expressed support or opposition but
because the officials have *anticipated* its reaction and have decided
accordingly. Policies that would exert a negative impact on the favorable business image of the community are rejected. According to this
perspective, public officials are also keenly aware of the fact that
business groups *could* marshal powerful opposition to any policy
decision. Because business interests command vast organizational
and economic resources, their favor is courted by local political leaders. If anything, business power is probably increasing in those cities
beset by economic decline. Policy options that would result in more
relocations of business and contribute to the further erosion of an
already depleted tax base are not likely to be seriously entertained.

The city is therefore heavily dependent on business interests
over which it has little control. It is forced to placate them. Fragmented government enhances the power of these private interests.
Business activity is essential to the vitality of any city, since it creates
jobs. If a city wants to keep established businesses and attract new

ones, it must be responsive to the demands of the business community. For those who believe that the role of government is to protect the business sector and encourage economic growth and development, the fragmentation of local government is a welcomed and advantageous situation. Fragmentation enhances the bargaining power of corporate (and upper-class) interests and reduces the political power of the poor. It forces city government to pay special attention to the demands of those who control the economic life of the city.

We do not suggest that business calls all the political shots in the city. It is unrealistic, however, to assume that the business community is only one of several equally powerful groups. Political leaders are too heavily dependent for the success of their programs on a thriving local economy to ignore business demands for long. That these demands may not be made explicitly does not lessen their impact on policy choices. All other things being equal, public officials are more likely to be sensitive to the preferences of the chamber of commerce than to the demands of a minority group. It is hard to argue with the assumption that what is good for business is good for the city as a whole.

Neighborhood Organizations   In general, political scientists do not know much about group participation in the city. They *think* that groups have a significant impact on the political process but do not have much information on the specifics of group influence. This is certainly the case with respect to neighborhood organizations. No one even knows how many such organizations there are in any city. There are probably thousands in a large metropolis. It is a fact that there are more citizen organizations in wealthier neighborhoods than in poorer ones. And neighborhood groups are organized around the concerns of individual homeowners. Nothing is more certain to arouse the anger of the average citizen and stimulate him or her to participate in political activity than perceived threats to personal property and family. Busing of school children, the relaxation of zoning restrictions, and proposals to raise the local property tax are guaranteed to move neighborhood associations to action. In fact, neighborhood groups are probably the most consistently active groups in the city with respect to political participation. Their relatively high rate of participation can be accounted for by the fact that they focus their efforts on those issues of direct concern to the local neighborhood. For example, proposed changes in deed restrictions and zoning ordinances that would allow for the construction of multifamily housing and bring poor people into the neighborhood are likely to be perceived as direct threats to property values and vigorously resisted. Political activity is high because the stakes are high and the payoff is limited to the immediate neighborhood. There is a strong incentive to participate to preserve the homogeneity of the community and the status quo.

Neighborhood organizations serve as watchdogs for their communities. They guard against encroachments by the poor and racial minorities. They are highly sensitive to infringements on their turf. Generally, their activities go unnoticed by the media. Visits to a bureaucrat's office to request better maintenance at the neighborhood park, appearances before the zoning commission to protest revisions, meetings with school officials to discuss educational policy, and talks with the planning board to influence the location of public facilities are unlikely to attract the attention of newspaper and television reporters. These routine group activities simply don't have the salience of major participatory events, such as elections. In the long run, however, their impact is likely to be more significant.

The importance of neighborhood organizations should not be underestimated. With hundreds and even thousands of these homeowners' associations, each defending the "integrity" of its neighborhood, public officials find it exceedingly difficult to pursue and implement changes in vital policy areas such as zoning, education, taxation, housing, and public services. Pressured at one end by business groups to create and maintain a climate conducive to economic growth and at the other by middle- and upper-class neighborhood organizations to protect residential property values, keep taxes low, provide public services, and defend exclusionary zoning, public officials find that their range of policy choices is severely limited. They cannot afford to antagonize either group because both enjoy the powerful participatory option of exiting the city for the suburbs. It is little wonder that local public policy is conservative and aims at maintenance of the status quo.

Labor Unions   Labor unions such as the AFL-CIO that organize private-sector employees aren't very active in local politics. There are good reasons for this. The issues that are of vital concern to unions—such as collective bargaining, minimum wages, closed versus open shops, unemployment benefits, and safety regulations—are resolved by state and national legislation. Mayors and city councils seldom consider policies that directly affect key labor interests. The fate of labor unions is debated and determined in places other than city hall.

The same cannot be said for public employees' unions. Within the past several years, they have become an increasingly potent force in city politics. A majority of the 9 million employees of state and local governments were members of union organizations in 1975. There were only twenty-eight work stoppages by employee unions in 1950, but this number increased to nearly 500 in 1975. Even though only seven states (Alaska, Hawaii, Minnesota, Montana, Oregon, Pennsylvania, and Vermont) allow their public employees even a limited right to strike, the use of the strike as a political tool is certainly not unknown even in those cities where it is illegal.

Police associations and teachers' organizations are consistently the most active and probably the most effective of all public unions. In cities such as Houston, the police have even become an independent political force to be reckoned with. They take positions on the selection of new police chiefs, actively campaign for pay raises (the Houston police union recently succeeded in getting a proposed pay hike placed before the voters and threatened that crime rates would rise if it was defeated), and speak out against perceived political interference in departmental affairs. In other cities, garbage collectors have allowed the trash to pile up while they demanded better pay and fringe benefits.

Public employees' unions present a dilemma. On the one hand, it is easy to sympathize with their argument that public employees are entitled to the same rights as other workers. From another perspective, however, a convincing argument can be made that the essential nature of public services precludes the right to strike. The public safety is seriously jeopardized when police officers and fire fighters refuse to perform their duties. They accepted their jobs fully aware of their legal obligations and, consequently, strikes and slowdowns cannot be tolerated.

There is also evidence that these unions have had an impact on the financial stability of American cities. Demands for higher pay, better fringe benefits, and more employees are one of the factors that have contributed to the fiscal crises in some cities. Employees' salaries and benefits account for a large majority of local governments' operating budgets, and employees' efforts to increase their share of the pie can impose severe strains on a city's ability to balance revenues and expenditures.

Municipal employees' unions may also have an impact in a more subtle but equally significant way. One of the problems with governmental bureaucracy is that elected officials frequently find it difficult to control the bureaucrats. The growing power of employees' unions contributes to strengthening the role of the bureaucracy as an essentially independent force in local politics. Even under the best of conditions, mayors and city council members experience difficulties in asserting control over vital service departments such as the police. These problems of control and accountability are compounded when police or other municipal employee unions demand a significant voice in important policy areas and threaten a slowdown or strike if these demands are not met.

NONVIOLENT PROTEST

Parades, demonstrations, pickets, and sit-ins are examples of non-violent protests. Voting and contacting are highly individualistic participatory acts. The citizen routinely conducts these kinds of political activity in the privacy of the voting booth or by simply picking up the phone. These forms of political behavior are routine, and their legitimacy is widely accepted. Citizens are expected to vote and to complain to bureaucrats and elected officials.

Nonviolent protest differs from these more common types of political participation in several ways. First, it involves the cooperation and collective effort of several or even hundreds and thousands of citizens. Second, the effort involved is often of a strenuous physical nature. Parade permits have to be obtained, the protest effort has to be carefully organized and orchestrated, publicity campaigns have to be coordinated, and the actual event has to be supervised, monitored, and directed. Nonviolent protest also differs from more routine forms of political participation in that it is unorthodox. It may not even be accepted as a legitimate means of political expression by many people. Protestors challenge the status quo. They upset the routine of politics. They block traffic and make noise. They may be perceived as weirdos, troublemakers, or malcontents. In fact, protestors may be so intensely resented by other groups that violence breaks out between them and hecklers.

Protest also differs from other types of participation in that it relies on a different set of mechanisms for success. There are several parties involved in a protest movement. In addition to the protesters and their organization, there is the target of the protest, which, for most types of politically directed protest, is an agency of government. Whether it is the mayor's office, the city council, the school board, the police department, or some other bureaucracy, the target ultimately has the responsibility and authority to redress the protesters' grievance.

It is significant, however, that protesters do not attempt to bring pressure to bear *directly* on the target. Instead, they exert pressure in an indirect fashion. For example, assume that black citizens are protesting alleged police brutality in their community. In order to express their outrage, they have held a series of demonstrations and marches. However, they do not really believe that police officials will take action as a direct result of their protest. Why? Because they are not sufficiently powerful to force meaningful change. The very fact that protesters are required to rely on such an unconventional and risky type of political participation demonstrates that they lack clout. More powerful groups use voting, contacting, and conventional group activity to get what they want. Only those who have exhausted or expect no results from orthodox forms of political participation turn to the protest.

Then how can nonviolent protest ever work? In order to be successful, protesters must elicit the sympathy and support of some ally that is sufficiently powerful to bring pressure to bear on behalf of the protesters through traditional forms of participation. But first a potential ally must be located. This is where another party becomes involved. The media—particularly television—are crucial to the success of many protest movements. Media coverage dramatizes and publicizes the plight of the protesters. Before sympathetic whites can exert political pressure on behalf of blacks outraged over police mistreatment, they have to be made aware of the blacks' grievances. Television and newspapers perform that function. Once such support is aroused, the protesters depend on their ally to obtain a redress of their grievances. This interpretation of the dynamics of protest activity helps to explain the sometimes bizarre behavior of participants. Since media coverage is crucial in the search for an ally, the protesters must do whatever is necessary to attract the attention of reporters and television cameras. Noise, outrageous statements, confrontations, and even the threat of violence are most likely to elicit such media attention (Lipsky, 1970).

Several parties, therefore, are essential to the successful protest. Since the protesters generally lack political power, they must seek out a powerful champion to press their claims on government. This support is most likely to be elicited as a result of widespread and sustained media coverage. It is ironic, however, that the heavy dependence of protesters on a powerful ally frequently limits the effectiveness of the protest. The policy changes that result are often more symbolic than substantive. This happens because the target (government) responds to the demands of the ally, not to those of the protesters. The ally brings pressure to bear on the target, and government responds to that pressure only as long as it is maintained. The problem is that frequently the ally is supportive of only *some* of the protesters' goals. It is willing to settle for much less than they are.

The grievances of minority citizens are focused on a variety of urban problems. When they protest, they are demanding that fundamental changes take place in areas such as employment opportunities, public services, discrimination, education, housing, and treatment by the police. To accomplish these goals through protest activity, they have to enlist the support of a powerful ally (liberal and moderate whites) who can force government to pursue change. However, even sympathetic whites are unlikely to insist on fundamental change if such change requires a large increase in taxes or a redistribution of resources. Consequently, white allies are willing to settle for what minorities see as nothing more than symbolic gestures: a mayoral commission to study the problems, a few more members of minority groups appointed to city jobs, a new park or two, or a pilot housing program.

We are not optimistic about the efficacy of nonviolent protest. It is far too heavily dependent on parties other than the participants for its success. If the media can't be convinced that the protest is newsworthy or if some ally isn't sufficiently outraged over the alleged grievances or injustices to champion the protesters' claims in high places, the protest will quickly fizzle out. This form of political participation is also difficult to sustain on any long-term basis. The negative attitudes that most citizens hold with respect to the legitimacy and appropriateness of nonviolent protest and the immense effort involved in organizing and directing protests severely limit the prospects for success. The best evidence in support of our argument that nonviolent protest is generally an ineffective political tool is that very few rich people are ever moved to strike, sit-in, parade, or demonstrate. Nonviolent protest is a weapon most often brandished by the politically powerless.

VIOLENCE AS POLITICAL PARTICIPATION

Violence has been used as a form of political participation throughout the history of urban America. The racial, ethnic, and religious violence in U.S. cities in the 1830s, the draft riots of the 1860s, the labor violence of the early twentieth century, and the white violence against blacks in the 1940s testify to that fact. Hundreds of ghetto riots in the 1960s suggest that violence, if not alive and well, is lurking beneath the surface of the relatively calm, contemporary political waters.

One of the several problems involved in analyzing violence as a political tool is that it is extremely difficult to determine whether a particular violent event is *politically* motivated. In fact, some have argued that the widespread urban riots of the 1960s were not politically directed at all. Instead, these riots provided an opportunity and justification for criminals to rampage and pillage. Participants were motivated by the chance to rip off a TV or stereo. Few were moved to take part as a result of outrage over perceived political injustices. Television is identified as the major culprit in the spread of these riots. Widespread media coverage of the initial riots stimulated individuals in other cities to duplicate the early efforts in their own ghettos. The breakdown of "law and order," the leniency of a "permissive society," and the eagerness of television to publicize violence combined to encourage the "criminal element" to take advantage of the opportunity that lay before them. A pattern of urban violence that endured for almost a decade was firmly established.

Social science research, however, challenges this interpretation. Riot participants were not atypical of their communities in terms of education, employment, and criminal background. Furthermore, blacks identified political factors as causes of the riots, including discrimination, police brutality, lack of jobs, inadequate housing, and inferior education. It is also significant that a majority of the blacks in those communities where the riots occurred disapproved of them, but a majority also believed that they would have beneficial effects. It is noteworthy, however, that whites tended to hold fundamentally different attitudes. White citizens were much more likely to attribute the riots to the activities of "Communist" and "Black Power" agitators. A much smaller percentage was inclined to link the urban violence of the 1960s to black frustration and outrage over widespread political and economic injustice.

These contradictory perceptions and interpretations are probably crucial in accounting for the apparent lack of impact of such violent behavior on public policies favorable to blacks. One study asked the following question: Did those cities that experienced riots change their expenditure patterns in ways that differed from the budgetary choices of cities that did not have riots? The answer was yes. Riot cities did begin to spend more than cities where no riots occurred. However, these increased expenditures primarily went to buy more police and fire protection. There was no evidence that riot cities diverted resources to financing programs and services designed to meet the needs and demands of blacks. Instead, those cities beefed up their protective services in apparent anticipation of an onslaught of more riots. In fact, some argue that white Americans were so outraged over the violence and destruction they saw on their television screens that they retreated from their previously sympathetic position. A white backlash ensued. According to this interpretation, the riots were actually counterproductive. They did more harm than good in advancing the interests of black Americans (Welch, 1975).

EXIT

It is significant that all of the forms of political participation except exit depend for success on the willingness and ability of political authorities to respond to the pressure exerted by citizens and groups. There is no guarantee that public officials will do what the voter, contactor, group member, or protester wants them to do. Sometimes the official doesn't agree with what the political activists want, sometimes he or she doesn't know what they want, sometimes he or she can't give them what they want because of a lack of resources or control, and sometimes political demands have to be ignored because there are other, competing demands. In any case, once a citizen casts a vote, complains to a government official, supports a group's political objectives, or participates in a riot, strike, demonstration, or sit-in, the resulting outcome is essentially out of his or her hands. Citizens can only hope that government renders a favorable decision. They are not likely to seize control of the machinery of government through a coup and consequently ensure that the outcome is a favorable one. Once they have participated in any of those ways, their role switches from active involvement to passive anticipation.

The tremendous popularity of exit as a form of political participation can be accounted for in part by the fact that it gives the individual great control over the outcome of his or her political activity. Citizens do not just move at random. The decision to sell one's home in one jurisdiction and buy another in a different jurisdiction is a rational and calculated choice, an action that is not undertaken lightly. Considerations include zoning ordinances, tax and crime rates, and the quality of schools and one's new neighbors. Citizens and their families know what they are getting into and what they are getting out of. They will not exit unless the new deal is better than the old. Just as many Americans in earlier times went west, millions of Americans today have headed to the suburbs.

A decision to exit can involve significant monetary and psychological costs. The new home in the suburbs may cost much more than the old one in the city and may be financed at a higher interest rate. The commute to work may require more time and effort. Both children and parents will have to give up established school and neighborhood ties and establish new associations and relationships. Consequently, the costs of using exit as a form of political participation are much higher than those attached to most of the other forms. Although the costs are greater, however, the advantages are also much greater. The citizen controls the outcome. If a citizen moves from a city to avoid living beside minorities, high taxes and crime, poor schools, inadequate services, or busing, then he or she will select a new home in a jurisdiction where the poor are excluded, where taxes and crime are lower, where the schools are excellent, and where busing is nonexistent because all the students are middle- and upper-class whites. That citizen does not have to *hope* that the political authorities will respond to demands for a redress of grievances. He or she solved the problem personally.

Exit is a highly effective and extraordinarily attractive form of political participation. If you vote, that action *may* help elect a mayor or other official who *may* do a little something about the problems that bother you. Even if your candidate is elected, there is absolutely no guarantee that he or she can or will do anything about your concerns. If you carefully select a new suburban residence, however, you can solve many of your problems with that one act. You can lower your taxes, decrease the probability that you or any member of your family will be a victim of a crime, protect your property values against an invasion of the poor and the black, upgrade the quality of your neighbors, send your kids to a better school, and insulate them from busing. Only the poor and the foolish ignore exit as a problem-solving mechanism. Developments in the nation's cities over the past few decades reveal that millions of Americans are neither.

THE EFFECTIVENESS OF POLITICAL PARTICIPATION

Political action sometimes works—under the right conditions and for certain types of people. Richer citizens are more politically effective than lower-income ones. People with money are more likely to participate, to believe that political activity is worthwhile, and to understand and manipulate the rules of the game. In addition, public officials are predisposed to identify with their goals and interests.

Contacting is the form of political participation that is least susceptible to this powerful class bias. There are good reasons for this. Contacting is a highly individualistic political act between a citizen and a public official. The outcomes of this kind of political relationship don't entail the redistribution of resources. Large numbers of citizens don't win or lose as a result of these decisions. Instead, citizen contacts are generally about housekeeping functions. Therefore, the impact of contacting is generally limited to the citizen and his or her immediate family and neighborhood. There is also no evidence to suggest that public officials are more responsive to contacts originating in wealthy neighborhoods. Instead, bureaucrats make decisions about whether and how to deal with citizen demands for assistance on the basis of apolitical factors such as technical-rational criteria, level of resources required to resolve the grievance, and professional values (Mladenka, 1981).

Voting exhibits a distinct class bias. The very small group that participates in local elections is dominated by middle- and upper-class voters. Since public officials are responsive to the most intense group of participators, it should not be surprising that local policy tends to emphasize the maintenance of the status quo.

Interest group activity also operates to the advantage of wealthier citizens. Effective group action requires resources: money, leadership skills, organizational abilities, sustained effort, information, and expertise. Groups composed of upper-income persons are much more likely to enjoy these resources in abundance. In addition, public officials are more inclined to identify with the political goals and objectives of those groups that represent upper-class and business interests.

Exit from the city as a form of political participation is also intensely class-biased. Only wealthier citizens can afford to move to the suburbs. Poorer persons are extremely limited in their ability to take advantage of this powerful participatory option.

When it comes to evaluating the effectiveness of different modes of political participation, we have to conclude that group activity and exit are the most successful and that violent and nonviolent protests are the least effective. Groups that represent business and propertied interests wield a major influence on local policy. Groups that attempt to advance the political objectives of lower-class citizens are considerably less influential.

Protesting is too heavily dependent on the strong support of other parties for success. The very act of engaging in nonviolent protest represents a challenge to the status quo and implies that the participants lack traditional political clout. Unless the protesters can fashion a coalition of powerful allies, they are apt to be received with indifference, scorn, or retaliation. Violent protest is the riskiest form of political participation. In fact, the costs are so high and the impacts so uncertain that violence qualifies as the least rational of political strategies. Violent protest is the political act most likely to do more harm than good. Voting, group activity, and nonviolent protest may not do much good, but most of the time, at least they do not make things a lot worse.

For the individual who can afford it, exit is the political act most likely to guarantee direct, positive results. No other participatory option can ensure the redress of personal grievances with the same degree of swiftness and certainty. In the short run, at least, protest, voting, contacting and group activity will not work. And even in the long-run, there is no guarantee that these types of political action will solve the individual's problems. Only exit allows the individual to simply move away from his or her problems. Only exit offers the opportunity of selecting an environment where crime rates are lower, public services (particularly the schools) are better, and the neighbors are all middle- or upper-class. Of course, one of the difficulties associated with exiting as a participatory act is that many cannot afford it. The cost of buying a home in a homogeneous, wealthy suburb is extremely high. Others simply may not want to move. For them, exit as political action is a decision of last resort.

CONCLUSION

Life in the city poses great challenges for both governments and residents. Those challenges have been growing in recent decades, and the exiting that has been the response of many individual residents and businesses has made many problems worse. Yet some of the changes in urban life, such as the fragmentation of political authority among many units of government, have their proponents as well as detractors. Thus, different people reach different conclusions about some of the changes American cities have been experiencing.

We have argued, however, that a citizen's point of view about these changes will largely depend on whether he or she can escape the worst consequences of life in the city. And only select individuals and families, those who are economically the most fortunate, are able to exercise the exit option. And even that action provides only short-run success. This nation and some of its citizens can temporarily delay solving the pervasive problems of central cities, but eventually those problems will have to be confronted. Similarly, scholars of state and local government must recognize the character of those problems. They define the political agenda for urban governments and residents, and they indicate the ways those governments and individuals can and cannot respond to the problems on that agenda.

REFERENCES

Alford, Robert R., and Eugene C. Lee. 1968. "Voting Turnout in American Cities," *American Political Science Review* 62 (September): 796–813.

Bish, Robert L. 1971. *The Political Economy of Metropolitan Areas.* Chicago: Markham.

Dye, Thomas R. 1964. "Urban Political Integration: Conditions Associated with Annexation in American Cities," *Midwest Journal of Political Science* 8: 430–446.

Downs, Anthony. 1973. *Opening Up the Suburbs.* New Haven, Conn.: Yale University Press.

Gray, Kenneth S., and J. David Greenstone. 1961. "Organized Labor in City Politics," pp. 64–86 in Edward C. Banfield (ed.), *Urban Government.* New York: Free Press.

Hamilton, Howard. 1971. "The Municipal Voter: Voting and Nonvoting in City Elections," *American Political Science Review* 65 (December): 1135–1140.

Hawkins, Brett, and Thomas R. Dye. 1970. Metropolitan Fragmentation: A Research Note," *Midwest Review of Public Administration* 4 (February): 17–24.

Hill, Richard. 1974. "Separate and Unequal: Governmental Inequality in the Metropolis," *American Political Science Review* 68 (December): 1560–1567.

Hirschman, Albert. 1970. *Exit, Voice, and Loyalty.* Cambridge, Mass.: Harvard University Press.

Karnig, Albert K., and B. Oliver Walter. 1989. "Municipal Voter Turnout during the 1980s: Continued Decline," paper delivered at the annual meeting of the Midwest Political Science Association, Chicago, April.

Keech, William R. 1968. *The Impact of Negro Voting.* Skokie, Ill.: Rand McNally.

Lipsky, Michael. 1970. *Protest in City Politics.* Skokie, Ill.: Rand McNally.

Lucy, William. 1975. "Metropolitan Dynamics: A Cross-National Framework for Analyzing Public Policy Effects in Metropolitan Areas," *Urban Affairs Quarterly* 11 (December): 155–185.

Mladenka, Kenneth R. 1980. "The Urban Bureaucracy and the Chicago Political Machine," *American Political Science Review* 74 (December): 991–998.

Mladenka, Kenneth R. 1981. "Citizen Demands and Urban Services," *American Journal of Political Science* 25 (November): 693–714.

Mladenka, Kenneth R., and Kim Quaile Hill. 1978. "The Distribution of Urban Police Services," *Journal of Politics* 40 (February): 112–133.

Newton, Kenneth. 1975. "Social Class, Political Structure, and Public Goods in American Urban Politics," *Urban Affairs Quarterly* 11 (December): 241–264.

Nivola, Pietro S. 1978. "Distributing a Municipal Service: A Case Study of Housing Inspection," *Journal of Politics* 40 (February): 59–81.

Orbell, John M., and Toro Uno. 1972. "A Theory of Neighborhood Problem Solving: Political Action vs. Residential Mobility," *American Political Science Review* 66 (June): 471–489.

Ostrom, Elinor. 1972. "Metropolitan Reform: Propositions Derived from Two Traditions," *Social Science Quarterly* 11 (December): 241–264.

Ostrom, Vincent, Charles M. Tiebout, and Robert Warren. 1961. "The Organization of Government in Metropolitan Areas: A Theoretical Inquiry," *American Political Science Review* 55: 831–842.

Schnore, Leo F. 1972. *Class and Race in Cities and Suburbs.* Chicago: Markham.

Sjoberg, Gideon. 1966. "Bureaucracy and the Lower Class," *Sociology and Social Research* 50 (April): 325–337.

Stone, Clarence N. 1980. "Systemic Power in Community Decision Making," *American Political Science Review* 74 (December): 978–990.

U.S. Bureau of the Census. 1990. *Statistical Abstract of the United States, 1990.* Washington, D.C.: U.S. Government Printing Office.

Verba, Sidney, and Norman Nie. 1972. *Participation in America.* New York: Harper & Row.

Welch, Susan. 1975. "The Impact of Urban Riots on Urban Expenditures," *American Journal of Political Science* 19 (November): 748–759.

Williams, Oliver P. 1967. "Life Style Values and Political Decentralization in Metropolitan Areas," *Social Science Quarterly* 48: 299–310.

Williams, Oliver P. 1971. *Metropolitan Political Analysis.* New York: Free Press.

Wirt, Frederick M. 1972. *On the City's Rim: Politics and Policy in Suburbia.* Lexington, Mass.: D.C. Heath.

Wood, Robert C. 1964. *1400 Governments.* Garden City, N.Y.: Doubleday Anchor.

Zisk, Betty. 1973. *Local Interest Politics: A One-Way Street.* Indianapolis, Ind.: Bobbs-Merrill.

10 *The Political Institutions of City Government*

The policy problems metropolitan areas in the United States typically face today, which were described in Chapter 9, arose in part because of the evolution of this nation's economy. Late in the nineteenth century, industrialization encouraged the rise of big cities because of the need for a large population concentrated in a single place—to provide workers for factories and other industrial plants. In recent years, postindustrial development began to minimize the need for such population aggregations. The factory began to be supplanted by the computer work station, which could be located at a considerable distance from the central office. That development made it possible for increasing numbers of workers to live and work outside of the central city. The prospects for suburban development and for the use of the exit option were also heightened.

But cities were affected in other ways by these economic changes. A new form of city government arose early in the industrial era, in response to some of the unusual social and economic pressures of that period. As we will explain in detail in this chapter, the urban political machine, a controversial form of government, was born at that time. Subsequently, other forms of government were proposed and adopted in the majority of American cities. There still exists today, however, a controversy between those who favor some of the features of machine government and those who attack those same features.

Furthermore, the various forms of city government have important and different consequences. They offer different prospects for representing the interests of particular groups of residents, for efficient as opposed to representative government, and even for leadership opportunities for elected officials. It is these complex but related matters that we will explore in this chapter.

THE REFORM OF CITY GOVERNMENT

The impulse toward reform that swept through American cities in the last decades of the nineteenth century and the first few of the twentieth had an enormous impact. In many ways the reform movement was reactionary—it sought to return cities to a less complicated past. In that sense the reformers failed. But in other ways they were successful in changing the very nature of urban life.

THE EFFECTS OF INDUSTRIALIZATION AND IMMIGRATION

The rapid industrialization of the United States in the latter part of the nineteenth and the early part of the twentieth century (described in Chapter 1) had profound consequences for its cities. They became the centers of economic expansion and change. Southern European and Eastern European immigrants poured into the cities in response to the need for a cheap, eager, and disciplined work force. This extraordinary population growth imposed severe strains on local governments. Cities became responsible for the provision of a complex array of public services essential to an industrial economy: streets, bridges, police and fire protection, sanitation, sewer systems, flood control, education, recreation, water, and transportation. This dramatic growth in the size and complexity of urban government would by itself have been a real test of existing political institutions.

However, the task of local government was made even more difficult by the fact that powerful political conflicts quickly developed between the newly arrived Irish, Russian, Italian, and Polish immigrants on the one hand and the already entrenched Protestant Anglo-Saxon Americans on the other. The immigrants presented a paradox. Although they filled a distinct need for a cheap supply of labor for the country's factories and mills, they also represented a potent threat to the social and political status quo. They were Catholics and Jews rather than Protestants. They spoke in alien tongues. As outsiders, they bore the brunt of many Americans' contempt. Racial, as well as social, discrimination was the norm. As Richard Severo and Lewis Milford observe (1989: 253),

> Italians were widely regarded as nonwhite, or, perhaps, subwhite. They were routinely called "wops" and "dagos" and told that it took two or three of them to do the job of a "white man." Their intellectual abilities were not more highly regarded than those of blacks.

One school superintendent was succinct in his evaluation. Italians, he said, "lack the conveniences for thinking" (Severo and Milford, 1989: 236). No less an intellectual eminence than David Starr Jordan, the president of Stanford University, wrote that Southern and Eastern European immigrants were "biologically incapable of rising either now or through their descendants above the mentality of a 12-year-old child" (Severo and Milford, 1989: 237).

Given the contempt in which they were held, it is not surprising that the immigrants were excluded from exercising a share of local political power. The existing institutions of city government turned a deaf ear to their demands. And their demands were great. They needed help in dealing with the police authorities. They needed help finding a job, getting their children an education, and protecting their families. They needed help when injured or disabled, when seriously ill, and in their old age. But they could not get any of that help from the government agencies that existed when they arrived. Government had not yet assumed responsibility for providing the vast array of social-welfare programs and services that later generations would come to expect as a given. There were no food stamps, no aid to families with dependent children, no minimum wage, no unemployment insurance, no disability and health care programs, no government programs to help unemployed workers find jobs. It would be a long time before government would accept substantial responsibility for helping the poor and the disadvantaged. The government that the immigrants found was one dedicated to minimal services and low taxes.

The Political Machine In order to gain access to local governance, immigrant groups were forced to create what was essentially a new form of urban government. This new form, which came to be known as the *political machine*, had the following characteristics:

- Executive power was concentrated in the hands of a popularly elected mayor.
- Machine bosses operated behind the scenes, wielded vast influence, and frequently did not hold elected office.
- The political machine was highly responsive to its constituent groups. In return for voter loyalty, it provided ethnic neighborhoods with tangible, material rewards: a job with city government, a place to live, a hod of coal in the winter, a helping hand when a family member ran afoul of the police, a little money and a food basket when the family hit hard times. The machine did not try to win elections on the basis of abstract policy proposals, ideological appeals, or moral judgments and pronouncements. Instead, it tried to develop a highly personalized form of government that thrived by sustaining a web of mutual obligations between citizen and public official.
- The machine accepted the status quo. It did not challenge the prevailing distribution of power and influence in society. It did not seek to fundamentally alter the economic and social structure of the city by creating a working-class party that would replace capitalism with socialism. Instead, it sought to improve the lot of its ethnic constituents by working within the system. Its goal was to improve the immigrants' lives during the difficult and extended transition from outsiders to mainstream participants.

Unreformed City Governments Although the urban political machine no longer exists in pure form, its legacy can still be found today in *unreformed city governments*. These governments have the following characteristics:

- Executive power is vested in a popularly elected mayor.
- Members of the city council are elected from wards or districts. They represent geographically defined areas of the city.

Consequently, racial and ethnic groups are more likely to enjoy some representation on council.

- Political parties nominate candidates for office and play a prominent role in politics and policy.
- Patronage is used to reward party loyalists. Many government jobs go to strong party supporters.

It is difficult, however, to find any city government in the United States with all of these characteristics. That fact testifies to the effectiveness of the assault on the political machine by reformers.

THE REFORM MOVEMENT

Historians disagree with respect to the precise motives of the reformers. They even disagree as to who they were. Richard Hofstadter (1955) argues that the reform movement was dominated by middle-class Americans: lawyers, teachers, ministers, newspaper editors, and owners of small businesses. According to Hofstadter, these middle-class professionals and businesspersons were appalled by the waste, favoritism, and corruption of the political machine. The behavior and goals of the machine clashed dramatically with traditional American values and notions of how local government should operate. According to this highly idealized perspective, government should be run like a New England town meeting, where neighbors gathered after work to discuss, debate, and resolve policy problems. The concern should be with the public interest rather than any narrow private interest. The larger interests of the city, rather than the particularistic interests of the individual neighborhoods, should prevail. Cooperation and consensus rather than conflict and controversy should be the bywords.

The reformers wanted to turn back the clock to a simpler time when purer motives held sway. Their opposition to the machine was more than a reaction to a corrupt political institution. The machine was a symbol of the profound change that had fundamentally altered the political, social, and economic landscape of the United States. The entire fabric of American life had dramatically changed during the course of a single generation. The reformers were dismayed by changes at every turn: from a close-knit, community-based way of life in which homogeneous groups of neighbors held common ground in terms of race, religion, and values to the great, impersonal, metropolis where alien tongues, nationalities, religions, and cultures challenged the dominant Anglo-Saxon tradition for political control; from small business to huge corporation; from limited government to vast bureaucracy; from the day when individuals controlled their own labor and found dignity in work to a time when factories and assembly lines made a mockery of the notion that the individual had value. Hofstadter also argues that the reformers were dismayed by their loss of status. The newly evolving social fabric did not allow them the same degree of power and influence that they had enjoyed in a less complicated society. Their attacks on the machine represented an effort to retrieve some of their lost power.

Samuel Hays (1964), however, offers a different perspective on the reform movement. According to Hays, the reformers consisted of powerful businesspeople and their allies. Their primary objective in abolishing the political machine was to create an urban environment conducive to economic growth and business expansion. The business community required low taxes, usable land, long-range planning, regulated markets, and essential public services such as streets, sanitation, water and sewers, transportation, and utilities. The corporate sector required a government staffed by highly skilled professionals and technicians who recognized that the lifeblood of the city was business and who were willing to enter into a partnership with the business community to create the conditions essential to economic development. The machine was seen as too beholden to working-class, ethnic neighborhoods.

Both perspectives on the reform movement are probably accurate. Both sets of reformers—middle-class professionals and powerful business interests—sought to wrest political power from the lower classes. The political machine was highly responsive to its working-class constituents. More so than any urban government before or since, it was keenly attentive to particularistic neighborhood interests. It was less interested in serving the needs of the middle class and responding to the demands of the business community.

The machine, however, was up against a formidable array of opponents. The reformers wanted a professionally staffed, management-oriented government that could maintain an environment conducive to economic growth. They dealt a severe blow to the machine by forcing a series of legal changes that crippled its ability to prosper. Taken together, these changes created a new form of government. *Reformed city governments* have the following characteristics:

- Executive and administrative authority is exercised by a professional city manager. The manager is appointed by, and can be removed by, the city council. The manager, in turn, appoints department heads and other key administrators. In principle, at least, the city manager administers and implements policy rather than makes it. Inevitably, however, the considerable discretion the manager enjoys in the implementation process ensures that he or she will exercise significant influence over policy outcomes. Increasingly, city managers are trained in graduate schools of public administration and are inculcated with certain values and norms deemed appropriate by various professional associations.

- The city council makes policy for the city. It appoints and removes the city manager.

- Elections are nonpartisan; that is, candidates are not identified on the ballot according to party affiliation. Political parties are not officially recognized and do not nominate and support candidates for local public office. Although political coalitions or factions may run slates of candidates, these coalitions operate behind the scenes, are loosely organized, and tend to dissolve once the campaign is over. They are only a weak shadow of the traditional party structure.

- Members of the council are elected *at large* rather than from districts or wards. That is, candidates are voted on by the entire electorate rather than by just the voters residing in a certain district. The intent is for local legislators to be responsive to the entire electorate rather than to an individual neighborhood and, consequently, to govern in the public interest rather than representing any private interest.

- Merit systems rather than patronage are used to staff municipal government. Allegedly objective indicators are relied on to select qualified personnel. These measures include standardized tests, training, education, and employment experience. The dynamics of personnel administration (selection, retention, promotion, and utilization) are effectively insulated from political influence.

The structural changes implemented by the reformers crippled the political machine for a variety of reasons. The transfer of executive authority from a popularly elected mayor to an appointed professional administrator destroyed the ability of the voters to control the chief executive and hold him or her responsible. In a reformed government, the executive is accountable to the city council rather than to the voters. Furthermore, members of that council are elected at large. Consequently, they are considerably less likely to be responsive to neighborhood interests. Since upper-class and conservative voters are the most active participants in city elections (Hamilton, 1971), at-large council members are inclined to be attentive to conservative interests. Generally, it is thought that ward-based electoral systems are representative of neighborhood concerns, and at-large arrangements operate to the advantage of business and the upper class.

Nonpartisanship also damaged the machine's base. In partisan elections, nominations are controlled by the parties, issues achieve greater significance, and candidates are identified on the ballot by a party designation. Nonpartisan elections, on the other hand, tend to be dominated by personalities rather than issues. In addition, voter turnout is lower for nonpartisan elections, particularly among those citizens likely to vote for Democratic candidates (Alford and Lee, 1968; Hamilton, 1971). The absence of political parties depresses turnout because parties undertake activities that stimulate interest, dramatize issues, and mobilize voters. For example, a party organization spends money on political advertising, organizes speeches and debates, passes out campaign literature, and conducts telephone and door-to-door canvassing. Also, the lack of any designation on the ballot of candidates' party affiliations contributes to frustration on the part of lower-income voters. These voters rely on party designation as a means to identify a candidate's positions on specific issues and political philosophy in general. In the absence of that information, such voters are more likely to be confused and frustrated. As a result, turnout declines.

The structural changes caused by the reform movement weakened the political machine since the machine relied on a core of working-class voters. The ward system also contributed to electoral loyalty because tangible, material rewards could be channeled to specific neighborhoods. In addition, the ward system guaranteed that ethnic neighborhoods would receive some level of representation on the city council. On the other hand, at-large arrangements weakened ethnic control over the council, and nonpartisan elections depressed turnout on the part of the machine's most loyal supporters. The reform movement also weakened the machine by replacing patronage with the merit system. Once the attainment of a job in city government was no longer dependent on one's support of, and connections with, the party in power, the machine lost a major source of influence. It could no longer use jobs to reward its friends and punish its enemies. Once job applicants had to clear a series of apolitical hurdles (examinations, training, education), the machine was considerably less crucial to their lives.

The reformers sought to remove political conflict from city governing. They forcefully argued that there is no Republican or Democratic way to pave a street. Such tasks present technical and managerial problems rather than political ones. However, the reformers had a hidden agenda. They wanted to wrest political power from ethnic, working-class groups, but they hid that goal by maintaining that their true intent was to introduce the tools and concepts of scientific management to the operations of city government. Like so many other significant changes that occurred during the reform period, this new set of management tools was a direct consequence of an industrial economy.

The new industrial workplace depended on organization, discipline, routinization, standardization, and coordination of production tasks and schedules. It placed a premium on interchangeability, efficiency, and effectiveness. The ultimate goal was for managers to exercise full control over materials, workers, and production. In order to rationalize and routinize the extraordinarily complex functions of the industrial workplace, managers increasingly turned to the universities for help. A variety of new disciplines, schools, and fields of study developed to accommodate the needs and demands of the corporate community. These included schools of business and public administration and new disciplines in psychology, industrial relations, and engineering. The methods of the scientific approach—observation, data collection, hypothesis testing, experimentation, and critical evaluation—were applied to the study and organization of the factory. How can productivity be improved? How can workers be better disciplined and controlled?

The reformers envisioned the techniques of scientific management being applied to the operation of city government as well. In fact, they saw little difference between the city and the business corporation. The citizens were the consumers and stockholders, the city manager was the chief executive officer, and the city council was the board of directors. The city was a business organization that delivered services to consumers. The tasks and functions of local government were primarily housekeeping ones. What was political about garbage collection and street repair? Political parties and a strong mayor simply engendered needless controversy and conflict.

Efficiency and effectiveness in the delivery of services suffered as a result. The obvious solution to the reformers consisted of replacing the political executive with an appointed professional housekeeper, removing control of the chief administrator from the voters and giving it to the company directors (city council), and insulating those directors from neighborhood control by establishing an at-large electoral system.

As we indicated earlier, the reform movement was highly successful. Today, two out of every three American cities have reformed governments. However, the structural changes accomplished by the reformers cannot account for the demise of the political machine. Certain changes that were taking place in society would have seriously eroded the strength of the machine, independent of reform activity. These changes included three important trends:

1. *Rise of the middle class.* As the country became increasingly prosperous, the children and grandchildren of the immigrants began to move up the economic and social ladder. As they did, they had less and less need for a party organization to serve as an intermediary between themselves and an alien environment.

2. *Rise of the welfare state.* The severe depression of the 1930s provided the impetus for the national government to assume responsibility for the provision of a vast and complex array of social welfare and income maintenance programs. After the era of cooperative federalism began, the needy citizen could turn to a public bureaucracy at the national, state, or local level for the type of help that earlier only the political machine could provide. Further, government could provide much more in the way of help since it commanded vast resources never available to the political machine.

3. *Increasing complexity of municipal government.* As the tasks and functions of city government grew more complicated, a need for highly educated and skilled managers, professionals, and technicians developed. As a result, the patronage system became quickly obsolete. In order to attract and retain the highly educated and qualified employees essential to the effective operation of municipal government, cities had to implement merit systems within their personnel departments. The implications of this development for the vitality of the political machine were significant. Since the machine was heavily dependent on using government jobs as a reward to loyal supporters, the move to a merit system weakened its ability to sustain voters' loyalty.

We have discussed the politics of reform fairly extensively because the reform movement continues to exert a powerful impact on city government in the United States. In fact, there is a constant struggle between the forces of reform and those groups and elements in the city that seek to fashion a more open and responsive set of local political institutions. We have already noted that a clear majority of cities have adopted reformed governmental structures. We can better understand the current significance of reform politics for urban governance if we first examine the impact of reformism on policy.

THE CONSEQUENCES OF REFORM

Perhaps the single most significant consequence of the reform movement is that it replaced the machine with another dominant political institution—the urban bureaucracy. The great bureaucracies that have arisen to administer public works, police and fire protection, city planning, education, and recreation are what Theodore Lowi calls *functional fiefdoms*. They are autonomous, independent centers of power in city government. (These bureaucratic organizations are so important and powerful in state *and* local governments that we will devote all of Chapter 13 to an extended discussion of their power.) They control vast amounts of money, personnel, and influence, and they have great discretion as to how those resources will be translated into services and programs. These bureaucratic empires are largely independent centers of power because bureaucrats enjoy the distinct advantage of being experts in their area of operations. They enjoy a virtual monopoly over information and are generally highly experienced, with long tenures in office. On the other hand, elected public officials tend to be generalists rather than specialists. Consequently, they are at a disadvantage when dealing with career experts.

Municipal bureaucracies represent the institutionalization of the philosophy of scientific management. The city's housekeepers are hired on the basis of their professional qualifications: experience, training, education, and expert knowledge. Once hired, they are largely insulated from public control and political pressure. Their jobs are not dependent on pleasing either the voters or elected officials. Instead, they can rely on their own professional judgments and apply their own professional norms as a guide to policy decisions.

Another impact of reformism is that voter turnout is lower in cities with reformed governments. It is also relatively lower among those citizens most likely to vote for the more liberal candidates. As a result, the active electorate is dominated by conservative voters. Since public officials tend to respond to the most active segment of the community (Verba and Nie, 1971), policy in reformed municipalities is more conservative than in unreformed ones.

Reformed governments are alleged to be less responsive than unreformed governments to the diverse racial and socioeconomic groups that populate a city. Reformed governmental structures represent the triumph of middle-class and business values. Reformed governments seek to minimize political controversy and conflict, to limit the influence of lower-class groups, and to reduce political problems to technical dimensions.

There is certainly evidence that unreformed governmental institutions are more open and responsive to the diverse racial and socioeconomic groups in a city. Robert Lineberry and Edmund Fowler (1967) analyzed two hundred cities and concluded that the structure of government was an intervening variable between socioeconomic characteristics and policy. Cities with reformed governments had lower tax and spending levels relative to income than those with unreformed governments. On the basis of this evidence, Lineberry and Fowler concluded that reformed cities were more responsive to middle-class preferences for lower taxes. Albert Karnig (1975) found that reformed governments were less responsive to civil rights groups, as indicated by spending policies in the areas of low-rent housing, model communities, and community action programs. William Lyons (1978) concluded that different linkage mechanisms exist in reformed and unreformed cities and that these mechanisms operate in favor of different groups. Since the poor and racial minorities have lower education levels and participation rates, they are helped by unreformed structures that are more responsive to lower-class groups. Lyons also found that unreformed governments were more sensitive to demands for higher expenditures. Since more spending was assumed to benefit poor and nonwhite residents, he concluded that unreformed cities are more responsive to these groups.

It should be noted, however, that other research challenges the notion that governmental structure makes a difference. Terry Clark (1968) analyzed fifty-one cities and found that reformed structures resulted in higher levels of spending. Roland Liebert (1974) concluded that the apparent relationship between structure and policy reported by Lineberry and Fowler was really a function of the number of services provided by the city governments. That is, reformed cities spend and tax less because they are less likely to have responsibility for the provision of welfare, hospitals, and education.

David Morgan and John Pelissero (1980) studied eleven cities that adopted reformed structures between 1948 and 1973. They compared spending patterns in those cities with patterns in a control group of unreformed cities. Significantly, the changes in the spending patterns of the reformed governments were similar to the changes observed for the control group. Still other evidence that challenges the impact of unreformed institutions on expenditure policy is reported by David Morgan and Jeffrey Brudney (1985). They found that the functional responsibility of a city as well as demographic variables exerted a greater impact on spending per capita than structural changes did. Finally, Peggy Heilig and Roger J. Mundt (1984) studied several cities that changed their electoral system from at-large to district elections. These researchers were hard-pressed to identify significant policy changes that occurred as a result. They observe that they were unable "to identify dramatic shifts in the overall distribution of goods and services in any of our cities following the adoption" of district elections; they conclude that "unless major shifts in power occur, symbolic satisfaction and stylistic modifications will be the primary, not simply the secondary, results of structural change" (Heilig and Mundt, 1984: 154).

Another perspective should also be considered. It is highly possible that major local institutions enjoy more power and autonomy in unreformed communities, and greater influence for well-established groups and organizations may operate to the detriment of minority interests. For example, Kenneth Mladenka (1989) found that municipal employees' unions exerted a negative impact on the level of public employment of blacks in unreformed cities with a substantial black population. As union coverage increased, black employment declined. Significantly, however, no such effect was observed in reformed cities. Mladenka found that blacks are not directly deprived by unreformed institutions. Instead, the role of unions in influencing employment policy is dramatically enhanced within unreformed cities. As noted, this relationship was particularly striking in those cities with large black communities. Apparently a small black population represents little threat to entrenched union interests. It is in cities with large numbers of blacks that union resistance to further minority inroads has been especially strong.

Unreformed cities are generally thought to be more responsive to the diverse racial and socioeconomic groups within them. However, the enhanced power enjoyed by some groups and organizations in unreformed communities may bring deprivation for others. Apparently, the relationship between reform structures and policy outcomes is more complex than was initially thought to be the case.

Reformism also influences the level of minority representation on the city council. Cities select council members from wards, at large, or from a combination of the two. Generally, it is thought that ward systems are representative of neighborhood interests, and at-large arrangements work to the advantage of business and upper-class interests. Most of the empirical evidence supports the conclusion that minority representation on city councils increases under ward systems (Robinson and Dye, 1978; Hamilton, 1978; Engstrom and McDonald, 1981; Vedlitz and Johnson, 1982). However, others have found no such relationship (MacManus, 1978; Karnig, 1979).

Arnold Vedlitz and Charles Johnson (1982) found that ward systems had a major impact on the election of blacks to city councils in segregated cities. They concluded that at-large electoral systems severely depressed the level of black representation in residentially segregated communities. However, the type of electoral system made no difference to blacks' representation on city councils in nonsegregated cities. Vedlitz and Johnson offer two explanations for this finding. First, racial segregation may also imply racial polarization in some cities. Such conflict may limit the likelihood of electoral success for black candidates under at-large systems. Second, at-large arrangements may require blacks to form coalitions with whites, and building such coalitions will be difficult in segregated cities.

Clearly, coalition building should prove to be a more difficult task in segregated communities than in nonsegregated ones. In addition, the political effectiveness of blacks is likely to vary on the basis of two dimensions: segregation and the nature of the electoral system. In segregated cities, blacks will have little opportunity to join the dominant coalition under either a ward or an at-large electoral system. Since the white majority will be unwilling to share substantial power with them, blacks will be forced to rely on other means to influence policy outcomes. These alternative methods may include attempts to develop alliances with other minorities and disaffected white liberals as well as efforts to increase the minority share of council seats. In segregated and racially polarized communities, black political power will prove to be the most effective under ward systems.

Minorities elected under at-large arrangements in segregated cities will exert little influence on policy because they will be excluded from the dominant political coalition. In addition, they will have little opportunity to explore alternative means of enhancing their power because in segregated communities at-large systems severely depress the election of minorities.

Differences are also likely to exist between ward and at-large cities with respect to the types of coalitions formed and the style of black leaders elected. The coalitions built in segregated communities under at-large arrangements are not apt to survive the electoral stage. Also, minority candidates recruited by such a coalition to run in at-large contests must be acceptable to the white majority. Consequently, it is unlikely that such candidates will vigorously champion a redistributive agenda on behalf of their constituents. On the other hand, minorities elected from wards in racially polarized cities will almost certainly take office with a clearly defined set of policy objectives. Thus, in segregated communities, minorities elected from wards are likely to exert a greater influence on employment outcomes than leaders selected at large.

In nonsegregated cities, however, the ward system may actually work to the disadvantage of blacks and other minorities. In communities where little racial polarization exists, blacks elected from wards may have no incentive to engage in coalition building. As a result, they may be ignored by the dominant coalition. In nonsegregated communities, black members of city councils will experience their greatest success in terms of influencing employment outcomes under at-large systems where exclusion is not a goal of the dominant majority but where coalition building is nonetheless essential to electoral victory.

LEADERSHIP IN THE CITY: MAYORS AND CITY MANAGERS

The mayor is traditionally viewed as the chief executive of the city. As such, he or she is expected to set the public agenda and address major problems confronting the municipality. When citizens have a problem, they demand that the mayor do something about it. When problems aren't solved, they hold the mayor responsible. Typically, the mayor is seen as an executive drawn from the same mold as the President and the governor. But mayors differ in several significant ways from these other executive officials.

First, two out of every three cities have reformed governments. Mayors in these cities have limited executive authority. Although some mayors are still able to exert effective leadership in the absence of formal powers, achieving that is exceedingly difficult. Second, mayors are frequently limited by the restrictions imposed by other levels of government. For example, state governments or state constitutions frequently impose tax ceilings on cities within their jurisdiction. Third, mayors are limited in their leadership opportunities because of the highly competitive environment in which cities exist. Unlike national and state governments, city governments have essentially no control over labor and capital. Citizens, businesses, and resources are highly mobile within a metropolitan area, as we explained in Chapter 9. A city is in constant competition with other cities for industry, jobs, and growth. Jobs and capital are free to relocate to any jurisdiction. Consequently, the mayor is constrained by the need to pursue programs and policies that will enhance the economic climate of the community.

Mayors are limited by the national and state governments in other ways as well. For one thing, many cities are heavily dependent on federal and state aid. When such aid is cut, these cities experience fiscal problems. In addition, many aid programs come with strings attached (as was illustrated in Chapter 3). These conditions limit mayoral action. The federal courts and the U.S. Justice Department also frequently intervene in municipal affairs. The mayor may be required to spend large amounts of time and energy dealing with a federal lawsuit challenging the constitutionality of a city's at-large election system. Or, he or she may have to defend the city against a Justice Department probe alleging racial discrimination in municipal employment.

Mayoral power is limited by various state laws. Some states, for example, restrict a city government's authority to annex unincorporated suburban areas. In such a case, the city is unable to combat the effects of the flight of people and jobs to fringe areas. Furthermore, some states impose mandated programs on their cities. For example, the state may require city government to provide particular education or welfare programs. Such requirements present potential problems for the mayor, since the state may not supply adequate financial aid to fund these programs.

The power of mayors varies greatly across cities. We have already noted that some mayors find it difficult to be effective leaders because they operate in cities with reformed governments. Other significant limitations are imposed by the restrictions that national and state governments put on aid programs, taxing authority, annexation powers, and services. Jeffrey Pressman (1972) has developed an additional list of three preconditions that account for differences in the strength of mayoral leadership across cities. These factors are revealed by the answers to the following questions:

1. Does the mayor have the resources to do the job? For example, does he or she have sufficient staff and an adequate salary?

2. Does the city government have adequate financial resources? If the city is experiencing fiscal problems, the mayor's ability to provide leadership is severely limited. Most of his or her time and energy will be devoted to attempting to locate additional revenues. Mayors in financially stable cities have the opportunity to be much more effective leaders.

3. Is there an active political party or other political organization available to support the mayor? A political party makes a mayor better able to provide effective leadership because it represents an organized constituency and can provide essential resources such as volunteers, money, and information. The mayor can call on the party for support of new or controversial programs.

Some mayors, therefore, have relatively few resources to utilize. In reformed cities, for example, they can't appoint and remove key administrators, they don't have a large staff, they aren't paid an adequate wage, and they can't turn to an active party organization for help. Other mayors are further handicapped by their city's precarious financial condition, and still others have to struggle to cope with state restrictions on taxing and annexation powers.

But even though many mayors are crippled by various limitations at the outset, some still manage to exert highly effective leadership. Henry Cisneros of San Antonio is a good example. Elected in a reformed city, Cisneros became one of the best-known and most influential mayors in the country. Even though most executive and administrative power in San Antonio is vested in a city manager, Cisneros took full advantage of a variety of informal sources of power to establish effective leadership. These include the following five resources:

1. *The power of personality.* Much can be accomplished through the sheer force of personality. Some mayors are shrinking violets, but others, like Cisneros, have the unique ability to generate enthusiasm

and even excitement over their policy proposals. The effectiveness of a mayor's personality is difficult to measure, assess, or predict. It is one of those intangibles that can make a significant difference, however, in the life of the city. San Antonio, for example, is a different city today than it would be if Cisneros had never run for office.

2. *The power of an idea.* Some ideas are more compelling than others. The mayor who possesses few legal powers but forcefully presents a plan for action will be a much more effective leader than the one who commands an imposing array of formal assets but is unable or unwilling to share a vision with constituents.

3. *The status of the office.* A mayor may enjoy few legal powers, but by acting in a forceful manner he or she can accomplish much. Citizens accord the office considerable respect. Members of the corporate elite take it seriously. The mayor who recognizes that simply occupying the office invariably bestows respect on the occupant can work to translate that status into influence.

4. *Access to information.* A mayor has access to a great deal of information. Even in a reformed city, the mayor can ask the city manager and key administrators for periodic reports and evaluations. Mayors are continuously in contact with leaders of interest groups and heads of major organizations in the city. Each of these encounters provides the opportunity to gather and test the validity of information. Information is a crucial political resource. The mayor who establishes an effective information network can use its feedback to enhance his or her leadership capabilities.

5. *Access to the media.* The city's newspapers, radios, and television stations pay attention to what the mayor says and does. The mayor can exploit that media coverage to mold public opinion, focus attention on important issues, and mobilize support for policy proposals.

In fact, it is even possible that, in terms of official-legal powers, a so-called weak mayor may actually be in a better position than a strong mayor to exercise long-term leadership. Most of a strong mayor's powers are associated with budgetary and appointive authority. In the short run, these powers have considerable impact. In the long run, however, control over the budget and supervision of departmental operations tie a mayor to a pattern of routine. They limit his or her discretion, consume energy and attention, and prevent him or her from devoting much time to future planning. The weak mayor, on the other hand, is essentially free to concentrate on the big picture, leaving the mundane tasks of budgeting, service delivery, and personnel administration to a city manager and professional staff. In that case, citizens' complaints about services and programs are not the mayor's responsibility. He or she is free to lead.

Again, Henry Cisneros illustrates the point. As a weak mayor in a reformed city, he could easily have been content to serve as a figurehead. Instead, the power of his vision for the city captivated his constituency, and the freedom he enjoyed gave him the time and energy to implement that vision. Cisneros's vision was captivatingly simple. As a Hispanic public official in a heavily Hispanic city, it would have been logical for him to call for better services for Hispanics, higher taxes to support those services, and a more equitable division of public resources across racial and class lines. Instead, he proposed something fundamentally different—a program that maintained his support among his natural constituents while making him the darling of the city's business elite as well. That program was a call for economic development. The solution to the problems of poverty, high taxes, declining revenues, and inferior services was a simple one— more jobs. Jobs provided income, took people off welfare, and improved the revenue base. In turn, better services could then be provided without raising taxes. And Cisneros did more than issue a call for action. He acted on his vision. For several years, he was one of this country's most prominent and forceful spokespersons on behalf of economic development. He traveled around the state, the nation, and the world touting San Antonio's natural and developed advantages. Cisneros demonstrated that a weak mayor in a reformed city could develop a national reputation and attain an extraordinary degree of political leadership.

The late Richard Daley of Chicago, on the other hand, is a good example of a mayor who relied on a powerful political group—the political machine—for support. The machine could be counted on to deliver the vote, to provide automatic support for mayoral programs and proposals, and to attack critics and detractors. In return for tangible, material rewards, such as patronage positions on the city payroll, legions of party workers toiled in hundreds of neighborhoods to maintain voter loyalty to the machine. In return for this electoral allegiance, municipal government under Daley provided a consistently high level of basic urban services. Known during the Daley regime as "the city that works," Chicago has witnessed a slow but steady decline of the political machine since his death. This erosion of the strength and vitality of a once powerful, even omnipotent, political organization can be attributed in large part to Daley's absence. The experience of the political machine in Chicago suggests that in local politics, at least, strong political organizations are as dependent on a charismatic leader as the leader is dependent on them.

THE SPECIAL CASE OF MINORITY MAYORS

Thirty years ago, blacks and Hispanics were almost totally absent from public positions in American cities. Today, blacks hold, or have held, the mayor's office in Atlanta, Baltimore, Chicago, Detroit, Gary, Los Angeles, New Orleans, Philadelphia, Richmond, and Washington, D.C. Several hundred cities have elected one or more blacks to city council. Hispanics have been elected as mayors of Denver and San Antonio. Many observers were confident that an increased level of political representation for blacks would produce substantial policy benefits for the minority community. More public jobs, better housing, and improved public services would be one major consequence. However, it is safe to conclude that those high expectations have not been met. At best, the evidence is mixed. Peter Eisinger (1982) studied the role of black mayors and found that they had only a slight impact on levels of public employment of blacks. Lana Stein (1986) discovered that minority executives had a positive impact on minorities' share of municipal jobs. Mladenka (1989), on the other hand, discovered that the level of minority representation on city councils made a significant contribution to minority employment. However, in all of these studies, the authors found that the black proportion of the city's population was a much more important factor than the political representation of minorities. Furthermore, Albert Karnig and Susan Welch (1980) reported that black mayors had only a small effect on municipal expenditure patterns.

At best, therefore, black mayors have only a limited effect in improving the lot of the black community. Why? First, minority mayors are constrained by their city's fiscal condition. Black mayors tend to be elected in cities experiencing serious financial problems. In the absence of adequate revenues, black mayors are hard-pressed to maintain the existing level of services. Diverting new programs, services, and resources to minority neighborhoods is simply out of the question. Second, many groups will strongly oppose a black mayor's efforts to substantially redistribute resources. This is particularly likely to be the case if gains for blacks come at the expense of whites. Third, blacks began to make significant electoral gains during a period when the great increases in federal programs of urban aid were coming to an end. In the absence of federal generosity, black city executives are severely hampered in their ability to deliver tangible, material rewards to thier minority constituents.

A fourth reason has to do with the mayor's powers. Even a strong mayor doesn't have the power to redistribute resources. Any mayor is limited by the influence of the city council, department heads, and interest groups. In addition, minority mayors are limited by the need to maintain the electoral coalition that brought them to office. Prominent members of this coalition—Hispanics and white liberals—will not necessarily support an agenda that calls for a redistribution of resources to the black community. Finally, minority mayors may pursue an agenda that differs from the one envisioned by their constituents. Again, Henry Cisneros of San Antonio illustrates the point. His goal was to seek vast infusions of outside capital to stimulate economic development and create new jobs. This agenda differed from that of many in the minority community, who expected Cisneros to champion an elaborate program of social welfare services for poor neighborhoods. Instead, the new mayor formed a powerful partnership with the business elite and became a staunch opponent of activities that he perceived might threaten economic growth (higher taxes, expensive new services).

An important point should be noted about the electoral prospects and achievements of the minority community. Blacks have made enormous progress in the past two decades in achieving elected office at all levels of government, as Tables 10-1 and 10-2 illustrate. For example, only 719 blacks held elected city and county positions

TABLE 10-1
NUMBERS OF BLACK
ELECTED OFFICIALS
BY TYPE OF OFFICE

YEAR	U.S. AND STATE LEGISLATURES	CITY AND COUNTY	LAW ENFORCEMENT	EDUCATION	TOTAL
1970	179	719	213	368	1,479
1973	256	1,268	334	777	2,635
1976	299	2,284	415	1,008	4,006
1979	315	2,675	491	1,155	4,636
1982	342	3,017	573	1,309	5,241
1985	407	3,689	685	1,531	6,312
1988	424	4,089	738	1,542	6,793

Source: U.S. Bureau of the Census, *Statistical Abstract of the United States, 1989* (Washington, D.C.: U.S. Government Printing Office, 1989)?

in 1970, but more than 4,000 did in 1988. The total number of black elected officials increased from 1,479 to 6,793 during that same period. Black electoral success has been particularly striking in the South. Although the enormous problems of the minority community should not be underestimated, the fact that blacks' political achievement has been substantial during the course of the past twenty years must also be kept in mind.

TABLE 10-2
NUMBERS OF BLACK
ELECTED OFFICIALS
BY OFFICE AND
REGION

REGION	U.S. AND STATE LEGISLATURES	CITY AND COUNTY	LAW ENFORCEMENT	EDUCATION	TOTAL
South	227	2,980	392	847	4,446
Midwest	93	733	139	320	1,285
Northeast	73	275	104	243	695
West	31	101	103	132	367

Source: U.S. Bureau of the Census, *Statistical Abstract of the United States, 1989* (Washington, D.C.: U.S. Government Printing Office, 1989).

DIFFERENCES BETWEEN CITY MANAGERS AND MAYORS

Although both city managers and mayors are the chief executives in their respective cities, these officials differ in some significant respects. One obvious difference is that managers are appointed and mayors are elected. City managers don't have to mobilize political support, raise money, develop a series of positions on every conceivable issue, and appeal for votes during arduous election campaigns. Nor do they have to repeat that process every two or four years. City managers are largely insulated from the type of political pressure a mayor is constantly subjected to. Not only are they exempt from the need to court voters' approval, but they are accountable to an at-large city council that is generally more interested in efficiency and effectiveness than political responsiveness. Consequently, managers can afford to be less sensitive than mayors to distinctly political concerns. Mayors, on the other hand, operate in politically charged environments—where parties are active, where interest group leaders scrutinize government's actions, and where council members are keenly attentive to the concerns of their wards and neighborhoods.

Managers are aware that they owe their primary allegiance not to the voters but to the city council. In fact, their ultimate loyalty may not even be to the council that hired them but to their profession. Unlike a mayor, who was moved to seek public office by some personal vision of what the city should be, a city manager may never even have visited the city before being interviewed by the search committee. Managers have to clear a different set of hurdles and pass a different series of tests. Their virtues are those of the effective administrator and efficient bureaucrat rather than those of the politician. The prospective manager will be graded and evaluated by a highly select group of economic and political elites on the basis of his or her resumé, education, job experience, and letters of recommendation. The voters will have no choice in the matter. The manager will attain his or her position not by convincing the voters, but by convincing the council that he or she can balance the budget, get along well with the city's elites, hold the line on taxes, and achieve efficiency and effectiveness in the delivery of public services. But the manager also knows that his or her current job is only a stop on a career path to an even larger city. The manager's ultimate goal is to achieve status and respect within the larger profession of city management.

Thus, the mayor's primary constituency is the diverse array of groups in the city. The city manager's constituency, in contrast, is the dominant economic, political, and bureaucratic elite. Because mayors and managers are accountable to fundamentally different constituencies, mayors are clearly likely to be more sensitive to political concerns, and managers will inevitably emphasize administrative and professional objectives. Mayors will be more interested in responsiveness and accessibility, and managers will pursue efficiency, effectiveness, and consensus.

We do not mean to imply, however, that mayors are political and city managers are not. Both executives are highly political. The difference is that mayors tend to be much more open about the inherently political nature of their jobs. Managers attempt to suppress conflict and controversy. They are strongly inclined to deny—or at least conceal—their political tasks, functions, and obligations. Even though managers adhere to professional norms, this loyalty itself incorporates a distinctly political bias. By emphasizing the goals of efficiency, effectiveness, fiscal stability, and economic growth, the manager identifies with the concerns and values of the business community and the dominant white majority. That identification represents a profound political choice that is fraught with significant political consequences.

CITY COUNCILS

Scholars have not been kind to city councils. The research on municipal budgeting paints a picture of a council eager to defer to the expertise of the executive and the bureaucrat, and recruitment studies (Prewitt, 1970) reinforce the image of council members as motivated by a sense of civic obligation and volunteerism. Successful candidates assume office without the benefit of a clearly defined policy agenda. Consequently, they are easy prey for experts and experienced mayors, city managers, and administrators. Typically, city councils are described as reactive institutions characterized by high turnover and inadequate staff support. Individual council members are poorly paid and inexperienced, devote only a few hours a week to the job, take office without clear policy goals, have little interest in staying in office, and are no match for professional politicians, managers, and administrators.

However, this bleak picture of the policy role of city councils is probably exaggerated. First, these conclusions are generally based on findings from case studies of only one or a few cities, which may not be representative of all communities. Second, the available research has largely ignored minority council members, who are apt to be much more diligent in their pursuit of redistributive policy objectives than white businesspeople who seek office out of a sense of civic obligation. Third, research has generally failed to distinguish between councils elected under ward and at-large systems. Ward systems significantly enhance the effectiveness of minority political power in segregated communities, and at-large arrangements boost minority influence in nonsegregated ones. It is probable that the behavior, activities, and influence of council members with respect to policy agendas varies significantly because of these differences in electoral system. Studies that have ignored the substantial impact of these differences on council members' behavior and effectiveness may have produced a distorted picture of the policy role of local legislatures.

In fact, several recent studies suggest that city councils may exert a greater influence on policy outcomes than was previously thought to be the case. Glenn Abney and Thomas Lauth (1986: 188, 193), in a survey of department heads in cities with populations over 50,000, found that 32 percent of department heads "perceived contacts by council members on behalf of constituents to result in a

CITY COUNCILS ARE IN EFFECT THE LEGISLATURES AT THE LOCAL LEVEL OF GOVERNMENT.

distortion of their priorities"; 37 percent reported that "requests from council members are important in their decisions about the pattern of service delivery"; and 42 percent of the department heads in reformed cities ranked the council as having the *most* impact on their departments relative to the chief executive and interest groups. Thomas Baylis (1983) studied the San Antonio council and found that, in addition to the selection of the city manager and the approval of the budget, the council exerted significant influence on the allocation of federal funds and on appointments to major municipal boards and commissions. Thomas Dye and James Renick (1981) analyzed employment patterns in forty-two cities and concluded that the level of minority representation on the city council was the most significant determinant of the variation in minority employment. Also, Rufus Browning, Dale Rogers Marshall and David Tabb (1984), in their study of ten California cities, found that the primary explanation of differences in minorities' share of public jobs was the extent to which minority council members had gained entry to the dominant political coalition. Finally, Kenneth Mladenka (1989) discovered that minority members of city councils were more important than minority mayors in accounting for the variation in minorities' share of municipal jobs in 1,200 cities.

Although existing research does not allow us to set up the city council as the dominant local policy-making institution, the evidence is sufficiently extensive to cast doubt on conventional wisdom. Councils are more than reactive bodies manipulated at will by executives and burcaucrats and disinclined to press their own policy agendas. At a minimum, minority council members play a crucial role with respect to at least some types of policy outcomes.

CONCLUSION

The form that city government has makes a difference in what cities do, how they respond to the needs of individual residents, and how elected officials are able to provide leadership in their communities. However, different interests are served by different forms of municipal government, so there will always be disagreement about which form is preferable. And these matters are of more than historical interest.

Even today there is controversy in a host of cities about how the local government should be structured. Those residents concerned principally with efficiency and with keeping the costs of government low argue for more use of the features of a reformed government. Advocates of minority interests push for some features of unreformed governments, in particular for the election of city officials from wards or districts. Thus, the concerns about structural arrangements discussed in this chapter are relevant to contemporary, lively controversies about how cities should be governed.

REFERENCES

Abney, Glenn, and Thomas P. Lauth. 1986. *The Politics of State and City Administration.* Albany: State University of New York Press.

Alford, Robert P., and Eugene C. Lee. 1968. "Voting Turnout in American Cities," *American Political Science Review* 62 (September): 796–813.

Baylis, Thomas A. 1983. "Leadership Change in Contemporary San Antonio," pp. 95–113 in *The Politics of San Antonio*, David R. Johnson, John A. Booth, and Richard J. Harris (eds.). Lincoln: University of Nebraska Press.

Browning, Rufus P., Dale Rogers Marshall, and David H. Tabb. 1984. *Protest Is Not Enough*. Berkeley: University of California Press.

Clark, Terry. 1968. "Community Structure, Decision Making, Budget Expenditures, and Urban Renewal in 51 American Cities," *American Sociological Review* 33 (August): 576–593.

Dye, Thomas R., and James Renick. 1981. "Political Power and City Jobs: Determinants of Minority Employment," *Social Science Quarterly* 62 (September): 475–486.

Eisinger, Peter K. 1980. *Politics of Displacement: Racial and Ethnic Transition in Three American Cities*. New York: Academic.

Eisinger, Peter K. 1982. "Black Employment in Municipal Jobs: The Impact of Black Political Power," *American Political Science Review* 76 (June): 380–392.

Engstrom, Richard L., and Michael E. McDonald. 1981. "The Election of Blacks to City Council: Clarifying the Impact of Electoral Arrangements on the Seats/Population Relationship," *American Political Science Review* 75 (June): 344–354.

Hamilton, Howard D. 1971. "The Municipal Voter: Voting and Nonvoting in City Elections," *American Political Science Review* 65 (December): 1135–1140.

Hamilton, Howard D. 1978. "Electing the Cincinnati City Council: An Examination of Alternative Electoral Representation Systems." Cincinnati, Ohio: Stephen H. Wilder Foundation.

Hays, Samuel P. 1964. "The Politics of Reform in Municipal Government in the Progressive Era," *Pacific Northwest Quarterly* 55 (October): 157–166.

Heilig, Peggy, and Robert J. Mundt. 1984. *Your Voice at City Hall*. Albany: State University of New York Press.

Hofstadter, Richard. 1955. *The Age of Reform*. New York: Random House.

Karnig, Albert. 1975. "Private—Regarding Policy, Civil Rights Groups, and the Mediating Impact of Municipal Reforms," *American Journal of Political Science* 19 (November): 91–106.

Karnig, Albert. 1976. "Black Representation on City Councils," *Urban Affairs Quarterly* 12 (December): 134–149.

Karnig, Albert, and Susan Welch. 1980. *Black Representation and Urban Policy*. Chicago: University of Chicago Press.

Liebert, Roland J. 1974. "Municipal Functions, Structure and Expenditures: A Re-analysis of Recent Research," *Social Science Quarterly* 54 (March): 765–783.

Lineberry, Robert L. 1977. *Equality and Urban Policy: The Distribution of Municipal Public Services*. Beverly Hills, Calif.: Sage.

Lineberry, Robert L., and Edmund P. Fowler. 1967. "Reformism and Public Policy in American Cities," *American Political Science Review* 61 (September) 701–716.

Lowi, Theodore J. 1967. "Machine Politics—Old and New," *The Public Interest* 9 (Fall): 84–95.

Lyons, William. 1978. "Reform and Response in American Cities: Structure and Policy Reconsidered," *Social Science Quarterly* 59 (June): 118–132.

MacManus, Susan S. 1978. "City Council Election Procedures and Minority Representation: Are They Related?" *Social Science Quarterly* 59 (June): 153–161.

Mladenka, Kenneth R. 1989. "Blacks and Hispanics in Urban Politics," *American Political Science Review* 83 (March): 165–191.

Morgan, David, and Jeffrey Brudney. 1985. "Urban Policy and the City Government Structure: Testing the Mediating Effects of Reform," paper presented at the annual meeting of the American Political Science Association, New Orleans, September 1–4.

Morgan, David R., and John P. Pelissero. 1980. "Urban Policy: Does Political Structure Matter?" *American Political Science Review* 74 (December): 999–1006.

Pressman, Jeffrey. 1972. "Preconditions of Mayoral Leadership," *American Political Science Review* 66 (June): 511–524.

Prewitt, Kenneth. 1970. *The Recruitment of Political Leaders: A Study of Citizen-Politicians*. Indianapolis, Ind.: Bobbs-Merrill.

Robinson, Theodore P., and Thomas R. Dye. 1978. "Reformism and Black Representation on City Councils," *Social Science Quarterly* 59 (June): 133–141.

Severo, Richard, and Lewis Milford. 1989. *Wages of War*. New York: Simon & Schuster.

Stein, Lana. 1986. "Representative Local Government: Minorities in the Municipal Workforce," *Journal of Politics* 48 (August): 694–713.

Vedlitz, Arnold, and Charles A. Johnson. 1982. "Community Racial Segregation, Electoral Structure, and Minority Representation," *Social Science Quarterly* 63 (December): 729–736.

Verba, Sidney, and Norman Nie. 1971. *Participation in America*. New York: Harper & Row.

11 Community Power

In several of the preceding chapters, we have discussed the role of private business in state and local politics, the relations between business and government, and the power of business in community politics. These topics have preoccupied many American social scientists for decades, and they have been addressed in a number of different ways. One particularly noteworthy body of scholarship, however, is that which focuses on the topic of community power. In this scholarship a passionate debate still rages—after more than four decades of research—over the question "Who rules American cities?" Two sharply diametrical answers have been offered in response to that question: one by the group of scholars known as the elitists, and one by the group known as the pluralists. This debate on community power offers an interesting exploration of the question of business power (a topic we raised in Chapter 1), as well as the power of a number of groups. Thus, we will explore the elitist and pluralist arguments to enrich and expand our earlier discussions of these matters.

THE ELITIST PERSPECTIVE

The elitists look at the government of the typical American city and see a closed system dominated by businesspeople. They believe that this elite wields immense influence because it occupies and controls key roles and positions in the economic structure. That is, the chairman of the board or chief operating officer of a major corporation exerts a significant influence over political decision making because he or she controls vast economic resources. Political power flows from economic power.

The elitists also believe that power relationships persist over time. The economic elite in the United States has always been powerful. It has never shared power with other groups. Although conditions and circumstances change, those who play key economic roles maintain a firm grip on the reins of power. Influence passes from one generation of economic elites to another, with little disruption. Just as the founding fathers of this country were men who controlled vast economic resources, the influential people of today are disproportionately drawn from corporate boardrooms.

The elitists also hold that the business elite is in consensus with respect to major issues and values. Although those in the elite may occasionally disagree, they are united on those issues that might pose a threat to their continued domination of and control over the system. This consensus is a major source of strength and contributes to the preservation of the status quo. The elite presents a united front.

The elitists further maintain that elected local government officials are simply "errand boys." The business elite makes the important political decisions and hands them to elected political authorities for implementation. Public officials do not constitute an independent source of power. This does not mean that government officials clearly recognize and accept their distinctly subordinate role. In fact, most would vehemently resist the characterization of errand boy. Whether they are aware of being used or not is irrelevant, however. Their primary purpose is to further the goals and objectives of the elite.

Another assumption of the elitist approach is that the masses exert negligible influence over important decisions. The masses are ignorant, apathetic, uninformed, and unconcerned. They are more interested in earning a living and enjoying leisure activities than in participating in the political process. Most citizens are not very interested in politics; they are much more concerned with the routines of their personal lives. As a result, the elite runs little risk in essentially ignoring public opinion. Elections pose little threat to the status quo. Even if the masses were inclined to participate, they would find themselves effectively excluded from the corridors of power. Political power flows from economic power, and the masses control little in the way of economic assets and resources.

It should be emphasized, however, that the elitists do not believe that the economic elite is dictatorial in its practices and politics. It is seen as being (or at least attempting to be) benevolent and as trying to take public preference into account in its deliberations and decisions. There are two factors that allow the elite to claim the role of benevolent dictator. First, members of the economic elite adhere to the democratic rules of the game. They believe that sensitivity to public preferences is an essential component of how a democratic society ought to work. Second, the economic elite fears the potential consequences of consistently riding roughshod over the masses. It tries to accommodate the desires of the masses in order to prevent popular discontent and the resultant potential for disruption and instability. However, the elite theorists claim that there are critical limits to this benevolence. The economic elite will bow to public preferences only so far as its own principal interests are not at stake.

THE PLURALIST PERSPECTIVE

The pluralists vigorously reject each of the elitist assumptions. First, the pluralists are in fundamental disagreement with the elitists over how to define political power. As we explained earlier, the elitist approach assumes that political influence inevitably flows from control over vast economic resources: employees, financial assets, markets, raw materials, organization, technology, investment opportunities, research, and information. It is self-evident to the elitists that command of this economic wealth ensures control of the political process. To the pluralists, such an assumption is neither self-evident nor accurate; instead, who holds power is an empirical question. Thus, the pluralists say that elitists *assume* what they wish to *prove*. The pluralists maintain that actual instances of decision making have to be studied before conclusions can be drawn about the distribution of influence. The exercise of power cannot be assumed and studied in the abstract. Only through the analysis of real people interacting in concrete situations can observations about power relationships be empirically verified.

The pluralists also deny that the power of the economic elite persists over time. Instead, they see a constantly changing array of power relationships. The influence structure is in a state of flux. Power relationships form and develop around particular issues and dissolve once the conflict is resolved; then new power relationships with different sets of actors emerge over new issues. The key participants in these power struggles and their characteristics change with the issues and with the circumstances under which they are debated and settled. To assume that the economic elite controls decision making with respect to all issues, under all conditions, and at all times seems both naïve and inaccurate to the pluralists. The distribution of power is much more complex than the elitists allow or recognize.

The pluralists also deny that there is a consensus among the business elites on major issues. In fact, they argue that business-people frequently disagree on public policy issues. The so-called corporate community encompasses a great deal of diversity, and businesspeople pursue a wide variety of sometimes conflicting goals. Consensus and unity simply do not exist. In any case, the pluralists believe that any consensus has to be empirically demonstrated rather than automatically assumed.

The pluralists also reject the assumption that political influence can only flow from economic power. They deny that control over economic resources is a sufficient or even necessary condition of political power. Although economic wealth helps, a variety of other factors are also significant in determining who is powerful and who is not. For example, personality traits are important in separating the powerful from the powerless. One of these traits is simply the degree of interest that the individual has concerning political participation. You cannot expect to be influential in political decision making unless you are sufficiently interested *and* act on that interest. Some citizens play a significant role in political decision making simply because they are keenly interested, knowledgeable, informed, and aware. Since most people are not so inclined, it is little wonder that most are powerless. In addition to interest, leadership skills may also be crucial. Some persons are much more effective leaders than others. They can mobilize popular support, marshal resources, and organize and structure issues. Frequently, skilled leaders with few economic assets but with detailed knowledge of the political rules of the game are able to outwit and outmaneuver their wealthy but less skilled opponents. Economic wealth alone is no guarantee of political influence.

The pluralists also emphasize the role of expertise in power relationships. Expertise is an invaluable asset. Other participants in political decision making frequently defer to an expert's knowledge. On many issues, the person of wealth is simply no match for the expert. In a society that is increasingly based on the collection and processing of information and whose government must grapple with increasingly complex technical problems, the significance and influence of experts will continue to grow.

According to the pluralists, organization is another asset that rivals wealth as a definitive factor in the power struggle. Wealth can be used to achieve an effective organizational structure, but it is also true that the less wealthy sometimes develop a potent organizational base. Although individual members of labor unions (such as the AFL-CIO or municipal and state employee associations) are not wealthy, these groups are powerful actors in the political process because of their organizational strength.

The pluralists also reject the argument that elected officials are simply errand boys for the economic elite. Public officials have an independent source of political power. In fact, they are consistently the most influential decision makers across a whole range of issues. To classify them as subordinate to and owned by the economic elite is absurd. Public officials are more than lackeys. Those who underestimate their significance for policy outcomes fundamentally misunderstand the political process.

The pluralists see the economic elite as only one of several powerful groups. The economic elite has to fight in the political arena with elected public officials, labor unions, citizen groups, and bureaucrats. Politics is group conflict. Groups compete, bargain, compromise, and accommodate. No group wins all the battles. Some win on some issues; others are more successful on other issues. Power is shared, and it shifts. The economic elite does not dominate.

The pluralists also believe that the masses influence important political decisions. Elections and public opinion polls establish limits beyond which decision makers cannot go. Elections also determine which individuals will hold office and wield the accompanying power. Although the masses do not participate directly in the shaping of public policy, they do exert significant influence. Key actors in the political process are sensitive to public opinion and mass preferences.

CRITICISMS OF THE ELITIST AND PLURALIST POSITIONS

How can the elitists and the pluralists look at the same situation and arrive at such fundamentally different conclusions? When the elitists analyze the governance of the American city, they see a closed system where important decisions are made by a small, cohesive business elite. Elected officials are errand boys, the mass of citizens is irrelevant, and political power flows from economic power. The pluralists look at the same city and marshal an array of evidence to support the opposite conclusion. They find an open system, in which there is intense competition among a variety of groups and to which a number of others could gain access if they would only try harder. Elected officials are important decision makers, the wealthy are often outclassed by those with few economic assets, policy is a result of conflict and compromise among competing groups, and elections and public opinion influence political deliberations and outcomes.

DEFINITIONS OF POWER

The elitists and the pluralists identify different power relationships largely because of differences in their definitions of power. The elitists assume that economic power determines political power. The pluralists challenge that assumption. They see the question of who has power as an empirical one. Actual instances of decision making have to be studied. Only careful observation and analysis of the participants in decision-making situations can determine the real locus of power.

These differences over the definition of power are crucial to an understanding of the elitist-pluralist debate. The pluralists define and study power in situational terms. Who exercises power in various situations? A major criticism of this perspective is that there are an infinite number of situations in which power is exercised. No single group can be or chooses to be powerful in every situation. Many or even most situations are trivial ones, and the power relationships involved are insignificant. For example, the typical college student is involved in a number of different situations on a daily basis. Each one is governed by a different power relationship. In the morning, a professor has power over the student with respect to activities and achievements in class. On the way home from class, a police officer has power when pulling the student over and issuing a speeding ticket. Later in the day, a landlord will exercise power in raising the rent on the student's apartment. According to the pluralist definition of power (A has power over B if he can get B to do something that B would not ordinarily do), different people are powerful at different times and with respect to different situations and issues.

Thus, neighborhood organizations may be the most influential actors in decision making about proposed changes in zoning ordinances. City bureaucrats will be powerful in determining service delivery patterns. The mayor and downtown businessowners will be influential with respect to decisions about urban renewal programs. Citizens' groups will defeat a proposed tax increase. Bureaucrats in the education system will be the key actors in the selection of a new school superintendent. To the pluralists, this sharing of power across different situations and over different issues provides strong evidence against the alleged control of decision making by an economic elite.

To the elitist, however, this interpretation of power relationships misses the point. To find that different actors are influential in different situations is irrelevant because there are many situations with which the economic elite is unconcerned. The elite controls the decision making only in those situations where the issues involved affect its vital interests. It has neither the time nor the inclination to make *all* decisions.

The elitist view of power has its own problems, however. Assuming that political power inevitably comes from economic position risks overstating that political power. It might result in confusing the reputation for power with the reality. Even many average citizens, that is, assume that economic leaders are politically very powerful. Yet they might not be. Even the elitists acknowledge that there are issues—trivial ones, they claim—over which the economic elite has no influence. There might be other issues, however, on which the elite might not be in agreement or other groups can compete effectively to control political decisions. Thus, the extent of economic power may not be as broad or as well-defined as the elite theorists claim.

METHODOLOGY

The different methodological approaches employed by the elitists and the pluralists also contribute to their differing conclusions with respect to the distribution of power and influence. The elitists rely heavily on what is known as a reputational methodology. One of the most influential studies of community power, Floyd Hunter's *Community Power Structure* (1953), employed this technique. Elitists ask key informants—persons in the community who are believed to have detailed knowledge and understanding of how things operate—to provide a list of the most powerful individuals. These lists generally show heavy representation of businesspeople. The pluralists maintain that this methodology simply gathers information on who has a *reputation* for power, not necessarily those who wield power in fact. Just because so-called knowledgeables identify prominent businesspeople as powerful does not make them so. The informants may be confusing reputation with reality.

The elitists retaliate by observing that the pluralists' emphasis on studying visible instances of public decision making produces distorted findings. First, many of the really important decisions are made in the private sector rather than in the public arena. By ignoring those decisions, the pluralists ignore the realities of power. Second, the economic elite conducts its decision making behind closed doors—in corporate boardrooms, shielded from public scrutiny. By concentrating on public decisions, the pluralists are misled by the smoke and noise of trivial displays of political influence. The vital arenas of decision making are boardrooms, country clubs, golf courses, business lunches, and cocktail parties. All but the economic elite are excluded from these arenas. Few, if any, significant decisions are made in meetings of the city council and the school board or in open debate before public agencies and commissions. Since many vital community decisions are made covertly, it is by definition impossible for the pluralists to gain a true understanding of the power structure.

NONDECISIONS AND ANTICIPATED REACTIONS

The elitists also maintain that the pluralists' findings are distorted by a failure to consider the crucial nature of *nondecisions*. According to the elitists, the decision not to decide is frequently a vital one, and the economic elite controls this process of nondecision making. By concentrating on observable public policy choices, the pluralists ignore a whole range of significant nondecisions. For example, assume that the business elite in a certain city is primarily concerned with continued economic growth and development. Through their control over nondecision making, those businesspeople will prevent any policies that might retard such development from ever reaching the stage of public debate. Since the pluralists study only actual instances of public decision making, they will not be aware that the most important decisions have already been made—through a determination that the opportunity to decide will not be allowed. Therefore, the pluralists will not have the chance to study which groups exercised power with respect to proposals for a tax increase, greater social welfare expenditures, more rigorous regulation of business activity, or policies designed to enhance minority participation in local affairs. This control over the public policy agenda is an extraordinarily potent and effective form of power. It is power exercised *prior to* the occurrence of any public decision making. To ignore the importance of nondecision making by studying only actual policy conflicts in public arenas is guaranteed to deceive and mislead the observer with respect to the distribution of influence.

The elitists also argue that economic elite's control over public officials is vitally affected by *anticipated reactions*. That is, public officials decide on one course of action rather than another because they *anticipate* the reaction of the elite. If they believe that the economic elite will oppose a tax increase, greater spending, or changes in zoning ordinances, then they will not introduce such policy proposals. Public officials seek out the position of the elite on major issues and then act accordingly. Their freedom to pursue an independent course of action is severely constrained by their perception that many decisions are simply unacceptable to the elite. Rather than risk the intense opposition of the elite, they will change their position to one that coincides with its wishes. Public officials either do or do not do many things because they anticipate the support or the opposition of the economic elite.

Furthermore, public officials identify with the elite because they themselves are disproportionately drawn from the upper strata of the community. Their manners, dress, and behavior are similar to those of the elite. They hold similar attitudes and values. This commonality of background, values, and purposes exerts a subtle but powerful impact on the policy choices of public officials. Their decisions will advance the interests of the rich rather than the powerless because they themselves are more like the rich (or prefer to be like them) than like the poor. In addition, public officials perceive that the interests of the economic elite are in the best interests of the city as a whole. The wealthy are associated with low taxes, growth and development, jobs, reasonable expenditure levels, and social stability (recall Lindblom's characterization of government officials' reaction to business interest groups, presented in Chapter 5). The poor are identified with high taxes, demands for expensive social welfare programs, rising crime rates, and white flight. What is good for the economic elite is good for the entire city.

The pluralists find these arguments unconvincing. How do the elites know that significant decisions are secretly made when, by definition, these covert choices cannot be observed and analyzed? How do they know that many vital decisions are really nondecisions and that so-called nondecision making is controlled by powerful businesspeople? How can they be so sure that anticipated reactions determine the behavior of public officials, particularly since there is evidence that these officials sometimes take on and defeat the elite on important policy issues? To the pluralists, the elitists make their case on the basis of arguments that cannot be verified or disproved. How can factors such as covert decision making, nondecision making, and anticipated reactions be empirically tested and then either accepted or rejected? Since these concepts cannot be scientifically analyzed, the elitists cannot make a legitimate claim as to their significance. According to the pluralists, what *can* be studied is actual decision making. And when real decisions are analyzed, the pluralist rather than the elitist interpretation of the distribution of power is affirmed.

RECONCILING THE ELITIST AND PLURALIST POSITIONS

The pluralists are correct when they maintain that the business elite is not the only powerful group in the community. They are also on sound ground when they emphasize the influence wielded by public officials in local affairs and the importance of elections, public opinion, expertise, leadership skills, and organization. Yet the pluralists are naïve to conclude that all political decision making is characterized by openness, competition, and compromise among a variety of different groups. Some groups *are* more powerful than others.

THE SPECIAL POSITION OF BUSINESS

To concentrate only on concrete, visible, and public instances of decision making ignores the subtle but powerful biases present in the system. One does not have to accept the premise that businesspeople control the outcome of every issue to recognize their pervasive influence in community affairs. In fact, they are probably unconcerned with a variety of the public decisions that attract the attention of the pluralists. They may not care a great deal about the selection of a new police chief or school superintendent or even about a debate over whether tax rates on residential property should be increased. It is difficult to deny, however, that businesspeople exert vast influence as a result of their control over jobs, money, and credit. No public official can long afford to antagonize the business community—the economic, financial, and social vitality of a city is heavily dependent on jobs provided by the private sector. The goal of providing and maintaining a good business climate operates as a powerful incentive for public officials to advance the policy interests of the business sector. The fact that the opposite goal—maintaining a good climate for poor people—strikes most people as absurd is indicative of fundamental biases in the system. Most public officials do not favor the interests of the economic elite because its members command great wealth

SPORTS STADIUMS ARE OFTEN SUBSIDIZED BY LOCAL GOVERNMENTS IN AN EFFORT TO BOOST THE ECONOMY OF AN URBAN AREA AND PROMOTE THE HEALTH OF ITS BUSINESS SECTOR.

and are entitled to deference. Instead, most officials genuinely believe that the best interests of all—including minorities, the poor, and the disadvantaged—are most effectively served by ensuring economic growth and stability. They may well be correct in that assumption.

The business and financial sectors also wield great influence through their control of credit. If financial institutions choose to invest in some city neighborhoods and not in others, then the former areas will thrive and the latter will decline. If banks and savings and loan associations provide investment capital for the development of fringe areas at the expense of rehabilitation of the inner city, then the suburbs will boom while the central city decays.

However, the various ways in which the elite exercises its power are not always deliberate attempts to impose its will on political decisions. In fact, the activities of the business elite are not often intended to influence political decision making. The primary goals of businesspeople are growth, profits, and economic development rather than political power. In the pursuit of these goals, however, they exert vast (if unanticipated) political influence. For example, suppose that an entrepreneur decides to develop a tract of uninhabited fringe land. He arranges financing with banks in the central city, purchases the property, and constructs a shopping mall with grocery stores, restaurants, boutiques, office space, and theaters. Businesses are attracted by the new economic activity and relocate to adjacent areas. Builders begin to construct residential housing projects in the vicinity. A new local government is created to provide streets, sewers, water lines, and utilities. Zoning ordinances are adopted, taxes are levied, and police, fire, sanitation, and library services are provided for. Many new opportunities are created as a result of this entrepreneurial effort. Some jobs will relocate from the central city. New business enterprises that previously would have located in the city may move to the new center of suburban activity. Property values will increase dramatically. Financing and investment capital will flow from the central city to the fringe area. Residential developers will respond to the newly created demand for upper-class, single-family housing.

If these economic changes had no impact on political issues and decisions, then they would be of little relevance to an understanding of community power. However, they do influence political decision making. When the scenario described above is played out dozens of times at different locales within an urban area, the whole structure of political conflict may change. The public agenda will shift fundamentally. In an effort to stem the flight of jobs, people, and investment capital to new suburban centers, public officials in the central city will drop some issues and take up others. Holding the line on taxes will become a major priority. Proposals for greater expenditures on social welfare and poverty-related programs will be ignored. The bargaining power of the business community and upper-class neighborhoods will increase, and the political influence of the poor will decline. Creating a favorable climate for business will become a primary goal. Political options will be evaluated in terms of how the economic elite will react. The nature and balance of political power will change in a fundamental way.

The economic elite will inevitably exert a major influence on politics. There is nothing particularly conspiratorial about the process; it is simply a fact of life. A central city in decline will turn to the business community rather than to the poor to stimulate economic activity and generate more jobs. Its elected officials will be more inclined to respond to the preferences of the wealthy than to those of the less well-off, because the former are identified as revenue providers and the latter are perceived as service demanders. Poor people do not create more jobs. They do not represent new sources of revenue. Instead, they demand costly services that place additional strains on the ability of the city to cope. Thus, they are less likely to be heeded.

THE IMPORTANCE OF THE ECONOMIC CLIMATE

Elitist theorists are wrong, however, to assume that the economic elite will be dominant at all times and in all places. In particular, the intimacy of the relationship between public officials and businesspeople will vary depending on the economic situation and the financial condition of the city. The economic elite will be less powerful in those cities where the population is stable or growing, where white flight is not a major problem, where employment is high, and where the tax base is sound. Under those conditions, elected officials will enjoy more discretion with respect to political choices. The needs and demands of the business community will not be their only concern. Other groups (ethnic minorities, neighborhoods, labor, and municipal employees) will be more likely to gain access to decision-making channels. Such a city can afford pluralist politics, characterized by competition, bargaining, and accommodation among multiple groups.

The opposite holds true in those cities beset by population and job losses, white flight, rising taxes, a declining revenue base, and soaring service demands. Under those conditions, public officials will conclude that the city cannot afford to accommodate the demands of all groups. The needs of minority neighborhoods for more and better public services will be ignored when the city lacks the resources to respond. During a period of decline and decay, accommodation of major corporations and financial institutions becomes the highest priority.

There is also evidence that the distribution of power in American communities undergoes long-term change as the economy evolves. Until the 1970s, the economies of Southern cities, as an example, were less industrialized and diversified than Northern ones. Major companies in the South tended to be locally owned. Minorities lacked influence. The fairly homogeneous white population was dominant. Under such conditions, a closed, elitist system of decision making prevailed. Today, however, the economy of the South is more diversified. National corporations in Sun Belt cities are run by professional managers who have relatively little stake or interest in local politics. Newcomers from other states bring new attitudes and values with them. The rise of the middle class shifts the balance of power. Newly emerging groups (such as minorities and municipal employees' unions) begin to challenge established power relationships. Thus, political life is more pluralistic in those cities today than it was in the past.

Ironically, the previously pluralistic Frost Belt is beginning to exhibit signs of increased business influence. The economic and financial difficulties experienced by cities such as Boston, Cleveland, Indianapolis, and New York have made them considerably more anxious to follow the preferences of major employers and large financial institutions. Public officials in those cities are heavily dependent on the corporate community for jobs, credit, investment capital, and loan guarantees. These observations are not meant to suggest that the economic elite will dictate the outcome of all political issues in Frost Belt cities. Even in a period of financial and economic distress, it is unlikely that businesspeople will be interested in many or even most political decisions. Dozens of important political choices are made in a major city on a weekly basis. For most of those decisions, pluralism will prevail. Different actors—elected officials, bureaucrats, minority groups, or neighborhood organizations—will emerge as influential with respect to different issues. Business interests may even suffer defeat at the hands of these groups over some issues. However, some decisions are more important than others. A decision affecting the availability of jobs, credit, and investment capital is simply more significant than that concerning who will be the next school superintendent, for example. That the pluralist interpretation may best explain the latter outcome does not alter the fact that the economic elite controls the former.

THE POWER OF PUBLIC OFFICIALS

The elitists see public officials as errand boys. The pluralists see them as one of several important groups. Their influence is underestimated by both sides. In fact, public officials sometimes exercise enormous power. Their influence derives from several sources. First, they control the city budget. They set spending priorities and decide which programs will receive emphasis. Second, they command attention. They can mobilize public concern and focus public attention on specific problems and issues. Third, they enjoy access to information and expertise. Finally, they play a crucial role in setting the public agenda. Which issues will be brought up for discussion and consideration? Which ones will be ignored?

The extent of elected officials' influence varies greatly from city to city. They are more likely to exercise substantial power in cities with unreformed governments and in those that are in good financial shape. Furthermore, personalities, goals, and values also play a role. Some elected officials are energetic and aggressive and have a clearly defined set of policy objectives when they take office. They are skilled and resourceful leaders who work tirelessly to accomplish their goals. Other officials are more passive in nature and are relatively unconcerned with changing the status quo.

Bureaucrats also have the capacity to exercise considerable influence over local politics. As we noted in Chapter 10, bureaucracies may be the new political machines. Their control over information, experience, and expertise makes them independent sources of power. The apparent power of bureaucrats cannot be dismissed by maintaining that they simply do the bidding of the business elite. Many programs are adopted and policies initiated because bureaucrats first proposed them. Similarly, some policies that are strongly supported by the business community are eventually vetoed because bureaucrats oppose them.

The media also constitute a potentially powerful force in local politics. Newspapers and television news programs have the power to focus attention on some issues and deny it for others. They can play an important role in ensuring that some problems are placed on the public agenda for debate and eventual resolution. Investigative reporters can have a major impact on the conduct of local politics through their exposure of gross waste and inefficiency, fraud, corruption, or immoral behavior. On the other hand, if the media are largely indifferent to or unconcerned with local political issues, this condition will contribute to a climate in which other actors and groups will dominate the political debate. An indifferent media will shield politicians and businesspeople from scrutiny and will allow these groups, rather than the public, to set and control the local agenda.

POLICY ARENAS AND POWER

In his influential book *City Limits,* Paul Peterson (1981) provides an additional argument intended to resolve the debate between the elitists and pluralists. According to Peterson, all city governments are guided by an overriding interest in economic growth. Since growth provides benefits to everyone, in the form of jobs, income, profits, and revenue, policies that promote economic development are in the best interests of the city. Only one type of policies, however, stimulates such growth—the so-called *developmental policies,* which can take several forms. One form of developmental policy is an attempt by a city to attract major new industries. Another developmental policy is a plan to revitalize a depressed downtown business district by seeking federal funds for rehabilitating the area. Renewal plans might include the proposed construction of a civic center, sports complex, or shopping mall.

Peterson claims that cities are driven by economic interests because they exist in a fiercely competitive environment. At the same time, they exert relatively little control over that environment. For example, labor and capital are highly mobile. People, businesses, and investors are not bound to a particular location. If they are unhappy with New York, they are free to move to Dallas or Denver. If Atlanta refuses to pursue policies designed to promote economic growth, then Chicago or some other city certainly will. The eventual result will be fewer jobs, lower incomes, rising taxes, declining revenues, and deteriorating services in one city, and increasing prosperity, lower taxes, and better services and programs in another.

But cities also pursue policies that have no effect on economic development. *Allocational policies* are ones that concern the level and distribution of basic public services, such as police, fire protection, sanitation, education, and street repair. Peterson argues that decisions about these policies do not generally affect the city's developmental prospects. Yet, as Peterson (1981: 44–45) notes, these are important policy areas:

> All members of the community benefit from the most valued aspects of police and fire protection, and from systematic, community-wide collection of garbage and refuse. These services reduce the likelihood of catastrophic conflagrations, wholesale violations of persons and property, community epidemics, and the use of public spaces as dumps and junkyards. The value each individual places on these services may vary, but all receive important benefits.

Allocational policies, then, concern some of the most traditional of urban public services. These are admittedly prosaic, but they are essential to the quality of everyday life in a city.

Redistributive policies, finally, are ones that Peterson argues will have a negative influence on economic growth. These are policies that redistribute income from the relatively wealthy to the relatively poor through, for example, welfare expenditures on health care and housing and income supplements for the indigent and aged. Redistributive policies have a negative impact on development because they attract more poor people to the city, cause higher public expenditures, and drive up taxes. As a result, the city may become less attractive to business and to middle- and upper-class residents. According to Peterson, cities have little capacity to engage in redistribution, and policies that would result in a substantial redistribution of resources seldom reach the public agenda. In fact, as we explained in Chapter 3, the federal government has largely coopted redistributive policies from state and local governments. Thus, most debates about such policies occur in Washington, D.C., instead of Chicago, Los Angeles, or Tampa.

When redistributive policies do get on the local agenda, however, not much is actually done about them. Michael Lipsky's (1970) study of a rent strike in New York City illustrates this point. The protesters were moved to action by the deplorable conditions in slum housing. They appeared to have a strong case with good prospects for a favorable response on the part of city government. The legitimacy of their grievances was widely recognized, they enjoyed widespread support from public officials, and their plight received extensive coverage in the media. As a result of all this political activity, however, nothing changed. No significant progress was made in terms of improving the deplorable housing conditions of the poor. Lipsky found that the measures taken to address the housing problem were largely cosmetic and symbolic. Federal grants were applied for, action was taken to deal with some of the most widely publicized horror stories (rats biting children), and commissions were formed to study the problems. However, steps that would have been required to substantially improve housing for the poor—such as having the city enforce its existing housing codes—were never seriously considered. If the city had enforced the codes, slum landlords would have been required to spend huge sums of money to rehabilitate their properties. But the tenants would have been unable to pay the higher rents that would have resulted, and the owners would have more incentive to abandon their properties than to repair them. The city government, in turn, would be unwilling or unable to pay for public housing to replace the substandard or abandoned buildings. Consequently, little change took place.

Peterson's framework is valuable because it demonstrates that the style and substance of decision making are likely to differ across types of policies. For developmental policies, consensus is apt to characterize the decision-making process. Since developmental initiatives are perceived to be in the best economic interests of all who reside or work in a city, the relationship between members of the economic elite and other political actors will be harmonious rather than conflictual. In addition, the elite, by virtue of its standing in the community and control over critical economic resources, will have a crucial effect on the successful conduct of development campaigns. Developmental policies enjoy widespread community support. Consequently, the difficulties they encounter on the route to adoption are apt to be of an organizational, managerial, or technical nature. Political conflict will play a relatively small role. From this perspective, we can see that Hunter's interpretation in *Community Political Structure* (1953) has considerable validity with respect to developmental policies. The economic elite does play a dominant role. The notion of conflict among competing interest groups is essentially irrelevant to an understanding of the policy-making process.

For allocational policies, however, the pluralist interpretation is more likely to be accurate. Since allocation has little effect on the overall economic health of a city but can affect individuals and groups dramatically, conflict rather than consensus prevails. In fact, Peterson (1981) argues that allocational decisions are rife with politics. Such decision making is characterized by group conflict, shifting allegiances, bargaining, accommodation, and compromise. The economic elite is only one of many competing groups participating in the process.

Finally, redistributive issues seldom even arise in city politics, according to Peterson. Cities are highly limited by their financial condition with respect to their ability to respond to such demands, and the existence of a network of federal redistributive programs probably attracts most demands to that level of government. But Peterson believes that the structure and normal political routines of city government are biased against sympathetic responses to demands for redistribution. And even the poor are often more interested in allocational issues concerning levels of city services.

CONCLUSION

The question of who rules American cities is a complicated and controversial one. The power wielded by any particular group—businesspeople, ethnic minorities, interest groups, or even elected public officials—is vigorously debated. The power of the business sector is especially important in light of the role that it might play as state and local governments tackle the economic challenge outlined in Chapter 1. We have suggested some ways in which this debate can be settled and the power of business explained, but we have surely not achieved a complete resolution of the matter. However, an understanding of the bases of community power offers insight into and additional perspective on a number of questions that are prominent throughout this book.

REFERENCES   Agger, Robert, Daniel Goldrich, and Bert Swanson. 1965. *The Rulers and the Ruled.* New York: John Wiley.

Anton, Thomas J. 1963. "Power, Pluralism, and Local Politics," *Administrative Science Quarterly* 7 (March): 425–447.

Bachrach, Peter, and Morton S. Baratz. 1962. "Two Faces of Power," *American Political Science Review* 56 (December): 947–953.

Banfield, Edward. 1961. *Political Influence.* Glencoe, Ill.: Free Press.

Dahl, Robert. 1961. *Who Governs?* New Haven, Conn.: Yale University Press.

Hunter, Floyd. 1953. *Community Power Structure.* Chapel Hill: University of North Carolina Press.

Lipsky, Michael. 1970. *Protest in City Politics.* Skokie, Ill.: Rand McNally.

Peterson, Paul. 1981. *City Limits.* Chicago: University of Chicago Press.

Presthus, Robert. 1964. *Men at the Top.* New York: Oxford University Press.

Sayre, Wallace, and Herbert Kaufman. 1965. *Governing New York City.* New York: W. W. Norton.

Stone, Clarence. 1980. "Systemic Power in Community Decision Making," *American Political Science Review* 74 (December): 978–990.

Wolfinger, Raymond. 1971. "Nondecisions and the Study of Local Politics," *American Political Science Review* 65 (December): 1063–1080.

12

The Delivery and Distribution of Urban Public Services

Public services are essential to the safety, health, and well-being of the citizens of metropolitan areas. City life in the United States could not proceed in any civilized form without them. Services such as police and fire protection, sewerage, refuse collection, flood control, and sanitation are so routine that we seldom consider how vital they really are. One of the myths about these services is that they have little to do with politics. What is political about picking up the garbage, patrolling the streets, educating children, providing an adequate water supply, or maintaining a fire protection system? In fact, the provision of routine public services is fraught with opportunities for political conflict. The political issues and choices inherent in decisions concerning service delivery are significant. Which services should be provided? How much of a particular service should be delivered? Which services should be assigned priority? Who should pay for each service? How should burdens and benefits be distributed among the population?

In this chapter we will consider those factors and conditions that complicate the delivery and distribution of public services. We will also evaluate competing conceptions of what constitutes equity in service distribution and analyze the value judgments implicit in each equity standard. We will examine evidence from a variety of cities concerning distributional patterns and comment on the role played by decision rules, professional norms, and technical-rational criteria. Finally, we will analyze the conflict between bureaucrats and elected officials over service delivery.

THE ENVIRONMENT OF URBAN GOVERNMENTS

Municipal governments in the United States are severely limited in terms of their ability to manage their environments. They are acted on by a variety of forces over which they have little or no control (Peterson, 1981). Many cities are unable to generate sufficient revenues because of state limitations on their ability to levy taxes. Frequently, cities are required to provide expensive state-mandated programs without being given sufficient financing for those programs. State limitations on cities' annexation authority further restrict their capacity to respond to change.

The role played by the federal government also illustrates the city's dependency. Many cities rely heavily on federal aid. Their fiscal health is closely tied to the structure and funding of federal aid programs. Furthermore, federal intervention in a variety of local activities and institutions impinges on the ability of the city to conduct and manage its own affairs. Examples range from involvement of the federal courts in local educational systems to federal rulings that dictate changes in cities' electoral systems. There are few areas of local government that are immune from the control or direct influence of state and federal authorities.

Cities are also particularly susceptible to the play of forces in the private sector. The circulation of jobs, money, and credit within a city and between the central city and suburbs exerts dramatic impacts on the destinies of metropolitan areas. Private investment decisions determine whether a city will grow or decay. The strength and vitality of the city are also heavily dependent on the personal choices and preferences of individual citizens. The massive exodus of middle- and upper-class families to the suburbs (and the continuing threat of further population erosion) has had a major impact on urban development.

Political authorities in urban areas are highly sensitive to business and upper-class goals because they perceive that achieving these is in the best interests of the city as a whole. They identify with the wealthy rather than the poor because the former are associated with economic growth, jobs, low taxes, reasonable expenditure levels, and social stability. The underclass is synonymous with white flight, high unemployment, rising taxes, increasing service demands, and social disorganization (Stone, 1980). The rather limited capacity of local public officials to deal with their city's problems is further restricted by the need to placate powerful economic interests. To antagonize a major employer is to risk weakening the tax base of the city. To pursue policies that will anger residents of middle- and upper-class neighborhoods is foolhardy when those citizens can simply relocate to a nearby suburb if they become sufficiently disenchanted with conditions in the city.

THE DIFFICULTIES OF SERVICE DELIVERY IN URBAN AREAS

We have argued that cities are severely limited in terms of their ability to shape and control their own destinies. Constitutionally, they are creations of their respective state governments. As such, they are heavily dependent on their state government for grants of power and for resources. The reliance of cities on federal aid further restricts their capacity to realize their policy agendas. Finally, the advantageous bargaining position of business interests and upper-class citizens greatly reduces the extent to which local public officials can pursue an independent course of action. However, one arena in which urban political authorities still maintain significant control is that of service delivery. Essential public services such as police and fire protection and education remain the responsibilities of local governments. Although many city governments are virtually powerless in major policy areas such as business regulation, income redistribution, and social welfare, they retain authority over vital services.

The effective provision of public services in urban areas is not an easy task. Several factors complicate the process. First, many of these services, such as education and police protection, can generate intense conflict. Many parents, for example, look to the public schools as an avenue of upward mobility for their children. Thus, the perception that certain policy changes will weaken the educational system may stimulate significant involvement of and conflict among citizens. Many people believe that they have a large, personal stake in public services. Consequently, their expectations for those services, as well as their propensity to express their grievances and discontents, are exceedingly high. When services are essential to people's safety, well-being, or hopes for the future, whether and how they are delivered can arouse widespread public concern and involvement. Citizen involvement complicates the service delivery process because public officials have less freedom to deliver services according to established decision rules and routines when citizens are presenting multiple and conflicting demands. Differing public preferences require that bureaucrats balance competing expectations.

Another factor that complicates service delivery is the divisible nature of many services. More and better-qualified police officers, fire fighters, garbage collectors, dogcatchers, and teachers may be assigned to some neighborhoods than to others. Some neighborhoods may have better schools, parks, libraries, and streets than others. The public perception that some receive more and others receive less increases the possibility for conflict over who does or should get what. Of course, such perceptions may be wrong. What is significant, however, is that service delivery is more difficult when some groups of citizens are consistently complaining than they are receiving less than others. If the expression of such grievances is sufficiently intense (taking the form of legal action, for example), public officials may be forced to redistribute service resources. Thus, the divisible nature of public services introduces another element of risk and uncertainty into the bureaucrat's environment. Citizens' demands for redistribution complicate service delivery because the public official is forced to pay more attention to political factors. Professional values such as efficiency, effectiveness, and impact are necessarily accorded a lower priority.

Provision of public services is also made more difficult by the considerable variation in citizens' needs and preferences concerning those services. For example, poor people may well prefer more parks and fewer libraries. Differences in preferences can even extend to the same service. Wealthy parents are likely to expect the public schools to serve as college preparatory institutions. Minority parents may prefer that more vocational training programs be offered and that their neighborhood be given more control over the way its schools are run—control that extends to the hiring, firing, and promotion of teachers and staff. Similarly, some neighborhoods expect police to devote the bulk of their time and resources to the enforcement of the law and the apprehension of criminal suspects. Other citizens expect that the police should perform a service function as well as an enforcement function.

The conflicting needs, preferences, and expectations of citizens are difficult to reconcile. That is, it is frequently impossible for local governments to please all, most, or even some of their constituents. For example, the police cannot be all things to all people. Many citizens expect them to spend most of their time enforcing the law and catching criminals. One study found, however, that 90 percent of police effort was devoted to functions other than the traditional one of law enforcement (Wilson, 1968). Even a single citizen may expect a particular service to achieve a variety of goals or a number of different and even conflicting objectives. Citizens want the police to regulate traffic, perform community relations, apprehend suspects, investigate crimes, come when they call (even though the call may have little to do with a criminal act or violation of a criminal law), and provide information. These wide-ranging expectations immensely complicate delivery of public services because the same service is required to perform a variety of functions and achieve contradictory goals. Since the service delivery system is simply incapable of satisfying all of the conflicting needs, preferences, and expectations, public officials make choices concerning service delivery in an atmosphere characterized by confusion and uncertainty. Effective implementation of service goals is difficult when they are unclear because citizens demand the accomplishment of conflicting objectives.

The conflict between elected officials and bureaucrats adds another layer of complexity to the service delivery process. Bureaucrats are a powerful force in local government. In many departments they enjoy a virtual monopoly over information, experience, and expertise. Elected officials come and go. Bureaucrats are career administrators who develop expertise in a narrow area of governmental operations. Frequently, elected officials are simply unequipped in terms of training, information, or inclination to challenge bureaucratic choices. Those authorities have too many services to provide and too many decisions to make to be able to exercise effective direction and control over dozens of separate agencies.

This observation is especially accurate in those cases where the issues under consideraton involve complex technical matters. Yet even decisions that appear to involve only routine choices may have significant political implications and consequences. Because bureaucrats have such extensive power, elected officials are often forced to rely on them for an evaluation of whether a policy change should be initiated. If public officials do order a new policy to be implemented, they must trust the bureaucrats to put the change into effect. Their powers to force compliance are severely limited.

Service delivery is further complicated by the fact that lower-level bureaucrats are often outside of the control of top-level administrators (Lipsky, 1976). How can the police chief know if the officer on the street is enforcing all laws rigorously and fairly? How can the department head determine whether the building inspector is performing his or her duties in compliance with the provisions of the building code? Establishing and maintaining control over the so-called *street-level bureaucrat* is immensely difficult—perhaps impossible. There are never enough supervisors to monitor performance. The problem is particularly acute for vital services such as police protection and education, since the policeman on the beat or the teacher in the classroom *is* the service. Directives from agency and bureau chiefs may be carefully followed by some street-level bureaucrats, partially implemented by others, and completely ignored by still others. Elected political authorities often cannot get the bureaucracy to do what they would like, but the heads of city agencies also frequently find it extremely difficult to modify the behavior of workers at the level at which tangible services are actually delivered to citizens (Lipsky, 1976; Nivola, 1978).

Control of the street-level bureaucrat is made even more difficult by the fact that goals for public services are frequently unclear. They are generally implicit rather than explicit—and conflicting rather than compatible. In the absence of clearly defined and expressed goals, however, the street-level bureaucrat is *forced* to exercise personal discretion and pursue his or her own vision of the appropriate organizational mission. For there to be upper-echelon control of employees, there must exist a shared set of expectations with respect to task performance. Objectives must be clearly stated. In fact, however, service delivery goals are frequently vague or unexpressed. Is the cop on the beat to enforce all the laws? If not, which violations should be ignored? How rigorously should laws be enforced? Should different standards be employed in some neighborhoods or for some groups? Should the law be uniformly applied even if such application appears to violate widely shared norms and values in some neighborhoods? Should the police officer concentrate on the most serious crimes or those offenses most likely to be successfully prosecuted? Should he or she respond to all citizen requests for service even if many of these are so-called nuisance calls and have nothing to do with violations of the criminal law? Generally, police departments provide little or no guidance to street-level officers with respect to these and other important questions. Consequently, the cop on the beat must make his or her own determinations and interpretations of departmental priorities and organizational goals. As a result, discretion at the street level is encouraged rather than restricted and controlled.

Some public services are easier to implement than others, however. For example, park and library services involve the delivery of tangible facilities and resources at fixed sites and locations. The use of the services is discretionary. Although the public employees who staff these facilities are not irrelevant to client utilization, they are certainly far less crucial than is the case for police, education, and building inspection services. Delivery is much easier to accomplish for public services that do not depend on upper-level control of the street-level bureaucrat (Mladenka, 1980).

GARBAGE COLLECTION IS AN URBAN PUBLIC SERVICE OFTEN TAKEN FOR GRANTED—UNTIL THE SERVICE IS NOT PROVIDED.

Still another factor that complicates effective delivery of basic public services is the multidimensional nature of service delivery systems. The service delivery process can be thought of in terms of at least three distinct stages: resources, activities, and results. For police, personnel and equipment are examples of resources. Patrolling, responding to calls for service, and investigating crimes are all examples of police activities. Results are exemplified by crime rates, number of crimes solved, levels of citizen satisfaction with police services, and public fear of crime. Delivery of public services is further complicated by the uniqueness of each of the three different stages and the multiplicity of the relationships among them. For example, demands for more and better police protection generally center on the need for additional staff and equipment, which are resources. However, greater numbers of police officers may have only a marginal impact on activities and no discernible effect at all on results. In fact, the relationship between resources and results is very poorly understood.

What is known is that a variety of factors other than resources exert significant influence on service outcomes. More police, for example, may have no effect on crime rates. Instead, those rates may show a much higher association with poverty, unemployment, and population density. The public, however, frequently misunderstands the relationships among the various stages of the service delivery process. For example, citizens expect that more police officers will translate into better police protection and lower crime rates. The typical citizen's failure to recognize the highly tenuous linkage between resources and results accounts in large part for public frustration and dissatisfaction with government services. When adding police officers (particularly when this resource augmentation is accompanied by a tax increase) does not automatically translate into quicker response times, more visible neighborhood patrols, lower crime rates, and more crimes solved, the result is apt to be public disenchantment. Citizens' expectations for dramatic improvements in service outcomes are raised by enhanced levels of resources. They are just as readily dashed when such results do not automatically materialize.

The degree of difficulty of delivering public services varies from city to city, as well as from neighborhood to neighborhood within a city. One significant factor is the level of fiscal resources available to the municipal government. Cities with substantial resources are better able to deliver services effectively than those experiencing fiscal strain. For example, governments with surplus resources are capable of responding to a wider range of citizens' expectations for the same service. For example, different groups may expect the police to perform different functions: fight crime, provide routine information on an individual basis, maintain order, enforce the laws, and regulate traffic. Cities in a healthy fiscal condition are in a much better position than others to employ enough police officers to fulfill most or even all of these expectations. Cities with inadequate public funds are forced to make choices among conflicting demands and goals. When they do so, the act is likely to antagonize some groups of citizens. If citizens become sufficiently disgruntled, they may express their grievances and discontents through increased participation in decision-making processes such as attendance at public hearings and lawsuits. Heightened citizen involvement complicates the provision of public services because it forces public officials to balance competing political demands.

It is also significant that the element of the discretionary power of the street-level bureaucrat assumes greater importance in heterogeneous cities. When citizens' values and preferences clash, the street-level bureaucrat is forced to choose among conflicting public expectations when discharging his or her duties. The individual police officer, teacher, or building inspector cannot satisfy all preferences when those wishes conflict. The preferences of some citizens will be satisfied by decisions about service delivery, and those of other citizens will be denied.

Whether the governmental jurisdiction constitutes a central city or a suburban area also makes a difference with respect to the ease with which public services are delivered. Central cities are more likely than suburban areas to contain heterogeneous populations. In addition, central city governments are generally subject to greater financial strains than suburban governments are. For reasons we have already mentioned, both of these factors complicate the service delivery process.

The concept of *coproduction* is also relevant to service delivery. Citizens share in the provision of public services by contributing to or detracting from the efficiency and effectiveness of delivery. For example, some citizens carefully package their garbage and place it in the appropriate location for collection; others simply toss it out in the direction of the curb. Some citizens take pains to maintain their neighborhood parks; others misuse the equipment, discard their trash, and even commit acts of vandalism. Some neighborhood residents make a significant difference to the quality of their public schools by contributing time, money, and effort as well as disciplined and well-prepared students; others do nothing. The quality of services delivered is determined, in large part, by citizens' contributions to the production of these services.

We have discussed a variety of factors that complicate the effective delivery of basic public services in urban areas. These factors include the fact that apparently mundane services involve strong human values and conflicting needs and demands. Other important factors are the divisible nature of municipal services, the insulation of the bureaucracy from political control, the wide discretion enjoyed by the street-level bureaucrat, the multiple stages of the service delivery process, the varying levels of wealth and heterogeneity, and the coproduction of services by citizens.

EQUITY IN SERVICE DELIVERY

Competing conceptions of equity further hamper the successful delivery of public services. Equity involves justice and fairness. From the perspective of service delivery, the major problem is that what constitutes fairness is open to a variety of differing interpretations. What appears to be indisputably fair to the public official and a majority of citizens may well strike a substantial minority of the population as eminently unjust. Public officials are forced to grapple with such normative concerns during the process of delivering public services.

CONCEPTIONS OF EQUITY

Every decision concerning service delivery involves an explicit or implicit standard of equity. This dimension is especially relevant at the distributional stage. How should service benefits be distributed across neighborhoods and groups? Should some receive more than others? Under what conditions? We can identify at least five competing conceptions of equity: equality, need, demand, preference, and willingness and ability to pay. Each will produce a distinctly different distributional pattern.

The standard of equality implies that the distribution of benefits will occur within some permissible or acceptable range of variation. The differences that are tolerated will be unrelated to the characteristics of the population and the conditions of neighborhoods. Dissimilar clients and environments will be treated similarly. And this standard of equality is relevant at each stage of the service delivery process: resources, activities, and results. For police services, equality would mean an equal number of police officers per every thousand in population (resources), equal response times to citizens' calls originating in different parts of the city (activities), and equal crime rates in all neighborhoods (results). Of course, there is an inherent contradiction here: equality of results would imply a highly unequal distribution of resources because many more police officers would be required in high crime areas.

Need as a standard of equity assumes that some citizens have a greater need for services than others and that the greater needs are entitled to preferential consideration. High crime neighborhoods, it could be argued, for example, need greater levels of police protection. One of the difficulties associated with employing need as the equity standard is that it is most likely to generate intense political controversy and conflict. Service delivery based on need obviously implies a highly unequal distribution of resources and benefits. Since many public services exhibit at least the potential for high divisibility, need frequently enters local deliberations concerning appropriate equity standards.

Demand as a standard of equity calls for public services to be distributed according to variations in citizen demand. Such demand can be expressed in a variety of ways. Use of services and facilities indicates demand. Requests for and complaints about services are also an expression of demand. The communication of citizen demands to political authorities is apt to vary widely across groups and neighborhoods (Eisinger, 1982; Verba and Nie, 1972). Therefore, distribution of service resources and benefits on the basis of demand will produce a highly unequal distributional pattern.

Another concept of equity with respect to service delivery is preference. Services could be distributed according to the variation in citizens' preferences for public programs and facilities. Differences in such preferences are closely associated with differences in personal incomes. Poor people are likely to have a greater preference than wealthier ones for public recreational programs and facilities because their access to private recreational opportunities is limited. Rich persons are apt to have a greater preference for library services and other publicly supported cultural activities. Responsiveness to variations in citizens' preferences will produce a highly uneven and involved pattern of public benefits.

A final standard of equity is willingness and ability to pay. Many local services are currently provided on that basis, including garbage collection, water, sewerage, and recreational facilities. All could be. No citizen would be allowed to consume a service unless he or she was willing and able to pay for it at the time of consumption. Individual assessment of specific costs, rather than tax and grant revenue, would be employed to finance service delivery. The intent would be to duplicate the operation of the private sector as closely as possible. Citizens' preferences would become susceptible to precise measurement.

IMPLICATIONS OF EQUITY STANDARDS

The fact that public officials must resolve the equity question immensely complicates service delivery because it increases the available choices. Each standard of equity produces a distinct set of winners and losers.

Equality as equity enjoys the virtue of simplicity because it ignores any variation in need. It is unlikely to generate much political conflict because poor persons are not singled out for preferential treatment. Under sone conditions, however, equality in distribution of resources is absurd. For example, neighborhoods with extraordinarily high crime rates or high numbers of fire hazards would not be allocated more resources than areas that seldom experience a crime or fire. Consequently, equality as a standard of equity is most apt to be employed for those services for which strong spillover effects are *not* perceived. That is, it is more likely to be used as a guide to distributional policy for recreational services than for so-called protective services such as police and fire.

Need as equity implies an array of difficulties regarding service delivery. For example, measurement of need is more complicated than it appears at first glance. How should the public's need for recreational services be determined? Variation in income levels may be too gross an indicator of differences in such a need. More precise and appropriate measures might include age, mobility, crime and delinquency rates, differences in access to private recreational facilities, and unemployment, welfare, and poverty levels. Another problem with need as equity revolves around the issue of how great a share of resources to provide to different groups once they have been created based on this criterion. Assume that need is measured according to income levels. How many more service resources should low-income neighborhoods receive than are provided in wealthy areas? Should middle-income citizens receive more than upper-income clients? How much more? Why? Should need as equity apply only to the distribution of resources, or should it be extended to service activities and results? Under what conditions? Who should control the operationalization and measurement of need—bureaucrats or elected officials?

As standards of equity, demand and ability to pay ensure that some citizens will receive higher service levels than others. However, use of these standards is less likely to stimulate opposition because the differential distribution that results from such use will disproportionately benefit the better-off. Need is unique in that its use as the determinant of service distribution tends to confer greater benefits on the disadvantaged. Consequently, arousal of the politically active segment of the population is most apt to occur in response to that use.

Demand is frequently used in American cities to determine the distribution of service benefits. It has several advantages from the perspective of the urban administrator. Unlike need, demand as the standard of equity does not require public officials to develop allegedly objective indicators. Instead, they gather data on user rates and the number of complaints/requests, and distribution occurs on that basis. In distributing service resources, they rely on such quantifiable information as the number of citizen calls for police service, circulation rates at branch libraries, user levels at neighborhood recreational facilities, and the incidence of complaints about the condition of streets. The higher the number, the larger the share of available resources. The local official is not required to undertake elaborate measurements of consumer need or preference. Resource distribution is simply matched to the variations in citizen demand.

Another virtue of using demand as the standard of equity is that it appears to emphasize rationality in the allocation of public resources. The administrator can easily defend such a criterion by pointing out to critics that the most efficient and effective use of available resources is to distribute them to areas of highest consumption. It is unreasonable to provide services to citizens who have not used them or asked for them. It is wasteful to distribute service resources on the basis of equality or need, since only the standard of demand allows the administrator to determine if the services will actually be consumed by the potential clients. All citizens have the opportunity to express demand by utilizing existing services or by communicating with political authorities. It would represent a gross misuse of scarce resources to provide citizens who fail to express demand with high levels of public services.

Another advantage of using demand as the standard of equity from the perspective of the governmental official is that it entails responsiveness to citizens' grievances. Local political authorities are keenly sensitive to the argument that their primary function as officeholders is to respond to and resolve the problems of their constituents. To impose one's own value judgments while determining the appropriate distribution of resources is to violate a canon of local government. As standards of equity, equality and need tamper with the sanctity of that pervasive and powerful premise. Demand does not.

However, using demand as the standard may impose severe penalties on some citizens. There is evidence to suggest that blacks and low-income persons are less likely than wealthier citizens to communicate complaints and requests to public officials. In addition, depressed use of existing service facilities may be attributed to factors other than lack of interest on the part of citizens. That is, some groups of citizens may use public services less than other groups because the facilities available in their neighborhoods are of poor quality. Since some people are less likely to express demand than others, application of that standard will produce a differential pattern of distribution. Frequently, that pattern operates to the disadvantage of the poor.

Utilizing preference as the standard of equity for service delivery also presents a variety of problems. It certainly appears rational to elicit and consult citizens' preferences concerning public services. Service facilities and programs that go unused because citizens are not interested in them represent a highly inefficient use of resources. However, preferences are exceedingly difficult to measure and respond to. First, preferences vary widely across groups on the basis of income, education, race, and age. Second, the variation in intensity of preferences is an issue that is difficult to resolve. Some citizens will feel very strongly about a particular service, and others will be lukewarm or indifferent in their expression of preference. Attempts to assign values to differing intensities of preference enormously complicate the service delivery process. Third, public preferences are highly volatile and subject to change. Since many public services frequently involve the heavy investment of resources at fixed sites, adaptation to shifting preferences that result from population movement or changing tastes is difficult to accomplish. Consequently, preference as the standard of equity is apt to violate established notions of efficiency in public sector allocation.

The conflicts among preferences, their differing intensities, and their volatility complicate the implementation of preference as the standard. This does not mean, however, that administrators never consult citizens' preferences when deliberating about the appropriate division of resources. In fact, responsiveness to demand ensures that some types of public preference will be incorporated into the distributional formula. What is significant is that public officials do not attempt to elicit citizens' preferences except in the most rudimentary and haphazard of ways. Consequently, the expressions of preference they rely on are highly unrepresentative of the general population. Since officials rely heavily on complaints and requests as indicators of public opinion about services, their knowledge about actual citizen preferences is limited. Rather than undertake the elaborate effort that would be required to accurately assess public preferences, local officials are content to accept the expressed demands of the upper strata as a guide to what different groups prefer.

Ability to pay is the final standard of equity. According to this notion of equity, no citizen would be required to pay for any service that he or she did not want. People would pay only for those services that they used. Government officials would not have to make efforts to measure variations in public demand and preference. Willingness and ability to pay incorporate precise measures of citizens' wishes. Specific costs are assessed at the time of consumption. Use is voluntary. The needs, demands, and preferences of some are not imposed on others.

Using ability to pay as a standard is an attempt to duplicate as closely as possible the operation of the private sector. The citizen-consumer chooses from among a variety of service options. The extraordinary service needs of some groups are ignored by government. Although it is likely that the standard of ability to pay enhances efficiency in service delivery, it is also the case that it is the least redistributive of the standards considered here. The system for service delivery in the public sector would make no effort to counteract the disparities produced by the operation of the private sector. In fact, those disparities would be duplicated.

There are also some unique problems associated with implementation of ability to pay as the standard of equity. Although some services (refuse collection, public transportation, water, and utilities) are highly amenable to delivery on this basis, others are not. Services for which unit costs and consumption can be easily measured and calculated are frequently provided according to ability to pay. A government employee simply reads a meter, counts a delivery, imposes a toll, or assesses a fee. For some services, however, such ease of measurement is simply not feasible or possible. For example, who should bear the costs when the police investigate a family disturbance—the neighbor who complained, the participants, all citizens who derive benefit? Should more be charged for the police to investigate a prowler report than for a residential burglary? How should relative costs be assigned for time involved and risks encountered? Because of the problems involved in measuring use and assigning costs to individual citizens, the standard of ability to pay is much more likely to be used for some services than for others.

The provision of each urban public service incorporates a particular conception of equity. Each standard of equity imposes a different set of distributional consequences. The choice of equity standard represents a significant decision because it determines the winners and losers of service benefits. Such choices are frequently made implicitly rather than explicitly, and there are good reasons why this is so. The provision and delivery of public services is the major task of city government. Distributing service benefits to citizens gives rise to immense opportunities for political controversy and conflict. When city budgets total billions of dollars, decisions about which neighborhoods and groups will receive services and at what levels assume vital significance. Will police, fire, education, sanitation, recreation, and other services be delivered on the basis of equality, need, preference, demand, ability to pay, or some other standard? Since each concept of equity will produce a distinct pattern of winners and losers, such decisions are the most significant political choices made by local governments.

THE PATTERNS OF SERVICE DISTRIBUTION

A prominent concern of both citizens and scholars has been the question of who benefits most from the distribution of public services in urban areas. And the most common version of that question focuses on whether the poor and ethnic minorities get worse services. However, there is little evidence that these groups are systematically deprived in the distribution of service resources. A number of studies have demonstrated that public schools in black and low-income neighborhoods receive less money, poorer facilities, and less-qualified teachers (Baron, 1971; Berk and Hartman, 1971; Burkhead, 1967;

Sexton, 1961). But other studies have concluded that schools in black and poor neighborhoods are advantaged in terms of resource distribution (Katzman, 1968; Lyon, 1970; Mandel, 1974). Still another group of researchers has reported a nonlinear relationship between income and service distribution, with both upper- and lower-income areas receiving the best services (Burkhead, 1967; Levy, Meltsner, and Wildavsky, 1974).

The evidence is also mixed with regard to the delivery of library services. Several studies have concluded that the library services provided to black and low-income neighborhoods are inferior to those received in wealthier areas (Levy, Meltsner, and Wildavsky, 1974; Mladenka and Hill, 1977). However, other research has demonstrated that inequality in the distribution of new acquisitions, periodicals, total bookstock, and library expenditures either did not correlate with the racial and socioeconomic characteristics of the population or tended to favor poorer sections of the city (Blank, 1969; Lineberry, 1977). Robert Lineberry (1977: 129) found:

> [The] quality of library services is very weakly related to attributes of neighborhoods in San Antonio. There is nothing particularly equal about the distribution of library services, but our capacity to relate these inequalities to neighborhood attributes is strained indeed. The best description would be to call it a system of unpatterned inequalities.

In addition, two studies found that poorer neighborhoods were favored with respect to the locations of branch library buildings (Lineberry, 1977; Mladenka and Hill, 1977).

A similar set of findings emerges concerning the distribution of recreational services. One study concluded that the allocation of such resources favored wealthier neighborhoods (Sexton, 1961), others reported an equal distribution across neighborhoods (Gold, 1974; Lyon, 1970; Mladenka and Hill, 1977), and still others have reported a pattern that favored poor areas (Fisk, 1973; Lineberry, 1977).

There is also little evidence to support the argument that city governments discriminate against black citizens in the distribution of police resources. In fact, John Weicher (1971) and Kenneth Mladenka and Kim Hill (1978) found that more police officers were assigned to black neighborhoods than to poor ones. Lineberry (1977) discovered an equal distribution of police officers across neighborhoods.

George Antunes and John Plumlee (1977) analyzed the rough-

*ARRESTING ALLEGED
WRONGDOERS AND
DEALING WITH
URBAN VIOLENCE
PUT POLICE
OFFICERS LITERALLY
ON THE FRONT LINES
OF URBAN SERVICE
DELIVERY.*

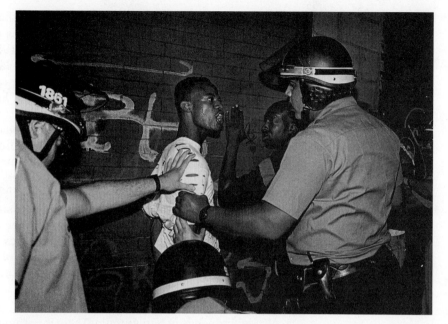

ness of 265 neighborhood streets in Houston. They also gathered data on the absence or presence of litter, sidewalks, curbs, and covered storm drains. These researchers concluded that no significant differences in street roughness existed between black and white neighborhoods or between wealthy and poor areas. However, they did find that black neighborhoods had a larger number of open ditches and were less clean than white neighborhoods.

In effect, then, there is no universal pattern to the distribution of urban public services based on income level, ethnicity, or class. Distributional patterns vary, instead, from city to city and from service to service.

THE DETERMINANTS OF THE DISTRIBUTIONAL PATTERN

Many public services in American cities appear to be distributed on the basis of bureaucratic *decision rules* rather than racial bias. These rules are used by bureaucrats to simplify their decision making. They are widely employed by municipal administrators because they appear to be reasonable and rational and can be used to defend decisions about the distribution of scarce resources. For example,

Mladenka and Hill (1978) found no evidence to support the argument that the police respond more quickly to calls from white neighborhoods than to those from black ones. Decision rules rather than racial bias determined the rapidity of response. Mladenka and Hill (1978: 126) concluded:

> The only independent source of variation in response to calls for police assistance appears to be the nature of the reported criminal activity. Incoming calls for service are not accorded equal consideration. Instead, the police dispatch system apparently evaluates each request for assistance in terms of the seriousness of the reported offense and the probability of an apprehension at the scene. These, rather than demographic considerations, determine the assignment of a response priority.

Mladenka and Hill also found that the assignment of police officers in Houston was determined by crime rates and calls for service. Since black neighborhoods had higher crime rates and more calls for service, they received higher levels of police patrols.

Several researchers have also reported that library departments allocate expenditures, books, periodicals, and personnel according to circulation rates (Blank, 1969; Lineberry, 1977; Mladenka and Hill, 1977). The higher the circulation rate in a branch library, the higher the resource levels allocated to that neighborhood facility. Therefore, libraries located in wealthier areas tend to receive higher levels of funds and more books and staff. The decision rule based on circulation rates heavily favors libraries in wealthier neighborhoods because reader levels are much higher at these branches.

Decision rules also influence the construction and repair of neighborhood streets. Frank Levy, Arnold Meltsner, and Aaron Wildavsky (1974), for example, reported that repair priorities were established on the basis of citizen demands. Citizens who complained the most to public officials got their neighborhood streets repaired first. Antunes and Plumlee (1977) discovered an identical decision rule being applied in Houston. In short, the squeaky wheel got the grease when it came to repairing residential streets. Another set of decision rules governed street *construction* in Houston. Antunes and Plumlee found that the developer of any new subdivision there is responsible for building the streets in accordance with city specifications. The cost of street construction is passed on to the buyers of the new homes. In established neighborhoods, deteriorated streets will be rebuilt by the city if 75 percent of those owning property along the street petition the city to do so. In that event, each property owner is required to pay for a share of the cost of construction.

In Detroit, Bryan Jones, Sadia Greenberg, Clifford Kaufman, and Joseph Drew (1978) also found decision rules to be operative in the sanitation department. Three rules were significant. First, the garbage was picked up once a week, each week. Second, refuse collection trucks and crews were allocated according to the amount of garbage neighborhoods produced. The third rule allocated additional resources to the central city. The first rule was neutral in its distributional consequences; the second and third rules favored the better-off and less well-off neighborhoods, respectively.

Mladenka (1980) examined the distribution of four services in Chicago and found different sets of factors and rules underlying the observed distributional patterns. For parks, past decisions and population shifts were important determinants. He concluded (Mladenka, 1980: 993):

> Many of the large parks in the system were acquired and developed in the last century. Much of the total parkland in the city is accounted for by a handful of giant sites. Decisions made many decades ago about where to locate these huge parks and the subsequent movement of the central-city population toward, around, and away from them offer the most convincing explanation of the present distribution of park acreage.

Mladenka also found that the distributional pattern for fire stations could be attributed to the recommendations made by a private consulting firm. The company analyzed the location of fire stations in the city and concluded that the inner city had an excessive number and outlying sections had inadequate fire protection. A redistribution of fire protection resources took place based on those conclusions. For education, Mladenka discovered that white schools were favored in terms of staffing costs, teacher experience, and teacher training. These differences were found to be a function of bureaucratic rules (Mladenka, 1980: 995):

> Teacher-assignment policy is highly decentralized. Transfer requests within the Chicago public school system are granted largely on the basis of seniority. White schools have the most experienced faculty because, when given the choice, teachers prefer to work in white schools. Transfer policy also determines the distribution of staffing costs and teacher qualifications. More experienced teachers also tend to be the best educated and teacher salaries are determined by experience and education.

For refuse collection, resources were allocated on the basis of the level of home ownership in the wards. Home ownership was a major determinant of the distributional pattern because a 1911 Chicago ordinance excluded multifamily structures from the service of refuse collection. The explanation can be traced to cost-efficiency concerns. During the nineteenth and part of the twentieth century, coal was the primary heating fuel. Its use resulted in major collection and disposal problems. Not only did tenement buildings produce tons of coal cinders, but the cinder heaps froze in winter and enormously complicated refuse collection. In order to economize, the city chose to deny collection service to tenement buildings. Although coal is no longer used as a major fuel, the 1911 ordinance continues to withhold that service from residents of apartments, high rises, townhouses, and condominiums.

Thus, the distribution of park, library, sanitation, street, and police and fire protection services does not seem to discriminate consistently against minority or low-income citizens. Although differences in service levels do exist across neighborhoods and groups, these differences do not appear to be a function of racial bias. Instead, they are what Lineberry (1977: 196) calls "unpatterned inequalities." This does not mean that the black and the poor receive service levels that are identical to those received by whites. However, research reveals that racial bias does not appear to be an explicit factor in distributional decisions. Municipal bureaucrats rely on decision rules to divide up scarce service resources. These rules are based on technical-rational criteria, and their application represents an effort to achieve administrative simplicity, efficiency, and rationality. For example, library resources are distributed on the basis of circulation rates, police resources on the basis of crime rates and citizen calls, recreational services according to user levels and citizen demand, garbage collection on the basis of tons of garbage generated, and street repairs on the basis of citizen complaints. However, the use of such decision rules does have distributonal consequences. That is, some groups and neighborhoods receive higher service levels because of the application of these rules. For example, wealthier neighborhoods receive more library resources under the circulation rate rule, and poorer areas are assigned more police officers under the crime rate rule.

Decision rules do not determine all aspects of the distribution of urban public services, however. For example, the actual quality of service provided to citizens by individual police officers, welfare caseworkers, teachers, and building inspectors is unlikely to be determined by decision rules. We have already pointed out the difficulty involved in controlling the behavior of these street-level bureaucrats (Lipsky, 1976). Decision rules are more likely to control the distribution of resources (library books, park equipment), expenditures, and personnel (police officers, maintenance crews).

Another finding from the research on the distribution of urban public services is that distributional outcomes do not appear to be influenced by elected public officials. Instead, bureaucrats control the decision-making process. Elected officials seem to be uninformed about the distributional pattern (Mladenka and Hill, 1977). They do not possess the detailed knowledge about service delivery that would allow them to challenge the bureaucrats' decisions. This pattern appears to hold in both unreformed and reformed cities (Mladenka, 1980). Consequently, a major responsibility of city government—making decisions about the equitable delivery of vital public services—is left to the discretion of appointed rather than elected officials.

HISTORICAL CHANGE IN DISTRIBUTIONAL DETERMINANTS

Distributional patterns for urban public services do change over time. Population shifts occur, new decision rules are implemented by bureaucracies, and budgetary priorities change.

Mladenka (1980) analyzed facilities, programs, and expenditures in Chicago during a period of twenty-two years. The results revealed a fundamental change in the distribution of recreational facilities over time. In 1962, racial bias was clearly the norm. By 1983, race was not a factor in accounting for the distributional pattern. In 1962, white wards received three times as many major recreational facilities as black wards. By 1983, the average number of facilities in black wards and in white wards was virtually identical. The progress experienced by black wards has been quite extraordinary. Mladenka concluded that population shifts have been a major factor contributing to this progress. As whites abandoned the central city for the suburbs, blacks moved in and began to use the recreational facilities originally provided for white neighborhoods. However, other factors were also significant. The heightened political awareness and activity of blacks had an impact on the distributional configuration. Public officials could no longer simply ignore black demands, which instead became a factor that had to be considered when making distributional choices. The national government also played a role. The courts were more likely to hear cases alleging discrimination in service delivery, and a variety of federal agencies were involved in the implementation of grant programs requiring nondiscrimination in service provision. In addition, the race riots of the 1960s had a particularly significant impact on the recreational system. More swimming pools, field houses, and athletic fields were built in minority wards as a result.

Another factor that accounts for the decline of race as a determinant of the distributional pattern in Chicago has been a change in the motivations of public officials. Public officials are more sensitive to the need to maintain the stability of middle- and upper-class neighborhoods than they were previously. Racial discrimination was the norm twenty years ago. Although class was not unimportant, it certainly did not rank in the same league with race as a characteristic on which winners and losers could be separated. Today, some black wards fare better than other black wards, and some white wards receive more than other white wards. Furthermore, black wards frequently fare better than white ones. Part of the explanation of why the level of home ownership has replaced race as a distributional standard in Chicago is that city officials fear further population losses. The vitality of the city is perceived to depend to a great degree on the maintenance of stable residential neighborhoods. Although population losses have been more severe among whites, public officials seek to retard flight from middle-class black neighborhoods as well. Therefore, they are more likely to use higher levels of public services as incentives to selected neighborhoods than was the case two decades ago.

One major conclusion from Mladenka's research is that white wards with a low level of home ownership fare very poorly in the distributional struggle. In fact, this group of wards constitutes the worst-off category, followed closely by black wards with low home ownership levels. The lowest white wards received only 30 major public facilities per ward. In comparison, black wards with medium and high levels of home ownership were allocated 51 and 48 major facilities, respectively. Further, racially mixed wards (20 to 80 percent black) received 67 major facilities per ward.

For recreational programs, however, a different pattern was revealed. Race is clearly a significant factor in determining the availability of such resources. Although the level of home ownership was the dominant explanation for differences in recreational services, fewer programs were offered in black wards. Program opportunities in the Chicago Park District are demand-driven. Further, they sometimes require that the participants pay the cost of equipment purchases. Because of the nature of the programs offered, both rules operate to the detriment of black wards.

Mladenka's analysis over a twenty-two year period reveals a fundamental redistribution of resources between black and white wards in Chicago. In fact, the worst-off category of wards in the city today is white rather than black, and although population shifts have played a major role in this redistribution, the changing perceptions of public officials have also been an important factor. The altered demographic and economic structure of the city has forced public officials to use urban services as a weapon in the struggle to combat the deterioration of the social fabric. Mladenka concludes that other scholars have underestimated the extent to which distributional patterns change over time. In addition, political influences are more significant and bureaucratic decision rules less important than was previously thought. Furthermore, poorer white neighborhoods may frequently be the major losers in the distributional struggle. Finally, class appears to have displaced race as the crucial determinant of distributional patterns. The deteriorating economic and social condition of many central cities has exerted a major impact on distributional politics.

RACIAL BIAS IN THE DISTRIBUTION OF MUNICIPAL JOBS

Jobs with urban governments can be seen as a public resource if not a public service. And, in contrast to the distributional pattern for public services in urban areas, the staffing of municipal departments reflects the operation of racial bias in great numbers of cities. Although racial bias may no longer be affecting the distribution of service resources and elected public officials play no significant role in decisions about the distribution of service benefits, there is strong evidence to suggest racial bias does affect the filling of positions with the city government. In addition, there is evidence that public officials do influence the extent to which black citizens obtain signficant shares of these jobs.

Research on municipal employment reveals substantial racial bias in the distribution of city jobs. One study (Mladenka, 1987) found that 306 cities in a sample of 1,224 cities with over 10,000 population did not employ a *single* black citizen! Further, 427 (35 percent) of those cities employed less than 1 percent blacks and 540 (44 percent) employed less than 2 percent. The numbers were much

worse for the key job categories of officials/administrators (department heads, directors), professionals, and protective service workers
(police officers). These positions are significant for several reasons.
First, they pay considerably more than clerical and blue-collar positions. Second, blacks in administrative and professional positions
have great potential to influence the recruitment and advancement
of other minority employees. In addition, the presence of blacks in
key decision-making positions significantly increases black influence
in vital areas of city government such as spending, taxing, zoning,
regulation, and public services. Finally, blacks in protective service
positions can have major substantive as well as symbolic value with
respect to the treatment of minorities in citizen encounters.

Given the importance of these key types of positions, it is significant that blacks fill an abysmally small proportion of such jobs. Of
the 1,224 cities studied by Mladenka, 842 (70 percent) didn't employ
a single black as an official or administrator in municipal government and 730 (63 percent) didn't employ any black professionals.
Furthermore, 507 cities (43 percent) didn't have a single black police
officer or firefighter, and 624 (53 percent) had less than 2 percent
blacks in protective service positions. In addition, the overwhelming
majority of the cities studied by Mladenka underrepresented blacks
on the municipal work force. For example, 1,080 of the cities (89
percent) underrepresented blacks in official/administrator positions,
and 1,009 (87 percent) underrepresented them in professional jobs.
On the other hand, blacks held a disproportionate share of menial
jobs such as laborer and garbage collector. As an example, 89 percent
of all menial city jobs in Philadelphia are filled by blacks even though
blacks constitute only 38 percent of the population. In San Francisco,
only 7 percent of white city workers are employed in menial jobs, but
49 percent of black employees fill these low-level positions.

What about the impact of political power on the distribution of
city jobs? Are black mayors and city council members able to reward
their constituents with a larger share of government jobs? The answer is yes. Several studies have concluded that the election of black
public officials increases the likelihood that blacks will obtain city
jobs (Dye and Renick, 1981; Eisinger, 1982; Mladenka, 1987; Stein,
1986). In fact, Thomas Dye and James Renick (1981) found:

> Employment in top city jobs appears to be a function of political
> power, as it is reflected in city council representation. Representa-
> tion on city council is more important in gaining city employment
> in administrative, professional, and protective service positions than

any other single factor. . . . We believe that black representation on city councils is a crucial link in improving black employment opportunities in city government.

CONCLUSION

The delivery of public services in urban areas poses numerous opportunities for political conflict; yet the distributional process is generally free of such controversy. Most of the time the allocation of public services is controlled by the bureaucracy and takes place in an environment where professional administrators enjoy a great deal of discretion in making distributional choices. These bureaucrats typically rely on one or more decision rules to simplify their decision making. Application of these decision rules, however, has significant consequences in terms of the pattern of service distribution. That is, some rules will generally benefit wealthier residents and neighborhoods; others will generally benefit poorer ones. Still others will benefit the most vocal and demanding residents. Each rule also incorporates some conception of equity, even though that standard may not be fully recognized by those who adopt the rule. Perhaps what is most important, however, is that no city currently appears to use only one decision rule for all its service-related decisions. Thus, the pattern of benefits and burdens is mixed. In the typical city every class and ethnic group is advantaged with respect to some services and disadvantaged with respect to others.

It would be misleading, however, to conclude that the application of decision rules entirely explains which residents get good service and which get poor service. The activities of street-level bureaucrats such as police officers, welfare caseworkers, and teachers are unlikely to be fully controlled by administrative rules intended to ensure consistent and uniform behavior. The individual values of these street-level bureaucrats and the cultural norms of their organizations are more likely to determine how they will respond to individual citizens.

Some resources of city governments are clearly allocated in a way that favors white residents more than minority ones. Employment opportunities probably offer the best example of the effect of racial bias—with minorities being disproportionately relegated to menial jobs and excluded from professional ones. However, minority residents can achieve a greater share of these benefits when they have elected representatives in city government to press their claims. In that sense the democratic process can work for many groups and citizens, at least for those who have sympathetic public officials to represent them.

REFERENCES

Antunes, George, and John P. Plumlee. 1977. "The Distribution of an Urban Public Service," pp. 51–70 in Robert L. Lineberry (ed.), *The Politics and Economics of Urban Services.* Beverly Hills, Calif.: Sage.

Baron, Harold M. 1971. "Race and Status in School Spending: Chicago, 1961–1966," *Journal of Human Resources* 6 (Winter): 1–24.

Berk, Richard A., and Alice A. Hartman. 1971. *Race and District Differences in Per Pupil Staffing Expenditures in Chicago Elementary Schools, 1970–1971.* Chicago: Center for Urban Affairs.

Blank, Blanche D. 1969. "A Comparative Study of an Urban Bureaucracy," *Urban Affairs Quarterly* 4 (May): 343–354.

Burkhead, Jesse. 1967. *Input and Output in Large City High Schools.* Syracuse: Syracuse University Press.

Dye, Thomas R., and James Renick. 1981. "Political Power and City Jobs: Determinants of Minority Employment," *Social Science Quarterly* 62 (September): 475–486.

Eisinger, Peter. 1982. "Black Employment in City Jobs: The Impact of Black Political Power," *American Political Science Review* 72 (June): 380–392.

Fisk, Donald M. 1973. *How Effective Are Your Community Recreation Services?* Washington, D.C.: U.S. Department of the Interior.

Gold, Steven D. 1974. "The Distribution of an Urban Government Service in Theory and Practice: The Case of Recreation in Detroit," *Public Finance Quarterly* 2 (January): 107–130.

Jones, Bryan D., Sadia Greenberg, Clifford Kaufman, and Joseph Drew. 1978. "Service Delivery Rules and the Distribution of Local Government Services: Three Detroit Bureaucracies," *Journal of Politics* 40 (May): 332–368.

Katzman, Martin T. 1968. "Distributions and Production in a Big City Elementary School System," *Yale Economic Essays* 8 (Spring): 201–256.

Levy, Frank S., Arnold J. Meltsner, and Aaron Wildavsky. 1974. *Urban Outcomes.* Berkeley: University of California Press.

Lineberry, Robert L. 1977. *Equality and Urban Policy.* Beverly Hills, Calif.: Sage.

Lipsky, Michael. 1976. "Toward a Theory of Street Level Bureaucracy," pp. 196–213 in Willis D. Hawley and Michael Lipsky (eds.), *Theoretical Perspectives in Urban Politics.* Englewood Cliffs, N.J.: Prentice-Hall.

Lyon, David W. 1970. "Capital Spending and the Neighborhoods of Philadelphia," *Business Review* (May): 16–27.

Mandel, Allen. 1974. "The Allocation of Resources in Urban and Suburban School Districts." Unpublished Ph.D. dissertation, University of Michigan, Ann Arbor.

Mladenka, Kenneth R. 1980. "The Urban Bureaucracy and the Chicago Political Machine: Who Gets What and the Limits to Political Control," *American Political Science Review* 74 (December): 991–998.

Mladenka, Kenneth R. 1987. "Black Jobs and Black Political Power in the American City." Paper delivered at the annual meeting of the Southwestern Political Science Association, Dallas, March 19–21.

Mladenka, Kenneth R., and Kim Quaile Hill. 1977. "The Distribution of Benefits in an Urban Environment: Parks and Libraries in Houston," *Urban Affairs Quarterly* 13 (September): 73–94.

Mladenka, Kenneth R., and Kim Quaile Hill. 1978. "The Distribution of Urban Police Services," *Journal of Politics* 40 (July): 112–133.

Nivola, Peter S. 1978. "Distributing a Municipal Service: A Case Study of Housing Inspection," *Journal of Politics* 40 (February): 59–81.

Peterson, Paul E. 1981. *City Limits.* Chicago: University of Chicago Press.

Sexton, Patricia C. 1961. *Education and Income.* New York: Viking.

Stein, Lana. 1986. "Representative Local Government: Minorities in the Municipal Workforce," *Journal of Politics* 48 (August): 694–713.

Stone, Clarence N. 1980. "Systemic Power in Community Decision Making: A Restatement of Stratification Theory," *American Political Science Review* 74 (December): 978–990.

Verba, Sidney, and Norman H. Nie. 1972. *Participation in America.* New York: Harper & Row.

Weicher, John A. 1971. "The Allocation of Police Protection by Income Class," *Urban Studies* 8 (October): 207–220.

Wilson, James Q. 1968. *Varieties of Police Behavior.* Cambridge, Mass.: Harvard University Press.

13

Bureaucratic Power in State and Local Government

Bureaucracies play a major role in Americans' lives. They provide police protection, put out fires, regulate land use, educate children, pick up the garbage, and maintain and operate the transportation system. They also propose new laws and ordinances, write budgets, and implement public policies. Given the vast influence of bureaucracies it is little wonder that horror stories abound. Charles Goodsell (1983: 3) recounts the following:

> A Chicago woman undergoing chemotherapy for cancer of the breast applied for Medicare. She received a computer-produced letter indicating she was ineligible since she had died the previous April.

> The Department of Energy set out to declassify millions of documents inherited from the Atomic Energy Commission. Eight of the released documents contained the basic design principles for the hydrogen bomb.

> A unit of what is now the Department of Health and Human Services sent fifteen chimpanzees to a Texas laboratory for the purpose of launching a chimp-breeding program. All were males.

And bureaucrats are not only perceived as inept and stupid; they are also thought to be dangerous, because they are essentially an independent force in government. They operate under little control by either elected officials or voters. Thus, it is believed that they thwart the democratic process.

Bureaucrats are also accused of elitism. They are said to serve the interests of the upper classes, ignoring the demands of the poor and disadvantaged. They seek to maintain the status quo. In addition, they are alleged to corrupt the policy process. Through their control over the implementation of public policies, bureaucrats often distort the true intent of elected decision makers.

Finally, bureaucrats are charged with dehumanizing individual clients. The citizen who has a problem or request is forced to deal with a huge organization where the emphasis is on impersonal, routinized behavior. Everyone is assigned a number. Special circumstances are ignored. Efficiency rather than responsiveness is the goal. Often, the relationship between the bureaucrat and the citizen is a confrontational one. Inevitably, the citizen is the loser.

In this chapter we will examine the evidence concerning these views of bureaucratic performance to determine whether state and local bureaucrats are responsive and accountable. We will also analyze bureaucratic decision making, examine the sources of bureaucratic power, and comment on the role of bureaucracies in a democratic society.

CHARACTERISTICS OF BUREAUCRACIES

All complex organizations exhibit eight characteristics:

1. Hierarchal structure
2. Chain of command and span of control
3. Division of labor
4. Specialization of labor
5. Routinized behavior and standardized production
6. Promotion on the basis of demonstrated performance
7. Goal orientation that emphasizes the efficient and effective attainment of objectives.
8. Control of employees according to specific rules and procedures.

That is, all bureaucracies are hierarchically arranged. Every employee has a superior. Specific tasks are assigned to each member of the organization. Communication is structured according to an established chain of command. Labor is divided and specialized. Intense specialization of functions is the norm. Bureaucracies are centers of complex knowledge and expertise. Employees are carefully trained to perform tasks in accordance with routinized procedures.

In principle, bureaucracies emphasize demonstrated performance and merit in the evaluation and promotion of employees. Ideally, at least, the bureaucracy is a meritocracy. Factors such as family connections, office politics, and personal relationships should play no role in the reward structure. That they obviously do does not repudiate the fact that the bureaucracy strives to minimize their influence. Bureaucracies emphasize demonstrated performance as the key to the evaluation of employees because complex organizations are geared to the attainment of goals. A system of rewards based on merit is considered to be conducive to the accomplishment of those goals. In fact, the bureaucracy is the best form of organization yet devised for the efficient and effective attainment of goals.

BUREAUCRATIC DECISION MAKING

How do bureaucrats make decisions? According to one school of thought, complex organizations cannot be the locus of rational decision making (Perrow, 1972). This state of affairs can be attributed to several factors that severely limit the bureaucrat's ability to pursue and make rational choices.

LIMITATIONS ON RATIONALITY IN BUREAUCRACIES

First, bureaucrats are unable to predict with any reasonable degree of certainty the impact of many decisions. What will be the consequences of choice A? How will those impacts differ from those attendant on choice B? Since the bureaucrat can only guess as to the likely effects of a particular decision, rationality is seriously endangered.

Another limitation on rationality in decision making revolves around the range of alternative courses of action. Any bureaucracy operates under real limits on time and available resources. Bureaucrats cannot afford to investigate the feasibility and effects of every possible decision or course of action. Also, some potentially attractive choices will never become known to the bureaucrat. Consequently, the decision taken may be selected from only a few options. Since the options never considered may have proven to be more rational than the one chosen, the decision-making process is not as rational as it could be.

A final limitation is that the bureaucracy cannot rank-order its priorities. It cannot specify which goals are most important and how much more important they are than others. For example, is the police department most interested in reducing crime, responding to citizens' calls, raising levels of public satisfaction with police services, maintaining officer morale, or increasing the size and budget of the department? Rationality requires that the organization specify its priorities and make decisions designed to enhance their attainment. There can be no rational decision making without clearly established and prioritized goals. The situation is further complicated by the fact that bureaucracies have symbolic as well as operational goals. In addition, they pursue long-term as well as short-term objectives. Also, different divisions and departments of state and local governments pursue different goals, and sometimes these are in conflict. And a deliberate, systematic attempt to specify a hierarchy of goals might well generate intense intraorganizational conflict. For example, a police department that established crime reduction as its primary goal and redistributed resources to accomplish it might well experience considerable opposition from its employees, who see salaries, fringe benefits, and working conditions as their top goals.

Because of these various limitations on rational behavior, the bureaucrat seeks workable decisions that will satisfy the various organizational components. Workable decisions do not happen by chance, however. Instead, the bureaucracy takes pains to establish a routinized set of procedures that will control the search for solutions to problems. *Standard operating procedures (SOPs)* are heavily relied on within bureaucracies. SOPs specify how employees are to behave when decisions have to be made. SOPs limit human discretion. They reflect the organization's experiences with past problems and transmit to the employee the appropriate course of action to pursue, based on that experience. Individual employees might well try to make decisions by following a rational approach that emphasizes the careful collection of data, systematic analysis, the setting of goals, and the evaluation of costs and benefits. The bureaucracy knows better.

It seeks to minimize individual involvement in decision making by invoking routinized and predetermined procedures.

Bureaucracies also rely on the training and indoctrination of employees to ensure the predictability and consistency of decision making. Employees are trained to accept certain assumptions and premises of behavior. They are conditioned to accept some information and ignore other information, to highlight some parts of reality and filter or reject other parts. Bureaucrats are indoctrinated to make choices based on a sensitivity to the organization's interests as a whole.

CHARACTERISTICS OF BUREAUCRATIC DECISIONS

The decisions that result from the process of bureaucratic decision making exhibit several distinctive characteristics. First, current decisions bear a marked resemblance to past decisions. This occurs because, when faced with a problem, bureaucrats search their memory for a similar situation. When they identify a workable past decision that fits the present situation, they imitate that earlier choice. As a result, the best predictor of present and future bureaucratic decisions is past decisions.

Since past decisions serve as a guide to present behavior, change in bureaucracies is incremental at best. A major characteristic of bureaucracies is that they seldom undertake comprehensive change or engage in innovative behavior. They are averse to risk taking. They hew a line that seldom departs from the status quo. They are disinclined to experiment and innovate. The reason can be traced to bureaucrats' pronounced tendency to rely on the past as a guide. Bureaucrats fear change because departures from the status quo are fraught with risk. Consequences cannot be predicted, and alternative courses of action are not obvious. Workable decisions require a sensitivity to what has served the organization's needs in the past.

However, bureaucracies do sometimes depart substantially from previous courses of action. Policies do change, and procedures are revised. Under what conditions are innovation and change apt to take place? A change in leadership is one such condition. A new director, bureau chief, or department head may bring different ideas into the organization and infuse it with a new sense of purpose and direction. Additional resources may be brought into the organization, available resources redistributed, existing policies revised, and new policies adopted. Disruptions in the organization's environment are also conducive to change. A dramatic increase in the crime rate and in public demands that the police do something about it may force a city council to provide higher resource levels and encourage police officials to alter existing priorities. Generally, however, bureaucracies exhibit a tendency to return to previous patterns of behavior as soon as such disruptions subside.

Thus, we can conclude that bureaucrats will generally rely on the past as a guide to present policy. Change will be incremental. The element of human discretion in decision making will be minimized by relying on standard operating procedures to guide choices. When a decision involves complex political issues, the bureaucracy will attempt to simplify the situation by reducing it to a technical and administrative task, thereby avoiding political conflict. For example, decisions about how to allocate police patrols across neighborhoods that differ on the basis of race, wealth, and need involve important choices as to equity and the appropriate division of scarce resources. The bureaucrat avoids these complicated political issues by distributing protective resources on the basis of technical criteria such as crime rates and calls for service. Decision making is routinized, the element of human discretion is minimized, and political controversy is avoided. Since reliance on technical criteria has provided workable decisions in the past, past choices continue to be invoked as a guide to the present.

THE CONTRADICTIONS INHERENT IN THE FUNCTIONING OF BUREAUCRACIES

Bureaucrats occupy an unenviable position in government. They are responsible for the delivery of a variety of essential public services. Since these services are vital to the health, safety, and well-being of the citizenry, the average individual often gets upset when they are not delivered or when the service provided is perceived as substandard. At the same time, bureaucrats are expected to be both fair and responsive. Fairness implies objectivity, impartiality, and even-handedness. Bureaucrats are expected to evaluate each case on its merits. They are not supposed to play favorites. Rich, white, or well-mannered citizens are not guaranteed preferential treatment. Instead, every person is entitled to courteous behavior and high-quality service.

However, bureaucrats are also expected to place a high priority on responsiveness. When citizens call the police, they expect them to come. When they complain about a pothole in the street, defective equipment at the neighborhood playground, or a clogged sewer line, they expect a prompt and favorable response. In fact, citizens place a premium on responsive behavior from bureaucracies. The problem for the administrator is that he or she cannot be both fair and responsive at the same time. Fairness requires impartial and evenhanded treatment; responsiveness means playing favorites. Resources are always limited. There is never enough time, money, or personnel to meet every demand and solve every problem. Therefore, responsiveness requires that some citizen demands be ignored or only partially responded to. Not all demands can be treated equally.

THE UNEMPLOYMENT LINE IS A PLACE WHERE INCREASING NUMBERS OF AMERICANS GET FIRST-HAND EXPERIENCE WITH THE FUNCTIONING OF GOVERNMENTAL BUREAUCRACY.

Unfortunately, there are no guidelines for the bureaucrat to follow in solving this dilemma. Elected public officials have not decreed that administrators should emphasize responsiveness rather than fairness. Instead, bureaucrats are left to their own devices to resolve the conflict between fairness and responsiveness. Generally, it appears that bureaucrats have opted for fairness over responsiveness since they rely so heavily on technical-rational criteria to distribute resources and solve citizens' problems. However, that choice has not protected bureaucracies from intense criticism. The citizen expects the bureaucrat to maximize both values simultaneously and exhibits little patience or understanding when he or she is unable to do so.

Another contradiction exists between efficiency and effectiveness. Citizens want bureaucrats to be efficient, to accomplish goals with a minimum outlay of resources. They want public employees to be hardworking, dedicated, and professional. They expect department budgets to be trimmed of all fat. The public is disgusted by reports of government workers with nothing to do and expects maximum effort and output from the smallest possible number of workers. At the same time the citizenry also demands effectiveness. Citizens not only want efficiency in production, they also want various goals to be accomplished. They want lower crime rates, clean, attractive, and well-equipped parks, and a good education for their children. Inevitably, however, a conflict arises between efficiency and effectiveness. Although citizens want good streets, schools, parks, and police protection, they are seldom willing (even if able) to pay the taxes necessary to support superior service levels. What they really want is high-quality service at a very low cost. Since that is impossible, it is more satisfying to blame the inefficiency of bureaucrats than to assume a heavier tax burden.

Still another contradiction arises from the conflict between the public's desire to create an independent bureaucracy on the one hand and the need to ensure accountability on the other. The public wants a professional bureaucracy equipped with the most sophisticated technology and armed with superior knowledge. However, a professional is also apt to be largely independent. He or she will be more likely to follow guidelines arising from his or her training, expertise, and professional norms than to accede to citizens' demands. The public is willing to tolerate a considerable degree of independence since that implies that the bureaucrat will also be insulated from political meddling. An independent bureaucracy is free to administer the laws and distribute resources on a fair and impartial basis. Americans are inclined to accept bureaucratic independence because it enhances efficiency and effectiveness as well as fairness.

But an independent bureaucracy protected from political interference on the part of interest groups and guided by professional norms and specialized knowledge is also likely to be insulated from public control. Citizens do not elect most administrators. Once these appointed officials have served a probationary period, it is exceedingly difficult to remove them from office. An official protected by tenure is less likely to be responsive to citizen demands than one dependent on public favor.

Thus, bureaucrats are frequently criticized by the public because the average citizen holds unreasonable expectations. Administrators cannot satisfy citizens' demands for both fairness and responsiveness. Similarly, bureaucrats cannot simultaneously maximize the values of efficiency and effectiveness. A high degree of effectiveness in the provision of public services will be very expensive. Finally, administrators cannot be both independent and accountable. However, citizens are apt to remain unaware that their expectations are contradictory. They want bureaucrats to be fair, efficient, and professional as well as responsive, effective, and independent.

THE POWER OF BUREAUCRACIES

It is easy to underestimate the power of bureaucracies. Bureaucrats' activities are seldom subjected to media coverage or public scrutiny. The life of the bureaucrat is far from glamorous; many people think that bureaucrats are nothing more than clerks who spend their careers buried in paperwork. However, the reality of bureaucratic power defies this image.

SOURCES OF BUREAUCRATIC POWER

The bureaucracy is a powerful force in American government (arguably the most powerful) for a variety of reasons. First, it controls the delivery of a variety of vital services. This control over the provision of protective, education, recreational, transportation, health, and welfare services confers great power. Every citizen is heavily dependent on the governmental bureaucracy. Its power derives from the fact that, within certain limits, it can deliver the service or withhold it, provide superior or substandard levels of service, and deliver the

Bureaucratic Size

One source of bureaucratic power is the sheer size of many of the separate agencies and organizations that make up the executive branch of a single city or state. Consider, as one especially remarkable example, the following breakdown of the employees of New York City. Undoubtedly, the mayor and other elected officials of the Big Apple face an imposing task in trying to manage and direct this huge bureaucracy.

Education employees	117,158
Financial and other general administrators	10,014
Fire department employees	12,974
Hospital workers	49,668
Judicial and legal employees	4,933
Parks and recreation employees	4,964
Police department employees	33,559
Road and highway workers	9,398
Solid waste management employees	12,217
Utility workers	52,877
All other employees	88,508
Total full-time city employees	396,270

Source: U.S. Bureau of the Census, *City Employment: 1989* (Washington, D.C.: U.S. Bureau of the Census, 1990).

service promptly or slowly. Administrators have a great deal of influence over how a given service will be provided, how much of the service will be delivered, and in what ways and to which neighborhoods and groups the service will be distributed.

Another source of power derives from the bureaucracy's control over budgeting (Crecine, 1969). Budgets are obviously major documents in government. They specify how much money will be spent for services and programs. They also specify how it will be divided among personnel, equipment, materials, maintenance, construction, and administration. Budgets set priorities and establish the direction of government activity. Bureaucrats are the dominant force in the budget-making process. Although elected officials approve total budget expenditures, they rarely scrutinize the programs and services of individual departments. Instead, the various bureaucratic agencies establish their own priorities and programs. They decide how the budget dollars will be spent. Generally, elected officials accept the judgments and evaluations of bureaucrats with respect to budgetary matters.

Another source of power stems from the bureaucrat's knowledge and expertise. Bureaucrats are the recognized experts in government. Many have years of specialized education and training. While on the job, they continue to stay abreast of the latest developments in their field by participating in professional associations, attending conferences, and enrolling in seminars and workshops. As a result, it is exceedingly difficult, if not impossible, for elected public officials to challenge expert administrators on many policy decisions. Instead, the tendency is to defer to the bureaucrat's expertise.

The bureaucrats' experience and tenure also contribute to their power and influence. Elected officials come and go. Some resign or choose not to run for reelection. Others are defeated at the polls. City managers may be fired. In cities with reformed governments, the jobs of mayor and council members are part-time. The same is also true of many state legislators. Their highest priority is pursuing a livelihood in a private occupation. Consequently, they do not have the time or the incentive to pore over budgetary details, gather independent information, and monitor departmental operations. Bureaucracies, on the other hand, have relatively little turnover. Their employees cannot be removed by an angry electorate. And once those employees have served a probationary period, it is exceedingly difficult to remove them for any reason. As a result, bureaucrats enjoy a monopoly over experience. The department develops a collective memory. That experience also translates into access to and control over vast amounts of information. Elected officials, in comparison, have little in the way of an organizational memory and institutional support and are much less likely to enjoy access to a vast array of information. Consequently, they are seldom able to mount an effective challenge to bureaucratic dominance in many decision-making arenas.

The element of discretion also gives administrators a powerful tool. There are two types of bureaucratic discretion. The first type is the discretion enjoyed by high-level administrators. They have a great deal of flexibility with respect to establishing new programs and setting departmental priorities. For example, a new police chief

Bureaucratic Expertise

As we have noted, one source of bureaucratic power is expertise. And a good illustration of that expertise comes from the kinds of occupations represented in state and local government executive branch agencies today. Consider, as a few examples, the following job openings recently advertised by the Virginia Department of Personnel and Training:

Accountant
Archaeologist
Clinical social worker
Computer systems senior engineer
Economist
Environmental engineer
Environmental program analyst
Hospital quality assurance coordinator
Industrial development marketing manager
Marine scientist

may decide to reassign officers from the traffic bureau to the patrol division. He or she may make crime reduction the top priority and reduce the emphasis on community relations. Or, the police chief may choose to improve officer morale by seeking a pay raise and better fringe benefits. Similarly, the director of parks and recreation engages in a major exercise of bureaucratic discretion when he or she lobbies for a bond proposal intended to finance a program of park improvement and site acquisition. When key administrators take advantage of the considerable flexibility inherent in the implementation of legislative policies, they are capitalizing on a major source of bureaucratic power.

There is another type of bureaucratic discretion. The so-called street-level bureaucrats (police officers, teachers, and welfare caseworkers, for example) also enjoy great flexibility with respect to how they do their jobs. For example, the police officer on the beat decides

Mental health physician
Occupational safety inspector
Planner
Public health nurse
Speech pathologist
Transportation engineer
Veterinary diagnostician
Visually handicapped education specialist
Wildlife biologist

All of these occupations require extensive, advanced education and can only be filled by an individual with highly specialized knowledge—unusual expertise, that is. Not every state and local government employee, of course, has such special expertise. But the bureaucracies of these governments employ very large numbers of such persons. The work of these experts is often the principal activity of many bureaucratic agencies. And the unique knowledge of these experts, which is often little understood by citizens or elected officials, gives them remarkable power over decisions about what government policies ought to be adopted and how they ought to be pursued.

which laws to enforce and how vigorously and whether enforcement will apply equally to all citizens. This type of discretion does not usually enhance the bureaucracy's power and influence, however. In fact, it may sometimes create serious organizational problems. If departmental supervisors cannot control the behavior of street-level employees, then the implementation of policy is threatened and the organization is subject to criticism (Lipsky, 1976).

Bureaucrats can also rely on their clientele to enhance their power. Every bureaucracy courts the support of its client groups, which range from neighborhood groups who use and support a city's park and recreation system to organizations of prominent businesspeople who support a state government's economic development program. Client groups increase the power of the bureaucracy in several ways. They may engage in fund-raising activities and provide volunteer staffing. For example, parent-teacher organizations frequently raise considerable sums of money and donate thousands of hours of labor to local public schools. In cities across the country, organizations called "Friends of the Parks" and "Friends of the Library" provide major assistance in the form of donated land, recreational equipment, and money. Similarly, various businesses contribute to state colleges and universities, which train prospective employees for and carry out research relevant to the needs of those businesses.

Client groups also enhance the power of the bureaucracy in other ways. When an agency is threatened with budget cuts, for example, its clients will be called on to come to its defense. Since many of these groups count large numbers of the social and economic elite among their membership, their assistance and support can prove to be invaluable. The members can write letters and make phone calls to elected officials and make personal visits to their offices. They can circulate petitions, they can contribute time and money to the campaigns of sympathetic candidates, and they can dramatize the issue at hand by conducting public relations campaigns.

LIMITS ON BUREAUCRATIC POWER

It would be wrong to leave the impression that the power of the bureaucracy is essentially limitless. Although that power is substantial, a variety of factors restrict it. First, administrative power is limited by the bureaucrats' own professional training and values. These officials are socialized to abide by the democratic rules of the game and to accept the distinction (at least in principle) between politics and administration. They are trained to distribute resources, implement policy, and solve problems on the basis of the rational application of sophisticated technology and expert knowledge. They adhere to the canon of fair and objective treatment. There is little in their education and training that would tend to foster capricious and arrogant behavior or encourage the usurption of power. In fact, bureaucrats are often confronted with the opportunity to make political choices. The fact that they tend to reduce political problems to technical puzzles that can be solved through the application of knowledge and technology testifies to their reluctance to assume distinctly political responsibilities.

Another limitation on bureaucratic power is imposed by the public. Both individual citizens and groups have the potential to influence bureaucratic operations directly as well as indirectly. If citizens are not satisfied with the performance of a certain department, they can express their grievances and discontents in a variety of ways. No bureaucracy wants an irate citizenry or a disaffected city council or state legislature. Bureaucracies seek routine and predictability and favor the status quo. They go to great lengths to avoid citizen complaints and public dissatisfaction.

Bureaucracies are also constrained by political parties. Parties provide an institutional and organizational layer that mediates between citizens and bureaucrats. Citizens' complaints are frequently communicated to a party official, who in turn forwards the demand to the bureaucracy and follows up on the resolution of the problem. The party in power is also likely to control various patronage appointments.

Budgets certainly impose limits on bureaucratic power. Although we have argued that administrators tend to dominate the budget-making process, financial resources are finite. Budgetary limitations curtail efforts at program expansion. In addition, an angry city council or legislature can threaten a department with budget cuts.

Incrementalism also imposes limits on bureaucratic power. As we discussed earlier, bureaucrats rely on past behavior as a guide to present and future decisions. Undertaking any comprehensive or significant change is fraught with risk because the impact of such change cannot be predicted with any reasonable degree of certainty. Therefore, bureaucrats avoid risk by doing in the present what has worked in the past. As a result, change tends to be gradual. This incremental tendency limits bureaucratic power because major changes and radical departures from existing routines, programs, and activities are highly unlikely. Bureaucrats are conservative. They hew to the status quo. Their actions tend to be consistent and predictable.

Elected public officials further limit bureaucratic power. These officials can reduce budgeted funds, and they can appoint and remove department heads and directors. In addition, they can pass laws to reorganize, consolidate, or even abolish administrative functions. Even though such actions are relatively rare, the potential for such oversight serves as a brake on agencies that might otherwise engage in conflicts with elected officials.

Still another check on bureaucratic power comes from media coverage. Television and newspaper reporters are eager to expose bureaucratic bungling, incompetence, arrogance, and capriciousness. Newspapers run many articles uncovering corruption, inefficiency, and insensitivity to citizens' problems. The scrutiny of departmental operations by local journalists and television reporters exerts a significant influence on bureaucratic behavior. Anyone who has studied government bureaucracies knows how difficult it is to obtain data about administrative operations. In part, the reluctance to release such data can be attributed to unpleasant experiences with journalists. Administrators are quick to note that reporters are not trained to analyze complex statistical information, are unfair in their interpretations, and are apt to quote remarks out of context. Bureaucrats are much more self-conscious about their behavior than they would be if an appearance on the front page or on the local evening news was only a remote possibility.

Finally, the federal government also constrains the power of state and local bureaucracies. For example, the U.S. Justice Department has filed suit against several cities concerning hiring practices that are allegedly racially discriminatory and has initiated investigations of a number of others. In the past the federal courts have scrutinized bureaucratic operations for alleged violations of civil rights, including police brutality, denial of voting rights, and unfair housing practices. And the federal government's cooptation of policy making (described in Chapter 3) has dictated many program activities of state and local bureaucrats.

ARE BUREAUCRATS RESPONSIVE AND ACCOUNTABLE?

One of the ultimate tests of bureaucratic performance is the extent to which public administrators are responsive and accountable. Even if bureaucrats were efficient and effective and treated clients fairly, many would hesitate to label their performance as satisfactory if they were not responsive and accountable as well. Much of the criticism of governmental bureaucracy is directed at the inability or unwillingness of public organizations to respond to public preferences. Yet this argument has been overstated and is supported by only limited evidence. There is reason to believe that bureaucracies are more responsive than the literature suggests.

Normative democratic theory is generally silent on the role of the bureaucracy in modern society. The emphasis of such theory is on process and procedure. However, we can distinguish several perspectives in the literature on bureaucratic responsiveness and accountability. Joseph Schumpter (1950: 68) takes an extreme view when he observes that the bureaucracy must be "strong enough to guide and, if need be, to instruct the politician. . . . In order to be able to do this it must be in a position to evolve principles of its own and sufficiently independent to assert them. It must be a power in its own right." A more orthodox position is held by Herbert Finer (1941: 342), who maintains that "the servants of the public are not to decide their own course; they are to be responsible to the elected representatives of the public, and these are to determine the course of action of the public servants to the most minute degree that is technically feasible." The middle ground is occupied by Carl Friedrich (1940: 17) who observes that a bureaucratic policy can be called irresponsible "if it can be shown that it was adopted without proper regard to the existing sum of human knowledge concerning the technical issues involved; we also have a right to call it irresponsible if it can be shown that it was adopted without proper regard for existing preferences in the community, and more particularly its prevailing majority."

Accountability and responsiveness can therefore be evaluated from a variety of perspectives. Should the bureaucracy enjoy virtual independence from political control, should administrative policy be closely monitored and directed by elected officials, or should bureaucratic choices be guided by attentiveness to majority preferences and allegiance to professional wisdom and technical knowledge?

Evaluating responsiveness can also be complicated if any of the following seven conditions exist:

1. Public preferences are not expressed.
2. Only a few citizens or a single group or class expresses preferences.
3. Preferences are widely expressed, but different groups have conflicting preferences.
4. Preferences are in conflict, and there are differing intensities of preference.
5. The preference of the majority favors one course of action, and that of one or more minorities advocates another.
6. Preferences are weakly held or volatile.
7. Technical knowledge conflicts with expressed preference.

Does the bureaucrat have a responsibility to elicit unexpressed preferences? Should he or she respond only to expressed preferences, even though those expressions may represent only a limited part of the population? Does the administrator have a responsibility to resolve conflicting preferences, and, if so, on what basis should choices be made? Is he or she required to discern differing intensities of preference, and what mechanism should be employed to measure those intensities? Should the majority opinion always prevail, regardless of the intense preferences of the minority? Should the bureaucrat be guided by attentiveness to public demands even if he or she believes that preferences are not strongly held or are subject to rapid change? Under what conditions is efficiency more important than responsiveness?

EVIDENCE FROM RESEARCHERS

Bureaucracies of urban governments, in particular, are alleged to be unaccountable to political authorities and unresponsive to public preferences (or to be responsive only to the interests of the powerful few) for a variety of reasons. These include the following:

1. The urban reform movement is held to have destroyed the basis for political control of the bureaucracy. According to Theodore Lowi (1967: 86–87), "the legacy of reform is the bureaucratic city state." He further observes that "the new machines are machines because they are relatively irresponsible structures of power. That is, each agency shapes important public policies, yet the leadership of each is relatively self-perpetuating and not really subject to the controls of any higher authority." The elimination of the political party, the advent of civil service reforms and at-large elections, and the triumph of professional management "destroyed the basis for sustained, central, popularly-based action" and substituted "formal authority" for "majority acquiescence."

2. Bureaucrats are thought to be unresponsive and unaccountable because of a bureaucratic monopoly on information, experience, and expertise and because of bureaucratic control over budgetary matters. Furthermore, elected officials lack sufficient ability to reward and punish administrators, and they lack the resources and motivation necessary to monitor bureaucratic operations (Crecine, 1969; Lupsha, 1974).

3. Bureaucrats' responsiveness to citizen demands is limited because institutional arrangements emphasize efficiency and economy rather than responsiveness as the appropriate performance criteria. The collective-goods nature of some urban services reduces information about public preferences and inhibits responsiveness (Ostrom, 1975).

4. Bureaucrats' responsiveness to individual citizens is limited by the tremendous variation in personal skills and resources among citizens. Gideon Sjoberg, Richard Brymer, and Buford Farris (1966: 327) maintain that "first and foremost, the lower-class person simply lacks knowledge of the rules of the game. Middle-class persons generally learn how to manipulate bureaucratic rules to their advantage . . . the lower-class person stands in awe of bureaucratic regulations and frequently is unaware that he [or she] has a legal and moral claim to certain rights and privileges."

5. Distinctive characteristics of the urban political system yield a situation that renders the concepts of responsiveness and accountability nearly meaningless. These characteristics include the divisible nature of urban services, tremendous variation in needs and demands for those services, the subjective nature of service evaluation, the multiplicity of neighborhood organizations, the weakness of the system of political representation, and the fragmentation of political authority. According to Douglas Yates (1976: 244), the result is a "political and governmental free-for-all that makes urban policy making chaotic and unstable. More precisely, the fragmentation of urban government at every level produces an almost anarchic structure of demands and policy conflicts."

6. Even if elected officials exerted considerably more control over bureaucrats than the literature suggests, those officials themselves are held to be unresponsive and unaccountable. Consequently, it is unlikely that political control of administrative operations would enhance responsiveness to public preferences. Kenneth Prewitt (1970: 211) concluded that the electorate is incapable of holding political authorities accountable because a significant percentage of city council members are appointed to their first term, four out of five incumbents who run for reelection are victorious, and a large number voluntarily retire. He observes that "if the elected official plans to exit from office in any case, why should he [or she] fear voter disapproval? And if he [or she] has no need to fear voter disapproval, what is the guarantee that he [or she] will feel accountable?"

Not only is bureaucrats' accountability problematic, but the equality of their response is doubtful as well. Howard Hamilton

(1971) found that the urban electorate is dominated by upper-class voters to a far greater extent than is the case for national elections. Kenneth Prewitt (1970) holds that the unrepresentative nature of those who are politically active ensures that the "constituency salient to the officeholders . . . will represent a restricted part of the population." Sidney Verba and Norman Nie (1972) concluded that the priorities of individuals who are active political participants differ from those of nonparticipants and that leaders are more likely to agree with the priorities of the former.

To this discussion of the limitations on responsiveness and accountability, we might add Robert Dahl's (1956: 131) warning that elections seldom reveal public preferences. "We expect elections to reveal the 'will' or the preferences of a majority on a set of issues," he observes. "This is the one thing elections rarely do, except in an almost trivial fashion."

We can draw at least three conclusions from this literature. First, elected officials are seldom capable of mounting an effective challenge to the bureaucracy's superiority. The bureaucracies are the new urban machines. Fragmented authority, nonpartisan and at-large elections, civil service reforms, the triumph of professional management, and the power of municipal employees' unions insulate bureaucrats from popular control. Elected officials do not control budgets or the distribution of resources and are ill-equipped and perhaps even uninterested in performing an effective oversight function.

Second, bureaucrats are unresponsive to public preferences. At best, their responsiveness is limited to the demands of client groups or to the interests of the powerful few. Professional administrators enjoy a monopoly over information, experience, and expertise. Institutional arrangements emphasize efficiency and economy to the detriment of responsiveness to public preferences. Inattentiveness to citizens' demands is particularly severe among street-level bureaucrats. Middle-class status ensures knowledge of the rules of the game—the procedures by which benefits are distributed—and confers a disproportionate advantage in dealing with the bureaucracy. In cities, the divisibility of urban services, the tremendous variation in citizens' needs and demands, the highly subjective nature of citizens' evaluations, the multiplicity of neighborhood organizations, and the fragmentation of political and administrative authority produce a chaotic situation that renders the bureaucracy incapable of responding to the immense variety of articulated and conflicting preferences.

Third, elected officials themselves are often unaccountable to the electorate and unresponsive to public preferences. The urban electorate, in particular, is highly unrepresentative of the population. Political authorities respond to the politically active, elections seldom reveal public preferences, and elected officials are little concerned with voter disapproval.

BUREAUCRATIC RESPONSIVENESS IN CHICAGO—
A CASE STUDY

Despite the above conclusions from a large and respected body of literature, we will argue that some urban bureaucracies are fair and impartial in their application of established policy, are responsive to articulated preferences, and are controlled by and accountable to elected officials. Critics have too readily discounted the potential for organizational responsiveness and accountability. For some urban bureaucracies, the alleged barriers to responsiveness are more myth than reality. In support of this argument, we will present the results of a study of the municipal bureaucracy in Chicago.

Demands for stop signs and traffic signals at neighborhood intersections, for example, are a major service priority in Chicago. In fact, these service demands represent the second largest category of citizen complaints in the city (Mladenka, 1981). Furthermore, citizens' preferences concerning this service area are clearly articulated to public authorities. Grievances about traffic signals are transmitted directly to ward aldermen, to city hall, and to the Bureau of Street Traffic. The level of demand is also fairly uniform across wards. Complaints about traffic control devices rank in the top five service priorities in white, mixed, and black wards as well as in poor, middle-income, and wealthy wards. Such complaints are particularly vehement when the location referred to is in the vicinity of a public school.

How does the bureaucracy react to citizens' grievances when preferences are clearly articulated, when the service demand represents a major public priority, and when the service deficiency has implications for danger to life and limb? An investigation of actual citizen-initiated contacts with public authorities in Chicago revealed that bureaucratic responsiveness to demands of this type is *equally* distributed across neigborhoods that differ on the basis of race, income, and a variety of other characteristics. Grievances concerning traffic control devices transmitted from poor black neighborhoods are as likely to be addressed as demands originating in wealthy white areas. However, very few demands for this kind of service are satisfactorily resolved. Only seven out of every hundred requests for the installation of a traffic signal are complied with. Although each citizen grievance is investigated and although the level of response is equally distributed, the individual citizen has little reason to believe that his or her complaint will be resolved satisfactorily.

At first glance, this failure to respond to citizen demands about a service matter of extreme importance to the individuals appears to be a function of the bureaucrats' reliance on technical-rational criteria and professional norms. An examination of standard operating procedures within the Bureau of Street Traffic reveals that a highly routinized system has been developed to process citizens' demands. The bureau rejects the argument that it "waits for someone to be killed" before a traffic control device is installed. It has specified in written form those premises that guide its decision making:

> It is the responsibility of the city's traffic engineers to develop recommendations from an analysis of factual information rather than upon emotional entreaties. A citizen often bases his [or her] request upon limited personal observation of a situation and does not have knowledge of all of the factors which contribute to traffic safety. In many cases a traffic control device can actually generate a higher accident rate. The traffic engineer with his [or her] technical training and experience is best qualified to make an objective evaluation.

The procedures further state that "the professional is the best qualified to decide when and how stop signs and traffic signals are to be used, and the citizen can help by recognizing this and offering his [or her] full support and cooperation." The bureau then outlines in great detail the steps to be taken in response to each demand. Each complaint is to be investigated. This investigation entails an elaborate series of studies including an analysis of the number and type of accidents at the proposed location within the past three years, various traffic counts, a field survey by a traffic engineer, and radar speed surveys.

Although the standards employed by the Chicago Bureau of Street Traffic to justify the installation of two-way stop signs are much less stringent than those for four-way stop signs and traffic lights, they serve to illustrate the importance of technical-rational criteria. Two-way stop signs may be installed if any of the following conditions are true:

A. Five or more accidents of a *correctable* type occurred at an intersection during the past three calendar years, with at least two occurring during the last twelve months.

B. The volume of vehicles through an intersection exceeds 200 vehicles during the eight highest hours of an average week day, provided that three or more accidents of a correctable type occurred during the past three calendar years.

C. The intersection is adjacent to a *primary* school, and . . . the combined vehicular and children crossing volumes exceed 200 units during each of three school crossing hours of an average week day.

Such criteria are hard to meet. The citizen is reminded that "near-misses and unreported accidents cannot be quantified and therefore cannot be considered in the analysis." Indeed, an examination of contacts with the Bureau of Street Traffic reveals that many demands are rejected because of a failure to comply with the specified criteria. Since the rules emphasize traffic volume, residential streets are accorded a lower priority. Thus, a bias exists in the system against neighborhood streets and in favor of arterial ones (streets that carry through traffic).

The scarcity of resources is another factor limiting bureaucratic responsiveness in this case. Many citizen demands for traffic signals survive the evaluation process, and a large number of installations on neighborhood streets are approved annually. Nevertheless, very few of these approved projects are ever carried out. There are approximately 2,500 intersections in Chicago with traffic signals. About one-half of these existing signals are in need of replacement or extensive repair. It is estimated that repair and replacement costs for the existing signals would approach $100 million. However, only $1 million a year is available for repairs *and* new installations. Consequently, the chances that a new signal will be installed even on a major arterial route are remote at best, and the likelihood that one will be added to a residential street is almost nonexistent.

Administrators in the Bureau of Street Traffic are primarily concerned with the efficiency of traffic flow and the reduction of the vehicular accident rate. Thus, the technical-rational criteria employed by the bureau reflect a clear bias against neighborhood streets. However, the organizational rules used by the bureau to resolve distributional issues are fair, rational, and objectively applied. Professional engineers in the bureau may be correct when they argue that in some cases the installation of a traffic control device would actually increase the accident rate. Moreover, that they *attempt* to respond to public demands is supported by the finding that each citizen complaint is investigated in detail and that many requests survive the evaluation process. That a substantive outcome is seldom forthcoming has to be attributed to factors external to the bureaucratic process.

The volume of complaints about residential streets in Chicago reveals that street conditions are another major service priority. An analysis of bureaucratic responsiveness to these citizen requests revealed that such responsiveness is also equally distributed. Again, however, the level of response is extremely low. Although some residential streets require nothing more than moderate repair, many others would benefit little from even extensive repair efforts. Nothing short of complete rebuilding would suffice. There are 347 miles of unimproved residential streets in the city. They lack curbs and paved shoulders. Drainage is inadequate. Citizens complain incessantly and in overwhelming numbers about them. Administrators in the Bureau of Streets agree that those streets are in atrocious condition. However, there is no reasonable expectation that public authorities will ever initiate action to reconstruct them.

A large part of the problem can be traced to the role played by the Works Progress Administration (WPA). During the 1930s, the WPA built many new residential streets in Chicago. The main purpose of the project was to put people to work, and a significant by-product of that emphasis was a failure to comply with professional design and construction specifications. Streets built by the WPA were constructed with inferior materials and lacked curbing and paved shoulders. They began to deteriorate almost immediately. The problem with residential streets was compounded when the city annexed a number of suburban neighborhoods in the 1940s and 1950s. In the process, the city assumed responsibility for many additional miles of poorly constructed streets.

Very few of these WPA-built and suburban streets have been rebuilt, and it is unlikely that they will be in the foreseeable future. The reason is primarily economic. Officials in the Bureau of Streets estimate that it cost $544,000 in 1978 to rebuild a single mile. If all unimproved residential streets were rebuilt, the total cost would approach $200 million (in 1978 dollars). City government is unwilling to assume this burden. Although money is available for street construction, such funds are always spent on major arterials. Officials in Chicago perceive two street networks. The so-called preferential network, consisting of streets in the downtown Loop area and arterial streets connecting with suburbs, consumes most of the resources of the Bureau of Streets. The other network, consisting of residential streets, is of secondary concern and can receive attention only when problems in the preferential network are solved. They never are; therefore, low-volume residential streets receive very little attention.

In fact, no general budget funds are designated for the rebuilding of residential streets. The only money available for this purpose comes from the State of Illinois Motor Fuel Tax Fund and from the federal government. Through 1977, $5 million in state and federal funds had been allocated for the reconstruction of neighborhood streets. This amount was sufficient to pay for the cost of rebuilding only 9 of the 347 miles of unimproved streets.

Assessment of property owners to pay for street improvements is another option. When citizens complain about unimproved neighborhood streets, they are informed that no action will be taken by city government until all of the property owners on the street agree to pay part of the cost of reconstruction. If this agreement is obtained, the citizens are required to assume 30 percent of the expense of rebuilding. Depending on the number of property owners involved, it is not unusual for each one on a street to be assessed from $1,000 to $2,000 for a reconstruction project. Thus, in effect, a decentralized and private-sector solution is invoked to resolve (or silence) this kind of citizen grievance. Whether or not a resolution occurs is largely a function of willingness and ability to pay. A satisfactory resolution of this service complaint requires that the citizen take the initiative and that the citizen commit significant private resources. It is an option that many citizens cannot afford to exercise.

Both the Bureau of Street Traffic and the Bureau of Streets are ultimately unresponsive to citizen demands. Very few traffic signals are installed and few miles of residential streets are rebuilt, even though citizen preferences concerning these service areas are clearly articulated. However, this insensitivity to public demands cannot be attributed to bureaucratic process or structure or to the inability or unwillingness of elected officials to control professional administrators. In fact, the mayor and city council are in clear control of both bureaucracies. But this control primarily takes the form of a refusal to provide sufficient resources to adequately fulfill service priorities. Even though the two service areas are extremely important to the citizens, Chicago's elected officials appropriate no money for them. The only available funds represent part of the city's share of the Illinois Motor Fuel Tax Fund and are grossly inadequate for the purpose of satisfying public demands.

In fact, Chicago's bureaucrats are more sympathetic to these public demands than are its elected officials. For example, administrators in the Bureau of Streets were responsible for shifting part of the cost of street reconstruction from the citizen to government. Until 1976, neighborhood property owners had to bear all, rather than 30 percent, of the total expense involved in rebuilding residential streets. Citizens' reduced financial burden in this area can be attributed in large part to the effectiveness of bureaucratic lobbying.

Citizens' demands for public services are unlikely to elicit a favorable response from government in Chicago because the priorities of elected officials are in fundamental conflict with those of citizens. Citizens emphasize the level and quality of routine municipal services (streets, traffic lights, rodent control) in their contacts with bureaucrats and ward aldermen. Elected officials are considerably less likely to view public services as the major priority. Their policy priorities are focused on issues such as taxation, fiscal stability, and loss of jobs and people. This conflict and the fact that political priorities are reflected in budgetary allocations explain the failure to respond to expressed citizen preferences far better than any combination of distinctly bureaucratic factors. And we suspect that this explanation would hold true for many policy situations in many state and local governments.

CONCLUSION

As government has taken on more and more challenging responsibilities in the twentieth century, it has come to depend very heavily on bureaucracies to carry on its work. Indeed, no alternative form of organization may be possible. Despite their failings, only relatively large, bureaucratized organizations can marshal the knowledge and concentrated energy necessary to pursue government's major goals or even to carry on its customary service activities. That bureaucracies do these things imperfectly and at times with great difficulty may be as much testimony to the complexity of the tasks as to their own shortcomings.

Nonetheless, bureaucracies pose fundamental challenges for democratic governance. How can citizens achieve appropriate control over them? How can elected officials do so? How can appropriate control even be defined, in light of the inevitable tension between bureaucratic responsiveness and fairness? We have surely not answered these questions in this chapter, but they may not even have clear answers. However, the relations among bureaucrats, citizens, and elected officials create one of the central tensions of modern American government. If you do not understand this tension—whether it can be resolved or not—you will be uninformed with respect to a major dimension of how government functions.

REFERENCES   Crecine, John. 1969. *Governmental Problem Solving*. Chicago: Rand McNally.

Dahl, Robert A. 1956. *A Preface to Democratic Theory*. Chicago: University of Chicago Press.

Finer, Herbert. 1941. "Administrative Responsibility in Democratic Government," *Public Administration Review* 1 (Summer): 335–350.

Friedrich, Carl J. 1940. "Public Policy and the Nature of Administrative Responsibility," *Public Policy* 1: 3–24.

Goodsell, Charles T. 1983. *The Case for Bureaucracy*. Chatham, N.J.: Chatham House.

Hamilton, Howard D. 1971. "The Municipal Voter: Voting and Nonvoting in City Elections," *American Political Science Review* LXV (December): 1135–1140.

Lipsky, Michael. 1976. "Toward a Theory of Street Level Bureaucracy," pp. 196–213 in Willis D. Hawley and Michael Lipsky (eds.), *Theoretical Perspectives on Urban Politics*. Englewood Cliffs, N.J.: Prentice-Hall.

Lowi, Theador J. 1967. "Machine Politics: Old and New," *Public Interest* 9 (Fall): 86–87.

Lupsha, Peter A. 1974. "Constraints on Urban Leadership or Why Cities Cannot Be Creatively Governed," pp. 48–64 in Willis D. Hawley and Dale Rogers (eds.), *Improving the Quality of Urban Management*. Beverly Hills, Calif.: Sage.

Mladenka, Kenneth R. 1981. "Citizen Demands and Urban Services: The Distribution of Bureaucratic Response in Chicago and Houston," *American Journal of Political Science* 25 (November): 693–714.

Ostrom, Elinor. 1975. "The Design of Institutional Arrangements and the Responsiveness of the Police," pp. 274–299 in Leroy N. Rieselbach (ed.), *People vs. Government: The Responsiveness of American Institutions*. Bloomington: Indiana University Press.

Perrow, Charles. 1972. *Complex Organizations*. Glenview, Ill.: Scott, Foresman.

Prewitt, Kenneth. 1970. *The Recruitment of Political Leaders*. Indianapolis, Ind.: Bobbs-Merrill.

Schumpeter, Joseph S. 1950. *Capitalism, Socialism, and Democracy*. New York: Harper & Row.

Sjoberg, Gideon, Richard A. Brymer, and Buford Farris. 1966. "Bureaucracy and the Lower Class," *Sociology and Social Research* 50 (April): 325–337.

U.S. Bureau of the Census. 1990. *City Employment: 1989*. Washington, D.C.: U.S. Bureau of the Census.

Verba, Sidney, and Norman H. Nie. 1972. *Participation in America*. New York: Harper & Row.

Yates, Douglas. 1976. "Urban Government as a Policy-Making System," pp. 235–264 in Louis H. Masotti and Robert L. Lineberry (eds.), *The New Urban Politics*. Cambridge, Mass.: Bollinger.

The Public Policies of State and Local Governments

To this point our principal concerns have been the social, economic, and political conditions within which state and local governments operate and the institutional characteristics of those governments. We have also discussed their public policies at various points but we have not done so systematically. Do the states differ remarkably in their policy efforts? If they do, what explains these differences? Answers to these questions should help you anticipate how individual states may respond to the contemporary policy challenges discussed at length in this book.

WHAT PUBLIC POLICIES ARE

Public policies are the sustained activities of governments in pursuit of specific goals. They can be distinguished by the strategies adopted to pursue particular goals and by the vigor with which such efforts are implemented. For example, all states have antipollution policies, but some have especially tough regulations and wide-ranging activi-

ties in this area. Furthermore, some states enforce their antipollution laws far more diligently than others. Those enforcement efforts
may be evident, too, in the activities of several branches of government: in legislative oversight of the efforts, in the attention of chief
executives such as the governor and city mayors to the subject,
in the efforts of executive branch bureaucrats in implementing the
policies, and even in the decisions of the courts on disputes under
these laws.

Public policies are, as indicated above, expressions of governmental goals or objectives, but merely having a policy goal does
not mean that it will be realized. Laws may be passed but not
enforced. In such a situation the policy on the books is not really
in force. At other times public policies may be ill-conceived. A
policy might be inadequately designed to solve the perceived
problem. And you should remember that many problems governments confront are quite complex ones for which there is little consensus on appropriate solutions. (For example, how can society
rehabilitate criminal felons or eliminate pollution at reasonable
costs?) Thus, the appropriate policy may not be self-evident in
many instances. Furthermore, the cost of the best policy may be
prohibitive, and the second-best one may be all that is financially
practical.

Alternatively, public policies may be well designed but may be
underfunded or otherwise provided with inadequate resources. In
still other instances the policy problem may itself be changing, ren-
dering the design of established programs ineffective. As one example, states could be successful with certain kinds of economic
development policies in the era of mature industrialism, but changes
in the economy might render those policies inappropriate under
emerging postindustrialism.

The preceding comments indicate some of the difficulties the
states face in formulating and implementing policies. Yet they also
suggest that the states can be distinguished in terms of the goals they
claim to be pursuing, the policy strategies by which they do so, and
the results of their efforts. Furthermore, any individual policy can be
described, again in terms of the kind of strategy employed and the
vigor with which it is implemented. It is also possible to evaluate the
results of individual policies in terms of whether they achieve their
intended goals, to what degree they do so, how quickly they do so,
and whether any good or ill *unintended* consequences arise in the
process.

CHARACTERISTICS OF STATE AND LOCAL GOVERNMENTS' POLICIES

State and local governments do many things, as we have pointed out repeatedly in this book. Thus, they have many policies and pursue many goals. We could describe here their policies on economic growth, education, protective services, welfare, business regulation, and the environment, along with a good many others. However, the limits of our publisher's projections for the length of this book and of your patience and attentiveness might be reached rather quickly were we to try to cover all that territory. And there are some other good reasons why such an extended discussion of public policies is not necessary.

We can identify certain general characteristics of state and local policies, which *summarize* the kinds and levels of effort pursued by the states in separate policy areas. We can evaluate, for example, how extensive a state's policy efforts are *in general*. States with generally extensive policy efforts will have extensive programs in most individual policy areas such as education, police, welfare, and so on. States with generally modest overall policy efforts will typically have modest commitments in those separate areas.

Adopting this focus on broad policy characteristics, we will evaluate the relative positions of the states on four general attributes: (1) the magnitude, or *scope,* of state and local policy efforts, (2) the *extractive efforts* states marshal to capture resources to pursue their policies, (3) the *distribution of benefits and burdens* among individual citizens through their policies, and (4) the *degree of innovativeness* that states exhibit in their policy choices. First, we will consider some of the reasons why states differ on these four attributes.

REASONS FOR THE DIVERGENCE AND CONVERGENCE OF STATES' POLICIES

Before turning to the comparison of the states on the four broad policy dimensions, we need to consider briefly some of the forces that tend to produce policy similarities *or* differences among the states.

States should be relatively similar in many of their public policies, for example, for several reasons. They share, by custom and by constitutional provision, some common responsibilities. Public education, business regulation, police protection, and the range of local public services discussed in earlier chapters are but a few of these. And these have been responsibilities of state and local governments in the United States since the founding of the republic. Thus, all states have policies in these areas, and it is not surprising if many of their policy efforts are quite similar.

Additionally, the states shoulder many responsibilities they have acquired through collaboration with or pressure from the federal government. As you'll recall from Chapter 3, the eras of cooperative and cooptive federalism led to many new responsibilities and policies for state and local governments. The decision that these policies should be adopted was often made elsewhere—in Washington, of course. Yet the result was to add items to the agendas of state and local governments. In these instances the policy activities of different states might easily be similar, for that was the intent of cooptive federalism. Problems of national scope were to be addressed through nationally uniform policy efforts.

Finally, the states have shared to some degree a number of social, economic, and political experiences that have directly shaped public policy. To use only examples from the principal themes of this book, shared experiences of industrialization, urbanization, and emerging postindustrial development have led to many common problems necessitating relatively similar policies.

Considering only the preceding rationales for policy convergence might lead to the conclusion that the states should be quite similar in their policy agendas. There are, however, some equally notable forces promoting divergence in policy making. One of those forces arises out of what the citizens and officials of different states *wish* to achieve by way of public policy efforts. In other words, public and elite preferences for government can differ from state to state, engendering different policies as a result. As you may recall, our discussion of state political cultures in Chapter 2 explained one basis on which such policy preferences might differ from state to state. Thus, although states may have some problems, such as environmental pollution, in common, their citizens may differ with respect to how serious they perceive a specific problem to be, whether they wish state government to address it, *and* what costs they are willing to bear to solve it.

The states might also face different policy problems, or they might choose or be forced to emphasize some problems over others. The state of New York, for example, has to be especially concerned, of necessity, with the large numbers of poor residents in its large cities, who are unable to fulfill their own housing, food, and health care needs. The relatively prosperous state of Connecticut, on the other hand, can be less concerned with this policy problem because of its smaller number of poor residents. Mississippians, as a final example, might be especially concerned with state policies aimed at expanding the industrial and business sectors of their relatively underdeveloped economy. Which problems are most prominent will differ to some degree, then, from state to state, shaping somewhat distinctive policy agendas.

States may also differ in their policies because of what they can *afford* to do. Rich states may have the luxury of adopting and vigorously pursuing many goals about which poor states can only dream. California can, no doubt, have a more expansive policy agenda than Alabama. Even strong public desires for particular policies or especially pressing problems may have to be ignored in some states for lack of sufficient resources.

Finally, states may differ in their present policies because of different experiences and decisions in their pasts. Past decisions may have determined policy directions for generations. This can be the case for several reasons. Past decisions may be venerated for their historical significance or wisdom, thus creating resistance to changing the policies based on them. Policies associated with past decisions also acquire bureaucratic expression: public agencies are created to carry them out. Those agencies grow, expanding their efforts *and* the state's commitment of money, time, and personnel. The size and momentum—or the inertia—of such bureaucratic institutions can be an impediment to change. Bureaucratic resistance to change can also arise because of the rigidity of many bureaucratic decision rules and standard operating procedures (discussed in Chapters 12 and 13).

Thus, the fact that Minnesota, Wisconsin, and California were at the forefront of the Progressive movement at the beginning of this century may have made a permanent impact on their governmental policies. The common heritage of the states of the Confederacy in the South—including slavery, insurrection, and defeat—produced a set of social and political policies that distinguished those states from the rest of the nation for generations. Some scholars have argued that the policies of Southern states are still distinctive (Tucker and Herzik, 1986).

In sum, the policy postures of state and local governments have been influenced by a host of forces, which have evolved over time. These forces give rise to both shared and quite distinctive policy orientations. In light of that fact, it is difficult to guess how the states will compare on our four general policy dimensions.

THE SCOPE OF STATE AND LOCAL POLICY EFFORTS

As a general policy dimension, scope refers to the overall size or breadth of the policy effort mounted by states and their local governments. Some states have especially big governments, and some do not. And the size of the governmental establishment may be a reflection of public preferences, the breadth of policy problems, or the extent to which a state has adopted the agenda of the positive state.

There is no ideal way to measure the scope of governmental policy efforts, but the figures in Table 14-1 represent the most typical

TABLE 14-1
STATE AND LOCAL GOVERNMENT REVENUES, FISCAL YEAR 1988–89

STATE	TOTAL REVENUES (BILLIONS)	REVENUES FROM OWN SOURCES (BILLIONS)	PER CAPITA REVENUES FROM OWN SOURCES
Alabama	$ 12.7	$ 10.7	$ 2,600
Alaska	6.6	5.9	11,204
Arizona	13.5	12.1	3,413
Arkansas	6.0	4.9	2,025
California	132.2	115.8	3,984
Colorado	12.8	11.4	3,438
Connecticut	13.7	11.9	3,677
Delaware	2.9	2.5	3,737
Florida	42.6	38.4	3,030
Georgia	21.8	18.8	2,920
Hawaii	4.8	4.2	3,820
Idaho	3.1	2.5	2,496
Illinois	39.6	34.5	2,958
Indiana	17.2	14.9	2,657
Iowa	10.1	8.7	3,053

| | | REVENUES | |
STATE	**TOTAL REVENUES (BILLIONS)**	**FROM OWN SOURCES (BILLIONS)**	**PER CAPITA REVENUES FROM OWN SOURCES**
TABLE 14-1 CONTINUED			
Kansas	$ 8.3	$ 7.3	$ 2,916
Kentucky	11.3	9.4	2,520
Louisiana	14.5	12.2	2,774
Maine	4.3	3.6	2,945
Maryland	18.1	15.8	3,359
Massachusetts	24.2	20.7	3,497
Michigan	35.7	30.9	3,337
Minnesota	19.8	17.3	3,980
Mississippi	7.6	6.1	2,342
Missouri	14.5	12.6	2,439
Montana	3.0	2.4	2,985
Nebraska	6.6	5.9	3,652
Nevada	4.3	3.9	3,522
New Hampshire	3.3	2.9	2,598
New Jersey	33.2	30.0	3,819
New Mexico	5.9	5.0	3,297
New York	101.5	88.1	4,911
North Carolina	21.3	18.4	2,804
North Dakota	2.4	2.3	2,856
Ohio	40.4	35.4	3,245
Oklahoma	10.2	8.6	2,670
Oregon	11.3	9.4	3,350
Pennsylvania	40.6	34.7	2,881
Rhode Island	3.9	3.2	3,328
South Carolina	11.4	9.8	2,792
South Dakota	2.2	1.7	2,403
Tennessee	16.8	14.2	2,874
Texas	55.1	48.7	2,865
Utah	6.2	5.2	3,041
Vermont	2.2	1.7	3,073
Virginia	20.8	18.4	3,012
Washington	21.7	19.1	4,011
West Virginia	5.2	4.3	2,331
Wisconsin	19.1	16.6	3,409
Wyoming	2.7	2.2	4,585
National average			3,334

Source: U.S. Bureau of the Census, *Governmental Finances in 1988–89* (Washington, D.C.: U.S. Bureau of the Census, 1991), pp. 20 and 97.

way of doing so.[1] The first column ("Total Revenues") shows the absolute magnitude of state and local governments' revenues for a recent year. Because the states must maintain balanced budgets and thus cannot spend more than they raise in taxes, these numbers also indicate the total cost of the states' policy and administrative efforts. The second column of the table provides the total revenues raised indigenously within the states—excluding federal aid, that is. This measure indicates what level of government the states have chosen themselves. The third column expresses the total of indigenous state and local revenues in per capita form—divided, that is, by the number of residents in each state who are presumably served by the policy activities supported by these monies.

The figures on the total magnitude of spending indicate a considerable range of governmental establishments. At the top are California and New York, whose total annual budgets exceeded $100 billion in the year being considered. At the bottom of the range are a number of states—mostly in New England and the West—whose expenditures were less than $4 billion. Obviously, the governmental and policy efforts of those states are tiny in comparison to those of the big spenders.

Much of the variation in total budget arises, of course, because the populations of the states differ so greatly in size. Thus, the per capita figures in the third column of Table 14-1 indicate a different ranking. Largely because of their small populations, Alaska and Wyoming rank high in per capita expenditures. However, not all the small states fall into this pattern. These two states are distinguished from most of the other small ones because they have exceptional sources of revenue to support their high levels of spending. They get considerable revenues from taxing the production of crude oil and natural gas. Some other states enjoy unusual revenue sources: Louisiana and Texas, as two examples, also earn large revenues from taxes on crude oil production; Nevada takes in a lot from taxes on its tourist and gambling industries. A good portion of the burden of such taxes is borne by out-of-state residents—those who purchase gasoline at retail throughout the United States and those who vacation in Nevada. So certain states enjoy relatively high levels of government spending somewhat at others' expense.

Alaska needs to be further distinguished in this comparison because the cost of living is so high there. All monetary comparisons between Alaska and the rest of the nation are somewhat misleading

The Cost of Living—and of Government—in Alaska

The high cost of living in Alaska is a factor that affects per capita government spending in that state. Just how high, one might ask, is the cost of living in Alaska? And how does it contribute to higher costs for government?

A study by the Alaskan Department of Labor provides answers to the first of these questions (State of Alaska, 1986). The study compares the cost of living in Alaska's two largest cities to that in 198 cities in the lower forty-eight. Also reported were figures on per capita personal income—in effect, a measure of salary differences—for selected metropolitan areas in the United States. A sampling of those results illustrates the distinctiveness of economic life in Alaska. The cost of living in Juneau and Anchorage was 40 percent higher than the national average and was even higher than the cost of living in New York City. And personal incomes of Alaskans in those two cities were 50 and 70 percent higher, respectively, than the national average.

The higher cost of living must be borne by Alaska's state and local governments as well as by its residents. When the state buys goods and services—from paper clips to airline tickets—it pays the same costs as individual Alaskans. Government employees' salaries must also be kept in line with the statewide average to make the state a competitive employer. Thus, the level of government spending in Alaska is in part a reflection of the general cost of living.

for that reason. The box on the cost of living in Alaska explains why this affects government spending in that state.

In addition to Alaska and Wyoming, California, Minnesota, New Jersey, New York, and Washington rank especially high in per capita spending. A number of mostly Southern, and therefore relatively poor, states rank at the bottom in per capita spending. The range on this measure is again remarkable. Per capita spending by New York is double that of Arkansas, Mississippi, Missouri, South Dakota, or West Virginia.

EXTRACTIVE EFFORTS OF THE STATES

Extractive effort refers to the extent a state takes private resources, principally through taxation, for its policy activities. One might initially think that the total amount of taxes raised or the per capita amount would be the best measure of extractive effort. Either of those figures would be misleading, however, for a reason suggested earlier. On average, wealthier states will raise higher amounts of taxes simply because their citizens can afford to pay them.

A better measure of extractive effort would be less subject to wealth differences and would, therefore, be more indicative of political choices. The U.S. Advisory Commission on Intergovernmental Relations (ACIR), a research agency supported by state and federal governments, has generated such a measure. The ACIR has developed the measure *tax effort*, which compares the dollar amount of taxes each state raises to what it theoretically could raise based on the value of taxable entities, goods, and activities in the state (Cohen, 1990).

The ACIR has accumulated a list of all those taxes commonly employed by state and local governments, and it has calculated the average rates at which states impose each kind of tax. With these data ACIR researchers calculate an estimated per capita *tax capacity* for each state, which is equal to the sum of the revenues the state could raise if it adopted all the common taxes at the average rate, divided by the number of state residents. (If, that is, a given state applied the average gasoline tax rate to the total of gas sales in its borders, the average sales tax rate to retail sales, and so on.) In effect, tax capacity is a measure of the per capita wealth of a state in terms of those things that have characteristically been taxed by state and local governments. Mathematically, then, tax effort is the ratio of actual per capita revenues to tax capacity, multiplied by 100. A score of 100 means that effort is equal to capacity—the state is raising exactly what it should be able to, applying all the common state and local taxes at average rates. A score above 100 means that the state is extracting private resources by taxation at a rate above the average rate. A score below 100 indicates a relatively low tax effort.

Table 14-2 reports the most recent scores on tax capacity and tax effort for all fifty states. There are considerable differences here on both measures. Alaska, Connecticut, Delaware, Massachusetts, Nevada, New Hampshire, New Jersey, and Wyoming are especially wealthy states; that is, they have very high tax capacity. Mississippi, on the other hand, is the poorest. Tax effort is especially high in Alaska, New York, and Wisconsin and is quite low in Nevada and New Hampshire. Tax effort in New York is more than double that in New Hampshire. Once again, the differences among the states are striking.

TABLE 14-2
TAX CAPACITY AND
TAX EFFORT OF
THE STATES

STATE	TAX CAPACITY	TAX EFFORT	STATE	TAX CAPACITY	TAX EFFORT
Alabama	76	84	Montana	85	102
Alaska	159	127	Nebraska	90	98
Arizona	99	96	Nevada	135	69
Arkansas	74	84	New Hampshire	126	66
California	116	94	New Jersey	124	101
Colorado	107	89	New Mexico	83	99
Connecticut	143	90	New York	109	143
Delaware	124	84	North Carolina	91	93
Florida	104	82	North Dakota	86	91
Georgia	94	89	Ohio	91	97
Hawaii	114	112	Oklahoma	89	89
Idaho	76	93	Oregon	91	99
Illinois	99	102	Pennsylvania	94	97
Indiana	87	93	Rhode Island	99	104
Iowa	83	113	South Carolina	79	96
Kansas	91	104	South Dakota	78	95
Kentucky	83	88	Tennessee	84	83
Louisiana	83	90	Texas	96	88
Maine	98	105	Utah	78	106
Maryland	109	108	Vermont	105	100
Massachusetts	129	94	Virginia	104	91
Michigan	95	112	Washington	98	102
Minnesota	104	112	West Virginia	78	88
Mississippi	65	94	Wisconsin	90	119
Missouri	90	86	Wyoming	123	94

Source: Carol E. Cohen, "State Fiscal Capacity and Effort: The 1988 Representative Tax System Estimates," *Intergovernmental Perspective* 16 (Fall): 17–22.

The Practical Meaning of High and Low Tax Effort

The most compelling way to grasp the meaning of high and low tax effort is to consider the actual amounts of taxes that the residents of different states pay. The figures given below estimate the totals of major state and local taxes (income, property, gasoline, and sales taxes, plus automobile registration fees) paid by average families (home-owning families of four) at two income levels in the largest cities in several states in 1987. In addition to states ranked high and low in tax effort, we have also included some that have unusual sources of revenue, which shift some of a state's tax burden to the residents of other states.

	TAXES PAID BY FAMILY WITH INCOME OF $35,000	TAXES PAID BY FAMILY WITH INCOME OF $75,000
States with High Tax Effort		
Detroit, Michigan	$4,102	$ 9,280
Minneapolis, Minnesota	3,393	11,291
New York, New York	3,932	10,199
Milwaukee, Wisconsin	4,671	10,620
States with Low Tax Effort		
Denver, Colorado	2,606	6,034
Manchester, New Hampshire	1,687	3,677
Oklahoma City, Oklahoma	2,362	5,621
Memphis, Tennessee	2,366	4,536
States with Unusual Revenue Sources		
Anchorage, Alaska	1,223	2,556
Las Vegas, Nevada	1,701	3,480
Houston, Texas	1,746	3,354
Casper, Wyoming	1,358	2,725

Source: Government of the District of Columbia, *Tax Rates and Tax Burdens in the District of Columbia: A Nationwide Comparison* (Washington, D.C.: Department of Finance and Revenue, 1988).

There is some variation within each of the three groups, but the differences across the groups are especially evident. The average families in the high-tax states bear as much as twice the tax burden of those in low-tax states. And the tax burdens in the states with unusual revenue sources are only about one-quarter to one-third of those in the high-tax states.

THE DISTRIBUTION OF BENEFITS AND BURDENS

The third general dimension of public policy addresses the question of who benefits most and least from public spending and taxation. One can imagine many ways of considering the distribution of benefits and burdens that result from governments' activities. We might compare the public benefits and tax burdens of the wealthy to those of the middle class and the poor. We might compare the benefits and burdens imposed on the business sector from state to state. We might even compare taxes on individuals to those on businesses. Of greatest continuing interest to American political scientists, however, has been the distribution of benefits and burdens by income class: the rich versus the middle class versus the poor. This is the aspect of the distributional dimension we will consider.

Like the other dimensions of public policy we have already discussed, this one is somewhat complicated. Some public programs dispense benefits directly to one class. Some dispense them to all. Yet even those public services enjoyed by all may be valued differently by different individuals or groups. If the police give all the residents of a city equal protection for their homes and property, that benefit is worth more to those who live in mansions than to those who live in slums. Alternatively, if local governments provide certain health care services, such as immunizations against childhood diseases, free of charge, those services will be used more by the poor than the relatively well-off (who will mostly go to their private physicians). These circumstances do not suggest how the value of public services to different income groups should be assessed or how the total value of the benefits enjoyed by any group should be calculated, but they indicate the complexity of attempting to do so.

Sorting out the burden of taxation is also complicated, but a bit less so than with expenditures. Some taxes are paid in equal dollar amounts by all state residents—the fee for registering an automobile, for example. Some vary in accordance with individual economic circumstances—with some income taxes, for example, the higher one's income, the higher a percentage of that income is paid in taxes. Similarly, property tax is typically based on the market value of one's physical assets: land, buildings, machinery, and so on. Thus, it is relatively straightforward to sum the taxes an individual pays directly.[2]

Recent research suggests a good way to measure the benefits from state and local governments' expenditures—by a measure of welfare spending levels (Dye, 1984; Jennings, 1979; Klingman and

Lammers, 1984). A high level of welfare spending indicates an emphasis on redistributive policy goals, or a desire to redistribute some income from the relatively wealthy to the relatively poor. Thus, we have calculated per capita welfare expenditures for all the states, presented in Table 14-3.

The second measure in Table 14-3 addresses the distribution of tax burdens across income groups. It indicates whether the major state and local taxes in a given state are progressive, proportional, or regressive with respect to income. With *progressive taxes*, the relatively wealthy pay a larger percentage of their income than the relatively poor do. Progressive taxes are hailed by many economists as especially fair, based on the idea that one's income level indicates one's ability to pay. *Regressive taxes* have just the opposite incidence—the poor pay a higher portion of their income than the rich do. *Proportional taxes*, finally, are those for which the burden—in terms of the percentage of one's income paid—is equal across all income levels. The measure of tax progressivity reported in Table 14-3 is derived by comparing the burden of major state and local taxes on relatively wealthy residents to that on relatively poor ones.

TABLE 14-3
WELFARE EXPENDI-
TURES AND TAX PRO-
GRESSIVITY OF THE
STATES

STATE	WELFARE EXPENDITURES PER CAPITA	TAX PROGRESSIVITY INDEX[a]
Alabama	$193	114
Alaska	682	120
Arizona	273	90
Arkansas	261	85
California	535	62
Colorado	287	93
Connecticut	466	114
Delaware	288	79
Florida	232	86
Georgia	293	92
Hawaii	328	89
Idaho	220	68
Illinois	363	110
Indiana	311	111
Iowa	336	92
Kansas	253	88
Kentucky	339	104
Louisiana	284	59

TABLE 14-3
CONTINUED

STATE	WELFARE EXPENDITURES PER CAPITA	TAX PROGRESSIVITY INDEX[a]
Maine	505	61
Maryland	358	96
Massachusetts	631	76
Michigan	496	98
Minnesota	546	49
Mississippi	267	88
Missouri	246	108
Montana	319	77
Nebraska	299	91
Nevada	179	132
New Hampshire	298	113
New Jersey	435	99
New Mexico	260	84
New York	814	69
North Carolina	254	90
North Dakota	414	92
Ohio	433	87
Oklahoma	325	80
Oregon	266	90
Pennsylvania	409	116
Rhode Island	526	87
South Carolina	211	82
South Dakota	242	138
Tennessee	241	139
Texas	198	137
Utah	219	91
Vermont	432	79
Virginia	220	95
Washington	347	128
West Virginia	286	82
Wisconsin	519	91
Wyoming	224	135

[a]The measure of tax progressivity is for 1987. It compares the state and local tax burden borne by a family of four living in the largest city in each state and earning $20,000 a year with the tax burden on a similar family earning $100,000. Taxes as a percentage of income for the poorer family are divided by taxes as a percentage of income for the wealthier family, and the result is multiplied by 100 to create the index (Government of the District of Columbia, 1988: 17).

Source: U.S. Bureau of the Census, *Governmental Finances in 1988–89* (Washington, D.C.: U.S. Bureau of the Census, 1991), p. 105.

Scores above 100 indicate a regressive burden, a score of 100 indicates a proportional one, and scores below 100 indicate varying degrees of progressivity.

The patterns of benefit and burden revealed by the table are quite variable. There are some states—California, Hawaii, Maine, Minnesota, and New York—that have both high per capita welfare spending and progressive taxation. One might say that the overall pattern of policy in these states is highly redistributive. The result of public spending and taxation in these states is to place a relatively light burden for the cost of government on the poor *and* to provide relatively high benefits to such people at the same time. At the other extreme are Nevada, South Dakota, Tennessee, Texas, and Wyoming, where there is just the reverse kind of redistribution. Welfare expenditures are quite low, and taxation is highly regressive. One could argue that the poor are subsidizing the rich in these states. The poor pay relatively high taxes and get low welfare services, and the wealthy pay especially low taxes and support little in the way of social welfare programs for the poor. There are also a number of states that have intermediate scores on both of the indices in Table 14-3 or have a mixed pattern. Consider, as an example of the latter case, the state of Connecticut. It has high welfare expenditures and relatively regressive taxes. In a sense the poor get what they pay for in Connecticut. Their benefits are relatively high compared to those in other states, but their taxes are also high compared to those of wealthier Connecticutians.

INNOVATIVENESS OF POLICY MAKING

Policy innovation refers to the development of new ways in which governments might pursue customary goals *and* the adoption of new goals to fit changing times and circumstances. One could restrict the label *innovative* to only those governments that pioneer such efforts. However, it is common for states to imitate one another in many of their policy efforts. Innovative ideas for policies will be quickly copied by many states, although such ideas will be ignored by still other states. The concept of policy innovation—as scholars of the subject view it—takes into account the reality of this responsiveness to new ideas. To be innovative, a state need not be the *first* to come up with a new idea. It can be innovative by quickly adopting new policies originated elsewhere. This is the sense of policy innovation that we use here.

A good measure of policy innovativeness should cover a relatively long time period so that it will reveal how rapidly, if at all, individual states adopt new ideas. It should also encompass a large number of innovative policies that states might adopt. A short or selective list of such ideas might produce biased results. Some states might be innovative in a single area—such as education policy or environmental policy—but parochial and unresponsive to new ideas in most others.

Robert L. Savage (1978) has produced a ranking of the states with respect to policy innovation, which meets the above criteria. His ranking compares the states with regard to how quickly, if ever, they adopted sixty-nine innovative policies that were originated by some state in the period 1930–1970. Table 14-4 reports his results.

TABLE 14-4
RANKING OF THE
STATES ON POLICY
INNOVATION, 1930–
1970

STATE	RANK	STATE	RANK
Alabama	44	Montana	27
Alaska	n/a	Nebraska	24.5
Arizona	41	Nevada	48
Arkansas	29	New Hampshire	33
California	5	New Jersey	18
Colorado	13	New Mexico	15
Connecticut	16.5	New York	8
Delaware	42	North Carolina	40
Florida	23	North Dakota	32
Georgia	45	Ohio	2
Hawaii	n/a	Oklahoma	22
Idaho	3	Oregon	6
Illinois	13	Pennsylvania	28
Indiana	10	Rhode Island	19.5
Iowa	26	South Carolina	47
Kansas	38	South Dakota	30
Kentucky	31	Tennessee	11
Louisiana	35	Texas	43
Maine	9	Utah	4
Maryland	16.5	Vermont	19.5
Massachusetts	21	Virginia	39
Michigan	13	Washington	1
Minnesota	7	West Virginia	37
Mississippi	46	Wisconsin	34
Missouri	24.5	Wyoming	36

Source: Robert L. Savage, "Policy Innovativeness as a Trait of American States," *Journal of Politics* 40 (February): 212–228.

Among the innovative policies Savage looked at were a number of efforts to regulate economic, business, and social behavior; several welfare programs for the needy; a variety of regulatory policies for workers' rights and labor union activities; and a host of interstate compacts in which the collaborating states agree to work together in some policy effort. Thus, the innovations encompassed in Savage's ranking make it reflective of the principal thrust of governmental policy in the twentieth century—the extension of the positive state in response to the social and political demands on government during the maturation of the industrial economy. This measure thus indicates the responsiveness of the states to the most notable policy problems of the times and their acceptance of new ideas about how to address those problems.

There are several familiar faces at both the top and the bottom of the ranking in Table 14-4. California, Idaho, Minnesota, New York, Ohio, Oregon, Utah, and Washington are the most innovative. Alabama, Georgia, Mississippi, Nevada, and South Carolina are the least so. In general, Southern states rank poorly, but they are joined in that low position by Arizona, Delaware, and Nevada. The high-ranking states, on the other hand, include some that show high scores on one or more of the other policy dimensions and several others that are best distinguished by their moralistic political cultures (such as Idaho, Maine, Minnesota, Utah, and Washington). States with traditionalistic political cultures are generally among the least innovative.

EXPLAINING THE STATES' RANKINGS

What accounts for the states' rankings on the four policy dimensions we have considered? Why do some states have large governmental sectors, high welfare spending, and innovative policies, and some have just the opposite? It is not possible to account completely for all the state-by-state rankings because research on state policy patterns is still incomplete. And the problems faced by the researchers are considerable. You can appreciate some of those problems if you recall our earlier discussion of the many reasons why states' policies might be similar and dissimilar. Many factors, some acting in concert and some in opposition, have worked to shape state policy making over more than two centuries. Sorting out the separate influences of these various factors is a difficult enterprise.

In spite of these difficulties, recent research explains some of the policy rankings in ways that mesh with earlier discussions in this book. Most notably, Gerald C. Wright, Robert S. Erikson, and John P. McIver (1987) have shown that the liberalism of government policy in a state is largely accounted for by the liberalism of public opinion in that state. States with relatively liberal residents, that is, have relatively liberal policies; states with conservative populations have relatively conservative policies. Liberalism should itself be reflected in all four of the policy dimensions discussed above. Liberalism, that is, means a greater scope of state and local policy efforts, more progressive taxes, greater welfare spending, and more innovative policies. This finding may seem unremarkable, but it is of considerable importance. Earlier scholarship had been unable to demonstrate a clear relationship between public opinion and state policy because of a number of conceptual and methodological problems.

If public opinion and public policy are relatively congruent, then political parties and elections would seem to be likely means by which that result is achieved. And, in a second research effort, Erikson, Wright, and McIver (1989) have demonstrated that party competition and elections are, indeed, central to achieving this congruence. As these researchers conclude, based on their analysis, "party [ideological] positions respond to state opinion," and "state elections reward and punish state parties based on their responsiveness to public opinion" (Erikson, Wright, and McIver, 1989: 743).

Other recent research has revealed further evidence of the linkage of partisan electoral factors to states' spending policies (Dye, 1984; Garland, 1985; Jennings, 1979) and to the progressivity of their tax policies (Lowery, 1987). Furthermore, a state's political culture has been linked to policy liberalism (Klingman and Lammers, 1984), to policy innovation (Hill and Hurley, 1988; Savage, 1985), and to tax progressivity (Lowery, 1987). The latter studies found that the more moralistic a state's political culture, the more liberal and innovative were its policies and the more progressive its tax system.

In spite of the gaps in scholars' understanding of states' policymaking processes, then, one important conclusion is clear. Public preferences can influence public policy at the state level, just as democratic theory indicates that they should. Yet the *quality* of the democratic process in the states—which will be discussed in detail in Chapter 15—is central to achieving this congruence of opinion and policy. The extent of public influence on governmental policy depends on the strength of democratic institutions and processes. Citizens can get the policies they collectively desire from state and local governments, but they are better able to do so in states whose political institutions are the most democratic.

THE MECHANICS OF STATE AND LOCAL FINANCES

Much of the preceding discussion in this chapter has been concerned with how or how much state and local governments spend and tax. The scope of government, extractive effort, redistributiveness, and tax progressivity are all abstract concepts derived from one or another aspect of state and local finances. If, however, we consider some of the practical details of these finances, we can better explain how states achieve their rankings on these policy dimensions.

STATE AND LOCAL TAXATION

State and local governments rely on a variety of sources in raising the revenues to pay for their policy efforts. The most important revenue sources are property taxes, sales taxes, income taxes, licensing and user fees, and federal aid.

Table 14-5 illustrates how these revenue sources sum to form the total pot of state and local governments' revenues nationwide. Property, general sales, individual income, and selective sales taxes are the greatest contributors to indigenously raised revenues. No other single internal source amounts to as much as 5 percent of total revenue for the average state. Federal aid, on the other hand, is the second largest source of revenue listed in the table. The pattern in individual states will differ from this average picture, of course, with particular taxes assuming greater or lesser importance. And the actual combination of revenue sources exploited in each state determines not just the total extractive effort but also the degree of progressivity or regressivity of the tax system.

Property Taxes   The so-called *ad valorem property tax* is an assessment charged to the owners of land, homes, buildings, and sometimes machinery and personal possessions such as automobiles and home furnishings. (*Ad valorem* means "according to the value.") The assessment is a percentage of the market value of the piece of property being taxed. Some form of property tax is used in all the states, most typically by local governments, for whom it has always represented a considerable portion of total revenues.

Property taxes are controversial for two reasons. First, they are difficult to administer fairly. The crux of this difficulty is the problem

SOURCE	REVENUE (IN MILLIONS)	PERCENTAGE OF TOTAL REVENUE
Own Taxes		
Property taxes	$142,525	18%
General sales taxes	112,598	14
Selective sales taxes[a]	53,418	7
Individual income taxes	97,807	12
Corporate income taxes	25,922	3
Death and gift taxes	3,510	<1
Severance taxes[b]	4,147	1
Licensing fees[c]	18,379	2
Other	10,341	1
Fees for goods and services		
Education	30,060	4
Hospitals	28,745	4
Sewerage	11,345	1
All other[d]	34,426	4
Miscellaneous[e]	86,797	11
Federal aid	125,824	16
Total	$597,719	

TABLE 14-5 GENERAL REVENUES OF STATE AND LOCAL GOVERNMENTS IN THE UNITED STATES, FISCAL YEAR 1988–89

[a]Principally on motor fuel, alcoholic beverages, tobacco products, and utilities.
[b]Principally on crude oil and natural gas production.
[c]Principally for motor vehicles, motor vehicle operators, and corporations.
[d]As for hospitals, highways, parking, parks, and sewerage.
[e]Principally taxes on interest earnings and special assessments.
Source: U.S. Bureau of the Census, *Governmental Finances in 1988–89* (Washington, D.C.: U.S. Bureau of the Census, 1991), p. 7.

of maintaining accurate estimates of fair market value for all taxable properties. Such estimates constitute the basis to which the tax rate is applied to determine individual assessments. Individual governments may have thousands of items of property on their tax rolls, some of which are seldom sold—thus providing no indication of the true market price. Thus, both the administrative difficulties of handling so many taxable items and the limited availability of information on their true market value make the assessment task difficult.

Although there is controversy among economists on this point, property taxes are also widely criticized for being regressive (Aronson and Hilley, 1986: 123–126; Pechman, 1985). That is, as we pointed out in our earlier discussion of regressive, proportional, and progressive taxes, their burden falls more heavily (as a percentage of income) on low-income persons than on high-income ones.

Despite these difficulties, property taxes remain essential, particularly for local governments. This is the case partly because of custom and an apparent lack of alternatives. Property taxes are also well entrenched because they are difficult to avoid—since the items subject to taxation are relatively immobile and highly visible.

Sales Taxes   A *general sales tax* is a percent duty added to the price of many goods purchased by consumers and businesses. It is collected by the retailer for the taxing authority, which is the state or local government. All the states except Alaska, Delaware, Montana, New Hampshire, and Oregon have a general sales tax. In many states there is a state sales tax *and* local ones added on top of that by particular local governments.

General sales taxes are also widely criticized for being regressive. Low-income individuals spend a larger proportion of their incomes than wealthier ones do on the items typically taxed—even though many states exempt food and medicines from their sales tax. Yet the ease and low cost of administration of sales taxes (private retail establishments do most of the work of tax collection) make them popular among state and local government.

Selective sales taxes are percent duties added to the purchase prices of particular goods, such as gasoline, alcoholic beverages, and tobacco products. Most states tax the sale of all of these goods, although the rates that are applied vary widely. These taxes, too, are regressive with respect to income.

Income Taxes   Like the federal government, many state and local governments impose a tax based on some calculation of a percentage of one's personal income, such as from salaries or wages. The typical state has only a modest tax of this kind—in terms of the actual percentage of income paid—when compared to the federal income tax. Yet this kind of tax is widely approved by economists because its rates can be structured progressively. Among all state and local taxes, the individual income tax can be most readily shaped to that end, and the extent to which a state relies on a progressive income tax is a major determinant of the overall degree of progressivity of its tax system. All the states except Florida, Nevada, South Dakota, Texas, Washington, and Wyoming have an individual income tax. This kind of tax raises only a very small fraction of the total revenues in Alaska, Connecticut, New Hampshire, North Dakota, and Tennessee, however.

Forty-six of the states levy a *corporate income tax* on corporations' net income, much like the federal corporation income tax. (The states without this kind of tax are Nevada, Texas, Washington, and Wyoming.) The rationale for corporate income taxes is that corporations enjoy many of the same legal rights and privileges as individuals, and they also benefit from many services provided by governments. Thus, these "citizens" should bear some of the burdens necessary to ensure such rights and services. The rates for corporate income taxes are relatively modest, largely because states fear that high rates will limit their ability to attract new business enterprises.

Licensing and User Fees

Licensing fees are charges imposed by a government for the licensing of an automobile, for an automobile operator's license, for the registration of a corporation to do business in the government's jurisdiction, or for the right to practice a given profession there. Such fees are intended to tax those individuals who benefit from a right or privilege granted by the governing authority. Those individuals granted licenses to practice law or accounting or medicine, for example, have a monopoly over the provision of certain professional services and an implied endorsement by the government as to their competence to do so. Thus, the licensing fee charged to those individuals is a tax for this privilege.

User fees are charges imposed on those individuals using certain services provided by a government. A familiar example is the tuition fees charged by state colleges and universities. Tuition does not cover the entire cost of a student's education in any state—the state government subsidizes the remainder of the cost. But tuition is justified because the students who pay it will get the most direct benefits from receiving a college education. The state benefits, too, by having an educated citizenry to participate in the democratic process and by having an educated work force that may attract new businesses. According to that rationale, the state's subsidy of a student's education is justified.

Other typical user fees include highway tolls, sewer fees, charges at public hospitals, fees to use public parks and recreational services, and parking fees. Every state has a variety of these charges.

Federal Aid

Another considerable source of revenue for state and local governments is, of course, federal aid. Although that aid has

Lotteries—A Recent Innovation in State Financing

A good example of policy innovation—one of the four general characteristics of public policy we discussed earlier—is the state lottery. State lotteries were popular in the early nineteenth century but were eventually forbidden by federal law because of widespread fraud and abuse. In the 1960s, however, revenue-hungry states rediscovered the lottery and eventually got the federal ban rescinded.

New Hampshire instituted the first modern lottery in 1963. The majority of the states have since followed that example, and lotteries have probably been debated in all of the states. And lotteries are big business. By 1989, twenty-nine states and the District of Columbia had lotteries, which collectively grossed over $17 billion in sales and provided over $7 billion in net revenues after deducting the costs of prizes and administration.

Lotteries have been popular with much of the public, presumably for the riches they promise and for their entertainment value. Many state officials also see lotteries as "painless" forms of taxation. But a lottery typically generates only 1 to 5 percent of a state's total revenue. And lotteries are widely criticized for being one of the most regressive means of raising government revenues.

Despite these criticisms, lotteries appear to have become permanent fixtures in a good number of states. They may soon be initiated in still more. However, their history also indicates that some policy innovations are controversial and are not universally endorsed.

been declining in recent years, as we observed in Chapter 3, it still constitutes a notable portion of total revenues in every state.

Other Taxes and Revenue Sources   Although the preceding are the most important sources of revenue nationwide, state and local governments have found a variety of other means of implementing taxation. Indeed, some of these other taxes give new meaning to an old folk proverb. The majority of the states have death and gift taxes, lending credence to the saying "nothing is certain but death *and* taxes thereon." In no state, however, do these two kinds of taxes bring in huge amounts of revenue. Perhaps you can get some small comfort from the fact that, although you can't take it with you, the state will not profit remarkably from your death either.

Still other revenue sources are used by only some states and have received more publicity in recent years than the income they generate would seem to justify. Lotteries, in particular, have gotten a good deal of public and media attention. However, in no state does a lottery contribute a notably large amount to total revenue. Lotteries

LOTTERIES HELP FILL STATE COFFERS WHILE FUELING THE DREAMS OF MILLIONS OF AMERICANS.

are often criticized, as well, for being highly regressive: the poor are more likely to spend their money on lottery tickets and do, in fact, spend a higher proportion of their total income in this way than do wealthier individuals. Nonetheless, lotteries are popular with citizens and governments. Whatever their faults, they may be an innovation in state government financing that is here to stay.

Other tax instruments are of considerable importance in a few states. Nevada and New Jersey raise a notable amount of revenue from taxes on gambling. Alaska, Louisiana, Montana, New Mexico, North Dakota, Oklahoma, Texas, and Wyoming benefit greatly from *severance taxes* on the market value of natural gas or crude oil when it is extracted (or "severed") from the ground. Both of these taxes bring a special benefit—a portion of the total tax burden is imposed on either tourists from other states who come to gamble or the consumers of the retail products made from oil and natural gas. Thus, part of the burden of these taxes is exported to the residents of other states. In addition, those states that enjoy a large tourist trade also export portions of their tax burdens, notably through the sales taxes on food, lodging, and gasoline paid by vacationers from other states.

STATE AND LOCAL SPENDING

We can now consider where state revenues are spent. Table 14-6 lists the most important categories of expenditures by dollar amount and percentage of total state and local spending nationwide. As the table indicates, education is overwhelmingly the largest activity of state and local governments. Slightly more than two-thirds of their expenditures are for elementary and secondary schooling. Welfare and highways are the next largest spending categories, and the remainder of total spending is divided among a variety of different activities, of which many are traditional functions that are readily identified with state and local government (such as police and fire protection) but that amount to modest portions of their total budgets. With the evolution of the positive state in the twentieth century, spending on these traditional functions has declined as a percentage of total spending. Spending on welfare, on the other hand, has grown dramatically since the 1960s. Health care spending has also grown considerably in recent years, in part because social welfare programs with a health care component have increased in number and in part because of rising health care costs. Spending in this category is projected to

	TOTAL SPENDING	PERCENTAGE OF
POLICY AREA	**(IN MILLIONS)**	**TOTAL SPENDING**
Education	$267,681	35%
Public welfare	97,879	13
Hospitals	47,073	6
Other health care programs	20,684	3
Other social services	3,093	<1
Highways	58,093	7
Airports	5,752	1
Water transportation	1,923	<1
Other transportation	1,157	<1
Police protection	27,771	4
Fire protection	11,932	2
Corrections	21,197	3
Other public safety programs	5,081	1
Natural resources	11,092	2
Parks and recreation	12,927	2
Sewerage and solid waste	25,773	3
Housing and community development	14,738	2
Governmental administration	40,923	5
Interest on debt	46,557	6
Other	40,985	5
Total	$554,161	

TABLE 14-6
GENERAL EXPENDI-
TURES OF STATE AND
LOCAL GOVERN-
MENTS IN THE
UNITED STATES,
1988–89

Source: U.S. Bureau of the Census *Governmental Finances in 1988–89* (Washington, D.C.: U.S. Bureau of the Census, 1991), p. 10.

grow even more in the future, since the average age of the American population is increasing.

Observe, finally, that Table 14-6 only reveals how the expenditure pie in the average state is sliced into portions. It does not indicate how big the pie is. Individual states differ from the average in how they allocate their funds. They have varying allocations to individual activities, such as welfare (one of the general dimensions of policy discussed earlier). And they differ in the sizes of their budgets and thus in the scope of their policy activities (also discussed earlier).

CONCLUSION

This chapter has indicated some general ways in which the public policies of state and local governments can be evaluated. Scope of government, extractive effort, distribution of benefits and burdens, and policy innovation constitute key characteristics of these policies. These are yardsticks by which we can compare the policies of different states.

Our discussion of state and local finances—of revenues and expenditures—provides some additional important details about policy making. And those details also help explain how states achieve their rankings on the four general dimensions of public policy by indicating the actual policy choices that combine to give states particular scores on scope of policy effort, extractive effort, and so on.

The most important observations in this chapter, however, are those that suggest an explanation for *why* states make the policy choices they do. Public preferences articulated through the democratic process and through elections and political parties play a central role in the shaping of these choices. Other factors such as wealth, pressure from the federal government, and even necessity are also influential. The character of the democratic process and the vitality of the associated representative mechanisms—especially public participation, elections, and parties—are critical to the making of public policy.

These findings should provide some comfort in light of the political problems the United States faces in making the economic transition beyond mature industrialism. That public preferences can influence the policy choices made in response to the challenge of this transition should be heartening. Yet Americans cannot be complacent about the prospects for public control of governmental policy making. In some states democracy is quite limited. There are powerful special interests in all states, which seek to ensure their interests or promote their version of the public interest. And there is a bias in many states and communities in favor of certain economic interests. In the next, and final, chapter we will explore the differences among the states with respect to the extent to which their governments operate by democratic processes and, therefore, the extent to which there is general public control over their policy choices.

NOTES

1. In this and all the succeeding tables in this chapter, state and local government revenues and expenditures will be combined. This practice is necessary in order to make fair comparisons of the overall policy efforts of the states, because they differ in the way they divide responsibilities between local and state governments. Using separate information on these units would therefore lead to some unfair comparisons.

2. What is more difficult about assessing tax incidence is estimating the amount of taxes that some taxpayers can shift to others. Landlords, for example, can pass along some or all of their property tax burden to their tenants in their rental rates. Similarly, businesses can pass along some portion of their taxes to those who buy their goods or services.

REFERENCES

Aronson, J. Richard, and John J. Hilley. 1986. *Financing State and Local Governments*, 4th ed. Washington, D.C.: Brookings Institution, 1986.

Cohen, Carol E. 1990. "State Fiscal Capacity and Effort: The 1988 Representative Tax System Estimates," *Intergovernmental Perspective* 16 (Fall): 17–22.

Dye, Thomas R. 1984. "Party and Policy in the States," *Journal of Politics* 46 (November): 1097–1116.

Erikson, Robert S., Gerald C. Wright, Jr., and John P. McIver. 1989. "Political Parties, Public Opinion, and State Policy in the United States," *American Political Science Review* 83 (September): 729–750.

Garland, James C. 1985. "Partisan Change and Shifting Expenditure Priorities in the American States, 1945–1978," *American Politics Quarterly* 13 (October): 355–391.

Government of the District of Columbia. 1988. *Tax Rates and Tax Burdens in the District of Columbia: A Nationwide Comparison.* Washington, D.C.: Department of Finance and Revenue.

Hill, Kim Quaile, and Patricia A. Hurley. 1988. "Uniform State Laws in the American States: An Explanatory Analysis," *Publius* 18 (Winter): 117–126.

Jennings, Edward T., Jr. 1979. "Competition, Constituencies, and Welfare Policies in American States," *American Political Science Review* 73 (June): 414–429.

Klingman, David, and William W. Lammers. 1984. "The 'General Policy Liberalism' Factor in American State Politics," *American Journal of Political Science* 28 (August): 598–610.

Lowery, David. 1987. "The Distribution of Tax Burdens in the American States: The Determinants of Fiscal Incidence," *Western Political Quarterly* 40 (March): 137–158.

Pechman, Joseph A. 1985. *Who Paid the Taxes, 1966–1985.* Washington, D.C.: Brookings Institution.

Savage, Robert L. 1978. "Policy Innovativeness as a Trait of American States," *Journal of Politics* 40 (February): 212–228.

Savage, Robert L. 1985. "Diffusion Research Traditions and the Spread of Policy Innovations in a Federal System," *Publius* 15 (Fall): 1–28.

State of Alaska. 1986. "The Cost of Living in Alaska," pp. 1–9 in *Alaska Economic Trends.* Juneau, Alaska: Department of Labor.

Tucker, Harvey, and Eric B. Herzik. 1986. "The Persisting Problem of Region in American State Policy Research," *Social Science Quarterly* 67 (March): 84–97.

U.S. Bureau of the Census. 1991. *Governmental Finances in 1988–89.* Washington, D.C.: U.S. Bureau of the Census.

Wright, Gerald C., Jr., Robert S. Erikson, and John P. McIver. 1987. "Public Opinion and Policy Liberalism in the American States," *American Journal of Political Science* 31 (November): 980–1001.

15 *Democracy in the States*

American government is supposedly democratic. In some sense this country has government "by the people"—as national mythology and high school civics texts maintain. To what extent, however, do the people govern? What are the limits, if any, on their control over their state governments? We have raised these questions in earlier chapters, but we have not fully answered them. Since these are complex and controversial questions, the conclusions we reach will surely be as well. But, despite these difficulties, concern with the extent of democracy goes to the heart of the political process and deserves extended consideration. Every American ought to have a considered opinion on this matter, and this chapter is intended to help you reach your own conclusion.

Besides its broad, almost philosophical, implications, this issue has practical relevance, too. In Chapter 14 we explained how the character of the democratic process is linked to the making of public policy in the states. But, as we will discuss in detail in this chapter, some states are far more democratic than others. In fact, some fall far short of the requirements for democracy. Knowing how democratic *your* state is will help you appreciate the likely extent of public influence over governmental responses to the socioeconomic transition described in Chapter 1. And that knowledge should help you gauge your prospects for influencing each of the various components of state and local government described in this book. In short, the degree of democracy in state government is relevant to immediate and substantial policy questions confronting the states today.

Is There Democracy in the United States?

Americans are taught at home and in school that theirs is a democratic government, but there is considerable disagreement over just how accurate that teaching is. Scholars have wrangled over that issue at greater length and with less resolution than most would willingly admit. Nor is there any greater agreement, we suspect, among average citizens. For every citizen who believes faithfully that democracy exists, there is probably another who is convinced that the phrase "government by the people" is a childish idea of how American government really works.

To begin to sort out this tangle, we must note some obvious practical matters. First, so-called *direct democracy* is not any more feasible in a state than in the entire nation. Direct democracy would exist if the entire citizenry sat together in one place—or perhaps gathered around their TV sets—to participate collectively in debates and decisions about what government should do. The entire citizenry, that is, would make all the important political decisions. This society is simply too big for such a form of government. Even the citizens of Alaska, Wyoming, and Vermont—the smallest states, each having between 500,000 and 600,000 residents—would find this process impractical. Not only are there too many citizens, but the number and the variety of governmental decisions that have to be made today are too imposing for direct democracy to work. American governments have accommodated to this reality from the first, for they have always been *representative governments*. The mass of citizens elects representatives to fashion governmental policies and then to stand for reelection, when they might be, in effect, graded on their efforts.

A second practical reality, derived from the first one, is that elections take on a crucial role in large, representative governmental systems. Some citizens do more than simply vote in elections to express their political preferences, as we noted in several earlier chapters. But elections are the only practical means by which the vast

IN A NEW ENGLAND TOWN MEETING, CITIZENS PARTICIPATE IN ONE OF THE LAST VESTIGES OF DIRECT DEMOCRACY IN THE UNITED STATES.

bulk of citizens can have direct influence over their governments. And, as we explained in Chapter 4, voting in elections is the only form of political participation practiced by a large percentage of Americans. Thus, the health of democracy in large modern nations must depend especially heavily on the satisfactoriness of the electoral process—which, we readily admit, has notable limitations as a tool for public control of government.

A third practical reality is that public influence and the electoral process can be greatly aided by the operation of political parties. These organizations can be thought of as specialized transmission mechanisms that help collect public preferences and then direct them to government. Political parties have been especially venerated in the United States as unique institutions that serve this and related purposes.

The preceding observations lay out some practical realities about how governments can function. We should next consider how they either theoretically could or actually do operate within those limits. Three different possibilities are applicable here.

DEMOCRATIC GOVERNMENT

What, first of all, would be the characteristics of a truly democratic government operating through representative mechanisms? Many definitions of such a government have been advanced, but all of them share certain key elements. One notable definition is that of Austin Ranney and Willmoore Kendall (1956: 18–39), who argue that a democratic government has four principal characteristics:

1. *Popular sovereignty*—governmental power is vested in the people at large.
2. *Political equality*—the power to influence government is shared equally by all citizens.
3. *Popular consultation*—government officials must periodically ascertain the public preference for governmental policy *and* then follow that preference.
4. *Majority rule*—when there is disagreement among members of the public over governmental policy, the preference of the majority should prevail.

Other, more specific, conditions are also necessary for democratic goverment in contemporary society. Some of those conditions concern the duties of citizens. Citizens have to be knowledgeable about existing governmental policies, emerging problems, and possible solutions. They have to form opinions about those matters and articulate their opinions to government leaders by voting and other means. In short, democratic government places serious burdens on the average citizen, but it also places heavy burdens on political institutions and leaders.

Political parties, as we noted above, are one type of institution with especially important responsibilities in a democracy. Parties can shape distinctive political points of view. They can provide a mechanism by which the preferences of like-minded citizens within a state (or, indeed, the entire nation) can be pressed on government. In a democracy, competing parties should form to transmit the preferences of those citizens not well represented by existing parties. Another common expectation for democracy is that there be at least two parties competing for control of government, and a good deal of research has posited several benefits that arise from that competition. It is a commonplace notion, of course, that the United States has traditionally had a two-party system.

Finally, political leaders have obligations under a democratic system, too. Their duty is, at minimum, to seek out public preferences, to assess the majority point of view in times of public disagreement, and to shape governmental policy in light of that point of view.

POLYARCHY

The requirements for a democratic system that we have discussed are highly demanding of citizens, leaders, and institutions. They may be so demanding that they are virtually impossible to attain. One scholar, Robert A. Dahl (1971), has argued that it is best to think of such requirements, even of democratic government itself, as *ideals* that real governments may strive to attain, but which they are unlikely to realize completely.

Dahl believes, however, that some governments at least approach the ideal of being democratic. They fall short in one or another aspect—political equality, popular consultation, or majority rule—yet they rate relatively highly on all these traits most of the time. Dahl (1971: 8) calls such governments *polyarchies*, meaning governments "that have been substantially popularized and liberalized, that is, [which are] highly inclusive and extensively open to public contestation." Dahl's primary intention is to describe the governments of nations; since he counts the United States as a long-standing polyarchy, by inference, he would judge the governments of the states similarly.

Polyarchy, then, is a second conception of how state governments in the United States might function. The idea of polyarchy accords at least generally with the civic education and traditional mythology of Americans. It recognizes that the states are not perfectly democratic, but it suggests that they should generally rate highly on most of the four indicators of democracy suggested by Ranney and Kendall (1956).

ECONOMIC DOMINANCE

Many scholars argue that even the polyarchic conception of American government is too charitable: the United States does not simply fall short of true democracy, it fails entirely. These critics say that it is not the general public but the most economically powerful members of this society who are in control of the most important governmental policies—much as the elite theorists view community power (discussed in Chapter 11). There are several different versions of this thesis, but two of them are especially prominent. Both of these are based on specific views of economic power in American society.

Marxist scholars argue that economic dominance results from the inevitable control of a capitalistic society by the small, narrow elite at the top of its economic system. As G. William Domhoff (1983: 1) explains, "there is a ruling class by virtue of its dominant role in the economy and government." This ruling class, according to Marxist theorists, is made up of roughly the most wealthy 0.5 percent of the population. It supposedly maintains its influence over government through the selection of candidates for political office, through the power of special-interest groups, and through infiltration of the policy-making positions in government. The capitalistic elite controls the government to ensure its own social and economic position and power (Greenberg, 1985).

The second version of economic dominance does not hold that there is a single, cohesive economic elite that controls American government. This second view does acknowledge that American governments traditionally defer to private economic power, that such power is very unequally held in this society, and that a small proportion of all Americans can therefore exercise disproportionate control over this country's governments (McConnell, 1966: 166–195). In this view the economic elite is somewhat diverse and does not share common goals on all major policy issues. Furthermore, although the economically powerful have exceptional political influence according to this second view, their political interests are thought to be relatively narrow and centered principally on their economic concerns.

There is a good deal of evidence that gives some support to the view that economic dominance is the correct conception of American government. Research on mass participation in American politics, for example, has found that large segments of the public fail by far to perform their civic duty as outlined under the requirements for democracy. Many Americans pay scant attention at best to political affairs, have little factual understanding of current policy issues, and seldom exercise their options for participation in or influence over their governments. (Recall our discussion in Chapter 4 of the limited extent to which most Americans engage in various forms of political participation.) The limited nature of public participation leaves considerable opportunity for those who *are* politically active to determine governments' agendas. And it is often prominent economic interests that take full advantage of this opportunity.

Similarly, other evidence indicates how elite and institutional behavior sometimes falls short of what is required for a democratic system. Elected officials sometimes appear to ignore majority preferences on policy issues. Political parties do not always take different stances on policy issues, nor do they necessarily represent all the major views of the general public. And those with a good deal of money can have disproportionate influence on politics and political leaders—as Chapter 4's discussion of the expenses of campaigning indicated.

Taken together, this evidence leads some to conclude that political power is highly *unequally* distributed in the United States. The preferences of the economically advantaged minority, these observers say, dominate governmental decisions. There is the appearance of democratic consultation, at elections, for example, but that appearance is belied by several facts. Limited public participation even by voting and disproportionate influence of the economically advantaged over nominations and elections as well as over the day-to-day operations of government suggest the reality that lies behind this appearance.

EVALUATING THE DEMOCRATIZATION OF THE STATES

There are, then, three competing interpretations of how state governments in this country should function to be considered democratic. To determine which of these interpretations is most accurate, however, we must establish some more specific criteria. Qualities such as "popular sovereignty" and "majority rule" are difficult to define precisely enough to be easily evaluated in everyday situations. It may even be impossible to produce a complete list of the attributes of government that would be (1) necessary for democracy, (2) readily and unambiguously observable, and (3) generally agreed on by all scholars of the subject. We can, nonetheless, compose a list of essential criteria for rating the democratization of the states. This list includes necessary but perhaps not entirely sufficient conditions for democracy. If states fall short of essential characteristics on this list, then they would surely do so on a longer and more elaborate list. If they rate highly here, then we may conclude that they exhibit the minimum essentials of democracy.

Democratic theorists are in agreement that three traits are essential for government to be considered democratic. First, *equal political rights* must be assured to all citizens. Second, there must be a very *high level of participation* among the citizenry in the electoral process by which representatives are chosen to govern and policy preferences may be communicated. Finally, there must be *competition among groups*, or especially among political parties, contending to control the government and its policies. We will use these three traits as our essential characteristics for rating the overall democratization of individual states.

If states have all these characteristics, then they satisfy the minimum criteria for democratic government. If some of them have only two of these traits, they may qualify as polyarchic governments. If other states lack most of these characteristics, then economic dominance may well characterize the process by which their political decisions are made.

We can draw on the results of previous chapters to make this evaluation. Chapter 4 presented information on competitiveness of political parties and public participation in elections. By adding an assessment of civil rights, particularly voting rights, we will be able to evaluate the three characteristics for each state.

THE STATUS OF POLITICAL RIGHTS

Equality of political rights is one of democracy's four essential elements. Indeed, the "civics text" image of American government is that all adult citizens are guaranteed the right to vote, as well as a variety of other individual rights and liberties included in the Bill of Rights and elsewhere in the Constitution. Although that image is generally accurate today, it has only recently become so in some states. Civil rights were not fully secure until the federal government coopted this policy area in the 1960s, as we described in Chapter 3. Before that time the civil rights of ethnic minorities, in particular, were widely violated. The federal government passed a number of broad-ranging civil rights laws and began to monitor the activities of state and local governments and private citizens to ensure that those laws were obeyed and enforced.

Of all civil rights, the right to vote is particularly important to democracy. Those people who cannot vote are excluded from political debates; their other civil rights may also be at risk. Those with the right to vote can participate in debates about governmental policies, but, equally important, they have the power to work toward ensuring their other civil rights. Before the passing of the federal civil rights laws in the 1960s, the right to vote was denied millions of American citizens, principally because of their race. In the eleven Southern states that formerly constituted the confederacy, a variety of restrictive suffrage laws that were discriminatorily enforced disfranchised most blacks. Hispanic-Americans, Native Americans, and Oriental Americans were frequently denied voting rights in several other states. The Voting Rights Act of 1965 (subsequently revised and extended in 1970, 1975, and 1982) swept away those restrictions. A revolutionary extension of voting rights occurred, and many Americans benefited. Blacks, Hispanic-Americans, a number of other ethnic minorities, the poor, the ill-educated, the elderly, and the handicapped won new voting rights guarantees.

The Voting Rights Act was intended to assure the right to vote to essentially all adult Americans (the only exceptions being convicted felons and the mentally incompetent in most states). There are a few states, however, where that goal has not yet been reached. When the 1982 extension of the Voting Rights Act was debated in Congress, considerable evidence was presented that some forms of voting rights discrimination were still common in several Southern states. The most succinct assessment of this discrimination was presented by the U.S. Commission on Civil Rights in its report *The Voting Rights Act: Unfulfilled Goals* (1981). The commission found that in Alabama, Georgia, Louisiana, Mississippi, North Carolina, South Carolina, and Texas there still existed frequent instances of (1) discrimination against individual minority citizens who attempted to register to vote, (2) the use of registration practices that discriminated against minorities and the poor, (3) selective discrimination against individual minority citizens who attempted to vote, (4) the manipulation of election procedures and locations to discriminate against minorities, (5) the manipulation of election district boundaries to weaken minorities' political influence, (6) the use of selective annexation practices by cities to weaken minorities' political influence, (7) harassment of minority political candidates, and (8) avoidance of the requirement of the Voting Rights Act that changes in state or local election laws be preapproved by the U.S. Department of Justice.[1]

There has undoubtedly been a revolution in voting rights in these Southern states in the last generation. What was once an entirely undemocratic system with respect to civil rights has become one that at least approaches the democratic ideal. No doubt, too, occasional instances of voting discrimination arise elsewhere. But in the seven states mentioned above such incidents occur regularly. For that reason, when compared to the rest of the nation, those states fall short of the democratic goal of equal political rights. Voting rights must be judged to be qualified and not assured in those states. In the remaining forty-three states, voting rights can fairly be characterized as generally assured to citizens of voting age.

A SCORECARD FOR DEMOCRACY IN THE STATES

With the preceding assessment of voting rights as well as information from Chapter 4, we can depict the democratization of each state in terms of the criteria of equal political rights, level of political participation, and party competitiveness. Table 15-1 brings together all that information in summarized form.

More important than the individual ratings presented in Table 15-1 is how the combination in each state compares to the democratic ideal. The results indicate several groups of states, which can be arrayed across a continuum with relatively polyarchic states at

TABLE 15-1
RATINGS OF THE STATES ON THREE DIMENSIONS OF DEMOCRACY

STATE	VOTING RIGHTS[a]	PARTICIPATION IN ELECTIONS[b]	PARTISAN COMPETITIVENESS
Alabama	Qualified	Low	Weak one-party
Alaska	Assured	Moderate	Two-party
Arizona	Assured	Low	Weak one-party
Arkansas	Assured	Low	Weak one-party
California	Assured	Low	Weak one-party
Colorado	Assured	Low	Weak one-party
Connecticut	Assured	Low	Two-party
Delaware	Assured	Moderate	Two-party
Florida	Assured	Low	Weak one-party
Georgia	Qualified	Low	One-party
Hawaii	Assured	Low	Weak one-party
Idaho	Assured	Moderate	Weak one-party
Illinois	Assured	Low	Two-party
Indiana	Assured	Moderate	Weak one-party
Iowa	Assured	Low	Two-party

	STATE	VOTING RIGHTS[a]	PARTICIPATION IN ELECTIONS[b]	PARTISAN COMPETITIVENESS
TABLE 15-1 CONTINUED	Kansas	Assured	Low	Weak one-party
	Kentucky	Assured	Low	Weak one-party
	Louisiana	Qualified	Moderate	Weak one-party
	Maine	Assured	Moderate	Two-party
	Maryland	Assured	Moderate	One-party
	Massachusetts	Assured	Low	Weak one-party
	Michigan	Assured	Low	Weak one-party
	Minnesota	Assured	Moderate	Weak one-party
	Mississippi	Qualified	Low	One-party
	Missouri	Assured	Moderate	Weak one-party
	Montana	Assured	High	Two-party
	Nebraska	Assured	Low	Two-party
	Nevada	Assured	Low	Weak one-party
	New Hampshire	Assured	Low	Weak one-party
	New Jersey	Assured	Low	Two-party
	New Mexico	Assured	Low	Two-party
	New York	Assured	Low	Two-party
	North Carolina	Qualified	Low	Weak one-party
	North Dakota	Assured	High	Two-party
	Ohio	Assured	Low	Two-party
	Oklahoma	Assured	Low	Weak one-party
	Oregon	Assured	Moderate	Weak one-party
	Pennsylvania	Assured	Low	Two-party
	Rhode Island	Assured	Moderate	Weak one-party
	South Carolina	Qualified	Low	Weak one-party
	South Dakota	Assured	Moderate	Weak one-party
	Tennessee	Assured	Low	Weak one-party
	Texas	Qualified	Low	Weak one-party
	Utah	Assured	High	Weak one-party
	Vermont	Assured	Moderate	Two-party
	Virginia	Assured	Low	Weak one-party
	Washington	Assured	High	Two-party
	West Virginia	Assured	Moderate	Weak one-party
	Wisconsin	Assured	Low	Weak one-party
	Wyoming	Assured	Low	Weak one-party

[a]The voting rights ratings are based on the preceding discussion in this chapter; the participation ratings are based on Table 4-4; the partisan competitiveness scores on Table 4-3.

[b]High participation is average turnout of 60 percent or more of the population of voting age in gubernatorial elections; moderate turnout is 50–59 percent; and low turnout is 49 percent or less.

one extreme and relatively undemocratic ones at the other, as shown in Table 15-2. Generally speaking, the higher the score a state has on any of the three characteristics of democracy, the higher it is rated in Table 15-2. But particular combinations of scores can raise or lower a state's rating, too. A relatively high score on one trait, two-party competition, for example, can compensate to some degree for a relatively poor score on another. Since the groupings of states are determined in this fashion, different combinations of traits can place a state at the same vertical level in the table.

No state qualifies as democratic—that would require very high scores on all three of the criteria. Furthermore, only three states merit the designation of polyarchy. Montana, North Dakota, and Washington have assured voting rights, two-party competitiveness,

TABLE 15-2
OVERALL PROGRESS
OF THE STATES
TOWARD
DEMOCRATIZATION

	States with assured voting rights, high participation in elections, and two-party competitiveness: Montana, North Dakota, and Washington	*Polyarchic States?*
More Democratic	States with assured voting rights, moderate participation in elections, and two-party competitiveness: Alaska, Delaware, Maine, and Vermont	States with assured voting rights, high participation in elections, and weak one-party competitiveness: Utah
	States with assured voting rights, low participation in elections, and two-party competitiveness: Connecticut, Illinois, Iowa, Nebraska, New Jersey, New Mexico, New York, Ohio, and Pennsylvania	States with assured voting rights, moderate participation in elections, and weak one-party competitiveness: Idaho, Indiana, Minnesota, Missouri, Oregon, Rhode Island, South Dakota, and West Virginia

TABLE 15-2 CONTINUED		

Less Democratic — States with assured voting rights, low participation in elections, and weak one-party competitiveness: Arkansas, Arizona, California, Colorado, Florida, Hawaii, Kansas, Kentucky, Massachusetts, Michigan, Nevada, New Hampshire, Oklahoma, Tennessee, Virginia, Wisconsin, and Wyoming

States with assured voting rights, moderate participation in elections, and one-party competitiveness: Maryland

States with qualified voting rights, moderate participation in elections, and one-party competitiveness: Louisiana

States with qualified voting rights and either low participation in elections with weak one-party competitiveness or moderate participation with one-party competitiveness: Alabama, North Carolina, South Carolina, and Texas

States with qualified voting rights, low participation in elections, and one-party competitiveness: Georgia and Mississippi

} *Economic Dominance States?*

and relatively high public participation in elections. Admittedly, the criterion for high public participation (at least 60 percent of the citizens of voting age going to the polls in the average election for governor) is not a very demanding one. True democracy requires a far higher level of participation, and the ratings of the states on this characteristic in Table 15-2 are somewhat generous ones. Nonetheless, Montana, North Dakota, and Washington are distinguished from all the remaining states in these terms.

Below the top three states in Table 15-2 are six levels of other states that are distinguished by decreasing degrees of democratization. The five states in the second level (divided into two subgroups because of the different patterns of their component scores) might be thought of as leaning toward polyarchy. Most of the states, however, are in the third and fourth levels from the top. They all have assured voting rights, but they also all have notable shortcomings in one or even two of the other criteria, significantly diminishing their ratings. At the bottom of Table 15-2, in the lowest three levels, are seven states that may well merit the label of economic dominance. The two states in the very lowest group—Georgia and Mississippi—are especially likely candidates for this designation because of their remarkably poor ratings on all three criteria. But the other five low-rated states—Alabama, Louisiana, North Carolina, South Carolina, and Texas—have sufficiently poor scores to raise strong doubts about whether broad public control of government can exist there.

These conclusions are buttressed by information from Chapter 5 concerning the strength of interest groups in these seven states. In six of them, interest groups are judged to enjoy some kind of dominant position of power; only in North Carolina is this not the case. In these low-rated states, then, democratic processes are quite weak, and the power of special interests is quite strong. And, as you may also recall from Chapter 5, the particular power of economic interests in *all* the states provides good reason to believe that those interests have preponderant power in these seven states. Thus, economic dominance appears to be justified as a characterization of their political systems.

No doubt, some of the categorizations of states both at the top and the bottom of Table 15-2 will be controversial. They depend, of necessity, on some judgmental decisions with respect to what constitutes a high, moderate, or low rating on each dimension. If anything, however, our judgments have erred on the side of generosity. And none of the states is a true democracy by these ratings. Only three of them qualify for the designation of polyarchy, and a large number either lean toward or must be classed as showing economic dominance. We must conclude, then, that after two centuries of progress toward democratic government in the United States, that goal has been fully attained in no state, is approximated in only a few, and remains quite a distant dream for a considerable minority. However, every state offers opportunities for public involvement in politics, and polyarchic government is within the reach of all—if citizens and public leaders wish to grasp it.

THE MEANING OF DEMOCRATIZATION IN THE EVERYDAY POLITICAL LIFE OF THE STATES

The preceding ratings of the states are based solely on judgments of their attainment of three characteristics of democracy. They are, then, relatively academic and abstract. However, the politics of the different groups of states differ in commonsensical, everyday respects. Imagine, for example, how different everyday political life in the polyarchic states is from that in the economic dominance ones. Contrast North Dakota with Georgia, for example. In North Dakota the right to vote is assured to all citizens, turnout at elections is high (and more than *double* that in Georgia), there is two-party competitiveness and only weak interest groups. In Georgia the right to vote is still at issue, turnout is quite low, there is little partisan competition, and interest groups are strong. Imagine, then, how different is the political climate experienced by average citizens in these two states. Levels of public interest in politics, of social and peer pressure to participate in politics, and of debate about political issues must be wholly different in the two. In North Dakota the political climate surely stimulates public interest in and concern with politics. It enhances democracy. Two-party competition increases public interest in elections and in government in general. A high level of political participation increases peer pressure to participate and the amount of discussion and debate about politics among average citizens. The political climate in Georgia, on the other hand, is likely to depress public concern and participation.

Imagine, too, how interest groups will be affected by different political climates. Where partisan competition and public participation are high, interest groups must pay far more attention to competing points of view. They will have to court public opinion rather than being able to ignore it. And they will more often have to give up part of their narrow, self-centered agenda to get a portion of it accepted by the public, the prevailing political party, or the government itself. Public officials will be affected differently, as well, by such differences in political climates. Elected officials in low-participation, one-party states have much more discretion in their policy choices. They need to worry far less about how the voters or the members of the other party might react. For that reason, too, they might be more readily influenced by special interests.

There is thus more to these ratings of democratization than mere academic counting of angels on pinheads. Real differences in political life are indicated here. However, since few Americans live at length in two or more states that are notably different in these terms *and* think systematically about how political life differs from state to state, the contrasts in their politics seldom strike anyone.

PUZZLES IN STATE POLITICS

The preceding summary of democracy in the states raises some questions about why the states have not made more progress in these terms as well as some apparent contradictions with conclusions from other chapters of this book. Three such puzzles are especially worthy of discussion here.

THE RELATIVE DISINTEREST OF CITIZENS IN STATE POLITICS

In no state is voter turnout exceptionally high. As you may know, in a number of other democratic nations, voter turnout is typically in the range of 80 to 90 percent of those of voting age. In the United States, turnout—whether for local, state, or national elections—has rarely approached that level. And turnout in a considerable number of states is embarrassingly low for even a pretense of democratic politics.

Furthermore, voter turnout has also been in decline nationwide since the early 1960s. An enormous amount of research has probed the reasons for this decline, but no clear explanation for it has emerged. The fact that many people do not vote has always been largely attributed to restrictive voting laws and individual demographic attributes, such as level of education, social class, and age (recall our discussion in Chapter 4). The recent period of decline, however, is coincident with the easing of registration requirements and a continued increase in the education level of the population. Thus, the puzzle of low public participation is an especially intriguing one. Various scholars have hypothesized that the decline in turnout is attributable to growing public cynicism about government and about the ability of citizens to influence government policies. These hypotheses have proven, however, to be difficult and controversial to test.

Does the level of public participation matter? Does it have any significance beyond being part of an academician's scorecard for state-level democratization such as Table 15-1? On this point we side with high-school civics texts. If democracy is to work, citizens must bear their share of the governmental burden. The government cannot submit to public preferences if those preferences are not expressed as clearly as possible. And if the participation rate of average citizens is low, it should come as no surprise if government responds principally to those who *do* press their claims vigorously. Many Americans like to complain about how special interests dominate government, but that complaint is hollow when it comes from those unwilling to play their part in the democratic process.

In sum, public participation in state politics is far short of the democratic ideal and, worse yet, has been on the decline in recent decades. Why this is the case we cannot say. But the implications for democratic government are unambiguous and unsettling.

THE LIMITED DEVELOPMENT OF TWO-PARTY COMPETITION

It has been widely hypothesized that two-party competition would inevitably increase in the United States in the last half of the twentieth century. This hypothesis is based on the following logic: First, at mid-century two-party competition typically existed in relatively economically advanced, highly urbanized states. In those states political interests were also especially diverse, so it seemed unlikely that a single party could represent all the legitimate interests. Thus, it was hypothesized that as other states became more economically advanced, urbanized, and modernized, they too would develop two-party competition. So far, however, this scenario has not been generally realized. In Chapter 4 we demonstrated that the number of states with competitiveness between parties *in state politics* has been roughly stable since the late 1940s. Strictly one-party states have declined in number, yet the overall trend has been more toward weak one-party (Democratic) control than toward two-partyism.

Perhaps there has simply not been enough time for enhanced economic and social complexity to exert their influence on partisan politics. That would mean two-party politics will eventually come to all the states, but "eventually" could be a long time away for many of them. Alternatively, the hypothesis could itself be wrong. One explanation for why that might be the case is suggested by the considerable number of scholars who argue that parties are generally in organizational decline in the United States (recall our discussion of this matter in Chapter 4). Other observers simply say that the parties are changing dramatically in their electoral functions to conform to the realities of the media age. Thus, two-party competition may not be increasing because the parties themselves are changing in their organization and functions—or perhaps even becoming irrelevant to modern-day American politics.

There is no consensus on the fate or future character of the political parties. What is most important, however, is the role they have played in democratic politics, rather than the specifics of how they do so. Parties have constituted the vehicle for presenting citizens with alternatives for government leadership and policy. A central plank of democratic theory has been that such alternatives are critically important. To the extent that two-party competition does not become a reality in individual states, that dimension of democracy will remain an unfulfilled ideal.

THE MISTRUST OF GOVERNMENT BY BUSINESS

We have indicated here and in Chapters 5 and 11 that special economic interests and the business sector, in particular, are quite powerful in all the states and may even dominate the politics of a significant number of states and communities. Why is it, then, that business leaders complain so much about government? Their criticisms and complaints are reported in newspapers and on television and radio. This high frequency of criticisms of government from the business sector implies a seeming contradiction with our characterization of business as powerful. Even academicians have recognized this fact and attempted to explain it. Several scholars have written at length about how critical American business is of government. Perhaps the best summing up of this situation comes from David Vogel (1978: 45):

> The most characteristic, distinctive and persistent belief of American corporate executives is an underlying suspicion and mistrust of government. It distinguishes the American business community not only from every other bourgeoisie, but also from every other legitimate

organization of political interests in American society. The scope of direct and indirect government support for corporate growth and profits does not belie this contention; on the contrary, it makes it all the more paradoxical. Why should the group in American society that has disproportionately benefited from governmental policies continue to remain distrustful of political intervention in the economy?

Why, indeed, is business so mistrustful of government if it is so politically powerful? That is a significant puzzle, which, in our judgment, no one has solved. Three arguments have been advanced, however, as possible explanations.

First, some have argued that much of business's criticism of government is simply a strategic exercise to keep government leaders on the defensive and concerned to demonstrate their goodwill toward business (Domhoff, 1983: 148; McConnell, 1966; 293–294). That is, businesspersons complain vociferously about government to ensure that their political demands will receive close attention. Although there is no conclusive evidence to support or reject this explanation, it may have something to do with Charles E. Lindblom's arguments (presented in Chapter 5) about the status of business as an interest group. Lindblom argued that business has a unique status in the eyes of government, which confers a guarantee of favored attention. If Lindblom's thesis *and* this first explanation for business's criticism are correct, then businesspeople could be likened to the spoiled but clever children of indulgent parents. By continuing to demand more and more, they know they will get exactly what they want.

A second proposed solution to this puzzle is that business interests are essentially undemocratic: they fear that true public control of government would usurp their own power (Prothro, 1954; Silk and Vogel, 1976: 189–217). Thus, they are wary of government because one day the rhetoric of democracy might be taken seriously and their own power substantially diminished. In addition, according to this argument, the business sector is quick to criticize specific actions of government that appear to favor the broader public interest over its own. Like the first explanation, this one has not been proven or disproven. We suspect, however, that there are some people who will accept it on faith, as well as those who will reject it on the same basis.

Finally, Grant McConnell (1966: 294) reminds us that American business is heterogeneous in its economic and political interests. Many government policies that harm certain business interests benefit others. Thus, some businesspersons will vehemently criticize policies that others will applaud. Yet, as we argued in Chapter 5, special-interest groups that benefit from particular governmental actions often try to downplay the extent to which they benefit. As a consequence, for any given policy, you may hear little of the applause and a good deal of the criticism from business. And because there are so many policies enacted by various levels of government, there will appear to be widespread business dissatisfaction with government.

Although this puzzle about business's attitude toward government may seem simply a matter of intellectual curiosity, there is a practical side to it as well. As we have noted elsewhere, business and government leaders have begun to work especially closely in pursuit of state economic development strategies. Those efforts are of particular importance to making the economic transition from the industrial era to the postindustrial future. Obviously, the success of these efforts is in part dependent on the ability of business leaders to work constructively with government. Even the willingness of business leaders to recognize their dependence on state and local governments for developmental assistance is crucial to these efforts. Thus, to the degree that business is critical of government, its ability to work cooperatively to encourage economic development will be impaired.

There are practical concerns for average citizens here, too. If business's criticism of government is merely strategic and designed to ensure policies favorable to its interests *or* if business is indeed undemocratic, Americans have special reason to worry because of current economic problems. Business leaders might successfully manipulate government's policy efforts to accommodate their interests more than those of the general public. But, in the present time, the economic stakes are especially high. Thus, there is much to be gained or lost by allowing business to control government's agenda.

CONCLUSION

Americans are taught from childhood that the United States is a democratic nation. In comparison with all the nations of the world, most of which are ruled by entirely nondemocratic regimes, state and national governments in this country do appear democratic. When the state governments are analyzed in terms of some specific requirements for representative democracy, however, they do not rate very highly. Only three states earn even the ranking of polyarchies. And the criteria used to compile those ratings were only a minimal set of necessary but perhaps not sufficient ones. Were we to develop a more comprehensive list of democratic traits and rate the states on that list, they would probably score somewhat lower.

Even though our overall conclusions are disappointing, it is important to acknowledge the progress that has been made in the last generation. The protection of individual rights, in particular, has been dramatically improved during this period. Although some states still fall short of the democratic ideal on that trait, those states and several others were entirely undemocratic in that respect as recently as the 1960s. Thus, notable progress has been made on this dimension of democracy, and participation in government has also improved in many states as a result.

Despite those gains, however, Robert Dahl may be correct in suggesting that true democracy is an ideal unlikely ever to be achieved. Perhaps, then, it is simply a myth that American governments ever were or ever can be democratic. The goal of polyarchy, on the other hand, is within the reach of every state—and the fact that some have achieved that status is testimony to its feasibility. Doing so, however, will require as much effort from citizens as from political leaders. In some sense, then, Americans get the government they are willing to accept.

NOTES

1. In addition to the U.S. Civil Rights Commission report, extensive evidence on restrictions on voting rights in the South is presented by the Committee on the Judiciary (1982; 1984) and Davidson (1984).

REFERENCES

Committee on the Judiciary. 1982. *Extension of the Voting Rights Act, Hearings before the Subcommittee on Civil and Constitutional Rights*, Parts 1, 2, 3. Washington, D.C.: U.S. House of Representatives.

Committee on the Judiciary. 1984. *The Voting Rights Act: Runoff Primaries and Registration Barriers: Hearings before the Subcommit-*

tee on Civil and Constitutional Rights. Washington, D.C.: U.S. House of Representatives.

Dahl, Robert A. 1971. *Polyarchy.* New Haven, Conn.: Yale University Press.

Davidson, Chandler. 1984. *Minority Vote Dilution.* Washington, D.C.: Howard University Press.

Domhoff, G. William. 1983. *Who Rules America Now?* Englewood Cliffs, N.J.: Prentice-Hall.

Greenberg, Edward. 1985. *Capitalism and the American Political Ideal.* Armonk, N.Y.: M.E. Sharp.

McConnell, Grant. 1966. *Private Power and American Democracy.* New York: Alfred A. Knopf.

Prothro, James. 1954. *Dollar Decade.* Baton Rouge: Louisiana State University Press.

Ranney, Austin, and Willmoore Kendall. 1956. *Democracy and the American Party System.* New York: Harcourt, Brace.

Silk, Leonard, and David Vogel. 1976. *Ethics and Profits.* New York: Simon and Schuster.

U.S. Commission on Civil Rights. 1981. *The Voting Rights Act: Unfulfilled Goals.* Washington, D.C.: U.S. Commission on Civil Rights.

Vogel, David. 1978. "Why Businessmen Distrust Their State: The Political Consciousness of American Corporate Executives," *British Journal of Political Science* 8 (January): 45–78.

INDEX

Ability to pay, as standard of
    equity, 366, 369–370
Access, 130
ACIR, 420
Ad valorem property tax, 430–432
Advertisers (legislator type), 165
Agricultural groups, 117–118
Agriculture
    decline in, with industrial-
      ism, 10
    economic problems in, 4
    relative dependence of states
      on, 19–20
Air pollution control, 62
Alabama, voting rights in, 449
Alaska, cost of living in, 418–419
Allocational policies, 350–351,
    352
Amendatory veto, 194
Annexation, 278–279, 322
Anticipated reactions, 292,
    343–344
Appellate courts, 225, 231–232
Article I, 49
At-large representation
    effects of, 330
    and minority representation,
      320–321
    and neighborhood interests,
      314
    and reformed governments, 313
Attorneys, 235–240

Bench trial, 234
Bias, of interest group sys-
    tem, 136
Bill
    blocking, 154–155
    drafting of, 150
Bill of Rights, 56, 57–58

Blanket primary, 83
Blocking bill, 154–155
Bribery, 126–127
Budgets
    and bureaucratic power,
      392–393
    and gubernatorial power,
      193–194
Bureaucracies
    characteristics of, 384–385
    decision making in, 385–388
    policy change in, 387–388
    power of, 391–398
    problems in, 388–391
    rise of, 317
Bureaucrats
    decision making by, 376
    power of, 349
    priorities of, 388–390
    responsiveness of, 398–403
    and service delivery, 359–361
    street-level, 360–361, 363,
      394–395
Bush administration, 53
Business
    elitist view of, 336
    mistrust of government by,
      458–460
    pluralist view of, 338
    role of, in reform, 312
    special position of, 345–347
Business groups, 115–116,
    129–130, 292–293

California, court system of,
    223–225
Campaign experts, 87–88
Campaigners, 103
Campaigns
    changes in, since 1950s, 86
    cost of, 88–90, 166

Campaigns—*Cont.*
  regulation of spending in, 91–93
  use of experts for, 87–88
Candidates, 84–85, 120–121
Carter, Jimmy, 208
Ceremonial leader, 183–184
Chicago
  bureaucratic responsiveness in, 403–408
  political machine in, 325–326
  service delivery in, 374–378
Chief executive officer, 182–183
Chief of state, 203
Cisnero, Henry (mayor of San Antonio), 322–323, 325, 327
Citizen legislatures, 159, 161, 165, 172
City councils
  minority representation on, 320
  power of, 330–332
  in reformed government, 313
  in unreformed government, 310–311
City government
  and political machine, 316
  reform of, 311–321
  reformed, 312–313, 318–319, 321–326
  unreformed, 310–311, 318–319
City managers, 313, 328–329
Civil cases, 218
Civil Rights Act of 1957, 1960, and 1964, 58
Civil rights policy, 56–59
Class
  and distribution of benefits and burdens, 423–426
  and economic dominance, 445–447, 454
  and political participation, 288–289, 291
  and segregation, 261–264
  and settlement of court cases, 239–240
Client groups, 395–396

Close scrutiny, 267
Closed primary, 82–83
Coalition building, 320–321
Committee review, 150–151
Communalists, 103–104
Community power
  changes in distribution of, 348
  elitist perspective on, 336–337, 340–344
  pluralist perspective on, 337–344
Company states, 131–132
Competition, among metropolitan governments, 259
Constituency service, 146–147
Constitution, U.S., 41–42, 48–49, 56–59, 267
Constitutions, state
  datedness of, 44–45
  and limits on state power, 37–39
  special interests' influence on, 42–44
  style and language problems in, 39–42
Contacting, 280–281, 287–290, 302
Cooperative federalism, 50–51
Cooptive federalism
  benefits and drawbacks of, 73–74
  and changes in states' lawmaking function, 143
  and civil rights policy, 56–59
  and environmental and pollution control policy, 59–60, 61–62
  and intergovernmental regulation, 60, 62–68
  methods of, 69–72
  and state and local governments, 51–52, 72–74, 414
  and welfare policy, 54–56
Coproduction, 363–364
Corporate income tax, 433
Councils of governments, 279–280

Courts. *See also* United States
Supreme Court
advantages of rich over poor
in, 241–242
appellate, 225, 231–232
extension of power of federal, 70
functions of, 218–219
judges in, 232–234, 242–247
juries in, 234–235
of last resort, 225, 232
litigants in, 240–242
organization of state and local,
223–228
as political institutions,
221–223
private attorneys in, 238–240
prosecuting attorneys in,
235–238
public understanding of,
219–221
trial, 224–228, 245–246
volume of work of, 228–232
Criminal cases, 218
Cross-cutting requirements, 66
Cultural regions, 32–35
Culture. *See* Political culture

Daley, Richard, 325–326
Debate, on legislation, 152–157
Decision making, by bureaucracies, 385–388
Decision rules, 372–376
Delaware, as company state, 131
Delegated powers, 49
Demand, as standard of equity,
365, 367–368
Democracy
characteristics of, 444–445, 448
direct, 105–108, 442
effect of business-government
collaboration on, 24–25
political parties and, 443,
444–445, 457–458
in states, 447–456
in United States, 442–447

Demographics, and service
delivery, 376–378
Developmental policies, 350
Direct democracy, 105–108, 442
Direct initiative, 106
District attorneys, 235–238
Division of power, 48
Dual federalism, 50

Economic dominance, 445–447,
454
Economic transition, 2–9, 13–16
Economy
development of, 7–8, 15
homogenous versus heterogenous, 132
influences on, 16–21
and political power, 347–349
Education
decision rules and, 374
distribution of, 370–371
factors affecting, 357–358
as percentage of state spending, 436, 437
as state-controlled policy area,
75–76
Elections
competition in, 96–99
costs of, 88–93, 166
general, 83–84
incumbents' success in, 167
participants in, 84–88, 99–102
primary, 82–83
rules of, 82–84
timing of, 83–84
Elitist perspective, 336–337,
340–344
versus pluralist perspective,
344–353
Energy industry, 4
Environmental and pollution
control policy, 59–60, 61–62
Equality, as standard of equity,
364–365, 366
Equity
concepts of, 364–366

Equity—*Cont.*
and service delivery, 366–370
Executive branches
characteristics of, 209–211
and governor, 190–191,
211–214
organizational control of, 191
reform of, 179
unified, 190–191
Exit, from the cities, 258–259,
271, 282–283, 300–301, 302
Expenditures, by state and local
government, 318, 436–437
Expertise, 339, 393
Extractive effort, 420–422

Fairness, versus responsiveness,
388–390
Federal Campaign Act of 1971, 89
Federal cooptation. *See* Cooptive
federalism
Federal government. *See* United
States government
Federal Housing Administration,
272–274
Federalism
cooperative, 50–51
cooptive. *See* Cooptive federalism
definition of, 47–48
dual, 50
evolution of, 49–53
original division of power in,
48–49
Fourteenth Amendment, 56, 267
Fragmentation, 254–257
attempts to combat, 277–280
competition and, 259
and freedom of choice, 258–259
and individual self-interest, 257
and lack of intergovernmental
cooperation, 268–269
and limited mobility, 264–268
segregation and, 261–264
Functional fiefdoms, 317

General election, 83
General jurisdiction courts,
224–225, 229–232
General sales tax, 432
Georgia, voting rights in, 449
Governors
budgetary power of, 193–194
characteristics of, 204–208
demands on, 185–188
and executive branches, 190–
191, 211–214
history of office of, 178–180
intergovernmental relations
of, 195
interstate comparison of
powers of, 199–201
and legislatures, 172–173, 194
organizational control and, 191
roles of, 180–184
size of staff of, 195–198
sources of power of, 188–203
tenure potential of, 189–190
veto power of, 157, 194
Gramm-Rudman-Hollings Deficit
Control Act, 53
Grange movement, 11
Great Depression, 50, 56
Group activity, as political participation, 281, 290–296, 302

Hawkins v. *Town of Shaw*,
267–268
Housing industry, 274–275

Ideology, 94–95
Immigrants, 28, 33–35, 309, 310
Income taxes, 432–433
Incrementalism, 397
Incumbents, reelection of, 167
Indirect initiative, 106
Industrialism, 2–3, 10–13,
308–311
Infrastructure, 7–8
Initiatives, 106
Innovation, by states, 76, 426–428

Interest groups
  and legislatures, 171–172
  and local government, 290–296
  and policy representation, 145
  power of, 127–136
  relative impact of, 134–136,
    455–456
  rich versus poor, 291
  strategies of, 120–127
  types of, 114–120
Intergovernmental regulation, 60,
    62–68
Intergovernmental relations, 195
Intermediate appellate courts,
    225, 231–232
Item veto, 194

Jacksonian era, 38, 242
Johnson administration, 51
Judges
  characteristics of, 245–247
  role of, 232–234
  selection of, 242–244
Juries, 234–235
Jury fixing, 236–237

Kennedy administration, 51

Labor unions, 294–296
Laissez-faire government, 35, 36
Lawmakers (legislator type), 165
Lawmaking
  changes in, 143
  as function of legislature, 142
  governor's role in, 182
  mechanics of, 148–157
Leadership, 76
Legislative committee, 150–151,
    153
Legislative leader, 182
Legislative reform movement,
    157–159
Legislators
  characteristics of, 163–170

feedback to, 145–146
  representation by, 144–148
  types of, 164–165
Legislatures
  citizen, 159, 161, 165, 172
  functions of, 141–144
  influences on, 170–173, 194
  professional, 160, 168, 169
  professionalization of, 158,
    160–161, 162
  quasi-professional, 160, 168
  reform of, 157–159
  second house of, 156
  turnover in, 167–169
Liberalism, 429
Library services, 371–372, 373
Licensing fees, 433
Limited jurisdiction
    courts, 224, 228
Litigants, 240–242
Lobbying, 121–126
Local government, 74–77,
    142–143. *See also* City
    councils; City government;
    City managers; Mayors
Long ballot, 178
Lotteries, 434, 435–436
Louisiana, voting rights in, 449

Mayors
  authority of, 321–326
  versus city managers, 328–329
  minority, 326–328
  in unreformed governments,
    310
Media, 297, 324, 349–350,
    397–398
Merit selection, of judges, 243
Merit system, 313, 314–315
Metropolitan areas, 256
  disparity of needs and re-
    sources in, 260–261
  effectiveness of political partic-
    ipation in, 301–303

Metropolitan areas—*Cont.*
exit from, 258–259, 271,
282–283, 300–301, 302
federal highway policy and,
275–277
federal housing policy and,
271–274
housing industry and, 274–275
lack of intergovernmental cooperation in, 268–269
political participation in,
280–303
Metropolitan Housing v. *Arlington
Heights*, 268
Metropolitan Statistical Areas,
254–255
Middle class, 311, 315. *See also*
Class
Minorities, 318, 327–328, 331. *See
also* Racial discrimination
Mississippi, voting rights in, 449
Mobility, and fragmentation,
264–268

National Defense Highway
Act, 275
National Housing Act of 1934, 272
Need, as standard of equity, 365,
366–367
Neighborhood organizations,
293–294
Nevada, executive branch of,
211–214
New Jersey, path of legislation
in, 149
New York, governor's office of,
196–199
Nominations, 82–83
Nondecisions, 342–343
Nonviolent protest, 282, 296–298,
303
Norm enforcement, 218
North Carolina, voting rights
in, 449

Occupational groups, 116–117
Occupations, fastest-growing, 4–6
Oklahoma, development strate-
gies of, 8–9
One-party states, 96, 171, 184
Open primary, 82–83

Parliamentary procedures,
156–157
Parochial participants, 103
Parties. *See* Political parties
Partisanship, of voters, 94–95
Partnerships, state-federal, 51
Patronage, 311
Plea bargaining, 238
Pluralist perspective, 337–344
versus elitist perspective,
344–353
Police services, 372, 373
Policies. *See* Public policies
Policy arenas, 350–353
Policy leader, 181–182
Policy representation, 144–146
Political action committees
(PACs), 89–90
Political climate, 455–456
Political culture, 27
individualistic, 28–29, 36
and interest group power,
133–134
moralistic, 28
and public policy, 429
of states, 28–32
traditionalistic, 29, 31
and voting turnout, 101
Political machine, 310, 313–316,
325–326
Political participation, 99–105
Political parties
and bureaucratic power, 397
and democracy, 443, 444–445,
457–458
electoral competition between,
96–99, 457–458
governor's role in, 184, 203

Political parties—*Cont.*
  influence of, 133, 171
  and interest group power, 133
  and public policy, 429
  and reformed city govern-
    ments, 313
  relative strength of, in states,
    94–95
  roles of, in elections, 85–87
  in unreformed city govern-
    ments, 311
  and voter turnout, 283–285
Political power, 340–342. *See also*
    Community power
  of bureaucracies, 391–396
  and distribution of city jobs,
    379–380
  and economic climate, 347–349
  and expertise, 339, 393
  of governors, 188–203
  of mayors, 321–326
  policy arenas and, 350–353
Political rights, 448–450
Polyarchy, 445, 452–453
Poor, mobility of, 264–268
Popular referendum, 106
Populists, 11, 35, 38, 179
Pork barrel politics, 147–148
Positive-state ethos, 35–37
Post industrialism, 2, 4, 6, 307
Power. *See* Community power;
    Political power
Preference, as standard of
    equity, 365, 368–369
Primary elections, 82–83
Private attorneys, 238–240
Professional legislatures, 160,
    168, 169
Professionalization
  of legislature, 158, 160–161, 162
  of public agencies, 209–210
Progressive movement
  and positive-state ethos, 35, 36
  reform by, 38, 179, 242
  and state policies, 415

Progressive taxes, 424
Property taxes, *ad valorem,*
    430–432
Proportional taxes, 424
Prosecuting attorneys, 235–238
Public defenders, 239
Public employees' unions, 295
Public hearings, 151
Public-interest groups, 118–119
Public policies
  allocational, 350–351, 352
  definition of, 411–412
  developmental, 350
  for distribution of benefits and
    burdens, 423–426
  effects of judicial branch
    on, 221
  innovation in, 426–428
  interstate differences in,
    413–416
  redistributive, 351–352, 353
  scope of, 416–420, 428–429
  social welfare, 54–56
  state government's control
    over, 74–76

Quasi-professional legislatures,
    160, 168

Racial discrimination, 267–268,
    309, 378–380, 448–450
Railroads, regulation of, 7
Reagan, Ronald, 52–53, 208
Recall, 106
Recreational services, 372,
    376–378
Redistributive policies,
    351–352, 353
Redlining, 273
Referendum, 105–106
Reform movement
  and bureaucratic power, 400
  and city government, 311–317
  consequences of, 317–321

Reform movement—*Cont.*
  legislative, 157–159
  and office of governor, 179–181
Reformed city government,
    312–313, 318–319, 321–326
Regressive taxes, 424, 431–432
Reluctants (legislator type),
    164–165
Representation
  at-large, 313, 314, 320–321, 330
  legislative, 142, 144–148
  ward, 310–311, 313, 314,
    320–321, 330
Representative government, 442
Reputational methodology, 342
Residual powers, 49
Resources, 405
Responsiveness, versus fairness,
    388–390
Revenues, 70–72, 416–418,
    430–436
Roe v. *Wade*, 58–59

Sales taxes, 432
San Antonio, 323–325
Sanitation, decision rules and,
    374, 375
Schools. *See* Education
Scientific management, 315, 317
Second house, role of, 156
Segregation, 261–264
Selective sales taxes, 432
Self-interest, 257
Service delivery
  changes in, 276–278
  difficulties in, 357–364
  distributional patterns of,
    370–380
  equity in, 364–370
  stages of, 362
Severance taxes, 436
Single-industry associations, 116
Single-interest groups, 119–120
Small claims courts, 224
Social lobbying, 124–125
Social welfare policy, 54–56

South Carolina, voting rights
  in, 449
Special districts, 279
Spectators (legislator type), 164
Spending, by state and local
  governments, 318, 436–437
Standard operating proce-
  dures, 386
State's attorneys, 235–238
Status, 129–130
Street-level bureaucrats,
    360–361, 363, 394–395
Street repair, 373–374
Suburbanization, 270–277
Suburbs, 260–261
Supercession, 70
Supreme courts. *See* Courts of
  last resort; United States
  Supreme Court
Suspect classifications, 267

Tax capacity, 16–18, 420–422
Tax effort, 420–422
Tax reductions, 7
Taxation
  level of, and type of city
    government, 318
  methods of, 430–436
  types of, 424
Technology, 20–21
Tenth Amendment, 49
Tenure potential, 189–190
Texas, voting rights in, 449
Trial courts
  of general jurisdiction,
    224–225, 229–232
  judges of, 245–246
  of limited jurisdiction, 224, 228
  specialization of, 227
Trial juries, 234–235
Turnover, in legislatures, 167–169

Unions, 294–296, 319
United States Advisory Commis-
  sion on Intergovernmental
  Relations (ACIR), 420

United States Constitution, 41–42, 48–49, 56–59, 267

United States government
aid provided by, 66–69, 70–72, 356, 433–434
economic dominance in, 445–447
growth of statutory law of, 58
highway policy of, 275–277
housing policy of, 271–274
regulatory powers of, 50–51
social welfare spending by, 55
and state implementation of policy, 76–77

United States Supreme Court
apportionment rulings of, 156, 173–174
extension of power of, 58
and powers of federal government, 53
and *Roe* v. *Wade*, 58–59
and voting rights, 59

Unreformed city government, 310–311, 313, 318–319

Urban government, 356–357. *See also* City government; Metropolitan areas

Urban growth, 12

User fees, 433

Veteran's Administration, housing policy of, 272

Veto, 157, 194

Violence, as protest, 282, 298–300, 303

Voluntary agreements, 279

Voters
partisanship of, 94–95
turnout of, 283–286, 317–318, 456–457

Voting behavior
effectiveness of, 286–287
and interest groups, 128
on legislation, 152–157
mass versus individual, 99–102
in metropolitan areas, 280, 283–287, 302

Voting rights, 59, 448–450

Voting Rights Act of 1965, 58, 448

Voting specialists, 103

War on Poverty, 55

Ward representation
effects of, 330
and minority representation, 320–321
and neighborhood interests, 314
in unreformed government, 310–311, 313

Water pollution, 60, 61

Water Pollution Control Act of 1948, 60

Welfare spending, 55, 424

Welfare state, and political machine, 316

Works Progress Administration, 406

Zoning
constitutionality of, 267–268
use of, 265–267

CREDITS

These pages constitute an extension of the copyright page.

Chapter 1

7, Photo © W. Marc Bernsau/The Image Works. All rights reserved.
21, Photo © Spencer Grant, FPG International Corp.

Chapter 2

30, Figure 2-1 from *American Federalism*, by Daniel Elazar. Copyright ©
1984 by Harper & Row, Publishers, Inc. Reprinted by permission of the
publisher. **33,** Photo by Robert Fox/Impact Visuals. **34,** Figure 2-2 from
Cultural Regions of the United States, by Raymond Gastil. Copyright 1975
by The University of Washington Press. Reprinted by permission. **40,**
Table 2-1 from *The Book of the States, 1989–1990*. Copyright © Council
of State Governments. Used with permission.

Chapter 3

57, Photo © Bob Daemmrich/The Image Works. All rights reserved.

Chapter 4

85, Photo © David Jennings/The Image Works. All rights reserved.
91, Table 4-1 from *The Book of the States, 1990–1991*. Copyright © Council
of State Governments. Used with permission. **95,** Figure 4-1 from
Gerald C. Wright, Jr., et al., "Measuring State Partisanship and Ideology
with Survey Data," *Journal of Politics*, Vol. 47:2, May 1985, p. 481. By
permission of the authors and the University of Texas Press. **103,** Photo
by Marilyn Humphries/Impact Visuals. **107,** Figure 4-3 from David B.
Magleby, *Direct Legislation: Voting on Ballot Propositions in the United
States*, copyright 1984 Johns Hopkins University Press. Reprinted
by permission.

Chapter 5

118, Photo by Jim West/Impact Visuals. **123,** "Youngsters Get Lobbying
Lesson; Massachusetts Gets State Muffin" reprinted by permission of
Associated Press. **124,** "It's Not All Play for Legislators on Annual Ski
Junket," copyright 1985 *The Denver Post*. Reprinted by permission. **135,**
Table 5-1 from *Politics in the American States: A Comparative Analysis*,
Fifth Edition, by Virginia Gray et al. Copyright © 1990 by Virginia Gray,
Herbert Jacob, and Robert B. Albritton. Reprinted by permission of
HarperCollins Publishers.

Chapter 6

149, Figure 6-1 from *New Jersey: Spotlight on Government* (Fifth Edition),
League of Women Voters Education Fund. Copyright © 1969, 1972, 1978,
1983, 1985 by the League of Women Voters of New Jersey Education
Fund. Reprinted with permission of Rutgers University Press. **153,** Photo

154, "Senate Should End Calendar Trickery," copyright 1985, *The Houston Post.* Reprinted by permission. **161,** Photo © Bob Daemmrich/The Image Works.

Chapter 7
181, Photo by Ron Sachs, copyright © 1990 Consolidated News/Archive Photos. **186,** "A Day in the Life of a Governor," reprinted with permission of National Governors' Association. **192,** Table 7-1 from *The Book of the States, 1990–1991.* Copyright © Council of State Governments. Used with permission. **196,** "Executive Department," from *New York Red Book, 1989–1990.* Copyright © New York Legal Publishing Corp. Used with permission. **200,** Table 7-2 from *Politics in the American States: A Comparative Analysis*, Fifth Edition, by Virginia Gray et al. Copyright © by Virginia Gray, Herbert Jacob, and Robert B. Albritton. Reprinted by permission of HarperCollins Publishers. **205,** Table 7-3 from "The Perks of the Governor's Office," from *The Book of the States, 1990–1991.* Copyright © Council of State Governments. Used with permission.

Chapter 8
226, Photograph by Peter Menzel, copyright © Stock, Boston, Inc. **233,** Photograph by Billy E. Barnes, copyright © Stock, Boston, Inc. **236,** Box item from Valerie P. Hans and Neil Vidmar, *Judging the Jury.* Copyright 1986 The Plenum Press. Reprinted by permission.

Chapter 9
262, Table 9-2 from Gary Orfield and Franklin Montfort, "Change in the Racial Composition and Segregation of Large School Districts: 1967–1986." Reprinted by permission of the author. **276,** Photograph by Spencer Grant, copyright © Stock, Boston, Inc.

Chapter 10
331, Photo © Bob Daemmrich/The Image Works.

Chapter 11
345, Photograph by Peter Menzel, copyright © Stock, Boston, Inc.

Chapter 12
361, Photo © George Gardner/The Image Works. **372,** Photo by Ricky Flores/Impact Visuals.

Chapter 13
389, Photograph by Spencer Grant, copyright © Stock, Boston, Inc.

Chapter 14
427, Table 14-4 from Robert L. Savage, "Policy Innovativeness as a Trait of American States," *Journal of Politics*, Vol. 40:1, Feb. 1978. By permission of the author and the University of Texas Press. **435,** Photo © Alan Carey/The Image Works. All rights reserved.

Chapter 15
443, Photo © Alan Carey/The Image Works. All rights reserved.

TO THE OWNER OF THIS BOOK:

We hope that you have found *Democratic Governance in American States and Cities* useful. So that this book can be improved in a future edition, would you take the time to complete this sheet and return it? Thank you.

Instructor's name: _____

Department: _____

School and address: _____

_____

1. The name of the course in which I used this book is: _____

_____

2. My general reaction to this book is: _____

_____

_____

3. What I like most about this book is: _____

_____

_____

4. What I like least about this book is: _____

_____

_____

5. Were all of the chapters of the book assigned for you to read?   Yes   No

   If not, which ones weren't? _____

6. Do you plan to keep this book after you finish the course?   Yes   No

   Why or why not? _____

_____

7. On a separate sheet of paper, please write specific suggestions for improving this book and anything else you'd care to share about your experience in using the book.

Optional:

Your name: _____ Date: _____

May Brooks/Cole quote you, either in promotion for *Democratic Governance in American States and Cities* or in future publishing ventures?

Yes: _____ No: _____

Sincerely,

Kim Quaile Hill
Kenneth R. Mladenka

- -

FOLD HERE

BUSINESS REPLY MAIL

FIRST CLASS   PERMIT NO. 358   PACIFIC GROVE, CA

POSTAGE WILL BE PAID BY ADDRESSEE

ATT: *Kim Quaile Hill & Kenneth R. Mladenka*

Brooks/Cole Publishing Company
511 Forest Lodge Road
Pacific Grove, California 93950-9968

- -

FOLD HERE